CorelDRAW™ 8 For Dummies®

W9-ANP-743

For CorelDraw

Note: Although some of these shortcuts work in other Corel programs, the stuff on this side of the Cheat Sheet pertains specifically to CorelDraw.

Toolbox and Toolbar Shortcuts

Tool	Icon	Shortcut
Arrow tool		Spacebar (or Ctrl+spacebar)
Shape tool		F10
Zoom tool		F2
Zoom Out		F3
Zoom to Selected		Shift+F2
Zoom to All Objects		F4
Zoom to Page		Shift+F4
Pencil tool		F5
Rectangle tool		F6
Oval tool		F7
Text tool		F8

Dialog Box Shortcuts

Dialog Box	Shortcut
Align & Distribute	Ctrl+A
Edit Text	Ctrl+Shift+T
Fountain Fill	F11
Options (Rulers panel)	Double-click on ruler
Guidelines Setup	Double-click on guide with arrow or shape tool
Insert Page	PgUp at beginning of document or PgDn at end
Options	Ctrl+J
Outline Pen	F12
Outline Color	Shift+F12
Options (Page Size panel)	Double-click on page boundary
Spell Checker	Ctrl+F12
Uniform Fill	Shift+F11

Roll-Up and Docker Shortcuts

Roll-Up/Docker	Shortcut
Blend	Ctrl+B
Envelope	Ctrl+F7
Extrude	Ctrl+E
Node Edit	Ctrl+F10
Object Properties	Select object and press Alt+Enter
Pen	Shift+F7
Position	Alt+F7
Rotate	Alt+F8
Scale & Mirror	Alt+F9
Skew	Alt+F11
Special Fill	Ctrl+F
Symbols	Ctrl+F11

Menu Command Shortcuts

Command	Shortcut
Close	Ctrl+F4
Copy	Ctrl+C (or Ctrl+Ins)
Cut	Ctrl+X (or Shift+Del)
Delete	Delete
Duplicate	Ctrl+D
Exit	Alt+F4
Group	Ctrl+G
Import	Ctrl+I
New Document	Ctrl+N
Open	Ctrl+O
Paste	Ctrl+V (or Shift+Ins)
Print	Ctrl+P
Redo	Ctrl+Shift+Z
Repeat	Ctrl+R
Save	Ctrl+S
Select All	Double-click on arrow tool icon
Snap to Grid	Ctrl+Y
To Back	Shift+PgDn
To Front	Shift+PgUp
Back one	Ctrl+PgDn
Forward one	Ctrl+PgUp
Undo	Ctrl+Z
Ungroup	Ctrl+U

...For Dummies®: Bestselling Book Series for Beginners

CorelDRAW™ 8 For Dummies®

Cheat Sheet

For Photo-Paint

Note: Although some of these shortcuts work in other Corel programs, the stuff listed on this side of the Cheat Sheet pertains specifically to Photo-Paint. The image window must be active for shortcuts to work.

Roll-Up and Docker Shortcuts

Roll-Up/Docker	Shortcut
Color	Ctrl+F2
Objects	Ctrl+F7
Scrapbook	Ctrl+F12
Tool Settings	Ctrl+F8

Menu Command Shortcuts

Command	Shortcut
Clear	Delete
Close	Ctrl+F4
Copy	Ctrl+C (or Ctrl+Ins)
Create Mask from Object	Ctrl+M
Create Object from Mask	Ctrl+up arrow
Cut	Ctrl+X (or Shift+Del)
Duplicate Object	Ctrl+D
Exit	Alt+F4
Feather	Ctrl+Shift+F
Full-Screen Preview	F9
Help Topics	F1
Mask Marquee Visible	Ctrl+H
Object Marquee Visible	Ctrl+Shift+H
Invert Selection	Ctrl+I
Level Equalization	Ctrl+E
Mask Select All	Ctrl+Shift+A or double-click on mask tool icon

Command	Shortcut
Mask Remove	Ctrl+Shift+R
New Document	Ctrl+N
Open	Ctrl+O
Options	Ctrl+J
Paste as New Object	Ctrl+V (or Shift+Ins)
Print	Ctrl+P
Repeat (last action)	Ctrl+L
Repeat (Effects command)	Ctrl+F
Rulers	Ctrl+R
Save	Ctrl+S
Snap Objects to Grid	Ctrl+Y
Undo (or Alt+Backspace)	Ctrl+Z
Zoom 100%	Ctrl+1
Zoom to Fit	F4

Toolbox Shortcuts

Tool	Icon	Shortcut
Arrow tool		0
Zoom In or Out		F2 or F3
Paint tool		F5
Rectangle tool		F6
Oval tool		F7
Text tool		F8

...For Dummies®: Bestselling Book Series for Beginners

TM

References for the Rest of Us!®

BESTSELLING BOOK SERIES

Are you intimidated and confused by computers? Do you find that traditional manuals are overloaded with technical details you'll never use? Do your friends and family always call you to fix simple problems on their PCs? Then the *...For Dummies*® computer book series from IDG Books Worldwide is for you.

...For Dummies books are written for those frustrated computer users who know they aren't really dumb but find that PC hardware, software, and indeed the unique vocabulary of computing make them feel helpless. *...For Dummies* books use a lighthearted approach, a down-to-earth style, and even cartoons and humorous icons to dispel computer novices' fears and build their confidence. Lighthearted but not lightweight, these books are a perfect survival guide for anyone forced to use a computer.

> *"I like my copy so much I told friends; now they bought copies."*
>
> — Irene C., Orwell, Ohio

> *"Quick, concise, nontechnical, and humorous."*
>
> — Jay A., Elburn, Illinois

> *"Thanks, I needed this book. Now I can sleep at night."*
>
> — Robin F., British Columbia, Canada

Already, millions of satisfied readers agree. They have made *...For Dummies* books the #1 introductory level computer book series and have written asking for more. So, if you're looking for the most fun and easy way to learn about computers, look to *...For Dummies* books to give you a helping hand.

IDG
BOOKS
WORLDWIDE

by Deke McClelland

IDG Books Worldwide, Inc.
An International Data Group Company

Foster City, CA ♦ Chicago, IL ♦ Indianapolis, IN ♦ New York, NY

CorelDRAW™ 8 For Dummies®

Published by
IDG Books Worldwide, Inc.
An International Data Group Company
919 E. Hillsdale Blvd.
Suite 400
Foster City, CA 94404
www.idgbooks.com (IDG Books Worldwide Web site)
www.dummies.com (Dummies Press Web site)

Library of Congress Catalog Card No.: 97-81453

ISBN: 0-7645-0317-0

Printed in the United States of America

10 9 8 7 6 5 4 3

1B/RZ/QW/ZZ/IN

Distributed in the United States by IDG Books Worldwide, Inc.

Distributed by CDG Books Canada Inc. for Canada; by Transworld Publishers Limited in the United Kingdom; by IDG Norge Books for Norway; by IDG Sweden Books for Sweden; by IDG Books Australia Publishing Corporation Pty. Ltd. for Australia and New Zealand; by TransQuest Publishers Pte Ltd. for Singapore, Malaysia, Thailand, Indonesia, and Hong Kong; by Gotop Information Inc. for Taiwan; by ICG Muse, Inc. for Japan; by Norma Comunicaciones S.A. for Colombia; by Intersoft for South Africa; by Eyrolles for France; by International Thomson Publishing for Germany, Austria and Switzerland; by Distribuidora Cuspide for Argentina; by Livraria Cultura for Brazil; by Ediciones ZETA S.C.R. Ltda. for Peru; by WS Computer Publishing Corporation, Inc., for the Philippines; by Contemporanea de Ediciones for Venezuela; by Express Computer Distributors for the Caribbean and West Indies; by Micronesia Media Distributor, Inc. for Micronesia; by Grupo Editorial Norma S.A. for Guatemala; by Chips Computadoras S.A. de C.V. for Mexico; by Editorial Norma de Panama S.A. for Panama; by American Bookshops for Finland. Authorized Sales Agent: Anthony Rudkin Associates for the Middle East and North Africa.

For general information on IDG Books Worldwide's books in the U.S., please call our Consumer Customer Service department at 800-762-2974. For reseller information, including discounts and premium sales, please call our Reseller Customer Service department at 800-434-3422.

For information on where to purchase IDG Books Worldwide's books outside the U.S., please contact our International Sales department at 317-596-5530 or fax 317-596-5692.

For consumer information on foreign language translations, please contact our Customer Service department at 1-800-434-3422, fax 317-596-5692, or e-mail rights@idgbooks.com.

For information on licensing foreign or domestic rights, please phone +1-650-655-3109.

For sales inquiries and special prices for bulk quantities, please contact our Sales department at 650-655-3200 or write to the address above.

For information on using IDG Books Worldwide's books in the classroom or for ordering examination copies, please contact our Educational Sales department at 800-434-2086 or fax 317-596-5499.

For press review copies, author interviews, or other publicity information, please contact our Public Relations department at 650-655-3000 or fax 650-655-3299.

For authorization to photocopy items for corporate, personal, or educational use, please contact Copyright Clearance Center, 222 Rosewood Drive, Danvers, MA 01923, or fax 978-750-4470.

is a registered trademark or trademark under exclusive license to IDG Books Worldwide, Inc. from International Data Group, Inc. in the United States and/or other countries.

About the Author

Deke McClelland is a contributing editor to *Macworld* and *Publish* magazines. He has authored more than 30 books on desktop publishing and the Macintosh computer, and his work has been translated into more than 20 languages. Deke also hosts *Digital Gurus,* a syndicated TV show about personal computing, from his home base in Colorado. He started his career as artistic director at the first service bureau in the United States.

Deke won a Society of Technical Communication Award in 1994, an American Society for Business Press Editors Award in 1995, and the Ben Franklin Award for Best Computer Book in 1989. He also won the prestigious Computer Press Association Award in 1990, 1992, 1994, and 1995.

Deke is the author of the following books published by IDG Books Worldwide, Inc.: *Macworld FreeHand 7 Bible, Macworld Photoshop 4 Bible, Photoshop 4 for Windows 95 Bible, PageMaker 6 For Windows For Dummies, Photoshop 4 For Dummies,* and *Photoshop 4 Studio Secrets.*

ABOUT IDG BOOKS WORLDWIDE

Welcome to the world of IDG Books Worldwide.

IDG Books Worldwide, Inc., is a subsidiary of International Data Group, the world's largest publisher of computer-related information and the leading global provider of information services on information technology. IDG was founded more than 30 years ago by Patrick J. McGovern and now employs more than 9,000 people worldwide. IDG publishes more than 290 computer publications in over 75 countries. More than 90 million people read one or more IDG publications each month.

Launched in 1990, IDG Books Worldwide is today the #1 publisher of best-selling computer books in the United States. We are proud to have received eight awards from the Computer Press Association in recognition of editorial excellence and three from Computer Currents' First Annual Readers' Choice Awards. Our best-selling ...*For Dummies*® series has more than 50 million copies in print with translations in 31 languages. IDG Books Worldwide, through a joint venture with IDG's Hi-Tech Beijing, became the first U.S. publisher to publish a computer book in the People's Republic of China. In record time, IDG Books Worldwide has become the first choice for millions of readers around the world who want to learn how to better manage their businesses.

Our mission is simple: Every one of our books is designed to bring extra value and skill-building instructions to the reader. Our books are written by experts who understand and care about our readers. The knowledge base of our editorial staff comes from years of experience in publishing, education, and journalism — experience we use to produce books to carry us into the new millennium. In short, we care about books, so we attract the best people. We devote special attention to details such as audience, interior design, use of icons, and illustrations. And because we use an efficient process of authoring, editing, and desktop publishing our books electronically, we can spend more time ensuring superior content and less time on the technicalities of making books.

You can count on our commitment to deliver high-quality books at competitive prices on topics you want to read about. At IDG Books Worldwide, we continue in the IDG tradition of delivering quality for more than 30 years. You'll find no better book on a subject than one from IDG Books Worldwide.

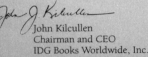

John Kilcullen
Chairman and CEO
IDG Books Worldwide, Inc.

Steven Berkowitz
President and Publisher
IDG Books Worldwide, Inc.

Eighth Annual Computer Press Awards ≥1992

Ninth Annual Computer Press Awards ≥1993

Tenth Annual Computer Press Awards ≥1994

Eleventh Annual Computer Press Awards ≥1995

IDG is the world's leading IT media, research and exposition company. Founded in 1964, IDG had 1997 revenues of $2.05 billion and has more than 9,000 employees worldwide. IDG offers the widest range of media options that reach IT buyers in 75 countries representing 95% of worldwide IT spending. IDG's diverse product and services portfolio spans six key areas including print publishing, online publishing, expositions and conferences, market research, education and training, and global marketing services. More than 90 million people read one or more of IDG's 290 magazines and newspapers, including IDG's leading global brands — Computerworld, PC World, Network World, Macworld and the Channel World family of publications. IDG Books Worldwide is one of the fastest-growing computer book publishers in the world, with more than 700 titles in 36 languages. The "...For Dummies®" series alone has more than 50 million copies in print. IDG offers online users the largest network of technology-specific Web sites around the world through IDG.net (http://www.idg.net), which comprises more than 225 targeted Web sites in 55 countries worldwide. International Data Corporation (IDC) is the world's largest provider of information technology data, analysis and consulting, with research centers in over 41 countries and more than 400 research analysts worldwide. IDG World Expo is a leading producer of more than 168 globally branded conferences and expositions in 35 countries including E3 (Electronic Entertainment Expo), Macworld Expo, ComNet, Windows World Expo, ICE (Internet Commerce Expo), Agenda, DEMO, and Spotlight. IDG's training subsidiary, ExecuTrain, is the world's largest computer training company, with more than 230 locations worldwide and 785 training courses. IDG Marketing Services helps industry-leading IT companies build international brand recognition by developing global integrated marketing programs via IDG's print, online and exposition products worldwide. Further information about the company can be found at www.idg.com. 1/24/99

Author's Acknowledgments

The author wishes to extend his grateful thank-you-very-kindly's to all the groovy folks who helped him with the book you now hold in your hands. Amy Thomas performed her usual miracles in revising this edition to keep everything up to date. Susan Pink did an exemplary job of ensuring that the text is unambiguous, humorous, and grammaticologically correct. And Colin Banfield did fine work as this book's technical editor.

No page of thank-yees would be complete without one directed at my charming and beautiful wife, Elizabeth. She's the cat's meow (which has confused our cat on more than one occasion).

Publisher's Acknowledgments

We're proud of this book; please register your comments through our IDG Books Worldwide Online Registration Form located at http://my2cents.dummies.com.

Some of the people who helped bring this book to market include the following:

Acquisitions, Development, and Editorial

Project Editor: Susan Pink

Acquisitions Editor: Michael Kelly

Technical Editor: Colin Banfield

Editorial Manager: Mary C. Corder

Editorial Assistant: Donna Love

Special Help

Suzanne Thomas, Associate Editor; Tina Sims, Copy Editor; Stephanie Koutek, Proof Editor

Production

Associate Project Coordinator: Karen York

Layout and Graphics: Lou Boudreau, J. Tyler Connor, Maridee V. Ennis, Angela F. Hunckler, Todd Klemme, Jane E. Martin, Heather Pearson, Anna Rohrer, Brent Savage, Deirdre Smith, Rashell Smith

Proofreaders: Kathleen Prata, Kelli Botta, Michelle Croninger, Brian Massey, Nancy Price, Rebecca Senninger, Janet M. Withers

Indexer: Richard Shrout

General and Administrative

IDG Books Worldwide, Inc.: John Kilcullen, CEO; Steven Berkowitz, President and Publisher

IDG Books Technology Publishing: Brenda McLaughlin, Senior Vice President and Group Publisher

Dummies Technology Press and Dummies Editorial: Diane Graves Steele, Vice President and Associate Publisher; Mary Bednarek, Director of Acquisitions and Product Development; Kristin A. Cocks, Editorial Director

Dummies Trade Press: Kathleen A. Welton, Vice President and Publisher; Kevin Thornton, Acquisitions Manager

IDG Books Production for Dummies Press: Michael R. Britton, Vice President of Production and Creative Services; Cindy L. Phipps, Manager of Project Coordination, Production Proofreading, and Indexing; Kathie S. Schutte, Supervisor of Page Layout; Shelley Lea, Supervisor of Graphics and Design; Debbie J. Gates, Production Systems Specialist; Robert Springer, Supervisor of Proofreading; Debbie Stailey, Special Projects Coordinator; Tony Augsburger, Supervisor of Reprints and Bluelines

Dummies Packaging and Book Design: Patty Page, Manager, Promotions Marketing

◆

The publisher would like to give special thanks to Patrick J. McGovern, without whom this book would not have been possible.

◆

Contents at a Glance

Cartoons at a Glance

By Rich Tennant

Fax: 978-546-7747 • E-mail: the5wave@tiac.net

Table of Contents

Introduction

● ●

*T*he *Guinness Book of World Records* doesn't seem to offer a category for the most immense software package. If it did, the prize would clearly have to go to CorelDraw 8. This ample, expansive, sprawling, capacious, comprehensive program is so large that it consumes three CD-ROMs.

Simply put, CorelDraw 8 is an all-in-one artist's studio. It enables you to create precise illustrations, draw free-form artwork, paint electronic masterpieces, edit digital photographs, and even design three-dimensional environments that look every bit as realistic — or surrealistic — as real life. The CorelDraw package also includes thousands upon thousands of pieces of clip art, fonts, digital photographs, 3-D models, and other valuable stuff.

All this combined with the program's reasonable price may explain the phenomenal popularity of CorelDraw. By some accounts, it's the most popular piece of graphics software for the personal computer.

Why a Book . . . For Dummies?

But all this power comes at a price. The CorelDraw 8 package comprises nearly a dozen programs. The central program is CorelDraw, which enables you to design professional-quality pages and artwork, but you also get Photo-Paint, Dream 3D, Scan, Texture, Trace, Capture, Font Navigator, and a bunch of others. If Corel could come up with a way to market its KitchenSink and SwissPocketKnife programs, they would be in the package as well.

Needless to say, there's no way to sit down cold with this many programs and figure them out overnight — in fact, there's really no reason why you should even bother to learn all of them. How can you tell which of these programs are worth your time and which you should ignore? I can tell you from years of personal experience that a few Corel programs are very interesting, some are somewhat interesting, and the rest are pretty darn forgettable — so forgettable that I have to consult the Corel press information to remember them.

So instead of packing your brain full of a bunch of utter nonsense about a bunch of programs you'll never touch, I cover just those aspects of those programs that I think you'll find exciting, entertaining, and ultimately useful. Being a generous guy by nature, I leave the boring stuff for another book.

By the way, I should mention that this book is specifically about CorelDraw 8. I suppose you could use it to learn about one of the other versions of the program, but quite a few commands would be different, some tools wouldn't be available, and your screen would look different than the ones pictured throughout this book. I can't say that I recommend this approach.

If you're using an older version of the program, your better bet is to look for an earlier edition of this book. Ask your bookseller for the edition that covers your version of the program. It'll make you smile again.

How to Use This Book

I tried to write this book so that you can approach it from several perspectives, depending on how you learn:

- ✔ If you're a reader — it's been my experience that only hard-core readers put up with book introductions — I hope you'll find my writing lively enough to keep you from falling asleep or collapsing into an information-age coma.

- ✔ If you just want to find out how a command works and then toss the book back into a dusty corner, look up the topic in the index and then turn to the appropriate page. The publisher of this book includes an ample, expansive, immense, sprawling, capacious, and comprehensive index, on par with CorelDraw itself.

- ✔ If you already know your way around CorelDraw, flip through the book, check out a few of the tips here and there, and pay special attention to the information marked with the CorelDraw 8 icon.

- ✔ If you hate to read anything without pictures, just read Rich Tennant's comics. I fall into this learning group. (Good news, huh?) Folks like you and me won't discover anything about CorelDraw, but by golly, we'll get in a few yucks.

- ✔ If you want to get a quick idea of what this book is like, read the four chapters in Part V. Each chapter contains a series of short sections that not only give you an indication of the high-falutin' caliber of information in this book but also mesmerize you with my enchanting style and wit. Well, perhaps *mesmerize* is the wrong word. How about *clomp you over the head?*

- ✔ If you don't much like the idea of reading a computer book but you're so confused that you don't even know what questions to ask, start at Chapter 1 and see where it takes you. I promise that I won't leave you wallowing in the dust.

This book has been read and reread by folks who don't know the first thing about CorelDraw, and to this day, they are only marginally confused. Considering that they all led happy and productive lives before they read *CorelDRAW 8 For Dummies* and that only three of them had to seek therapy afterwards, I think this is one heck of a book.

How This Book Is Organized

I've divided *CorelDRAW 8 For Dummies* into five digestible parts, each of which contains three to six chapters, which are themselves divided into gobs of discrete sections, which contain these funny little letter-units called *words*. I thought about including a synopsis of every sentence in the book in this introduction, but then I thought, no, it'd be better if you had a chance to read the book before the next Ice Age sets in. So here are brief descriptions of the parts instead.

Part I: The Stuff Everyone Pretends They Already Know

We're all dumb about some things and smart about others. But however smart we may be about our key interests in life, we're afraid that our dumb topics will be the death of us. At any moment, someone may expose us for what we truly are — congenital half-wits. You know what I'm saying here? (Sob.) Pass me that tissue, would you? (Sniff.) Thank you. (Honk.)

So this part of the book is about answering all those questions you had and didn't know you had, and even if you did know, you wouldn't have asked anyone because all your friends would have laughed at you and branded you an Industrial Age cretin. These chapters are like a CorelDraw information pill. Swallow them and be smart or, at least, better informed.

Part II: Let the Graphics Begin

In this part, you can start expressing yourself and creating some bona fide computer art. Not an artist? Not to worry. Neither are thousands of other folks who use this program. In fact, CorelDraw is specifically designed to accommodate artists and nonartists alike, enabling you to express the uniquely individual creative impulses that surge through, well, all those places that things tend to surge through. That is to say, you'll be able to get the job accomplished. You can even throw in a few special effects for good measure.

Part III: Getting the Message Out There (Wherever "There" Is)

Many of us feel the special need to share things with other people. Reports, newsletters, and internal memos allow us to show off our personalities and mix in a bit of our literary expertise. Bold headlines such as "Joe Bob Receives Employee of the Month Award" or "Sales up in March" tell a little something about who we are and how we live.

CorelDraw knows that it's not enough to draw pretty pictures; you have to be able to back up those pictures with hard-hitting text. In these chapters, you'll discover that CorelDraw is half drawing program and half document-creation software. You can enter and edit text, design logos and special text effects, create multipage documents, and print the whole thing on 20-pound bond paper. You can even prepare documents to be published on the World Wide Web.

Part IV: Corel's Other Amazing Programs

As I mentioned earlier, I try to steer you away from the boring and mostly useless Corel programs and concentrate on the good ones. This part of the book covers two good programs you're sure to want to check out, Photo-Paint and Dream 3D. In fact, I devote three full chapters to Photo-Paint, a program that is growing in popularity and is second only to CorelDraw in usefulness and artistic prowess.

Part V: The Part of Tens

This part of the book is a savory blend of real information and the sort of chatty top-ten lists that prevent us all from understanding too awfully much about anything. These chapters offer lists of special effects, obscure features, file formats, and advice for everyday living. Prepare to be entertained as you learn. Prepare to laugh and be studious. Prepare to chortle until factoids come out your nose.

Icons Used in This Book

To alert you to special passages of text that you may or may not want to read, the National Bureau of Wacky Graphics has designed the following universal margin icons and thoughtfully interspersed them throughout the book.

Here's an example of something you may want to avoid. This icon highlights a close encounter of the nerd kind, the variety of information that could land you in the intensive care ward if you were to utter it at the Annual Gathering of Hell's Angels. In other words, read if you must, but don't repeat.

Here's something you didn't know, or if you did know it, you're smarter than you thought. Don't be surprised if a single tip makes you fractions of a percentage point more efficient than you were before. It's been known to happen to people just like you.

This may be some bit of information I've already mentioned. But you may have forgotten it, and I want to drill it into your head. Metaphorically, of course. Or it may be something I just thought you would like to know — a friendly gesture on my part.

This icon spells danger — or at least something to be watchful for. Try to steer clear of the stuff I describe here.

If you're at all familiar with CorelDraw 3, 4, 5, 6, or 7, you may be keenly interested in how CorelDraw 8 differs from its predecessors. This icon lets you in on the newest features so that you can make the transition to Version 8 in record time. I also point out a few old features that have been changed so dramatically that you may not recognize them without a little help.

Where to Go from Here

Different people read in different ways. You may want to check out the index or table of contents and look up some bit of information that has been perplexing you for the past few days. Or you might just close the book and use it as a reference the next time you face an impasse or some horrible, confusing problem. Then again, you could just keep on reading, perish the thought. Personally, I couldn't put the book down, but you may have more willpower than I do.

How to Bug Me

If you want to ask me a question, tell me about a mistake, or just share your opinions about this book, feel free to write me at one of these handy e-mail addresses:

America Online: DekeMc

Internet: DekeMc@InternetMCI.com

Don't be discouraged if I don't respond for a few weeks. It just means that I'm in over my head with projects and deadlines (as usual). I eventually respond to every e-mail I get.

Good luck with the book, and may CorelDraw treat you with the dignity that you — a superior, carbon-based life form — deserve.

Part I

The Stuff Everyone Pretends They Already Know

The 5th Wave · By Rich Tennant

SOFTWARE DEVELOPMENT

"WE SHOULD HAVE THIS FIXED IN VERSION 8."

In this part . . .

*I*magine this: You're enrolled in an introductory computing course. The professor asks you to write a simple computer program. Let's say you're to create a program that types out a series of *A*s in a column or something equally pointless. Who cares. It's not important. Anyway, the professor takes time to carefully explain the language and logic behind the exercise. Because you secretly harbor an unusually immense brain — granted, you use it only on special occasions — you understand thoroughly. No sweat.

But when you sit down in front of a terminal at the computer lab, you realize that you lack a key bit of information. How are you supposed to get to the point where you start entering your programming instructions? The computer is on, but it just sits there blinking at you. Anything you enter results in an error message. You're so utterly clueless and overwhelmingly frustrated that you don't even know how to ask one of the pompous lab assistants what the heck is going on.

I've been there. I empathize. It stinks. The fact of the matter is, any amount of knowledge is worthless if you don't know the basics. The difficulty, of course, is that lots of folks act as if they already know the basics because they don't want to look like, well, a dummy. But let's face it, when it comes to computers, remarkably few people know what's going on. And those who do tend to be insufferable.

So here are the basics. The following chapters explain all the easy stuff you've been pretending to know, little realizing that 90 percent of the people around you don't know it, either. Soon, you'll be welcomed into the ranks of the Insufferable Computer Dweebs, a group we're all dying to join.

Chapter 1

What's with All These Programs?

*O*nce upon a time, when dinosaurs roamed the earth, CorelDraw was a single program — weird, huh? Nowadays, the CorelDraw box includes nearly a dozen separate programs, each of which you can use independently or in tandem with its little electronic friends. This chapter introduces many of these programs and explains their relative benefits and degrees of usefulness, which range from truly stupendous to barely worth yawning over. I also tell you which chapters in this book, if any, contain more information about each program.

CorelDraw

CorelDraw started it all. Not only is CorelDraw the program after which the package is named, it's the most powerful and useful program of the bunch. Not surprisingly, therefore, it's the one I talk about in the most detail.

What can you draw with CorelDraw? Why, anything. Free-form graphics of butterflies or unicorns engaged in some ridiculous activity, architectural plans for a bathroom off the linen closet (I wish I had one of those), anatomical illustrations that show food going down the trachea (and the ensuing coughing fit). . . . The list is endless, or at least close enough to endless that I'd run the risk of boring you into a coma if I were to continue.

Thar's math in them thar objets d'art

Math is the driving force behind CorelDraw. I know it's sick, but it's true. When you draw a wiggly line, for example, CorelDraw notes the coordinates of the first and last points and calculates a mathematical description of the curve between the two points. CorelDraw thinks of each line, shape, or character of text as a mathematical object, which is why the program and others like it are sometimes called *object-oriented software*. When you print your drawings, the program explains all this math to the printer, which in turn draws the objects as smoothly as it can so that they all look like you drew them by hand and not with a computer.

If your printed drawings look jagged, you're using a cheap printer. You can improve the appearance of your drawings by buying a better printer or by paying to have your drawings printed at a service bureau. Both options involve the outlay of some additional cash, of course. For the whole story on printing, read Chapter 13.

Wait, there's more. You can open and edit clip art — you know, those drawings that other people create specifically so that you can mess them up. You can create wild text effects, such as a logo or two for Stuckey's. You can even design documents such as advertisements for Stuckey's, fliers for Stuckey's, and posters for Long John Silver's. (What does Stuckey's need with posters, anyway? We're all familiar with their pecan logs.)

Corel Photo-Paint

The primary purpose of Corel Photo-Paint, discussed in Chapters 15 through 17, is to enable you to make changes to photographic images. You can change the color scheme of a photo so that everyone in your family looks like they had the sense not to wear bright orange and avocado green in the '70s. You can apply special effects so that Grandma Edna's face appears molded in lead. You can retouch subtle or bothersome details such as Junior's unusually immense chin wart. You can even combine the contents of two photos so that Uncle Mike and Aunt Rosie are standing shoulder to shoulder, even though the two of them would rather take a flying leap into the Grand Canyon than hang out in the same room together. And if that sounds like an accurate description of your family, you need all the help you can get.

Finding photos to edit

The following list explains a few ways to get photos on a floppy disk or a Photo CD so that you can edit them in Photo-Paint:

✔ You can take a photograph to a service bureau and have it *scanned* onto a floppy disk, which means to read the photo and convert it to a digital image, sort of like recording music onto a CD. Some folks call scanning *digitizing.* Scanning is generally a pretty expensive proposition, around $2 to $10 per photo, depending on whether you scan the photo in black and white or in color.

✔ To locate a service bureau, look in the Yellow Pages under "Desktop Publishing." Some cities have many service bureaus. San Francisco, Los Angeles, Seattle, Chicago, New York, and all those other coastal towns have as many service bureaus as they have adult bookstores. But in rural areas, service bureaus are a little harder to come by. You may have to search around a bit. If you have friends in the computer graphics biz, ask them for recommendations.

✔ If you intend to do a great deal of scanning, you may want to purchase your own scanner. Top-of-the-line scanners run $1000 and up, but you can get a decent scanner for under $500.

✔ The Kodak Photo CD technology provides a better alternative to scanning your images to disk, both in terms of quality and economy. For around $100, you can transfer up to 100 photos from slides, negatives, or undeveloped rolls of film to a compact disc that's identical in appearance to CDs that play music. Of course, to take advantage of Photo CD, you need a CD-ROM drive.

✔ For service bureaus that can put your images on Photo CD, look in the Yellow Pages under "Photo Finishing — Retail."

✔ You can also buy CDs filled with photographs shot by professional photographers. Called *stock photos,* these images run the gamut from famous landmarks to animals, from textures to people engaged in people-like pursuits. Corel sells its own line of stock-photo CDs, which you can buy for less than $20 a pop. You can also purchase individual images from Corel by visiting the Corel World Wide Web site at www.corel.com.

✔ If you have Internet access or subscribe to an online service such as CompuServe or America Online, you can download photos using your modem. Watch out, though. Because of their large file size, photos take several minutes — or several hours — to download. You can waste some major bucks in access charges if you're not careful.

Painting from scratch

You don't have to edit photos in Photo-Paint. You can also paint images from scratch. The difference between drawing in CorelDraw and painting in Photo-Paint is that the painting process is more intuitive. In fact, you don't need my help to paint an image. You just sketch a little here, erase a little there, fill in some details, and keep working on your image until you get it right. Kids love painting on a computer. You'll love it, too. Painting is the easiest thing you can do with any computer program, I swear.

CorelDraw and Photo-Paint Duke It Out

Although drawings and images are both forms of computer artwork, the two are distinct. Drawings created in CorelDraw feature sharp edges, as demonstrated in Figure 1-1. The second half of the figure shows an enlarged detail so that you can see what a difference math makes. Even when printed at a really large size, a drawing retains its detail.

Images created with Photo-Paint feature softer edges. One shade flows continuously into the next. *C'est magnifique, très* artsie fartsie, *n'est-ce pas?* But like Achilles — you know, that Greek guy with the bad heel — images have a fatal flaw. They look better when printed at small sizes. When images are printed at a large size, you can see the jagged transitions between colors, as illustrated in Figure 1-2.

Picture yourself done up in pixels

Ah, even in the Simple Simon world of computer painting, Technical Stuff rears its nerdy head. Remember that I said CorelDraw defines lines, shapes, and text using complex mathematical equations? (If not, and assuming that you care, check out the sidebar "Thar's math in them thar objets d'art," earlier in this chapter.) Well, Photo-Paint defines the entire image — whether it's a photograph or something you painted from scratch — using thousands or even millions of tiny colored squares called *pixels*.

A Photo-Paint image is similar to a mosaic. When you get close to a mosaic, you can see the individual colored tiles. When you get far away, the tiles blur into a recognizable picture. Pixels work like those tiles. When you magnify an image in Photo-Paint, you can see the individual pixels. When you restore the image to its regular size, the pixels blur together.

Figure 1-1:
No matter how large or small you print a drawing, you get smooth lines and high contrast.

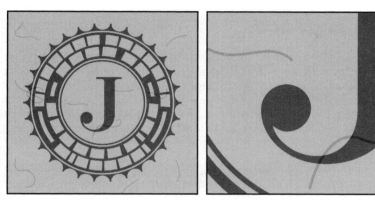

Figure 1-2:
When printed small, paintings look fine (left), but when printed in a large size, they look like a stinky pile of goo (right).

You can place scanned photos into a CorelDraw program and even do some minimal editing to the photos, such as enlarging or reducing the image and applying some photographic effects. Likewise, you can open a drawing in Photo-Paint. Photo-Paint automatically converts the drawing into a pixel-based image (also called a *bitmap*), which means you can then use Photo-Paint tools to edit the drawing-turned-image. But for best results, don't edit a drawing in Photo-Paint or an image in CorelDraw. Instead, edit in the appropriate program: CorelDraw for drawings and Photo-Paint for scanned images.

Corel OCR-Trace

Corel OCR-Trace is a conversion program. It converts Photo-Paint images to CorelDraw drawings by tracing the outlines of lines and shapes in the image. Suppose that you put pen to paper and sketched out that plan of the bathroom off the linen closet discussed earlier. Now you want to convert the plan to a CorelDraw drawing. How can you get your hand-drawn sketch into CorelDraw? Scan it, open and modify it in Photo-Paint, and then convert it using Corel OCR-Trace, that's how.

Unfortunately, converting an image to a drawing is an iffy proposition. This process relies on something called artificial intelligence, which is about as reliable as you'd expect. You have to be prepared to edit the drawing in CorelDraw.

In a time when magazine articles, TV commercials, and CNN news blips remind you on a daily basis how much new stuff is out there that you're totally unaware of, isn't it nice to know that you can get away with not knowing something? The fact is, most folks don't need to learn to use Corel OCR-Trace.

Corel Capture

Corel Capture takes pictures — called *screen shots* — of your screen. This book is chock-full of such pictures. Unless you're documenting a program like I am in this book, Corel Capture is probably of no use to you.

Oh, yes, that's the word, *ojoucd* — no, wait, it's *qohoot*

Corel OCR-Trace can also read. If you scan in a page of text, the program can convert the page to a computer text document that you can open and edit in a word processor such as Corel WordPerfect or Microsoft Word. This capability is called *optical character recognition,* or simply by its initials, OCR.

Unfortunately, OCR involves even more artificial intelligence than converting images to drawings. Depending on the quality of the page you want OCR-Trace to read, the program can easily confuse one letter for another. For example, the word *optical* may be read as *optkal, ogucd, ojoucd,* or *qohoot.* Don't get me wrong; Corel OCR-Trace is as good as most other OCR programs on the market. But it's highly unlikely that the program will read any page 100 percent correctly. In some cases, entering the text from scratch is easier.

Just in case you find yourself loving this program in direct violation of my specific instructions, here's a little something you should know: You can use Photo-Paint to edit the pictures you shoot with Corel Capture. In fact, that's exactly what I did to refine many of the figures in this book.

CorelDream 3D

When most folks think of computer graphics, they conjure up vivid three-dimensional images, the sort of stuff you can't create without computers. You know, like the animation in the movie *Toy Story,* which was created using nothing but computers.

With CorelDream 3D, you can create your own hyper-realistic Bizarro-World 3-D graphics. The problem is that CorelDream 3D is pretty darn complicated — like any 3-D drawing program. First you have to build a model of an object, which is roughly equivalent to constructing a geodesic dome out of Tinker Toys. Then you have to wrap a surface around the shape, which is kind of like stretching a balloon or some other elastic plastic around your Tinker Toys. Next, you have to amass all your models together and set up lights and camera angles. And when you're finished, you don't print the drawing. That would take too long. Instead, you render it to an image file, which may take a few minutes or a few hours, depending on the complexity of the graphic. After that little process is completed, you can open the image in Photo-Paint and print it.

Sounds hard? Well, it is hard. The truth is that 3-D drawing is one of the most complicated pursuits humans and computers can tackle. But what the heck, CorelDream 3D is worth a look-see anyway, which is what Chapter 18 is all about. There I tell you how to get to first base with this powerful but difficult program. The rest of the bases are up to you.

Corel Texture

CorelDraw includes a program called Corel Texture, which you can use to create custom digitized textures that resemble marble, wood, liquids, and metals. The question is: What are you really going to do with a custom texture, anyway? If you were enterprising and had a lot of time on your hands, I suppose you could create a texture and then use it as a background for your Windows desktop, a Photo-Paint image, or a CorelDream 3D scene. But really, you have better things to do with both your time and your enterprising urges — don't you?

And the Rest . . .

Remember the intro to the early episodes of *Gilligan's Island*, in which the Gleeful Castaway Singers sang "and the rest" instead of "the Professor and Mary Ann"? Well, that's how I feel about the other programs bundled with CorelDraw 8, including Corel Script, CorelScan, and the others: They're not really worth special mention. These programs are about as effective as the Professor was at fixing the *Minnow* — and that's why I don't cover them in this book.

But Wait, There's More

That's right, if you act now, you also receive thousands of clip-art drawings, hundreds of typefaces, lots and lots of photos, and more animation, sound, and movie files than you can shake a Douglas Fir at. No other program comes close to providing this variety of ready-to-use stuff. These goodies are truly amazing and well worth the price of admission on their own. I feature much of this artwork throughout this book in the hope that doing so helps you to follow along. I'm just that kind of guy.

Feeling Overwhelmed?

If you're feeling a little bewildered, I don't blame you. Corel went a little nuts in the value department. But the fact is, CorelDraw and Photo-Paint are far and away the most useful programs of the bunch. Frankly, few users would even buy a program like OCR-Trace or Corel Texture if it weren't bundled with CorelDraw.

To wit, most of this book is devoted to CorelDraw, with the secondary emphasis going to Photo-Paint. But I'll bet you ten comes a-runnin' to five (actually, I don't gamble, so I'm a little rusty on the vocabulary) that after you find out how to use these two wonderful programs, you could pick up on most of the others with remarkable ease. No doubt, then, you'll want to take a gander at my next book, *CorelDRAW For Bionic-Brained Ultra-Dweebs*. I'll probably devote the whole thing to Corel Texture.

Chapter 2

See CorelDraw Run

In This Chapter

▶ Starting Windows 95 and CorelDraw 8

▶ Exploring the CorelDraw interface

▶ Using the mouse

▶ Getting acquainted with the drawing tools

▶ Choosing menu commands from the keyboard

▶ Working with dialog boxes, roll-ups, and dockers

CorelDraw is one son-of-a-gun program. But you don't have a prayer of mastering it until you and the program get a little better acquainted. You have to discover its nuances, understand some of its clockwork and gizmos, study its fruity yet palatable bouquet, and make yourself familiar with its inner psyche. In short, you need to read this chapter. Herein lies the answer to that time-honored question, "What makes Draw draw?"

Draw on the March

Entering the world of CorelDraw is a mysterious but surprisingly straightforward process. It goes a little something like this:

1. **Turn on your computer.**

   Imagine how embarrassed you'd be if you skipped this step.

2. **Wait for your computer to start up.**

   Be patient, it'll finish soon.

3. **Enjoy a close encounter with Windows 95.**

   Yes, CorelDraw 8 requires Windows 95. If you're looking at some older version of Windows (or DOS, heaven help you), you can't use CorelDraw 8. That's just the way it goes, I'm afraid.

4. Start up CorelDraw.

The easiest way to start the program is to use the Windows 95 Start menu. Click on the Start button in the lower-left corner of the screen. A menu of items appears. Click on the Programs item in the menu to display a list of folders and programs you can run. Next, click on the CorelDraw 8 item to display yet another submenu, and click on the CorelDraw 8 item in that submenu. CorelDraw should pop up on your computer screen momentarily.

Don't panic if you have problems with menus and mouse clicks. I cover this stuff in more detail later in this chapter.

Interface in Your Face

When you first start CorelDraw, the program produces a Welcome screen that contains a bunch of buttons. You have the option to start a new drawing, open a drawing saved to disk, peruse the on-screen tutorial, or check out a description of features new to Version 8.

You can check out the tutorial or Version 8 preview, if you so desire, by clicking on the CorelTutor button or the What's New button. You can also click on the New Graphic button to start a new drawing, the Open Graphic button to edit an existing drawing, or the Open Last Edited button to edit the last drawing you worked on in CorelDraw. For now, click on the New Graphic button.

To make the Welcome screen disappear forever — really, you don't need to be bothered with this screen every time you start the program — click on the Show This Welcome Screen at Startup check box in the Welcome screen. Or, if you want CorelDraw to automatically perform one of the Welcome screen options each time you start the program, do this: Click on the Tools menu and then click on the Options command to display the Options dialog box. In the tree display on the left side of the dialog box, click on General. In the middle of the dialog box, make a selection from the On CorelDRAW! Start-up pop-up menu, which controls what happens when you start the program. (Selecting stuff from menus, dialog boxes, and so forth is covered in other sections in this chapter if you need help.)

What you see next and what I show you in Figure 2-1 is the CorelDraw 8 *interface* (pronounced *in-tur-face*). The interface is your means for working in and communicating with CorelDraw 8. All the bits and pieces you see labeled in Figure 2-1 are bravely covered at great length and personal risk in the following sections.

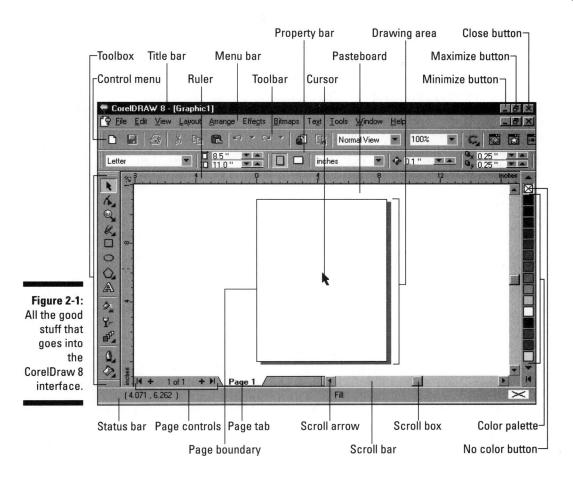

Figure 2-1:
All the good
stuff that
goes into
the
CorelDraw 8
interface.

If you set your monitor's screen display to 640 x 480 pixels, some buttons on the right edge of the toolbar and property bar appear cut off, as in Figure 2-1. Don't worry about it: You can still access all the program's commands; you just can't do so using the toolbar and property bar buttons. The CorelDraw interface appears in its entirety only if you use a screen display setting of 800 x 600 pixels or higher.

To change the screen display, right-click on the Windows 95 desktop, click on the Properties command, and then click on the Settings tab of the Display Properties dialog box that appears. Drag the Desktop Area slider to the right to raise the resolution of your monitor. But remember that the higher the monitor resolution, the greater the strain on your computer's resources. Also, on-screen things appear smaller than when you use the 640 x 480 pixels setting.

Just for the record, all the screen shots you see in this book were created using the 640 x 480 pixels setting to make the important components of the interface easier to see. Most folks who work with CorelDraw on a regular basis use a higher setting. If I were to shoot the figures at a higher resolution, however, the various buttons, bells, and whistles in the interface would be too tiny to be of much help to you.

See the "Property bar" section later in this chapter for instructions on how to move, reorganize, and resize your property bar and toolbar so that all the buttons are visible even at the lowest screen display setting.

Title bar

The title bar tells you the title of the program — CorelDraw 8 — followed by the name of the document you're working on. Until you assign a specific name to your document, CorelDraw gives it the name Graphic 1.

On the left side of the title bar is the Control menu. On the right side of the title bar is the Minimize button, which has a little bar at the bottom of it. To the right of the Minimize button is either the Maximize button (a box with a bar at its top) or the Restore button (two little boxes). And to the right of that button is a Close button with an X in it. These items are common to all Windows 95 programs, but the following list tells you how they work, just in case you're new to all this:

✔ When you first start CorelDraw 8, the interface appears inside a window that hovers in front of the Windows 95 desktop and any other programs you may be using. How distracting! To cover up all that background stuff, click on the Maximize button. Now the interface fills the screen in floor-to-ceiling cinematic splendor.

✔ To restore the CorelDraw interface to its cramped quarters in a floating window, click on the Restore button, the button displaying two little boxes. The background stuff becomes accessible again.

✔ You can move the floating CorelDraw window around by dragging the title bar — that is, pressing and holding the left mouse button on the title bar while moving the mouse.

✔ To change the size of the floating window, position your cursor over one of the window's four corners or one of its four sides. Your cursor changes to a line with arrowheads at either end. Drag the corner or side as desired.

✔ If you want to get CorelDraw out of your face for a moment, click on the Minimize button to hide the CorelDraw window entirely. A CorelDraw button appears in the Windows 95 taskbar at the bottom of the screen to show you that CorelDraw is still running but is hiding. Click on the button to bring the interface back into view.

> ✔ To quit CorelDraw 8, click on the Close button. For more on this topic, see the "Put Your Drawing to Bed" section of Chapter 3.
>
> ✔ All the aforementioned options are available as commands from the Control menu, but you'd have to be a nut to use them when the title bar and buttons are so much more convenient.

Menu bar

A single menu bar appears just below the title bar. The menu bar is another one of those traits CorelDraw shares with all other Windows 95 programs. Each word in the menu bar — File, Edit, View, Quagmire — represents a menu. A menu contains a list of commands you can use to manipulate the various lines and shapes you've drawn, change the way text looks, and initiate other mind-bogglingly sophisticated procedures.

On either side of the menu bar are the familiar Control menu and buttons that you find on the title bar. I discuss the Control menu and buttons in the preceding section. They work the same way as the title bar Control menu and buttons, with one exception. Instead of controlling the entire program interface, these controls affect only a single open drawing. If you click on the Minimize button, for example, the drawing shrinks to a little title bar in the lower-left corner of the CorelDraw window. To see the drawing again, click on the Maximize button in the little title bar or double-click anywhere on the little title bar.

Menus are a pretty big topic, so I talk more about them later in this chapter.

Toolbar

The toolbar is a bunch of buttons you can click on to access certain commands or functions, such as New, Open, and Print. If you want to find out what one of these buttons does, just pause your cursor over it. A little label appears, saying something helpful, such as "Copy."

Quite frankly, I hate the toolbar. It's a stupid Microsoft idea that serves no real purpose and just clutters up the interface. Why do I harbor such hostile feelings? I'll tell you why:

> ✔ Anything you can do with the toolbar you can do also with the menu bar. Instead of clicking on the Open button, for example, you can choose File⇨Open. Better yet, you can press the keyboard shortcut, Ctrl+O.
>
> ✔ The little button icons are so dinky that you can hardly tell one from another, and when you can, you can't tell what they do. Call me an anarchist, but I reckon that such buttons make the program harder to use, not easier.

> ✔ The toolbar reduces the size of the drawing area, which is really a problem when you're working on a 13- or 15-inch monitor.
>
> ✔ Corel implemented the toolbar out of peer pressure. All the other Windows programs were doing it, so Corel hopped on board. Just imagine what would happen if all the other Windows programs jumped off a cliff.

The only redeeming quality of the toolbar, in my opinion, is that you can change the zoom magnification and view mode using toolbar pop-up menus, as explained in Chapter 3. But I don't think these options warrant full-time display of the toolbar, which is why the toolbar doesn't appear in any figures after Chapter 3.

If you share my feelings about the toolbar and want to get rid of it, right-click on the toolbar between any two icons. A pop-up menu appears. Click on the Standard option to hide the toolbar.

Alternatively, you can choose the View⇨Toolbars command. Inside the Toolbars dialog box, click on the Standard option to turn the toolbar off and then press Enter. Either way, the toolbar vanishes and frees up valuable screen space. If you want to bring the toolbar back, choose the View⇨Toolbars command again.

Property bar

Beneath the toolbar (or beneath the menu bar, if you follow my advice and hide the toolbar as I suggest) lies the property bar. The property bar holds controls that you can use to quickly make all kinds of adjustments to your drawing, from changing the page size to rotating an object.

The controls on the property bar change depending on which tool you're using. For example, when you use the text tool, the property bar offers controls that let you select a font and type style.

In many cases, changes you make by using the property bar controls are automatically applied. For example, if you click on the little up- or down-pointing arrows next to an option box, drag a slider bar, or click on an icon, CorelDraw immediately alters your selected object in response. But if you enter a new option box value from the keyboard — that is, if you click inside the option box and type in a new value — you must press Enter to apply the value. (For the full scoop on option boxes and other dialog box elements, see the section "The Incessant Chatter of Dialog Boxes" later in this chapter.)

Like the toolbar, the property bar duplicates commands and options you can also access by choosing commands from the menu bar. So if you're working on a tiny screen and want to conserve space, you may want to turn off the property bar. To do so, right-click on an empty spot on the property bar to display a pop-up menu. Then click on the Property Bar item. To bring the property bar back into view, choose the View⇨Property Bar command.

You can move the property bar and toolbar to different on-screen locations if you want. Just press and hold the left mouse button on a blank spot on the bar in question and then drag the bar to its new home. Or double-click on a blank spot. Either way, the bar becomes a miniature floating window, complete with a title bar and a Close button. You can resize and reshape the bar — a good fix for the screen display problem discussed at the very beginning of the "Interface in Your Face" section. To resize or reshape a floating bar, place your cursor on a corner until you see a two-headed arrow. Then drag the edge of the bar. To move the bar, drag its title bar. If you want to return the bar to its default position — anchored across the top of the window — double-click on the title bar.

You can also easily rearrange or remove buttons from the property bar or toolbar. Just hold down the Alt key while you drag the button. You can even drag toolbar buttons onto the property bar and vice versa. If you drag a button off the toolbar or property bar, the button is removed and the remaining buttons scoot over to fill the empty space.

If you prefer using the 640 x 480 monitor resolution, you can remove buttons you don't use very often to make room for buttons previously hidden from view. To return to the default toolbar or property bar layout, choose View⇨Toolbars. Select the check box for the bar you want to change, and click on the Reset button.

Tools

The CorelDraw 8 toolbox — that strip of tools running down the left side of the drawing window — offers an abundance of tools for your drawing pleasure. To select a tool, click on its icon. Then use the tool by clicking or dragging inside the drawing area. To find out more about tools and even give one or two a test run, skip to the "How to Deal with Complete Tools" section. Or better yet, just keep reading. You'll get there soon enough.

Drawing area

Smack dab in the middle of the drawing area is the page boundary, which represents the physical size of the printed page. If you position a shape inside the page boundary, it prints. If you position a shape outside the page boundary, it doesn't print.

The area outside the page boundary is called the *pasteboard.* It's the surface on which the page sits. Think of the pasteboard as a kind of drawing repository because you can temporarily store shapes there while you figure out what to do with them.

Rulers

By default, CorelDraw displays horizontal and vertical rulers along the top and left edge of the drawing area, respectively. The rulers can be helpful when you need to position objects precisely. For more about rulers, including how to turn them on and off, see Chapter 6.

Scroll stuff

The scroll bars enable you to navigate around and display hidden portions of your drawing inside the drawing area. CorelDraw offers two scroll bars: one vertical bar along the right side of the drawing area and one horizontal bar along the bottom. If you click on a scroll arrow, you nudge your view of the drawing slightly in that direction. For example, if you click on the right-pointing scroll arrow, an item that was hidden on the right side of the drawing slides into view. Click in the gray area of a scroll bar to scroll the window more dramatically. Drag a scroll box to manually specify the distance scrolled.

 For an even easier way to view different portions of your drawing, check out the hand tool, discussed along with other screen navigation options in Chapter 3.

Page controls

To the left of the horizontal scroll bar is a clump of page controls, which let you advance from one page to another inside a multipage drawing. I explain the nuances of these controls in Chapter 12. In the meantime, just ignore them.

Color stuff

You can change the colors of the outlines and interiors of shapes in the drawing area using the color controls on the right side of the CorelDraw interface. Click with the left mouse button on a color in the color palette to change the color assigned to the interior of a selected shape, known as the fill color. Click with the right mouse button to change the color of a shape's outline. Use the No Color button to make the fill or outline transparent.

This topic is another biggie. I cover it in my usual rough-and-tumble style throughout the rolling sagebrush and hilly terrain of Chapter 7.

You can move the color palette to a different on-screen location and display additional color swatches by using the techniques described in Chapter 7.

Status bar

The status bar keeps you apprised of what's going on. For example, any time your cursor is in the drawing area — the place where you create your drawing, naturally — the status line tells you the exact coordinate location of your cursor. Cool, huh? The status bar also tells you a load of information about selected shapes or anything else you may want to create.

For more information about this splendid feature, check out Chapter 6.

The Mouse Is Your Willing Slave (And Other Children's Stories)

Very likely, you've already noticed that when you move the mouse, the cursor moves on the screen — way to use those deductive reasoning skills. But that's not all the mouse does. In fact, the mouse is your primary means of communicating with CorelDraw. Oh sure, the keyboard is great for entering text and performing the occasional shortcut, but the mouse is the primo drawing and editing tool. In other words, you need to become familiar with the thing.

The typical mouse features two buttons on top, which register clicks, and a trackball underneath, which registers movement. If your mouse offers three buttons, the center button doesn't work in CorelDraw.

Here's a quick look at some common mouse terminology (not how mice talk, mind you, but how we talk about them, sometimes behind their furry little backs):

- ✔ To *move* your mouse is to move it without pressing any button.

- ✔ To *click* is to press the left button and immediately release it without moving the mouse. For example, you click on a tool icon to select a tool.

- ✔ To *right-click* is to press and release the right mouse button. In the old days, you rarely right-clicked — just to apply color to an outline and that sort of thing. But in Windows 95 and CorelDraw 8, the right mouse button takes on new meaning. In fact, I recommend that you take a moment and right-click on everything you can see. Every time you right-click, a pop-up menu appears, offering a list of specialized options. When in doubt, right-clicking may very well solve your problem. It can also save you a trip or two to the menu bar.

✔ Some mice let you switch the mouse buttons so that the right button serves the purpose of the left mouse button and vice versa. In this book, I assume you haven't switched your mouse buttons. If you have, remember that whenever I tell you to click the left mouse button, you need to click the right mouse button instead. And if I tell you to right-click, you need to left-click.

✔ To *double-click* is to press and release the left button twice in rapid succession without moving the mouse. Some programs even accept triple- and quadruple-clicks. CorelDraw does not go to such extremes.

✔ To *press and hold* is to press the button and hold it down for a moment. I refer to this operation rarely — an example is when some item takes a moment or two to display.

✔ To *drag* is to press the left button and hold it down as you move the mouse. You then release the button to complete the operation. In CorelDraw, for example, you drag with the freehand tool (known in many camps, including this one, as the pencil tool) to draw a free-form line.

You can also use the keyboard and mouse in tandem. For example, you can draw a perfect square by pressing the Ctrl key while dragging with the rectangle tool. You can press Shift and click on shapes with the arrow tool to select multiple shapes. Such actions are so common that you often see key and mouse combinations joined into compound verbs, such as Ctrl+dragging or Shift+clicking. Don't you love the way computer marketing and journalism abuses the language? i THinX IT/z Grait.

How to Deal with Complete Tools

You can liken the CorelDraw tools to the pencils, compasses, and French curves that technical artists used back in the bad old days. The difference is that in CorelDraw, a tool never wears out, stains, runs dry, gets lost, or gets stepped on. The tools are always ready to use on a moment's notice.

A quick experiment

To familiarize yourself with the basic purpose of tools as a group, try this brief exercise:

1. Click on the freehand tool icon.

The freehand tool is the fourth one from the top of the toolbox. The freehand tool icon looks like a pencil drawing a wiggly line. In fact, I'm going to call this tool the pencil tool from now on because if I call it the freehand tool, you'll never remember which icon you need to click to get to the tool. The pencil tool works like a pencil, its icon is a picture of a pencil, and it ought to be called a pencil — so in this book, it shall.

Anyway (and thank you for allowing me to spew forth from my tiny soapbox), after you click on the tool in the toolbox, the tool is ready to use.

2. Express yourself.

I don't want to give away too much stuff about the pencil tool — I'd spoil the many surprises awaiting you in Chapter 5 — but you drag with the tool to create free-form lines. So draw something. Figure 2-2 shows a line I drew, if that's any help.

3. Roam freely. Recognize no boundaries.

Even though I stayed inside the page boundaries in Figure 2-2, you don't have to. You can draw anywhere you want inside the drawing area, either in the page boundary or on the pasteboard. Just remember, if the object you draw is outside the page, it won't print.

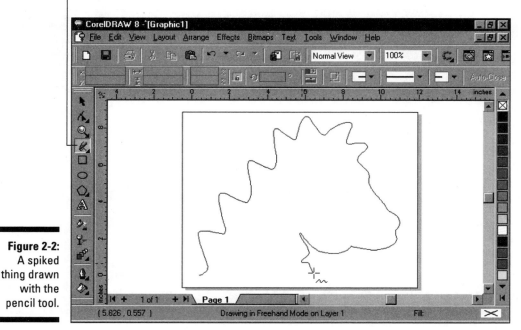

Figure 2-2:
A spiked thing drawn with the pencil tool.

4. Keep on drawing.

Don't stop. After you finish drawing one line, start another one. Draw something complicated or really messy. Drawing with a mouse can be a chore if you're not experienced with it. So I suggest you spend some quality time moving your mouse around. I want you two to get acquainted.

5. Okay, that's enough already.

I mean, don't get obsessed with it or anything.

6. Grab the arrow tool.

Click on the arrow tool — at the top of the toolbox — to select it. (Corel calls this tool the pick tool. But once again, I think this name is confusing, and therefore I refuse to fall in line. If the tool looks like an arrow, I say call it an arrow. Besides, I don't like to talk about "picking" in mixed company.) The arrow tool lets you manipulate the stuff you draw.

7. Select one of the lines.

Click on some line that you added to the drawing area. Make sure to align the tip of the arrow with the line before you click. The tip of the arrow is the hot point. I selected my wacky animal's wacky eye, as shown in wacky Figure 2-3.

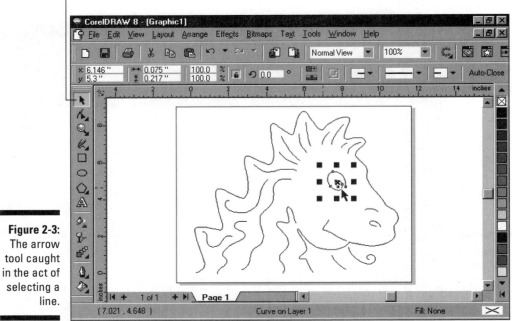

Figure 2-3:
The arrow tool caught in the act of selecting a line.

8. This is the end of the line, folks.

See those enormous squares that surround the line you just clicked on? They show that the line is selected. Try pressing Delete. Oops, the line's gone. You just killed it. Way to go.

See, that was pretty easy, huh? With some time, effort, patience, and a few other rare commodities, you'll have the whole drawing-with-a-mouse thing down cold.

How to find buried tools

If you click on the bottom two icons in the toolbox — the icons for the outline and fill tools — CorelDraw displays a *flyout menu,* which is simply a row of icons for options related to the tool. Click on an icon inside the menu to select the option you want to use. For example, the options on the outline tool flyout menu, shown in Figure 2-4, affect the color and thickness of the outline around a selected shape.

Five other tools — the ones that have little triangles in their lower-right corners — also offer flyout menus. But rather than simply clicking to display the flyout menus for these tools, you have to press and hold on the tool icon. Then click on an icon in the flyout menu to make that tool the active tool in the toolbox.

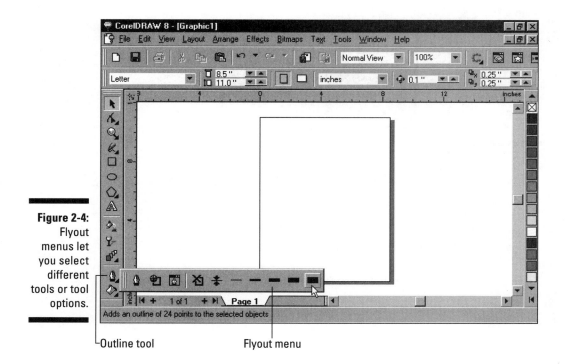

Figure 2-4:
Flyout menus let you select different tools or tool options.

Outline tool   Flyout menu

For example, the polygon tool is one of the tools that offers a flyout menu. Press and hold on the tool to display a flyout menu filled with three icons — polygon, spiral, and graph paper. If you click on the spiral or graph paper icon, it becomes the new occupant of the polygon tool slot.

More tool tricks

Normally, the toolbox adheres to the left side of the CorelDraw interface as if it were stuck there with denture adhesive. But you can easily move the toolbox: Simply drag it by its left or right edge, as illustrated in Figure 2-5. (Or drag any empty area around the tool icons.) After you release the mouse button, you get an independent, free-floating toolbox complete with a title bar. You can drag the title bar to move the toolbox around on-screen.

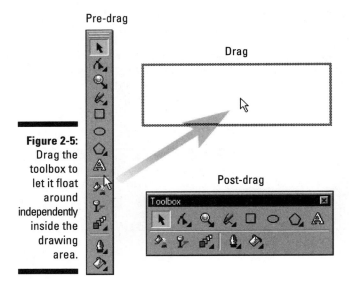

Figure 2-5: Drag the toolbox to let it float around independently inside the drawing area.

Just for laughs, here are some things you can do with the toolbox:

✔ Another way to make the toolbox float independently is to double-click in the gray area around the tools.

✔ You can resize the toolbox by dragging any side or corner.

✔ To restore the tools to their original moorings, double-click on the toolbox title bar or in the empty area around the buttons.

✔ If you want to make the tool icons larger or smaller, right-click on the gray area around the tools and select the Toolbars option. (Alternatively, you can choose View➪Toolbars.) The Options dialog box appears, as shown in Figure 2-6, offering a Button slider bar that affects the size of icons in the toolbox and toolbar. Drag the little tab on the slider bar to change the icon size.

✔ If you have trouble remembering what all the icons in the toolbox represent, never fear. If you hover your cursor over any tool in the toolbox, a little box appears displaying the name of the tool and the status bar displays a brief description of its purpose. In fact, CorelDraw displays the name and purpose of most interface items when you hover over them with your cursor.

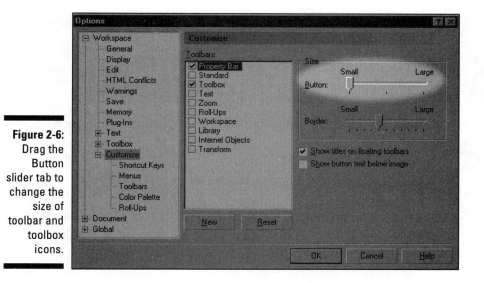

Figure 2-6: Drag the Button slider tab to change the size of toolbar and toolbox icons.

Les Menus sans Soupe du Jour

Instead of listing hors d'oeuvres and other tasty morsels, CorelDraw menus enable you to do stuff, such as open a drawing, abuse the drawing so that it's no longer recognizable, and save it to disk under the name Mud.

To choose a command from a menu, click on the menu name and then click on the command name. For example, if I ask you to choose File➪Open, click on the File menu name to display the File menu, and then click on the Open command.

Les équivalents du keyboard

In the case of File⇨Open (and many other commands), there's no reason to go to all the effort of using menus. You can simply press Ctrl+O — that is, press and hold the Ctrl key, press the O key, and then release both keys. This technique is called using a *keyboard equivalent*.

Most keyboard equivalents are listed along the right side of a menu. Some keyboard equivalents select tools and perform other functions instead of accessing menu commands. Either way, I keep you apprised of keyboard equivalents throughout this book. If you take the time to memorize a few shortcuts here and there, you can save yourself a heck of a lot of time and effort.

Alt, ma chère amie, oui?

You can also use the Alt key in combination with other keys to access menu commands. The following steps (with French translations) demonstrate one scenario for exploiting Alt:

1. **Press the Alt key plus the underlined letter in a menu name to display the menu.**

   For example, press Alt+F to display the File menu.

2. **Use the arrow keys to navigate the menus.**

   Press the down- and up-arrow keys to highlight commands in a menu. Use the left- and right-arrow keys to display neighboring menus.

3. **If the command has a submenu, press the right-arrow key to display that menu.**

   A submenu is simply an additional list of commands designed to further refine your choice of operations. Press the left-arrow key to hide the menu.

4. **Press Enter to choose the highlighted command.**

5. **To abandon the whole menu bit, press Alt again.**

   Or press the Esc (Escape) key. Each time you press Esc, CorelDraw hides a level of menus.

Alternatively, after pressing Alt and the key for the underlined letter in the menu name, you can press the key for the underlined letter in the command name. For example, to choose File⇨Open, press Alt, followed by F, and then O. (Those underlined letters are known as *hotkeys,* by the way.)

The Incessant Chatter of Dialog Boxes

Some menu commands react immediately. Others require you to fill out a few forms before they can be processed. In fact, any command that's followed by an ellipsis (three dots, like so: ...) displays a dialog box, a roll-up, or a docker. A dialog box asks you to answer some questions before CorelDraw implements the command; roll-ups and dockers stay on-screen so that you can perform an operation repeatedly without having to choose the command over and over again.

Figure 2-7 shows a sample dialog box.

The dialog box options work as follows:

✔ Many dialog boxes contain multiple panels of options. To get to a different panel, click on one of the tabs at the top of the dialog box.

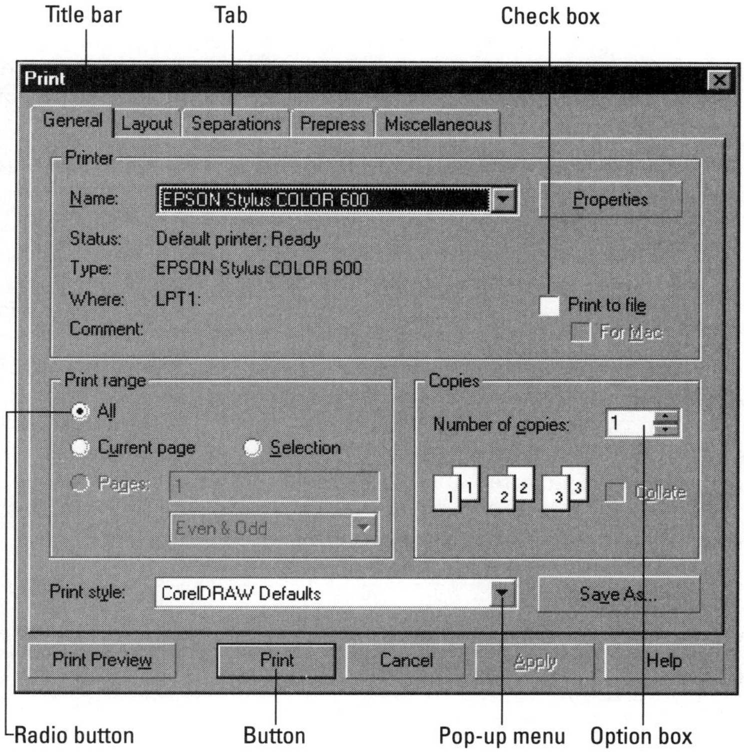

Title bar   Tab   Check box

Figure 2-7:
The anatomy of a dialog box.

Radio button   Button   Pop-up menu   Option box

✔ An option in which you can enter numbers or text is called an option box. (Propellerheads also like to call these options *fields,* strictly because it sounds more technical.) Double-click on an option box to highlight its contents and then replace the contents by entering new stuff with the keyboard. Or, if you prefer, use the arrow icons to the right of an option box or press the arrow keys on the keyboard to incrementally raise or lower the value in the option box — all without hydraulics, mind you.

✔ To conserve space, some multiple-choice options appear as pop-up menus (also known in some circles as drop-down lists). Click on the down-pointing arrow to display a menu of options. Then click on the desired option in the menu to select it, just as if you were choosing a command from a standard menu. (Note that menus that appear when you right-click on a screen element are also referred to as pop-up menus.)

✔ You can select only one circular radio button from any gang of radio buttons. To select a radio button, click on the button or on the option name that follows it. The selected radio button gets a black dot; all other radio buttons are hollow.

✔ You can select as many check boxes as you want. Really, go nuts. To select a check box, click on the box or on the option name that follows it. A check mark in the box shows that the option is turned on. Clicking on a selected check box turns off the option.

✔ The normal, everyday variety of button (not to be confused with the radio button) enables you to close the current dialog box or display others. For example, click on the Cancel button to close the dialog box and cancel the current command. Click on the OK button to close the dialog box and execute the command according to the current settings. If a button name includes an ellipsis, clicking on it brings up another dialog box.

As you can with menus, you can select options and perform other feats of magic inside dialog boxes from the keyboard. To advance from one option to the next, press the Tab key. To back up, press Shift+Tab. To select any option, press Alt along with the hotkey (the underlined letter). Or, if no option box is highlighted, just press the hotkey by itself. Press Enter to activate the button that's surrounded by a heavy outline, such as OK. Press Esc or Alt+F4 to choose the Cancel button.

Roll-Ups, Now in Dozens of Fruity Flavors

Roll-ups, like the one shown in Figure 2-8, are basically dialog boxes that can remain on-screen while you work with other functions in CorelDraw. They float above the surface of the drawing area, just like the toolbox. CorelDraw 8 offers more than two dozen roll-ups that you can display on-screen all at once, just a few at a time, or whatever. (The more roll-ups you display, the more you eat up your computer's memory, however.)

Close button⌐

Roll-up button⌐

Anchor button⌐

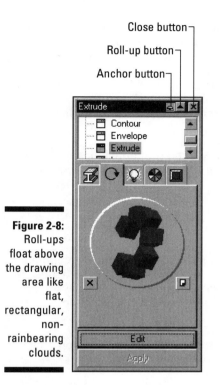

Figure 2-8:
Roll-ups
float above
the drawing
area like
flat,
rectangular,
non-
rainbearing
clouds.

Each roll-up provides so many individual options that there's no point in running through them all here. Suffice it to say that roll-ups let you do some pretty amazing stuff. The roll-up in Figure 2-8, for example, lets you add depth to an otherwise two-dimensional shape. You can stretch the shape off the page, much like you'd . . . well, frankly, no real-life equivalent exists. The process is way cool, which is why I describe it in Chapter 9.

To display a roll-up, choose it from the View⇨Roll-Ups submenu or press its keyboard shortcut (if it has one), conveniently located to the right of the roll-up's name. If you have more than one roll-up displayed on-screen, switch to the one you want to use by clicking on its roll-up button (labeled in Figure 2-8). The roll-up magically pops to the front of any other roll-ups that may be obscuring it from view.

Roll 'em up and tack 'em down

Roll-ups are called roll-ups because you can roll them up — strange but true. Click on the up-pointing arrow in the upper-right corner of the roll-up window to hide everything but the title bar. This way, you can have several roll-ups on-screen at once without cluttering up the interface. Click on a roll-up's arrow again — it's a down-pointing arrow now — to restore the full window.

By default, a roll-up is anchored so that it remains on-screen regardless of other activities you perform. However, if you want the roll-up to disappear after it's used once, click on the anchor button (it looks like a thumbtack) just to the left of the roll-up arrow in the title bar. The thumbtack appears to raise up, showing that the roll-up is no longer anchored. The next time you apply an option or a command from the roll-up, the roll-up disappears. If you're having problems with screen clutter, this approach is another way to eliminate it.

But if you want my opinion, you should leave the thumbtack down. Having the roll-up disappear every time you use it can be terribly disconcerting and is rarely useful.

Breakaway roll-ups

Because CorelDraw 8 offers so many roll-ups, some roll-ups are combined into related groups. For example, the Blend, Contour, Envelope, Extrude, and Lens roll-ups are all included in a single roll-up, as shown in Figure 2-9. Here are a few tidbits to keep in mind about working with these multiple roll-up roll-ups:

✔ You can switch to a different roll-up in the group by clicking on its name in the scrolling list at the top of the roll-up window.

✔ To separate an item in the group into an independent roll-up, right-click on the item's name in the scrolling list. Then select Ungroup, as in Figure 2-9. Give me your roll-ups, yearning to be free.

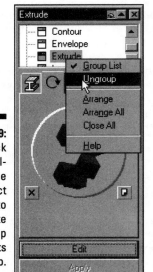

Figure 2-9:
Right-click
on a roll-
up's name
and select
Ungroup to
separate
the roll-up
from its
group.

> ✔ You can also combine roll-ups into your own groups, whether the roll-ups are related or not. Alt+drag the title bar of one roll-up and drop it onto another roll-up. Or, to move a roll-up from one group to another, drag the roll-up's name from the scrolling list onto the other roll-up.

Dockers you can't wear

CorelDraw 8 sports a special variety of roll-up, called dockers. *Dockers,* like the one shown in Figure 2-10, are roll-ups that can be "docked" to the side of the screen for quick and easy access while you work.

Dockers function just like roll-ups because, as I just said, they *are* roll-ups. To display a docker, choose it from the View⊅Dockers submenu. The docker appears neatly anchored to the right side of the document window and remains on-screen while you do whatever it is you're doing. If you want to reclaim your screen real estate while keeping a docker close at hand, click on the two right-pointing arrows in the upper-left corner of the docker window to roll it up (or, I should say, roll it right). To undock a docker, drag the top of the Docker window away from the edge of the document window.

Docker

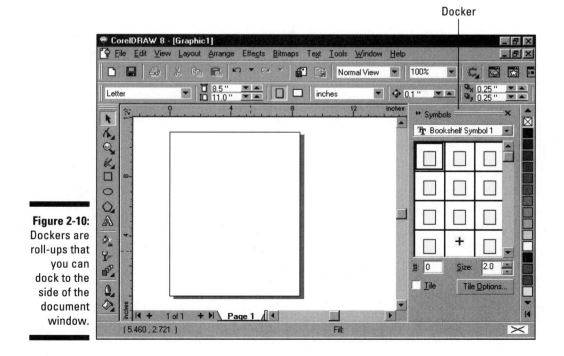

Figure 2-10: Dockers are roll-ups that you can dock to the side of the document window.

Chapter 3

Ladies and Gentlemen, Insert Your Pocket Protectors!

· ·

In This Chapter

▶ Creating a new document

▶ Importing and opening clip art

▶ Magnifying your drawing for a closer look

▶ Using other zooming options

▶ Exploring the past and present virtues of scrolling

▶ Modifying the screen display

▶ Looking at a rat in startling ways

▶ Saving a drawing to disk

▶ Updating files and making backups

▶ Shutting down CorelDraw

· ·

*W*ith CorelDraw, you're the master of your creation. You can add whatever flair or flourish you deem appropriate, using whatever tool strikes your fancy. You have total artistic freedom (as much as your client or boss allows, that is). But you can't experience the heady joys that come with this absolute power until you master three basic tasks: creation, navigation, and storage.

Creation is giving birth to the drawing; navigation is tooling around the on-screen landscape, moving from one part of your drawing to the next; and storage is the small but essential ceremony that ensures that all your hard work doesn't go in the tank when you quit the program. This chapter gets you up to speed on all three subjects, plus a few others for good measure.

Spank the Baby

You probably don't remember this, but when the doctor whisked you out of your mom, he or she smacked your rump to make you take in that first lungful of air and bellow like a stricken — well . . . baby. Now here you are, several thousand days later, wondering why I'm bringing up such a painful subject. The truth is, you have to perform a similar maneuver before you can begin drawing in CorelDraw.

Here's your chance to see whether you've managed to absorb anything about computers so far. Which of the following actions do you suspect results in a new document in CorelDraw?

A. Gently but firmly slap the disk drive. There's no time like the present to teach your computer who's boss.

B. Taunt the computer mercilessly until it cries.

C. Choose File➪New or File➪Open.

Four out of five computer scientists agree that B is the best way to humble your computer into producing a new document. But recently, dissenting scientists have come out in support of answer C. In the interest of fair and unbiased journalism, I test this strange theory in the following pages.

How do I start a new document?

If you turn off the welcome screen as I instruct in the "Interface in Your Face" section of Chapter 2, CorelDraw automatically produces an empty drawing area after you start the program. (If CorelDraw does something else after you start it, choose Tools➪Options or press Ctrl+J. After the Options dialog box appears, click on General and select Start a New Document from the On CorelDRAW! Startup pop-up menu, and press Enter. From now on, an empty drawing area greets you every time you start CorelDraw.)

The empty drawing area represents a brand new document. This area has no preconceived notions of what a drawing is or what it should be. You can mold it into anything you want. The problem is, an empty drawing area can be terrifying. Being confronted with a blank page is like looking inside the deepest recesses of your soul and seeing nothing — except the experience isn't nearly so profound. Thankfully, you have other options available, as covered in the next section.

If for some reason — like, you're a masochist or something — you want to start a document from scratch after you've been working in the program for a while, all you need to do is choose File➪New or press Ctrl+N.

The enlightening Chihuahua scenario

Starting a brand new drawing isn't the only route to success in CorelDraw. You can approach your drawing from a different angle by opening or importing an existing drawing that can serve as a starting point for whatever you want to create.

Suppose you want to draw a Chihuahua. Now there's a puzzle for you. You're stuck in a tiny cubicle on the third floor of an air-conditioned building in an office park — not the sort of place where a yippy little dog is likely to stroll by anytime soon. And even if you had a Chihuahua willing to serve as an artist's model, you wouldn't have a hope of drawing the animal, because the degree of difficulty for creating a realistic Chihuahua from scratch in CorelDraw is somewhere in the neighborhood of 13 on a 10-point scale.

So what's the solution? Well, in the vast CorelDraw library of clip art, you can find a drawing of a small animal that is generally accepted to be the direct ancestor to the Chihuahua. I am referring, of course, to the rat. All you have to do is shorten the tail, snip the claws, enlarge the ears, remove some whiskers, bulge out the eyes, reduce the size of the brain cavity, and add a little balloon above the creature's head that says "Yip yip," and the evolutionary transformation is complete.

But before you can do any editing, you have to open the rat drawing using the File⇨Open command, discussed next. You can find the rat on the second CD-ROM included in your CorelDraw 8 package.

How do I open a piece of clip art?

Corel ships its clip art in the CDR format, which means you can use the everyday, ordinary File⇨Open command to open a piece of clip art (despite what the product manual tells you). Back in Version 6, the clip art came in the CMX format, which required you to use the Import command to place a piece of clip art in your drawing.

The following steps tell you how to open one of the clip-art drawings in the CorelDraw package. You can use the same process to open any existing drawing, whether it's stored on a CD, a floppy disk, or your hard drive.

1. **Choose File⇨Open or press Ctrl+O.**

   The Open Drawing dialog box, shown in Figure 3-1, appears.

2. **Select a disk drive from the Look in pop-up menu.**

   Click anywhere on the option box at the top of the dialog box to display a pop-up menu. Then click on the drive in which your file is stored. To find the rat, select your CD-ROM drive, which is probably the D drive but can also be identified by the CD-ROM icon that accompanies the letter.

Up One Level┐   List ┌Details

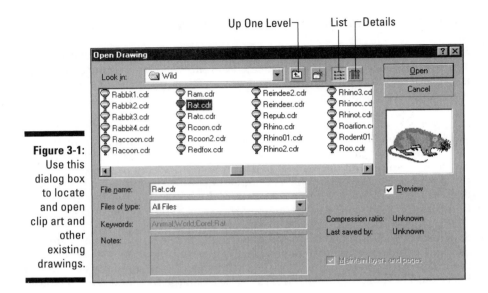

Figure 3-1:
Use this
dialog box
to locate
and open
clip art and
other
existing
drawings.

3. Open the desired folders in the central scrolling list.

Double-click on a folder name to open it. The list then displays all files
and folders inside that folder. Double-click on another folder to open it,
and so on. For example, to open the folder that holds the rat drawing,
first double-click on the Clipart folder, then on the Animals folder, and
finally on the Wild folder.

4. Select the drawing you want to open.

To open the rat, first click on any filename in the scrolling list. Next,
press R to scroll to the drawings that begin with that letter, including
such hits as Rabbit, Raccoon, and Ram. Then click on the right scroll
arrow a few times to advance to the Rat.cdr file. Click on the file to
select it. Assuming that the Preview check box is selected, a preview of
the drawing appears on the right side of the dialog box so that you can
see what the drawing looks like.

5. Click on the <u>O</u>pen button or press Enter.

You can also double-click on a filename to open the file. Whichever
method you choose, CorelDraw opens the rat inside a new drawing
area. Black squares called *handles* surround the rat, showing that it is
selected and ready to edit. You can now manipulate the rat at will.

I wish I could tell you how to change a rat into a Chihuahua in five easy
steps, but I can't. Instead, I devote Chapters 4 through 9 to the topic of
drawing and editing in CorelDraw. I don't specifically address Chihuahua
illustrations, but you can tell that they're constantly in the back of my mind.
In the meantime, here are a few additional notes on opening drawings to
carry you through your working day:

✔ To close a folder and look at the contents of the folder that contains it, click on the Up One Level button (labeled in Figure 3-1).

✔ To find out more information about a file — such as its size on disk and the last time it was modified — click on the Details button (also labeled in Figure 3-1). You can then change the order in which the files are displayed by clicking on the buttons that appear along the top of the list. For example, to list the files alphabetically, click on the Name button.

✔ To hide that technical stuff and see just the filenames again, click on the List button.

You can open a file also using the Scrapbook, as I discuss in the section "Opening and importing from the Scrapbook."

Adding a drawing to an existing drawing

The File⇨Open command opens a piece of clip art as a new drawing. But if you want to add a clip art drawing to an existing drawing — say, to place the rat into a pretty field of wildflowers that you created earlier — you need the Import command. You can add as many pieces of clip art to a drawing as you like. To place the rat or any other existing drawing into an open drawing, just perform the following easy-as-pie steps:

1. **Choose File⇨Import or press Ctrl+I.**

   The Import dialog box, which is nearly identical to the Open Drawing dialog box just discussed, appears.

2. **Locate and select the drawing.**

   Use the method described in the preceding section to hunt down the drawing and then click on it in the scrolling list.

3. **Click on Import or press Enter.**

   Alternatively, you can double-click on the drawing name in the scrolling list. Your cursor turns into a half-rectangle (kind of like a picture frame without the right and bottom sides) with the name of the file you are importing in the middle.

4. **Position your cursor where you want to insert the drawing, and click.**

   CorelDraw plops the drawing inside the drawing area. Your drawing is surrounded by black boxes (called *selection handles*), which indicate that the drawing is selected and ready to edit.

CorelDraw always imports all the little bits and pieces of stuff that go into a clip-art graphic as something called a *group*. If you want to select and edit individual elements in a group, you must use some special techniques, which are covered in the "Gang Behavior" section of Chapter 6.

If CorelDraw can't import a file, the file may be damaged and no longer usable. More likely, though, the file was stored in some file format that CorelDraw doesn't want to accept. Ask around and see whether anyone knows anything about the file, including where it came from. You may need to install an import filter for the file format.

Opening and importing from the Scrapbook

You can open and import clip art also from the Scrapbook, shown in Figure 3-2. To display the Scrapbook, choose View⇨Scrapbook⇨Clipart.

In CorelDraw 8, the Scrapbook is a docker rather than a roll-up as it was in Version 7. But don't let this throw you. Remember, dockers function just like traditional roll-ups; the only difference is that they can be anchored to the side of your document window.

Use the Folder pop-up menu and Up One Level button to locate the Clipart folder on the second CorelDraw CD-ROM. Double-click on the Clipart folder to display all the different clip-art folders; double-click on a folder to display thumbnail views of the drawings in that folder.

Folder pop-up menu ┐ Up One Level

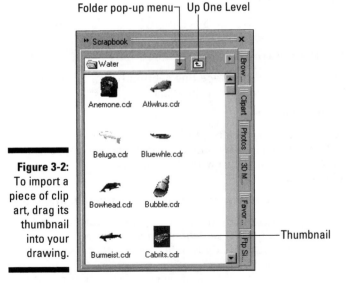

Thumbnail

Figure 3-2:
To import a piece of clip art, drag its thumbnail into your drawing.

When you find a piece of clip art you like, double-click on its thumbnail to open the clip art as a new drawing. To import the clip art into an open drawing, drag the thumbnail onto the drawing page. Alternatively, you can right-click on the thumbnail and choose Open or Import from the pop-up menu that appears.

If the file you want to use isn't on the CorelDraw CD, choose <u>V</u>iew⇨<u>S</u>crapbook⇨<u>B</u>rowse to display the Browse tab in the docker window. After locating the file, use the same methods just discussed to open or import the file. From this tab of the Scrapbook, you can open regular drawing files as well as clip-art files.

You also can use the Scrapbook to apply special fills and outlines to your shapes (as discussed in Chapter 7) and open photos (as discussed in Chapter 15).

CorelDraw has to generate thumbnails for each folder you open in the Scrapbook, a process that can take a bit of time if you're using a slow computer. For that reason, you may find it quicker to rely on the catalog provided with the CorelDraw 8 package to hunt down an appropriate piece of clip art rather than browsing thumbnails in the Scrapbook.

Tools for Getting around the Drawing Area

Ah, getting around, a favorite pursuit of the Beach Boys. Of course, we all know that in reality, the Beach Boys were about as likely to get around as a parade of go-carting Shriners. I mean, it's not like you're going to confuse a squad of sandy-haired Neil Bush lookalikes with the Hell's Angels.

Now that I've offended everyone who's ever surfed or enjoyed falsetto harmonies, I will say two things in the Beach Boys' defense. First, "Help Me, Rhonda" and "Good Vibrations" are crankin' tunes. And second, even a bunch of squares like the Beach Boys can get around in CorelDraw. (Nice tie-in, huh?)

Miracles of magnification

When you first open a drawing, you see the full page, as in Figure 3-3. To fit the page entirely inside the drawing area, CorelDraw has to reduce the page so that it appears considerably smaller than it will print. It's as if you're standing far away from an image, taking in the big picture.

Zoom tool

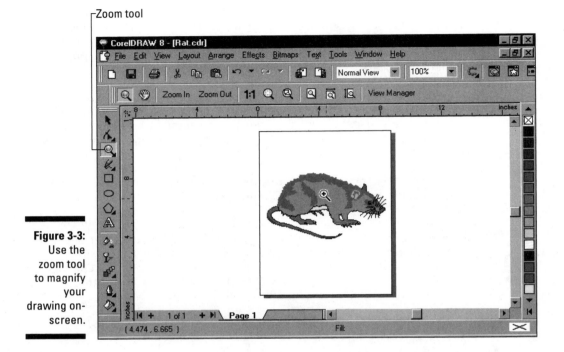

Figure 3-3:
Use the
zoom tool
to magnify
your
drawing on-
screen.

Although the big picture is great, it lacks detail. Imagine trying to edit the claws, the eyes, or some other minute feature of the rat from this vantage point. That's why CorelDraw lets you zoom in to magnify the drawing and zoom out to make it smaller.

Version 8 offers a multitude of ways to zoom in and out on a drawing, with the primary tool being the zoom tool, which you use as follows:

1. **Click on the zoom tool.**

   The zoom tool is the one that looks like a magnifying glass. Just click on the zoom tool icon in the toolbox to select the tool. The cursor changes to a little magnifying glass.

   To access the zoom tool temporarily when another tool is selected, press F2. The zoom cursor appears, and you can then click once to zoom in on your drawing. After you click, the tool that was previously selected becomes active again.

2. **Click in the drawing area.**

   CorelDraw magnifies the drawing to twice its previous size. The program centers the magnified view at the point where you click. In Figure 3-4, for example, I clicked on the eyeball to center the magnified view on the eyeball.

Alternatively, you can drag with the zoom tool to surround the area you want to magnify with a dotted outline. CorelDraw fills the drawing area with the area you dragged around. Using this technique, you can zoom in to more than twice the previous level of magnification.

3. Repeat Steps 1 and 2 until your wrist gets tired.

If you select the zoom tool by clicking on its icon in the toolbox, you can use it as many times as you like. If you select it by pressing F2, CorelDraw reverts to the previously selected tool after you finish zooming. You have to press F2 each time you want to zoom.

Zooming doesn't change the size at which your drawing prints. It affects just the size at which you see the drawing on-screen.

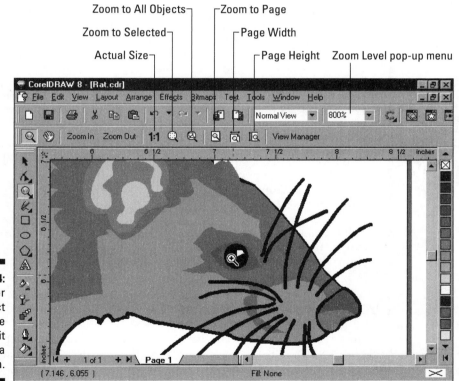

Figure 3-4:
The closer you inspect the rat, the more it looks like a Chihuahua.

CorelDraw also offers several automatic zoom controls that zoom in and out to predefined intervals. Here's the scoop:

- ✔ To zoom out, Shift+click with the zoom tool. CorelDraw reduces the drawing to 50 percent of its former glory.

- ✔ You can zoom out also by pressing F3. The screen zooms at the touch of the key. No clicking, soaking, or whittling is required.

- ✔ To zoom in on a selected portion of your drawing, press Shift+F2. For example, select the rat's nose by clicking on it with the arrow tool. Then press Shift+F2 to get a close-up view of the critter's nostrils.

- ✔ To reduce the view so that every line, shape, and character of text is visible, including objects on the pasteboard, press F4.

- ✔ To return the view so that you can see the entire page, press Shift+F4.

- ✔ As covered in Chapter 2, I prefer to keep the CorelDraw toolbar turned off so that I have more screen space available for my drawing. But as I also mention in Chapter 2, the toolbar does offer a valuable control for zooming. You can select a preset zoom ratio from the Zoom Level pop-up menu, labeled in Figure 3-4. More importantly, you can double-click on the Zoom Level box, enter a zoom value from the keyboard, and then press Enter. This method enables you to zoom to a specific zoom level — say, 73 percent — not available on the pop-up menu or with the zoom tool.

If you want to be able to access the Zoom Level pop-up menu but you don't want to display the toolbar, do this: First, select the zoom tool. Now Alt+drag the pop-up menu off the toolbar and onto the end of the property bar. Now you can access the menu from the property bar whenever the zoom tool is selected.

You'd think that this cornucopia of zooming options would be enough. But evidently CorelDraw didn't because the program offers still more ways to zoom in and out, as covered in the next three sections.

Zoom up to the property bar

If trying to remember all the keyboard shortcuts for zooming makes your brain hurt, you can use the zoom tools on the property bar, labeled in Figure 3-4. The tools become available when you select the zoom tool. From left to right, the property bar controls work as follows:

- ✔ Clicking on the Zoom In and Zoom Out buttons does the same thing as clicking and Shift+clicking with the zoom tool. Click on Zoom In to magnify your view to twice the previous size. Click on Zoom Out to reduce the view by 50 percent.

- ✔ Click on the Actual Size button — the one labeled 1:1 — to view your drawing at close to the size it will print.

- ✔ The Zoom to Selected button zooms to the currently selected area in your drawing.

- ✔ Click on the Zoom to All Objects button to see the entire drawing on-screen.

- ✔ Click on the Zoom to Page button to view the entire drawing page.

- ✔ The Page Width button zooms your drawing so that you can see the entire width of the page. The Page Height button zooms your drawing so that the entire length of the drawing is visible.

- ✔ Don't worry about the View Manager button. View Manager gives you another way to zoom in and out on your drawing. But because View Manager eats up more of your already precious screen real estate, you're better off using the other zoom controls.

Your very own zoombox

If you're trying to save screen space and you want to turn off the property bar (as explained in Chapter 2), you can still access the zoom icons discussed in the preceding section. Right-click in the gray area surrounding the toolbox to display a pop-up menu and select the Zoom option. The result is a free-floating palette of zoom tools, as shown in Figure 3-5.

The tools are twins of the tools found on the property bar, discussed in the preceding section. (Figure 3-5 provides a handy reference to the tools and their keyboard equivalents.) You also get one additional tool, which Corel calls the pan one-shot tool and ordinary folks are sure to refer to as the temporary hand tool. Clicking on the tool icon temporarily accesses the hand tool, discussed later in this chapter. After you use the tool, the previously selected tool becomes active again.

Double-click on a gray area in the Zoom palette to make it float independently. To fix the palette along the right side of the window, drag it to the right edge of your screen. Click on the Close button to put the palette away.

The secret magnification menu

If you don't like any of the kazillion zoom options already discussed, select the zoom tool and right-click anywhere in the drawing area. Up pops a menu that offers you a series of zoom options. You can even select from a submenu of specific zoom ratios from 10 to 400 percent.

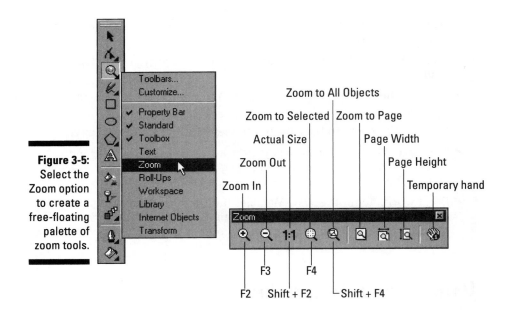

Figure 3-5:
Select the
Zoom option
to create a
free-floating
palette of
zoom tools.

Pull Your Image into View

As you doubtless have already noticed, you can see only bits and pieces of your drawing when it's magnified. The scroll bars and the hand tool allow you to control which bits and pieces are visible.

Corel refers to the hand tool as the pan tool, presumably in reference to the term *panning,* which is a word used in the television and movie business. To pan the camera is to move the camera to capture a different view of the action. However, no cameras are involved in CorelDraw, and I'm guessing that you work in an office, not on a movie or television set. Therefore, I refer to the pan tool as the hand tool because the tool's icon and cursor look like a hand and just about every other program on the planet with a similar navigation tool calls the thing the hand tool.

Anyway, suppose you can see only the nose of the rat, as shown in Figure 3-6. You want to view the animal's face and neck, an inch or so to the left. To do so, you can do any the following:

✔ Drag the scroll box on the horizontal scroll bar to the left. The drawing moves in the opposite direction.

✔ Select the hand tool from the zoom tool flyout or from the property bar, as shown in Figure 3-6. Then drag to the right with the hand tool, as in Figure 3-7. As you drag with the tool, the drawing moves to the right.

Hand tool

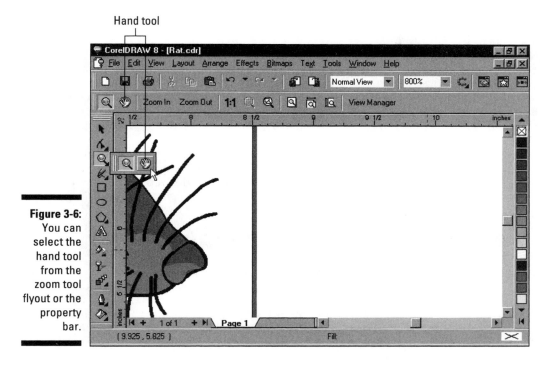

Figure 3-6:
You can select the hand tool from the zoom tool flyout or the property bar.

Figure 3-7:
Drag with the hand tool to scroll the drawing in the direction of your drag.

✔ You can temporarily select the hand tool from the Zoom palette, shown in Figure 3-5. After you use the tool once, the previously selected tool becomes active again.

✔ CorelDraw also offers a nifty keyboard shortcut for moving around your drawing. Press Alt plus an arrow key to scroll in the direction of the arrow key. Keep pressing Alt and the arrow key until you reach the area you want to view. The neat thing about this trick, called auto-panning, is that you can use it when any tool is selected, not just the hand tool.

If you get lost when scrolling your drawing and can't figure out where your drawing went, just press Shift+F4 to zoom all the way out so that the page fits inside the window. Then zoom and scroll as desired.

The Screen Is What You Make It

Another way to change how CorelDraw shows you a drawing on-screen is to switch display modes. Normally, you see the drawing in full, glorious color, with all fills and outlines intact. This view is called normal mode. This mode is excellent in that it shows the drawing as it will print. The only problem with this mode is that it can be slow, especially when you're viewing a complex drawing. As a remedy, CorelDraw provides a few other display modes for your viewing pleasure.

Show me a rough draft

One way to speed up the screen display is to switch to draft mode, which you can do by choosing View➪Draft or selecting the Draft View option from the View Quality pop-up menu on the toolbar. In this mode, CorelDraw displays any complex special effects — such as bitmap fills — as simple, two-color patterns instead of displaying the actual fill. If your drawing doesn't incorporate any of these effects, you don't see any difference between normal mode and draft mode.

String art revival

Another option for faster screen display is to choose View➪Wireframe. Or if your toolbar is displayed, select the Wireframe option from the View Quality pop-up menu on the toolbar, labeled in Figure 3-8. In wireframe mode, CorelDraw displays each shape in your drawing as if it were transparent and endowed with only a thin black outline, as shown in Figure 3-8.

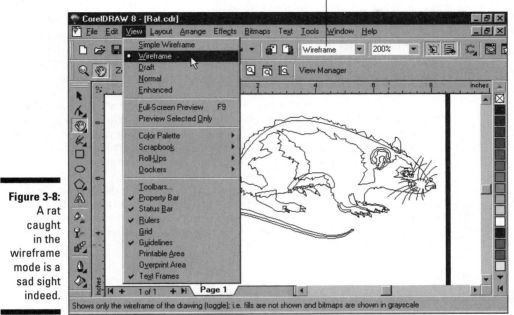

View Quality

Shows only the wireframe of the drawing (toggle): i.e. fills are not shown and bitmaps are shown in grayscale

Figure 3-8:
A rat
caught
in the
wireframe
mode is a
sad sight
indeed.

CorelDraw also offers a simple wireframe mode, which displays even less of your drawing's skeletal system than wireframe mode. (Depending on how complicated your drawing is, you may not see much difference between wireframe mode and simple wireframe mode.) To switch to simple wireframe mode, choose View⇨Simple Wireframe or select the Simple Wireframe option from the View Quality pop-up menu on the toolbar.

Wireframe and simple wireframe modes speed things up considerably because CorelDraw can display a bunch of black outlines way faster than colors, gradations, arrowheads, and other attributes that you find out about in Chapter 7. But both modes can also make it more difficult to edit the drawing. Using either of the wireframe modes is like trying to imagine how a house will look when still in the framing stage.

You need to use the wireframe mode only if CorelDraw is running exasperatingly slowly. And even then, you need to regularly switch back and forth between wireframe mode and normal mode to keep track of what's going on.

Pressing Shift+F9 switches you from the current view mode to the mode you used last. (A single command that switches you back and forth like this is known as a *toggle*.) So if you switched directly from normal mode to wireframe or simple wireframe, you can press Shift+F9 to return to normal mode. Otherwise, you need to choose View⇨Normal.

Die, you gravy-sucking interface

Although the interface is absolutely essential to communicating with CorelDraw, it can occasionally prove distracting. To temporarily hide everything but the drawing itself, as in Figure 3-9, press F9 or choose View⇨Full-Screen Preview. No matter what view mode you were previously using, CorelDraw shows the drawing in full color.

I like to call this mode the hands-off preview mode because you can't do anything in it besides look at the drawing. The second you click the right mouse button or press a key on the keyboard, CorelDraw exits the hands-off preview mode and restores the interface. Clicking the left mouse button forces CorelDraw to refresh the screen, but that's the extent of it.

Occasionally, novices get all panicky when the interface disappears, and they assume that the only way to return to CorelDraw is to turn off the computer, pawn it, and buy a new one. I don't want this to happen to you. So at the risk of sounding repetitive, I'll repeat myself: Just press any key on the keyboard, and the interface returns.

Preview bits and pieces

CorelDraw provides one additional method for previewing a drawing. When you're working with a complex drawing, some shapes can get in the way of other shapes. You may be tempted to delete shapes just to get them out of your way. But don't, because CorelDraw offers a better way:

Figure 3-9:
Unencumbered by the CorelDraw interface, the rat appears perceptibly more at ease with its surroundings.

1. **Select the lines, shapes, and text you want to preview.**

   I don't explain how to select stuff until Chapter 4. But to get you started, you can select a single object by clicking on it with the arrow tool. You select multiple objects by clicking on one and then Shift+clicking on the others.

2. **Choose <u>V</u>iew⇨Preview Selected <u>O</u>nly.**

   After you choose this command, it remains in effect until you choose the command again. Notice that a check mark appears next to the command name to show that the command is active.

3. **Press F9.**

   Only the selected objects appear on-screen.

Figure 3-10 shows the result of selectively previewing a few shapes that make up the rat. The poor animal looks like a gang of field mice stripped it down to its underwear.

Save or Die Trying!

Saving your drawing is like locking your car. After you get in the habit of doing it, you're protected. Until then, life can be traumatic. A stereo stolen here, a crucial drawing lost there. During my formative desktop publishing years, I managed to lose so many drawings that I finally taped the motto "Save or die trying" to the wall above my computer. If you're new to computers, I suggest that you do something similar. You look up, you save your drawing, and you live happily ever after.

Figure 3-10:
Transforming a rat into a mole through selective previewing.

After all, there's nothing like spending an hour or so on a complex drawing that you've neglected to save only to be greeted by a system error, power outage, or some other electronic tragedy. Losing a drawing makes you want to beat the old fists on the top of the monitor, strangle the computer with its own power cord, or engage in other unseemly acts of computer terrorism. To avoid the trauma, save your document to disk early and update it often.

Saving for the very first time

The very first time you save a new drawing, you have to name it and specify its location on disk. Here's how:

1. **Choose File⇨Save or press Ctrl+S.**

   The Save Drawing dialog box appears, as shown in Figure 3-11.

2. **Enter a name into the File name option box.**

   Gone are the days when filenames could be only eight characters long. Now you can go as high as you like. Heck, you can name the file Scurvy, Flea-Bitten, No-Good Chihuahua Wannabe if you like. As long as the name is shorter than 256 characters, you're okay.

   It's also worth noting that you don't have to enter .CDR (known as the *file extension*) at the end of the filename. CorelDraw does that for you without you ever knowing. Isn't progress wonderful? (If you want to save the file in some format other than the CDR format, select the format from the Save as type pop-up menu. The proper file extension is automatically added for you in that case, too.)

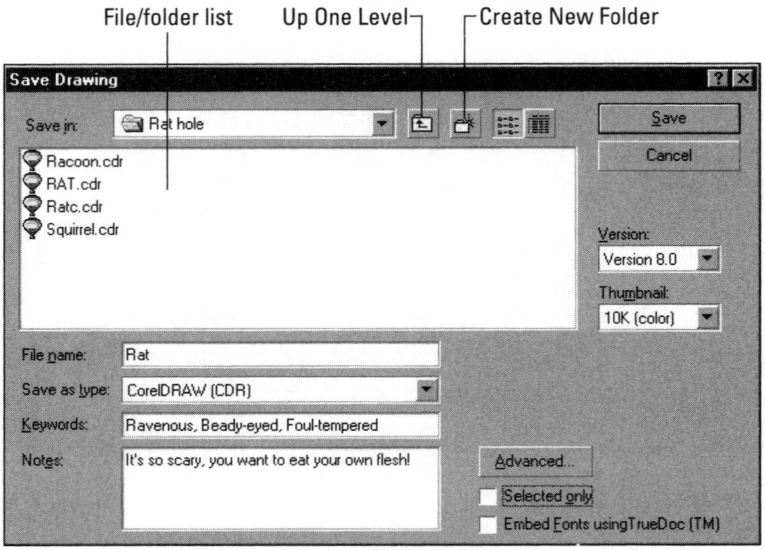

File/folder list   Up One Level┐   ┌Create New Folder

Figure 3-11: Use this dialog box to name your drawing and specify its location on disk.

Save Drawing		? ☒
Save in:	🗀 Rat hole	▼ 🔼 🗂 🔳 🔲	Save
			Cancel
💡 Racoon.cdr			
💡 RAT.cdr			
💡 Ratc.cdr			Version:
💡 Squirrel.cdr			Version 8.0 ▼
			Thumbnail:
			10K (color) ▼
File name:	Rat		
Save as type:	CorelDRAW (CDR)	▼	
Keywords:	Ravenous, Beady-eyed, Foul-tempered		
Notes:	It's so scary, you want to eat your own flesh!		Advanced...
			☐ Selected only
			☐ Embed Fonts usingTrueDoc (TM)

3. **Select a disk drive from the Save in pop-up menu.**

   Use the pop-up menu to select the drive where you want to store your drawing. Incidentally, you can't save a drawing to CD-ROM (unless, of course, you're one of those well-financed folks who own one of the new writable CD drives). If you opened a piece of CorelDraw clip art, you need to save it to your hard drive or some other disk.

4. **Select a folder inside the scrolling list of files and folders.**

   Double-click on folder names to open the folders, just as you did when opening a drawing (explained earlier in this chapter). If necessary, you can use the Up One Level button to navigate to a different folder, just as in the Open dialog box. If you want to create an entirely new folder, click on the Create New Folder button, labeled in Figure 3-11.

5. **Click on the Save button or press Enter.**

   Your drawing is now saved! Come heck or high water, you're protected.

Updating the drawing

After you name your drawing and save it to disk for the first time, press Ctrl+S every time you think of it. Pressing Ctrl+S automatically updates your drawing on disk without requiring you to work your way through dialog boxes, options, or any other interface artifacts. If you remember to update your drawing regularly, you won't lose hours of work when something goes wrong — notice that I said when, not if. You'll lose a few minutes, maybe, but that comes with the territory.

If you don't trust yourself to save your drawing every five to ten minutes, you can tell CorelDraw to do it for you. Choose Tools⇨Options (or press Ctrl+J), and click on Save in the dialog box that appears. If you see a check mark in the Auto-backup check box, the automatic saving function is turned on. If you don't see a check mark, click on the check box to turn on the option. To specify how often CorelDraw automatically saves your drawing, enter the number of minutes between saves into the option box just to the right of the check box. Then press Enter. Now your saving worries are gone.

Creating a backup copy

If you spend longer than a single day creating a drawing, you should create backup copies. That's not a hard-and-fast rule, mind you, but it is a sound principle of drawing management. The reasoning is, if a drawing takes longer than a day to create, you're that much worse off if you lose it. By creating one backup copy for each day that you work on the project — for example, Rodent 01, Rodent 02, Rodent 03, and so on — you're much less likely to lose your work. If some disk error occurs or you accidentally delete one or two of the files, one of the backups will probably survive the disaster, further protecting you from developing an ulcer or having to seek therapy.

At the end of the day, choose File⇨Save As. The Save Drawing dialog box opens, as when you first saved the drawing. Change the filename slightly and then click on the Save button — way to be doubly protected!

Put Your Drawing to Bed

To leave CorelDraw, choose File⇨Exit or press Alt+F4. I know that Alt+F4 doesn't make anywhere near as much sense as Ctrl+O to open and Ctrl+S to save, but Corel isn't to blame. Microsoft demands the Alt+F4 thing from all its Windows programs. Where Microsoft came up with Alt+F4 is anyone's guess. I think they made this shortcut confusing on purpose. This is the same company that brought you DOS, so what do you expect?

Microsoft decided to make a little more sense with Windows 95, however. In addition to using Exit and Alt+F4, you can now click on the Close button in the upper-right corner of the CorelDraw interface. This method wins my vote as the easiest way to quit the program.

Anyway, when you press Alt+F4 or click on the Close button, CorelDraw may warn you with a message that asks whether you want to save the changes you made to the current drawing. Unless you have some reason for doing otherwise, press Y or click on the Yes button. The program saves the drawing and then shuts itself down.

Part II
Let the Graphics Begin

The 5th Wave   By Rich Tennant

"Of course graphics are important to your project, Eddy, but I think it would've been better to scan a _picture_ of your worm collection."

In this part . . .

Traditional art tools are messy. Real-life ink, for example, bleeds into the fibers of the paper, goops and glumps onto the page, and stains if you accidentally spill some on your clothes. Real-life pens clog; real-life paintbrushes need washing; and real-life paintings flop over accidentally and get dust and hairs stuck all over them. Real life, in other words, is for the birds (which is only fitting because birds are wholly unequipped to use CorelDraw, what with their puny little brains and their sad lack of opposable thumbs).

CorelDraw, being a figment of your computer's imagination, is very tidy and orderly. There's nothing real to deal with. The pencil draws a line that remains the same thickness throughout its entire length. Whoever heard of such a thing? You can edit lines and shapes after you draw them. Unbelievable. And if you make a mistake, you can choose the Undo command. The real world has no equivalent. CorelDraw provides a flexible, forgiving interface that mimics real life while at the same time improving on it.

In the next six chapters, I show you how to draw, how to edit what you've drawn, how to apply colors, how to duplicate portions of your artwork, and how to create special effects. By the time you finish with Chapter 9, those Number 2 pencils you've been storing all these years will be history.

Chapter 4

The Secret Society of Simple Shapes

• •

In This Chapter

▶ Drawing rectangles, squares, ovals, and circles

▶ Introducing nodes

▶ Rounding off the corners of rectangles

▶ Converting ovals into pies and wedges

▶ Moving shapes with the arrow tool

▶ Scaling and flipping shapes

▶ Deleting shapes and subsequently freaking out

▶ Using the Undo command

• •

*E*ver try to draw a perfect square the old-fashioned way? Regardless of how many metal rulers, drafting arms, and absolutely 100 percent square stencils you have at your disposal, you're liable to miss the mark to some extent, however minuscule. And that's if you kill yourself over every corner and use the highest-grade engineering pens and acetate.

If you want to keep the Euclideans happy — and God knows, none of us wants to attract the wrath of an angry Euclidean — there's nothing like a drawing program for accuracy, simplicity, and downright efficiency. Suddenly, squares and circles are as easy to draw as, well, those smiley faces that little girls frequently use in their letters as punctuation at the end of jokes. You know, a semicircle mouth and two dots for eyes. Not even a circle to identify the boundaries of the head. Just a face in space, like some minimalist version of the Cheshire cat.

Well, anyway, the point is, smiley faces are ridiculously easy to draw, and so is the stuff in this chapter.

Shapes from Your Childhood

Wow, is this going to be easy! In about five minutes, you're going to laugh out loud at the idea that you once feared computers, thinking of them as cold-blooded machines intent on the overthrow of humanity. It's not that computers aren't cold-blooded machines intent on the overthrow of humanity, mind you, but at least they won't seem quite so menacing.

Rectangles and squares

Click on the rectangle tool (labeled in Figure 4-1) to select it. Or if you prefer, press F6. Now drag in the drawing area. A rectangle grows from the movement of your cursor, as demonstrated in Figure 4-1. One corner of the rectangle appears at the point at which you begin dragging. The opposite corner appears at the point at which you release. What could be simpler?

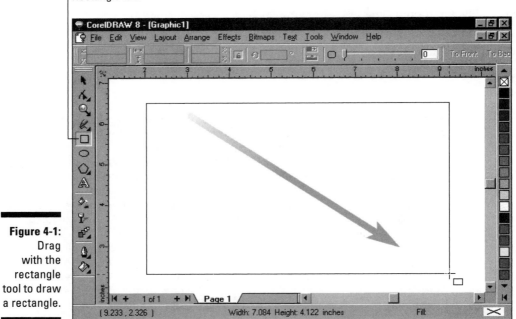

Figure 4-1:
Drag
with the
rectangle
tool to draw
a rectangle.

Here's some more stuff you can do with this tool:

- ✔ Press and hold the Ctrl key while dragging with the rectangle tool to draw a perfect square. The Ctrl key constrains the rectangle so that all four sides are the same length. Be sure to hold the Ctrl key down until you release your mouse button.

- ✔ Shift+drag with the rectangle tool — that is, press and hold the Shift key while dragging — to draw the rectangle outward from its center. CorelDraw centers the rectangle about the point at which you begin dragging. A corner appears at the point at which you release.

- ✔ Ctrl+Shift+drag to draw a square outward from the center.

- ✔ Double-click on the rectangle tool icon in the toolbox to draw a rectangle the size of the drawing page.

Ovals and circles

The ellipse tool, labeled in Figure 4-2, works the same way as the rectangle tool. The ellipse tool even has a keyboard equivalent, which is F7. You drag inside the drawing area to define the size of an oval, as shown in Figure 4-2. You can draw a perfect circle by Ctrl+dragging with the ellipse tool. Shift+drag to draw an oval from the center outward.

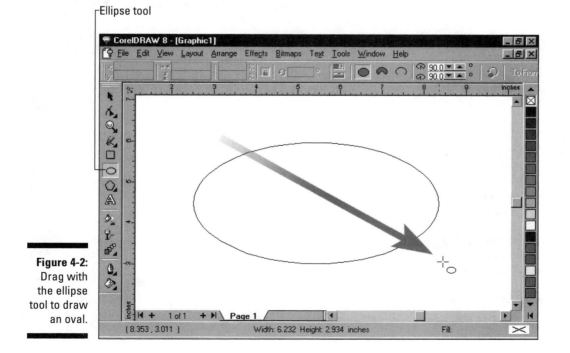

Ellipse tool

Figure 4-2: Drag with the ellipse tool to draw an oval.

Shapes with many sides

With the polygon tool, labeled in Figure 4-3, you can draw shapes with multiple sides, such as triangles, pentagons, octagons, and all those other 'gons. You can even draw stars — boy howdy.

To draw a polygon — the generic name for any shape with three or more straight sides — select the polygon tool by clicking on it. Then drag away, as shown in Figure 4-3. Ctrl+drag with the tool to draw a shape in which all sides are the same length (called an *equilateral polygon,* for those of you interested in tossing about the technical lingo). Shift+drag to draw the shape from the center out.

By default, CorelDraw creates a pentagon, which is a polygon with five sides. But you can draw as many sides as you want. To change the number of sides, do either of the following:

✔ To change the setting for any new shapes you draw — in other words, the default setting — double-click on the polygon tool icon in the toolbox. CorelDraw opens the Options dialog box with the settings for the polygon tool displayed.

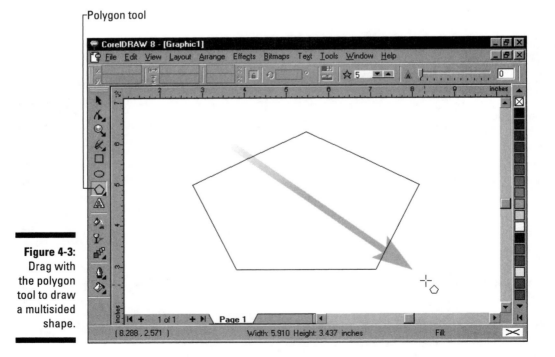

Polygon tool

Figure 4-3:
Drag with the polygon tool to draw a multisided shape.

✔ To change the number of sides assigned to an existing shape, first click on the shape with the arrow tool to select the shape. Then press Alt+Enter to open the Object Properties docker, shown in Figure 4-4. (You can also open the docker by right-clicking on the shape and selecting the Properties option from the bottom of the pop-up menu that appears. Or choose View➪Dockers➪Object Properties.)

You'll notice that the Object Properties docker doesn't appear docked on-screen automatically when you open it. Most likely, this is because there are so darn many tabs that the docker won't fit neatly on the right side of the document window. In fact, if you try to dock it by dragging, it docks at the top of the document window.

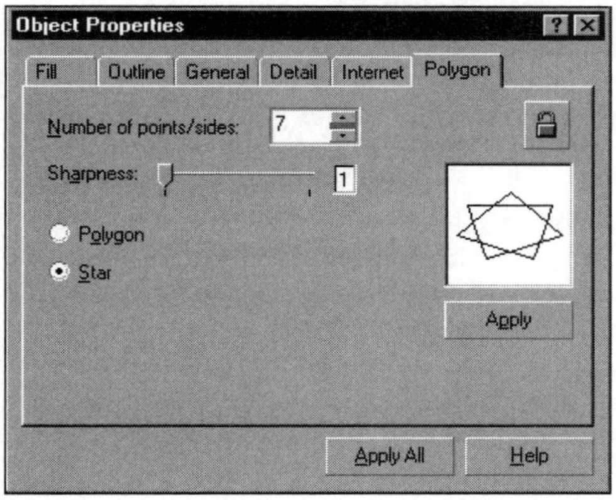

Figure 4-4:
You can decide whether to draw polygons or stars by using this docker.

Although the Options dialog box and the Object Properties docker look different, both offer the same polygon tool options, with one exception. Here's a look at your choices:

✔ Select a radio button to determine the shape of the polygon. The Options dialog box has three radio buttons: Polygon, Star, or Polygon as Star. If you select the Polygon as Star option, you create a star in which the lines of the star don't cross. But more important, the option gives you absolute control over the sharpness of the star's points. Suffice it to say, if you can't get the shape you want by selecting the Star option, try Polygon as Star instead.

The Object Properties docker doesn't offer the Polygon as Star option. If you want to convert an existing polygon to a Polygon as Star, you have to do it manually with the shape tool, as explained in "Making a wacky shape wackier," later in this chapter. Nor can you change an existing Polygon as Star shape into a regular Polygon shape; again, you must use the shape tool to edit the shape.

- ✔ The Number of Points/Sides option box establishes the number of sides for your shape. You can go as low as 3 for a triangle or as high as 500, which is, of course, an insanely large value.

- ✔ The Star option is unavailable in both the Object Properties docker and the Options dialog box if the Number of Points/Sides value is lower than 5; by definition, a star has at least five sides.

  Remember, when an option box is active, you can raise or lower the value in the box by pressing the up- or down-arrow key.

- ✔ If you select Star and set the Number of Points/Sides value as 7 or larger, the Sharpness option becomes available. The Sharpness value is available also if you select Polygon as Star. A higher Sharpness value increases the sharpness of the star's points.

- ✔ If you're changing the settings for an existing polygon with the Object Properties docker, click on the Apply button to apply the settings to your shape. If you don't like the effect of your settings, change the settings and click on the Apply button again.

When you select the polygon tool, the property bar offers controls for the same options as the Object Properties dockers. If you're using a 640 x 480 screen resolution, one of the vital controls is cut off the right side of the screen, a problem I mention in Chapter 2. If you want to use the property bar controls, just drag the property bar into the drawing window to convert the property bar to a floating window, shown in Figure 4-5, where you also see each of the controls labeled.

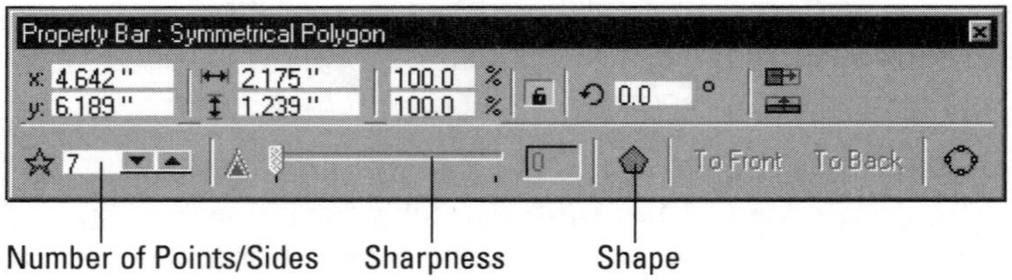

Figure 4-5:
The property bar controls for polygons.

Property Bar : Symmetrical Polygon

x: 4.642 "   2.175 "   100.0 %
y: 6.189 "   1.239 "   100.0 %   0.0 °

☆ 7

Number of Points/Sides   Sharpness   Shape

If no shape is selected when you change the property bar controls, the settings affect the next shape you draw — using the property bar in this way-is the same as changing the options in the Options dialog box. If a shape is selected, your settings affect only the selected shape. Just as in the Object Properties docker and the Options dialog box, the Star option is unavailable until you raise the number of sides for the shape to 5 or higher.

I should mention that you can similarly change the properties of rectangles and ovals. In other words, you can display the Ellipse tool panel of the Options dialog box by double-clicking on the ellipse tool, or you can display the Object Properties docker by right-clicking on a rectangle or oval in the drawing area and selecting the Properties option. But frankly, the changes you can make inside these dialog boxes are easier to apply by using a special tool called the shape tool, which I describe in the next section.

Ways to Change Shapes

After you finish drawing a rectangle, an oval, a polygon, or a star, take a look at it. You can see one or more tiny, square *nodes* on the outline of the shape. At least that's what Corel calls them. My dictionary says that a node is a "knotty, localized swelling." If I were you, I'd try not to think about that.

As illustrated in Figure 4-6, different shapes include different numbers of nodes (the nodes are highlighted in the figure):

✔ A rectangle sports a node on each of its four corners.

✔ An oval features just one node. If you draw the shape by dragging the cursor downward on-screen (as shown back in Figure 4-2), the node appears along the top of the shape, as in Figure 4-6. However, if you drag upward to draw the oval — which almost no one does — the node appears along the bottom. Either way is okay.

✔ A polygon or a star has one node in each corner and one in the middle of each side. So a triangle has six nodes, and a pentagon, or five-pointed star, has ten.

Although nodes are certainly decorative and particularly festive during the holidays, they also provide a bona fide function. You can change a shape by dragging a node with the shape tool, the mysterious tool of a thousand faces. Were he alive today, Lon Chaney would undoubtedly sue.

If you want to reshape an object whose nodes aren't visible, just click on the object with the shape tool. The nodes pop into view.

Sanding off the corners

When applied to one of the nodes of a rectangle, the shape tool (labeled in Figure 4-7) rounds off the corners of the shape. Here's how to perform this trick:

1. Draw a rectangle.

You can't edit a rectangle until you draw it.

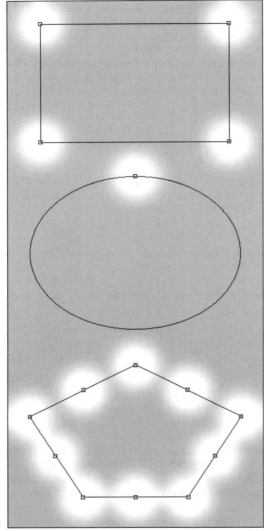

Figure 4-6:
Rectangles,
ovals, and
polygons
include
nodes you
can drag
with the
shape tool.

2. **Click on the shape tool to select it.**

Or press F10 to select the tool from the keyboard. Some particularly nerdy folks refer to the shape tool as the node edit tool, by the way.

3. **Drag one of the rectangle's nodes toward the middle of the shape.**

Regardless of which node you drag, CorelDraw rounds off all four corners in the shape to the same extent. Notice that you now have eight nodes, which mark the transitions between the straight and curved edges of the shape.

4. **Release the mouse button when you have sufficiently rounded off the corners.**

To restore the rectangle's sharp corners, drag any of the nodes back to the corner position. Your corners should now be considered dangerous. Don't play too close to the rectangle or run around it with scissors in your hands.

When you select the shape tool, the property bar offers controls that give you another way to round off the corners of your rectangle. Drag the roundness slider, labeled in Figure 4-7, to the right to make the corners more round; drag to the left to square up the corners again. You can also enter a value in the option box to the right of the slider bar, if you're feeling the need for precision. A value of zero gives you perfectly square corners.

Turning an oval into a tempting dessert

I speak, of course, of a pie. When you drag the node of an oval with the shape tool, you change the oval to a piping hot pie with a node on each side of the wedge. Truth be told, you can actually create either a pie or an arc, depending on how you drag the node, as illustrated in Figure 4-8.

- ✔ Move the shape tool cursor inside the oval during your drag to create a pie shape (top two objects in Figure 4-8). Like any shape, the pie has an interior that you can fill with a solid color, gradation, or what have you. (Chapter 7 talks about fills.)

- ✔ Move the cursor outside the oval during the drag to create an arc (bottom two objects in Figure 4-8). Notice that with an arc, the slice segments that form a V between the two pie nodes disappear. An arc is therefore a curved line with no scrumptious filling.

- ✔ Drag the node to the right to draw a pie with a wedge cut out of it or a long arc, as with the left two objects in Figure 4-8. (This instruction assumes that you created the oval by dragging downward from left to right, which most folks do without thinking. If you create your ovals by dragging from right to left, you nonconformist you, drag the node to the left to cut out a wedge.)

- ✔ Drag the node to the left to throw away most of the pie and retain a slim wedge or a short arc, as with the right-hand objects in Figure 4-8. (If you created the shape by dragging right to left, drag the node to the right instead.)

- ✔ Press Ctrl while dragging to constrain the wedge angle to the nearest 15-degree increment. Because a circle is 360 degrees — I don't know where Euclid got that number, maybe he had 36 toes or something — Ctrl+dragging ensures 24 equal increments around the perimeter of the oval. (360 ÷ 15 = 24, in case you're interested.)

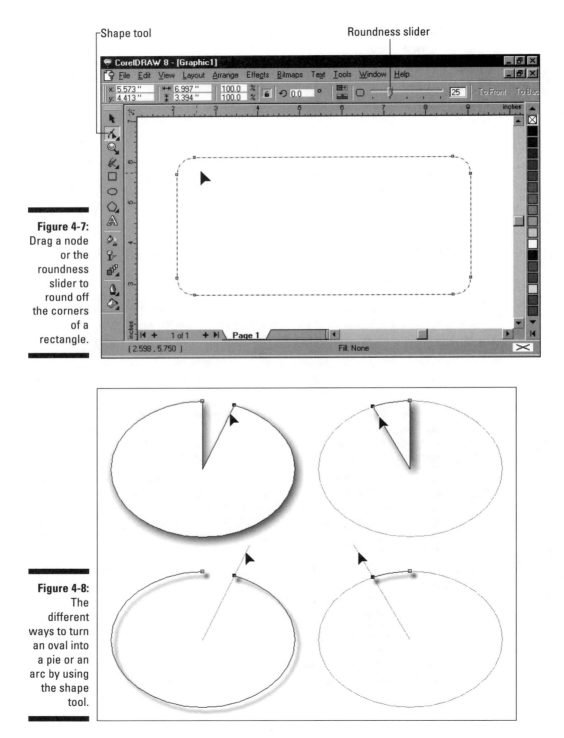

Figure 4-7:
Drag a node or the roundness slider to round off the corners of a rectangle.

Figure 4-8:
The different ways to turn an oval into a pie or an arc by using the shape tool.

✔ After you change the oval to a pie or an arc, you can continue to apply the shape tool to either node, creating all sorts of wedges and curves. To restore the pie or arc to a circle, drag one node exactly onto the other while keeping the cursor outside the shape. Don't worry about positioning the cursor directly over either node during the drag; the two nodes automatically snap together when they get close.

✔ If you have trouble dragging nodes to get the shape you want, try using the property bar controls, shown in Figure 4-9. These controls are available when the ellipse tool is selected or when the shape tool and an oval are selected. Click on the pie or arc icon to convert the oval into a pie or arc shape. Then click on the up- and down-pointing arrows next to the starting and ending angle option boxes to create the exact pie, arc, or wedge shape you want. Click on the clockwise/counterclockwise button to reverse the starting and ending angle values. (This button appears dimmed in Figure 4-9 because it's available only if you selected the pie or arc icon.) Click on the ellipse icon to return to your original ellipse.

Figure 4-9:
The property bar when the ellipse tool is active.

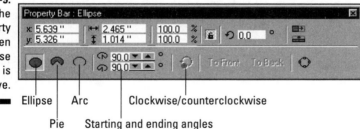

Ellipse   Arc   Clockwise/counterclockwise

Pie   Starting and ending angles

Giving the pie a wedgie

Creating a pie is pretty straightforward. But because of the right/left thing discussed in the preceding section, creating the pie-and-floating-wedge effect shown in Figure 4-10 is kind of difficult. I mean, you drag one way for the pie and the other way for the wedge, so how are you supposed to get the pie and wedge to match? Well, I can tell you how, but the job involves a few tricks I haven't discussed yet.

Assuming that you're willing to jump boldly into the unknown, here's how the procedure works:

1. Select the ellipse tool.

Remember, you can select the ellipse tool by pressing F7.

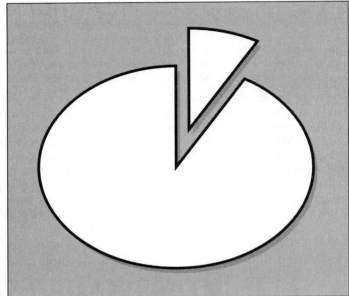

Figure 4-10:
The very
popular pie
shape with
a floating
wedge.

2. Draw an oval.

Make sure to drag from the upper-left portion of the drawing area to lower-right. Otherwise, things will get screwed up in steps to come.

3. Click on the shape tool or press F10.

Either process selects the shape tool.

4. Ctrl+drag the oval's node to the right. Be sure to keep your cursor on the inside of the shape.

This step creates a slice in the pie. Because the Ctrl key constrains your drag in increments, matching the wedge to the slice is easier later on. Otherwise, it's all up to you. How far you drag doesn't matter. You can create a thin slice or a big chunky one depending on what you want to represent — or how hungry you are.

You can also use the property bar controls, discussed in the preceding section, to create your pie slice.

5. Press Ctrl+D or choose Edit⇨Duplicate.

The Duplicate command makes a copy of the shape. I discuss this command in Chapter 8, but for now, just accept it.

6. **Reselect the shape tool (F10) and Ctrl+drag the right-hand node of the new shape to the left.**

   Ctrl+drag past the upper node and toward the inside of the shape to create a wedge that matches the slice out of the original pie, as shown in Figure 4-11. Alternatively, use the property bar controls to create your wedge.

7. **Click on the arrow tool to select it or press the spacebar.**

   I explain how to use the arrow tool with rectangles, ovals, pies, and all the rest in the next section. But for now, notice that the wedge becomes selected, with big corner handles around it.

8. **Press Alt+F9 or choose Arrange⇨Transform⇨Scale & Mirror.**

   Either way, the Scale & Mirror roll-up appears on-screen, as in Figure 4-12.

9. **Click on the Mirror Horizontal button, labeled in Figure 4-12.**

   Then press Enter or click on the Apply button. The wedge flips itself over, as the figure shows. Alternatively, you can simply click on the Mirror Horizontal button on the property bar to flip the slice without displaying the Scale & Mirror roll-up at all.

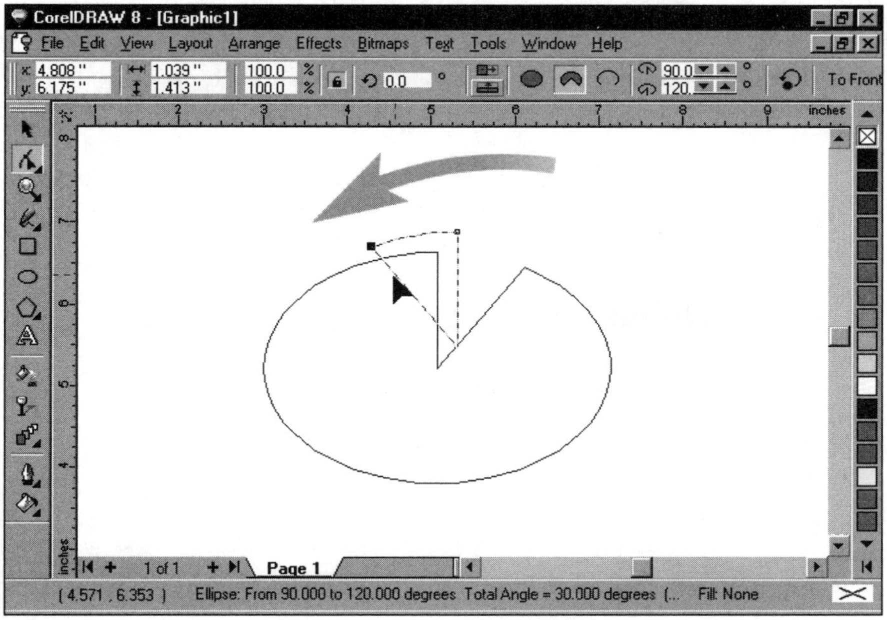

Figure 4-11: Ctrl+drag with the shape tool or use the property bar controls to create a wedge that matches the slice.

Object Position   Mirror Horizontal

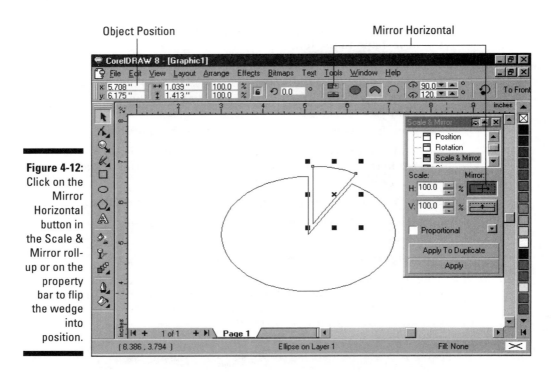

Figure 4-12:
Click on the
Mirror
Horizontal
button in
the Scale &
Mirror roll-
up or on the
property
bar to flip
the wedge
into
position.

10. Press the arrow keys to move the slice into place.

The arrow keys nudge the shape incrementally. The wedge is now moved into place. You can also use the Object Position option boxes, labeled in Figure 4-12, to shift the slice into place. The X value moves the slice left to right; the Y value moves it up and down. (You're moving the slice along an imaginary X and Y axis, you see.)

Making a wacky shape wackier

Reshaping rectangles and ovals is a great way to while away the occasional rainy day, but you can have the most fun reshaping polygons and stars. Here's how it works:

✔ Regardless of which node you drag in a polygon, the related nodes move in kind. All side nodes move together (as you can see in shapes 2, 3, and 4 in Figure 4-13), and all point nodes move together (shapes 5 and 6). This feature ensures that the polygon or star is forever symmetrical. Just so you can impress your friends, this kind of symmetry is known as *radial symmetry*.

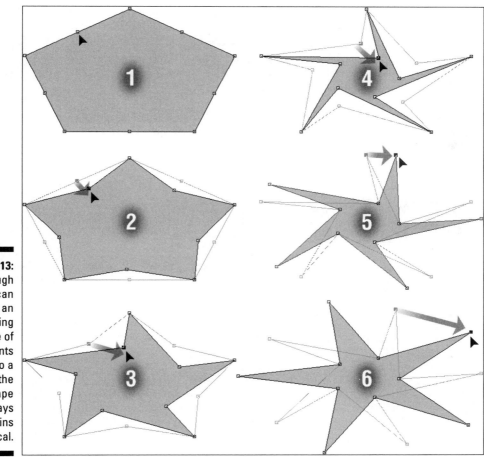

Figure 4-13:
Although you can apply an amazing range of adjustments to a polygon, the shape always remains symmetrical.

✔ Try dragging a side node past a point node or vice versa to create cool geometric effects, including double stars. The effects look really great on shapes with ten or more sides.

✔ You can add or subtract sides by pressing Alt+Enter or right-clicking on the polygon and choosing the Properties option, as discussed earlier, in the section "Shapes with many sides." You can change the number of sides also by using the Number of Points on Polygon control on the property bar. The polygon retains its new, weird shape regardless of how you change the Number of Points/Sides value.

✔ Click on a side node and then Shift+click on a point node. Both nodes become selected. Now when you drag one of the two nodes, both side and point nodes move together.

✔ Ctrl+drag a node to move side or point nodes in and out along a constrained axis. Ctrl+dragging is great if you want to keep things from getting too out of hand.

More than any other option I've discussed so far, reshaping polygons is something you should experiment with a great deal. There's simply no limit to the number of wild effects you can achieve.

Arrow Tool Techniques (Or Tricks of the Pick)

Every drawing and desktop publishing program on the planet offers a tool that looks like an arrow. Some companies call their arrows selection tools. Others call them edit tools. But wouldn't you know it, Corel — roughly the 500th company to implement such a tool — went and renamed the thing the pick tool. So when you select something, you're actually "picking" it. Just imagine if I had employed official Corel vernacular when instructing you to select the rat's nose in Chapter 3.

Everyone I know calls the tool that looks like an arrow the arrow tool. First tool among tools, the arrow tool is an editing tool, much like the shape tool. However, instead of enabling you to change details in an object like the shape tool does, the arrow tool enables you to make changes to the object as a whole.

Select the arrow tool and then click on a shape to select the shape. Be sure to click on the outline of the shape. (Up to this point in the book, all the shapes you've drawn are transparent, unless you've been experimenting without me.) After you select a shape, it becomes surrounded by eight big black handles (called *selection handles*) with an X in the middle, as shown in Figure 4-14. This is called a *bounding box*. The handles enable you to change the dimensions of the shape, and the center X enables you to move the shape from its center axis. (If you just drew the shape or you were editing it with the shape tool, you don't need to click on it with the arrow tool. The shape remains selected automatically.)

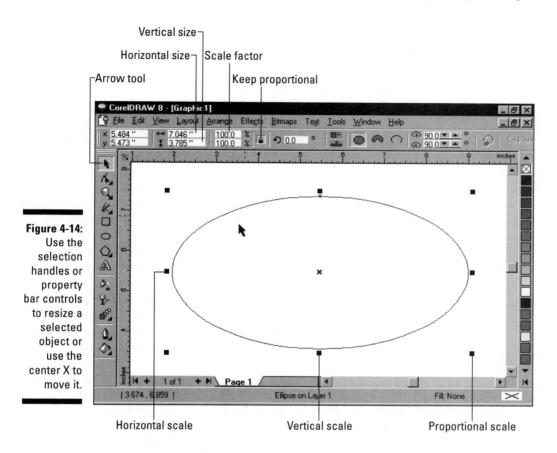

Vertical size ┐
Horizontal size ┐ Scale factor
┌Arrow tool Keep proportional

Horizontal scale Vertical scale Proportional scale

Figure 4-14:
Use the selection handles or property bar controls to resize a selected object or use the center X to move it.

You can also select shapes by selecting the arrow tool and then pressing Tab. CorelDraw selects one of the objects in your drawing. Press Tab to select the next object in the drawing. Keep pressing Tab until the object you want to select is surrounded by the black handles. To select the shape that was previously selected, press Shift+Tab.

To switch between the selected tool and the arrow tool, just press the spacebar. Press the spacebar again to return to the previously selected tool. If text is active, press Ctrl+spacebar to switch between the selected tool and the arrow tool.

To select two or more shapes so that you can manipulate them at the same time, click on the first shape and then Shift+click on the others. Or drag around the shapes with the arrow tool. To select all objects, double-click on the arrow tool icon or choose Edit⇨Select All.

The following list explains some basic ways to change a selected shape with the arrow tool:

- To scale the shape horizontally, drag the handle on the left or right side of the shape. Drag toward the center of the shape to make the shape skinnier; drag away from the shape to make it fatter.

- To scale the shape vertically, drag the handle on the top or bottom side of the shape. Drag in to make the shape shorter; drag away to make it taller.

- You can also use the horizontal and vertical size controls on the property bar, labeled in Figure 4-14, to resize an object with precision. Use the little arrows to the right of the controls to change the values in preset increments. Or double-click on one of the option boxes, enter a value from the keyboard, and press Enter.

- To scale the shape proportionally, so that the horizontal and vertical proportions remain equal, drag one of the four corner handles. Drag in to reduce; drag away to enlarge.

- If you're a property bar fan, click on the little lock icon to maintain the object's original proportions when you use the horizontal and vertical size controls. Note that clicking on the lock icon *doesn't* keep the object proportional when you drag the selection handles; the lock icon affects only the property bar controls.

- If you press Shift while dragging a handle, you scale the shape about its center. In other words, the center of the shape remains stationary throughout your drag. Normally, the opposite side is stationary.

- Ctrl+drag a handle to scale in 100 percent increments. You can scale a shape to twice, three times, or four times its previous size and even larger. You generally need a lot of extra room on-screen to pull this off. Try zooming out a few times (by pressing F3) before embarking on a Ctrl+drag.

- You may find it easier to use the property bar's horizontal and vertical scale controls to scale the object. Double-click on the option boxes, enter scale values from the keyboard, and press Enter. A value of less than 100 percent reduces the object's size; a value of more than 100 percent increases the size. Also, remember that the setting of the lock icon discussed earlier affects the scale options. If the lock icon is selected, the horizontal scale factor changes when you change the vertical scale factor and vice versa.

- Ctrl+drag a side handle past the opposite side to flip the shape. For example, if you Ctrl+drag the left handle rightward past the right handle, you flip the shape horizontally. Drag the top handle down past the bottom handle to flip the shape vertically. Be sure to press Ctrl when you drag, or you can distort your object. Pressing Ctrl ensures that your object remains the same size when you flip it.

- ✔ Notice that Ctrl+dragging has different results than using the mirror buttons on the property bar or in the Scale & Mirror roll-up, discussed earlier in this chapter. Compare the two techniques to see the difference in how your object flips.

- ✔ To move a shape, drag its outline (not on the handles) or drag the center x in the bounding box.

- ✔ You can also use the X and Y coordinate controls on the property bar to reposition the shape. The X value moves the shape left and right; the Y value moves the shape up and down. Remember that the X and Y values reflect the position of the center of the object.

- ✔ If you click on the outline of a selected shape, the handles change to double-headed arrows. These arrows enable you to rotate and slant the shape, as discussed in Chapter 9. To return to the big black handles, click on the shape again.

Kiss It Good-bye

To delete a shape, press Delete. It doesn't matter whether you selected the shape with the shape tool or the arrow tool or whether you just finished creating it with the rectangle or ellipse tool. Don't press the Backspace key, by the way. Backspacing doesn't do anything except cause your computer to beep at you.

Aaaugh, It's Gone!

Relax. Everything I discuss in this chapter — as well as in most other chapters — can be undone. You can undraw a rectangle or an oval, restore a shape that you changed with the shape tool, return a shape to its original size, and even bring back a shape you've deleted. To undo something, choose Edit⇨Undo or press Ctrl+Z or Alt+Backspace. The name of the Undo command changes to reflect the operation you're about to undo; if you choose the command after filling an object, for example, the command name is Undo Fill.

Not only can you undo the last operation, you can undo the one before that and the one before that. In CorelDraw, you can undo multiple operations in a row. For example, if you draw a rectangle, round off the corners with the shape tool, scale it, and then flip it, you can press Ctrl+Z three times, first to return the rectangle to its original position, then to return it to its original size, and then to restore its sharp corners.

If you then change your mind, you can restore operations that you undid by choosing Edit⇨Redo or pressing Ctrl+Shift+Z.

WARNING!

After you save a drawing, you lose the opportunity to undo any changes you made before you chose the Save command. Also, it is possible to run out of undos; for more information, see the sidebar "Raising the Undo ceiling until the rubble falls on your head."

TIP

Raising the Undo ceiling until the rubble falls on your head

You can find out for sure how many operations you can undo in a row by pressing Ctrl+J (or choosing Tools⇨Options), clicking on General in the tree display, and looking at the Regular value in the Undo levels option box. You can raise or lower the value to suit your own tolerance for risk. But be aware that CorelDraw may not function as well if you use a high value. Your system may crash more often, or you may not be able to use other Windows 95 programs while you're running CorelDraw.

I recommend that you set the Undo levels value no higher than 10 unless someone who is familiar with the inner workings of your computer tells you to do otherwise. And even then, ask for credentials. Those computer know-it-alls always tell you to do something and then go on vacation when the entire system breaks down.

Chapter 5

Drawn It, Shaped It, Ready to Go Free-Form

. . . .

In This Chapter

▶ Meeting Shenbop, crazed adventure seeker

▶ Drawing with the pencil tool

▶ Taking the natural pen tool for a spin

▶ Finding out all about paths, segments, and control points

▶ Going on a rampage with the shape tool

▶ Waking the neighbors with your endless curve bending

▶ Facing the Node Edit roll-up without fear

▶ Hacking away extraneous nodes

▶ Converting simple shapes to free-form paths

. . . .

*R*emember those Mountain Dew commercials from a few years back? A bunch of guys poke their faces into the camera and express with virile bravado that they've "Jumped it," "Scaled it," yada yada yada, while images of stunt men flinging themselves into and off everything imaginable reel across the screen. Restless daredevils overcome nature. Fledgling Odysseuses on dangerous doses.

I'm not a parent, but if I were, I think I would have been unnerved. These young men, juiced up on too much caffeine, overconfident beyond their levels of skill and endurance, were obviously destined to crack their skulls open during miscalculated bungie jumps, pound their kayaks into unyielding underwater boulders, smash their ultralights into low-flying crop dusters, and invite blood blisters when constructing spice racks without adult supervision. I mean, are we comfortable handing over the leadership responsibilities of this great nation to a bunch of super-charged yahoos? Haven't we learned anything from the super-charged yahoos currently at the helm?

I'm not sure what all this is leading up to, but I think it's a cautionary note. Some of you, Mountain Dews in hand, are naturally pumped about the skills you acquired in the first four chapters of this book. (That's assuming that you're reading this book from cover to cover.) You're drawing pies with flying wedges and polygons with sharp corners while bandying about terms such as *ellipse* and *node* like a veteran CorelDraw hack. With the maddening rush of adrenaline surging through your temples combined with the dizzying sensation of newfound knowledge, you're practically psycho to throw off the chains of geometric shapes. You're itching to go free-form!

Okay, I see nothing wrong with that. Just don't overdo it the first time out. I think that Edgar Allan Poe said it best: "Quoth the raven, 'Chill, homey.'"

Do Some Doodling with the Pencil

Figure 5-1 shows an amphibian of dubious heritage whose name happens to be Shenbop. The major factor in Shenbop's favor is that he's ridiculously easy to draw. After selecting the pencil tool — which you can do by clicking on the tool's icon or by pressing F5 — you can draw Shenbop in six steps, as demonstrated in Figure 5-2. Just drag with the tool as if you were doodling with a real pencil. Your lines may look a little shakier than mine — not that mine are all that smooth — but you can do it. (For tips on drawing with the pencil, see the upcoming section "Mastering the pencil.")

In response to your drags, CorelDraw creates a series of lines and shapes, known in CorelDraw lingo as *closed* and *open paths,* as explained next.

Understanding paths, lines, and shapes

Anything you draw — whether it's with the rectangle tool, the ellipse tool, the pencil tool, or some other tool — is called a *path.* The origin of the term has to do with the way some printers draw mathematical objects, but just think of it this way: If you blew up a rectangle or some other line or shape onto a sheet of paper the size of a city block, the shape's outline would become as wide as a sidewalk. You could follow this sidewalk outline around the block; hence, it's a *path.* The only difference is that paths in CorelDraw are for extremely small people.

In each of Steps 1 through 4 of Figure 5-2, you draw an *open path,* in which the beginning and end of the path don't touch. An open path is, therefore, the same as a *line.* Steps 5 and 6 show *closed paths,* which are paths that loop around continuously with no obvious beginning or end. In laymen's terms, a closed path is a *shape.* For me to define common words such as *line* and *shape* may seem silly, but these terms lie at the core of CorelDraw. In fact, everything you draw falls into one of these two camps.

Pencil tool

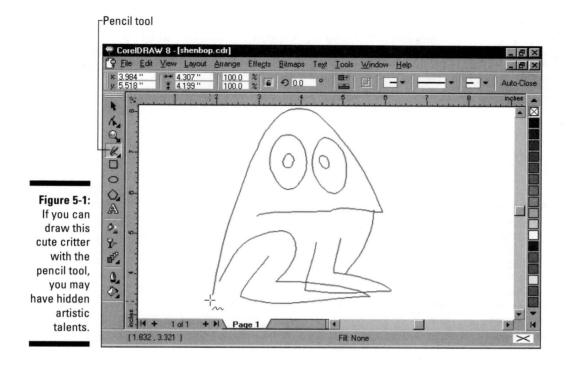

Figure 5-1:
If you can draw this cute critter with the pencil tool, you may have hidden artistic talents.

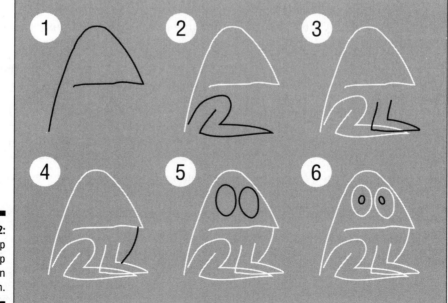

Figure 5-2:
The six-step Shenbop creation program.

In Chapter 1, I introduce the term *object,* which can also mean either a line or a shape. But unlike a path, an object can also be a block of text. For an object to qualify as a path, you must be able to edit its outline. So paths are a subset of objects that include lines and shapes only. Figure 5-3 shows the family tree of CorelDraw objects.

Figure 5-3:
Objects
include
paths and
text. Paths
include
lines and
shapes.

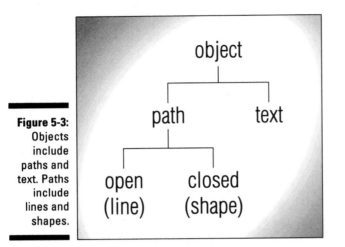

Coming to grips with nodes and segments

Immediately after you draw a line or a shape, CorelDraw performs some intense calculations and assigns nodes to the path automatically, as I discuss in Chapter 4. The length of the path from one node to the next is called a *segment.* (See Figure 5-4.) And you thought you were finished with the vocabulary. Here's the lowdown on nodes and segments:

- ✔ If the path is fairly simple — say, requiring ten nodes or fewer — CorelDraw displays all the nodes. If the path is more complex, the program shows only the first and last nodes. It's just a display thing; all the nodes are present but hiding. (If you were a node, wouldn't you be shy?)

- ✔ After you select the shape tool, the total number of nodes for a path appears in the middle of the status bar at the bottom of the screen.

- ✔ CorelDraw has a habit of depositing nodes based on the speed at which you draw. When you draw quickly, CorelDraw lays down a node here, another there. When you draw slowly, the program riddles the path with nodes because it thinks you're slowing down for emphasis. Unfortunately, densely concentrated nodes result in abrupt transitions and zigzags that make the path look jagged and irregular, as demonstrated in Figure 5-4. So try to maintain a quick and consistent drawing speed.

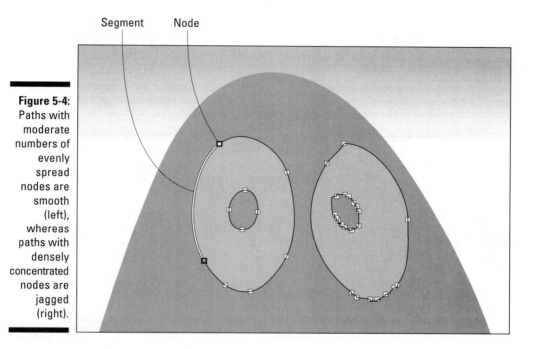

Segment   Node

Figure 5-4:
Paths with
moderate
numbers of
evenly
spread
nodes are
smooth
(left),
whereas
paths with
densely
concentrated
nodes are
jagged
(right).

Mastering the pencil

If you're inexperienced at drawing with a mouse, nearly all your first hundred or so paths will be jagged and irregular. What can I tell you? Becoming a competent computer artist takes time and practice. But don't let little flaws in your drawing bother you. As long as you draw approximately what you want, you can shape and mold it as I discuss later in this chapter.

Here are some additional tips for creating successful pencil paths:

- ✔ To draw a straight line, click with the pencil tool to establish the first node, and then click at a new location to establish the second node. CorelDraw automatically draws a straight line between the two nodes.

- ✔ To constrain your line to a 15-degree angle, Ctrl+click at the point where you want to end the line.

- ✔ To draw an irregular polygon — such as a triangle in which every side is a different length — click to create the first node, double-click at a new location to create the second node, and continue double-clicking to establish additional nodes in the path. The program draws a straight segment between each pair of nodes. To end the polygon, click once.

✔ You can erase part of your path as you draw by pressing the Shift key and dragging backwards along the path. But you have to Shift+drag before you release the mouse button to end the path. Keep the mouse button pressed to resume drawing the path again.

✔ To complete a closed path, you have to connect with the point at which you began dragging or clicking. If you miss, the path won't close properly. You can't fill an open path. (See Figure 5-5.)

✔ If a path does not close as you had hoped, you can press Delete and redraw the path. But you can also close the path with the pencil. Immediately after drawing an open path, drag from the first node to the last node to add a few more segments and close the path to form a shape. To close the path with a straight segment, click on the first node and then click on the last.

✔ You can extend any open path with the pencil. After drawing the path, drag from either the first or last node. Or click on either node to add straight segments.

Closed path   Open path

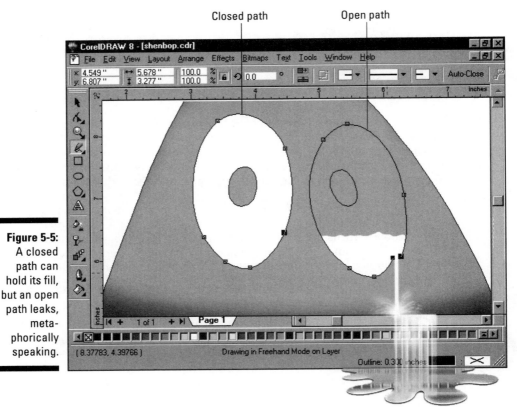

Figure 5-5:
A closed path can hold its fill, but an open path leaks, meta-phorically speaking.

Experimenting with the natural pen tool

The natural pen tool, which resides on the pencil tool flyout menu, is designed to create closed paths that look like curves. You can set the tool to work in several ways; to establish settings for the tool, select it from the pencil tool flyout and double-click on the tool icon to display the Options dialog box. Here are your choices:

- ✔ Select Fixed to draw curves that are one width along their entire length. Set the width by changing the Maximum width value.

- ✔ The Pressure option enables you to vary the width of the curve as you draw. If you use a pressure-sensitive pen and drawing tablet, the curve width varies depending on the pressure you apply to your pen. If you draw by using the mouse, you can change the width of the curve by pressing the up- and down-arrow keys. With this option, the Maximum width value determines how thick the curve can become.

- ✔ Select Calligraphy to create curves that resemble those you can create with a calligraphy pen. The width of the curve changes based on the direction of the curve. The Angle value controls the angle of the pen "nib" — changing the value is like changing the angle at which you hold a regular calligraphy pen against the paper's surface.

- ✔ The Presets option enables you to choose from a variety of preset line types. Select the line type you want from the pop-up menu that appears after you click on the Presets radio button. As you draw the curve, CorelDraw displays what appears to be a standard line, but after you release the mouse button, the program creates the curve according to the line type option you selected.

Figure 5-6 shows samples of curves created by using the four different tool options and then filled with black.

As you drag with the natural pen tool, CorelDraw displays what appears to be a simple line. But after you release the mouse button to complete your drag, the curve turns into a closed path. You can't draw an open path with the natural pen tool.

The controls in the Options dialog box are also available on the property bar when you select the natural pen tool, as labeled in Figure 5-6.

Nodes as You Never Knew Them

As I discuss earlier in this chapter, it's no big deal if you don't draw your paths correctly right off the bat. Even the best and most knowledgeable CorelDraw artists spend a significant portion of their time editing and generally rehashing paths with that tool of tools, the shape tool. You can

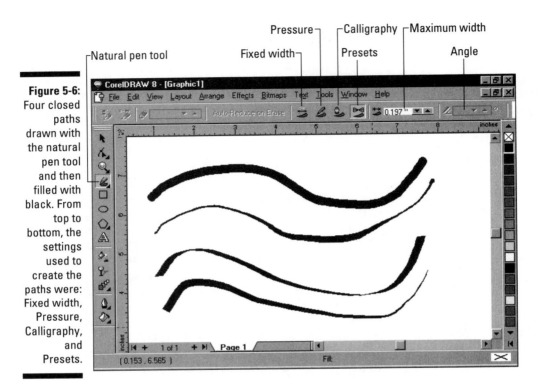

Figure 5-6: Four closed paths drawn with the natural pen tool and then filled with black. From top to bottom, the settings used to create the paths were: Fixed width, Pressure, Calligraphy, and Presets.

move nodes, change the curvature of segments, add and delete nodes, close open paths, open closed ones, and otherwise change a haphazard scrawl into a gracefully sinuous line or shape.

Bringing nodes into view

To view and edit the nodes in a pencil or natural pen path, click on the shape tool in the toolbox — or press the shortcut key, F10 — and click on the path. The nodes in the path light up like candles on a Christma . . . er, tree of ambiguous religious origin. (We must always be PC when discussing PCs.)

Click on an individual node in the path to select the node. The node changes from hollow to black. You may also see one or two *control points* extending from the node, as shown in Figure 5-7. A purely decorative dotted line — called a *lever* — connects each control point to its node.

Control points determine the curvature of segments. And yet, unlike nodes, control points don't actually reside on the path; they float above the path like little satellites. In fact, a control point tugs on a segment in much the same way that the moon tugs at the ocean to create tides. Control points are like a detached ethereal force with special gravitational powers. But unlike the moon, a control point doesn't inspire people to howl or turn into werewolves when it's full.

Using nodes to reshape your drawing

The following items explain how to use the shape tool to select nodes and control points as well as how to change the appearance of a path. I also toss in a few general notes and bits of wisdom to help you along your way:

- ✔ Click on a node to select it and display any control points associated with the node. A node can have no control points, or it can have as many as two (one for each segment).

- ✔ Segments need control points to bend them. If a segment is not bordered on either side by a control point, the segment is absolutely straight.

- ✔ Drag a node to move it and its control points. The segments that border the node stretch to keep up, as demonstrated in Figure 5-8. You can drag the node as far as you want; segments are infinitely stretchy.

- ✔ Drag a control point to bend and tug at the corresponding segment, as shown in Figure 5-9. Notice that the node remains stationary, anchoring the segment.

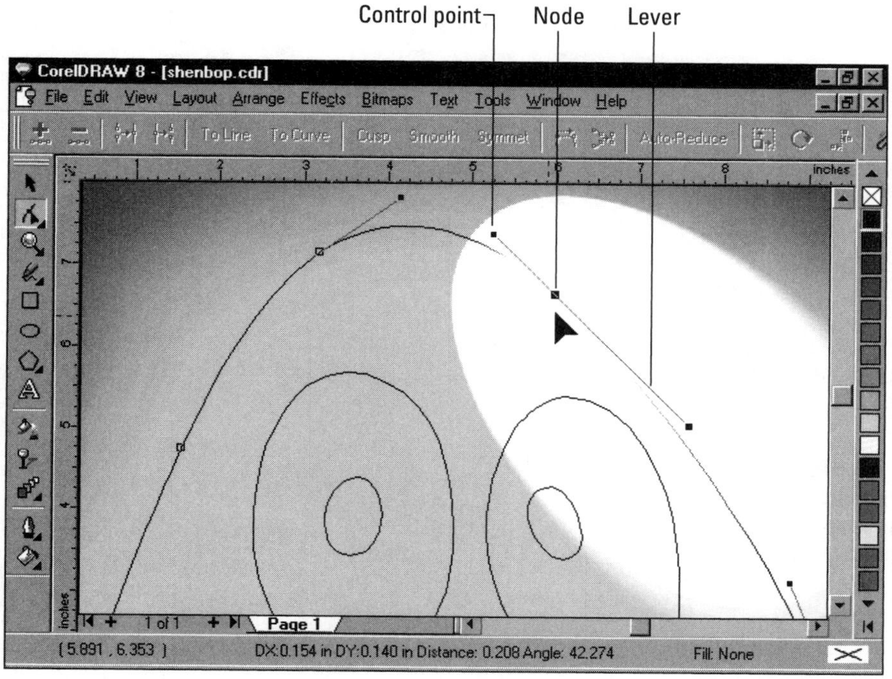

Figure 5-7:
Control points flank most nodes in a path drawn with the pencil or the natural pen.

Control point — Node   Lever

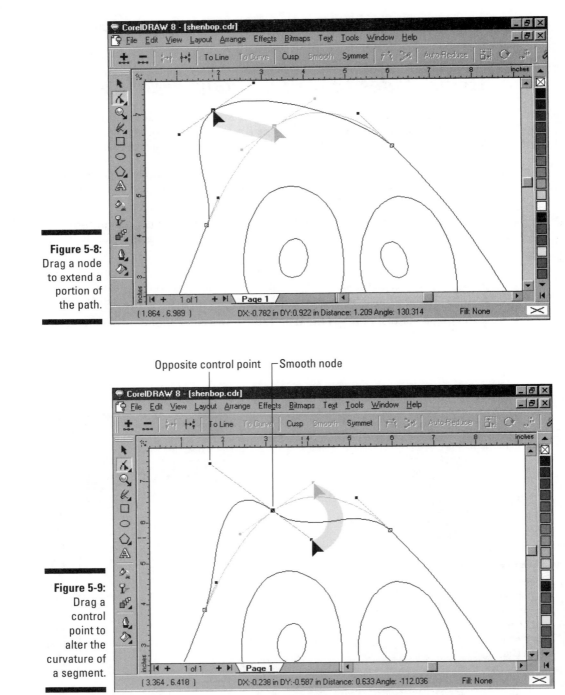

Figure 5-8:
Drag a node to extend a portion of the path.

Opposite control point ─Smooth node

Figure 5-9:
Drag a control point to alter the curvature of a segment.

- If the node is a *smooth node,* the opposite control point also moves, bending its segment, as in Figure 5-9. In a smooth node, the control points are locked into alignment to ensure a seamless arc. If the node is a *cusp node,* you can move one control point independently of its neighbor. The cusp node permits you to create corners in a path. (More on cusp and smooth nodes later in this chapter.)

- Are you still vague on the whole control point thing? Try envisioning a typical pencil path as a rubber band wrapped around a pattern of nails, as dramatized in Figure 5-10. The nails represent nodes in the path; the rubber band represents its segments. A sample control point appears as a round knob. The rubber band is stretched to give it tension and prevent it from crimping. A path in CorelDraw likewise bends evenly in the direction of its handle.

- If you don't want to deal with control points — believe me, everybody hates them — you can drag directly on a curved segment. The segment bends and stretches as shown in Figure 5-11.

- When you drag a segment bordered by a smooth node, the segment on the other side of that node bends and stretches with your drag. In Figure 5-11, both bordering nodes are smooth nodes, so three segments are affected.

- You can't drag a straight segment.

- To drag a node, a control point, or a segment in a strictly horizontal or vertical direction, press the Ctrl key while dragging.

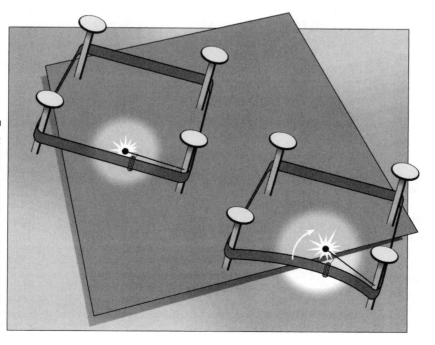

Figure 5-10: By dragging the control point from its original position (left), you bend the rubber band segment in that direction (right).

✔ To select more than one node, click on the first node and Shift+click on each additional node. Then drag any one of them to move all the selected nodes at the same time.

✔ If the nodes you want to select border each other, you can select them by dragging around them. As you drag, CorelDraw displays a dotted rectangle called a *marquee,* shown in Figure 5-12. Any nodes surrounded by the marquee become selected.

✔ Don't forget to press Ctrl+Z or choose Edit➪Undo if you make a mistake. Or, if you prefer, you can press Alt+Backspace. No change is irreparable if you catch it in time.

Meet the Node Edit Thingies

To perform any other node-editing function, such as adding and deleting nodes, joining and splitting paths, and all the rest of that stuff, you use the trusty Node Edit roll-up, the shape tool, or the property bar. To display the roll-up, featured in Figure 5-13, double-click on the shape tool or press Ctrl+F10.

In early versions of CorelDraw, most buttons in the Node Edit roll-up were labeled with words. The meanings of the buttons weren't always crystal clear — To Line and Symmet took some figuring out — but at least you had a

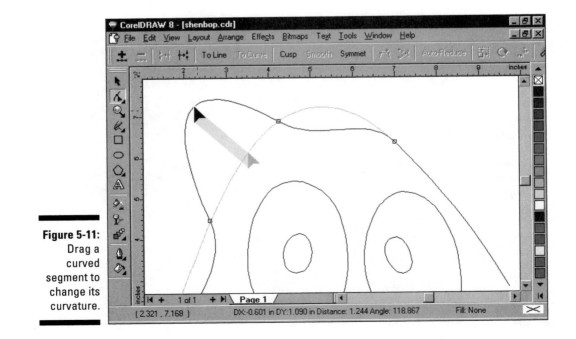

Figure 5-11: Drag a curved segment to change its curvature.

Marquee

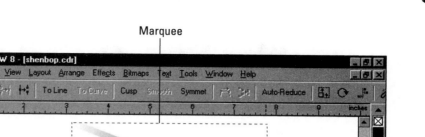

Figure 5-12:
As you
drag,
CorelDraw
creates a
marquee
outline.

clue. In CorelDraw 6, 7, and 8, the labels are replaced by icons, few of which are the least bit recognizable.

Fortunately, Figure 5-14 includes helpful labels for each button. I also describe all the buttons in detail in the following three sections and show each button in the margin when discussing it. And in case that's still not enough, I refer to each button in the text by its order in the Node Edit roll-up. The fourth button in the first row, for example, is the one labeled *Break one node in two* in Figure 5-15. I hope the result is a crystal-clear discussion of this wacky roll-up.

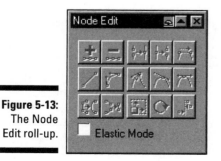

Figure 5-13:
The Node
Edit roll-up.

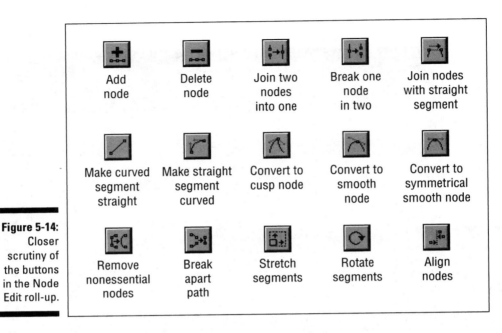

Figure 5-14:
Closer
scrutiny of
the buttons
in the Node
Edit roll-up.

You can identify each button in the Node Edit roll-up also by hovering your cursor over a button when the roll-up is active. A little box displaying the name of the button appears next to your cursor. Unfortunately, the status bar doesn't include a description of the button's purpose. You have to rely on the next three sections for that.

CorelDraw offers an additional avenue for working with nodes. When the shape tool is selected, the property bar offers the same controls as the Node Edit roll-up. Unfortunately, if you use the 640-x-480-pixel display setting for your monitor, some of the controls are hidden. To gain access to all property bar controls, drag the property bar into the drawing area to create a free-floating palette of shape tool controls, as shown in Figure 5-15.

To further complicate things, some controls on the property bar use the old text labels discussed earlier instead of using the same icons found in the Node Edit roll-up. Figure 5-15 sorts things out by labeling the property bar buttons that look different from those in the roll-up.

You may notice when looking at the Node Edit roll-up or property bar that many of the controls seem always to be dimmed. In many cases, the option is already in effect. For example, if you select a cusp node, the convert to cusp node button is dimmed because the cusp can't be any cuspier than it already is. Other times, the control isn't applicable. The align nodes button is dimmed if fewer than two nodes are selected because you can't align a single node to itself. Well, I guess you could, but what's the point?

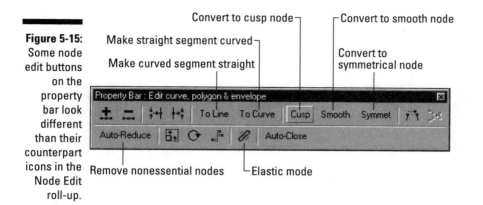

Figure 5-15: Some node edit buttons on the property bar look different than their counterpart icons in the Node Edit roll-up.

Your first tentative node edits

The following list explains how to use the most essential buttons in the Node Edit roll-up to add nodes, delete nodes, and otherwise wreak havoc on the whole node-oriented world. (You can also use the corresponding buttons on the property bar, labeled in Figure 5-15.) Get psyched, because this list is about the most exciting one you'll ever read — short of the phone book, of course.

- ✔ To add a node to a path, click on the spot in the segment where you want to add the node. A round sort of blob appears. It's not a node yet; it's sort of a fetal node. Then click on the add node button to bring the node into the world of the living.

- ✔ You can also add nodes to a shape drawn with the polygon tool. Try this: Draw a polygon, select the shape tool, and drag one of the side nodes to make the shape look like a star. Now click on any segment to create a fetal node and click on the add node button. Not only does a new node appear at the spot where you clicked, but additional nodes also spring up at symmetrical points around the shape. Drag any of these new nodes, and all the new nodes move in kind. It's very cool.

- ✔ To delete one or more nodes, select all the nodes you want to delete and then press Delete. Why bother with that delete node button when the Delete key is so much more convenient?

- ✔ If you can add nodes to a polygon, it stands to reason that you can select a polygon node and delete it as well.

- ✔ You can also press the + or – key on the numeric keypad to respectively add or delete a node. These keys work even when the Node Edit roll-up and property bar are hidden.

CorelDraw 8 offers an even easier way to add and delete nodes. Using the shape tool, you can double-click on a segment to add a node or double-click on an existing node to delete it. So why bother with buttons or keystrokes?

Excuse me for interrupting, but I feel it is my duty to come out in hearty support of the flagrant clear-cutting of nodes. The fact is, CorelDraw invariably assigns too many nodes to paths drawn with the pencil or natural pen. It's not unusual to see nodes stuck one right on top of the other, like procreating cockroaches, or wet Skittles, or some equally disgusting fluke of nature. As a rule, you need a cusp node for every corner in a path. You need a smooth node for every quarter-circle's worth of curve. Anything beyond that is garbage. Figure 5-16 shows a path before and after deleting extraneous nodes.

How to open, split, close, and join paths

In previous sections, I explain how to add and delete nodes, which amounts to super common stuff. If only for the sake of strip-mining paths, you may be engaging in these operations frequently. The next functions I describe are slightly less common, but rank right up there nonetheless. The following items describe how to open closed paths, close open ones, slice and dice paths without the aid of a Vegematic, and join them back together as effortlessly as a supercollider bonds kernels of creamed corn back onto the cob.

Figure 5-16:
Bad
Shenbop's
nodes are
many and
crowded.
Good
Shenbop's
nodes are
few and far
between.

Bad Shenbop   Good Shenbop

A little something you don't need to know

When you draw with a real pencil, you smudge graphite directly onto the page. It's a cause-and-effect thing, a simple law of nature. When you draw with the pencil tool, CorelDraw tries to imitate nature by using math. But because math isn't the natural state of anything except computer programs and high school calculus teachers, the line must undergo a conversion. You can tweak this conversion — thereby affecting how the pencil tool draws — by using the good old Options dialog box.

Double-click on the pencil tool icon in the toolbox to display the Options dialog box. Three options have a bearing on pencil paths, as spotlighted in the figure. The first, Freehand Tracking, controls how accurately the path follows your drag. The second, Corner Threshold, helps prevent CorelDraw from following its natural tendency, which is to insert jagged corners in a path. And the third, Straight Line Threshold, determines the likelihood of straight segments in a path.

In all three cases, the values in the option boxes can vary between 1 and 10. If you develop uncanny dexterity with the mouse, you may want to test lower values, which — taken to their extremes — encourage the path to follow every nuance and jiggle in your drag. If your drags exhibit the kinds of tremors normally associated with small earthquakes, or if folks have a tendency to ask why you write your letters in moving vehicles — and you actually write at a desk during the stillest of evenings while listening to endless loops of Pachelbel's *Canon in D minor* — you may want to avail yourself of higher values, which result in smoother and less jagged paths, however less accurate.

Options		? X
Eraser Tool	**Freehand/Bezier Tool**	
Zoom, Pan Too		
Freehand/Bezi	Freehand tracking: 5	pixels
Natural Pen To	Autotrace tracking: 5	pixels
Dimension Too		
Angular Dimen:	Corner threshold: 5	pixels
Connector Too		
Rectangle Too	Straight line threshold: 5	pixels
Ellipse Tool	Auto-join: 5	pixels
Polygon Tool		
Spiral Tool		
Graph Paper T		
Text Tool		
Outline Tool		
Fill Tool		
Customize		
Document		
Global		
		OK Cancel Help

✔ To open a closed path, select a node that you want to split into two nodes and click on the break one node in two button. What was once one node is now two nodes. You can drag each node wherever you want. If the closed path was filled with a color before you opened it, the color disappears.

✔ To split an open path into two independent paths, select the node at which you want the split to occur and then click on the break one node in two button. The path is now split, but CorelDraw continues to think of the path as a single unit. To finalize the divorce, click on the break apart path button. Or you can choose Arrange⇨Break Apart or press Ctrl+K. The two paths can now go their separate ways.

✔ To close an open path, select both the first and last nodes in the line and then click on the join two nodes into one button. The two nodes are fused into one, and the line is transformed into a shape.

✔ The problem with the join two nodes into one button is that it moves the nodes when joining them. If you want the nodes to remain in place and connect them with a straight line, click on the join nodes with straight segment button.

Joining two independent open paths into a single longer path is a little tricky. Here's the step-by-step process:

1. **Select the arrow tool.**

   See, this operation is tricky already.

2. **Click on the first open path that you want to join.**

   Don't try this technique on a closed path. If you want to extend a shape, make sure that you first open the path by selecting a node with the shape tool and clicking on the break one node in two button.

3. **Shift+click on the second open path that you want to join.**

   Now both paths are selected.

4. **Press Ctrl+L or choose Arrange⇨Combine.**

   CorelDraw now recognizes the paths as a single unit.

5. **Press F10 to select the shape tool.**

   Getting trickier.

6. **Click on the first or last node in one path and then Shift+click on the first or last node in the other path.**

   In other words, select the two nodes you want to fuse together.

7. **Click on the join two nodes into one button.**

   The two short lines are now one long line.

More ways to make a break

You can also use the knife tool or the eraser tool to break apart segments and paths. Both tools are available from the shape tool flyout menu, shown in Figure 5-17. Click on and hold the shape tool icon in the toolbox to display the flyout and then click on the tool you want to use:

- ✔ If you select the knife tool, you can click on a path to cut it apart at that point. (If you miss the path, CorelDraw beeps at you in a highly irritating manner.) You can click on a node or on a segment. Either way, a precise incision is made.

- ✔ By default, the knife tool closes any path it touches, whether the path was originally open or closed. If you click on a line drawn with the pencil tool, for example, CorelDraw automatically adds new segments to the severed paths and creates two closed shapes. Makes about as much sense as cutting a piece of string and getting two pieces of dinnerware.

  To instruct CorelDraw to stop this nonsensical closing of knifed paths, double-click on the knife tool icon in the toolbox. The Options dialog box comes to the rescue. Turn off the Automatically Close Object option and press Enter.

Knife tool ─ Eraser tool

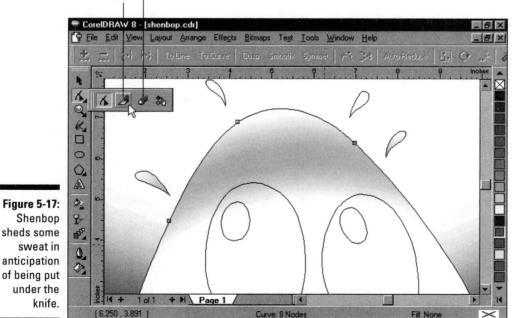

Figure 5-17:
Shenbop
sheds some
sweat in
anticipation
of being put
under the
knife.

✔ The eraser is another cutting tool, but instead of using it to cut at a point, you use it to slice a wide gash through the path. Select the eraser and drag across the path. The eraser tears through the path and splits it in pieces.

✔ The eraser tool leaves closed paths closed and leaves open paths open. What a sensible tool.

✔ To specify the width of the opening cut with the eraser tool, double-click on the eraser tool icon in the toolbox. You see the Options dialog box. Enter a new value into the Thickness option box — the default is $\frac{1}{4}$ inch — and press Enter. (Changing the value in the first option box on the left side of the property bar accomplishes the same thing.)

When you slice paths with the knife tool, CorelDraw breaks them into two separate objects. But when you use the eraser tool, the bits and pieces of the path remain combined into one path, which means you can't drag the pieces separately with the arrow tool. To break the pieces apart, press Ctrl+K or click on the break apart path button (labeled back in Figure 5-14) as described in the preceding section.

Options you need once in a blue moon

I'm tempted to end my discussion of the node edit buttons right here. The buttons I didn't discuss earlier aren't entirely useless — not all of them, anyway — but they're more specialized. Most beginners and intermediates barely touch these buttons. But the buttons do serve a purpose, so you may as well know about them. The upcoming list explains the remaining options (in order from most useful to least useful) in the Node Edit roll-up and on the property bar.

You can apply the node edit buttons to nodes and segments drawn with the polygon tool as well as to paths drawn with the pencil and natural pen tools. Throughout, CorelDraw maintains the symmetry of the polygon, which can make for some pretty entertaining effects.

✔ The first button in the second row of the Node Edit roll-up straightens out a curved segment. (This button is labeled To Line on the property bar.) To use the option, click on a too-curly segment with the shape tool. A round node-wannabe appears to show that the segment is selected. Click on the button, and the segment becomes straight.

✔ The next button in the second row of the roll-up fulfills the opposite function. (The button is labeled To Curve on the property bar.) Click on a straight segment to get the round fetal node, and then click on the button to make the segment a curve. Although the segment still looks straight, you can drag the segment with the shape tool to stretch it.

✔ To change a smooth node so that it represents a corner in the path, select the node and click on the convert to cusp node button (third button, second row of the Node Edit roll-up, labeled Cusp on the property bar). You can then move the control points of the cusp independently of each other.

✔ To change a corner to a smooth arc, select the node and click on the convert to smooth node button (fourth button, second row in the Node Edit roll-up, labeled Smooth on the property bar). CorelDraw locks the control points into alignment so that the transition between neighboring segments is seamless.

✔ The fifth button in the second row of the Node Edit roll-up (labeled Symmet on the property bar) locks the control points of a node into symmetrical alignment, so that the two levers are always the same length. The result is a variation on the smooth node that has almost no relevance in today's world. I think Peking Man used it in some sort of greet-the-dawn ritual, but nowadays, forget it.

✔ The stretch and rotate segments buttons are marginally useful. You can scale, rotate, flip, and slant individual segments in a path by selecting two or more nodes, clicking on one of these buttons, and dragging a handle. To find out about the standard transformation functions, read Chapter 9. Then come back to these options and try them out.

✔ The align nodes button aligns multiple nodes in horizontal or vertical formation. You can find out more about alignment in Chapter 6.

✔ The first button in the last row of the Node Edit roll-up (labeled Auto-Reduce on the property bar) wins my vote as the least useful of the node edit options. This option is supposed to remove nonessential nodes automatically. But think about it for a moment. If CorelDraw were smart enough to eliminate extraneous nodes, it wouldn't have put them in there in the first place. You can rearrange some settings in the Options dialog box (as explained in the "A little something you don't need to know" sidebar a few pages back) and get some remarkably disappointing results. But for the most part, this option doesn't do squat.

Bouncy paths made of rubber

At the bottom of the Node Edit roll-up, you see an Elastic Mode check box (refer to Figure 5-13). The option also appears on the property bar, in the form of a button that looks like a rubber band (labeled back in Figure 5-15). In the past, I've been a tad unfair to this option, making libelous suggestions such as "People who know how to use Elastic mode are dumber for it." That's true, of course, or I never would have said it. But still, being dumb can be fun, so I may as well tell you how the doggone thing works.

When Elastic mode is on, CorelDraw moves, stretches, and rotates all selected nodes with respect to the node that is farthest away from the node you drag. Even if the faraway node is selected, it remains stationary, while the other nodes stretch away or toward it to varying degrees depending on their proximity. This option produces a spongy effect, as if the faraway node is snagged on a nail or something and the rest of the path is made of rubber.

If you turn off Elastic mode, the selected nodes move, stretch, and rotate a consistent amount, without any rubbery stuff happening. This mode is less amusing, but it may be more useful if you're trying to achieve a specific effect. In other words, if you don't like the way a path is behaving, switch the Elastic mode setting and see whether you like things any better.

How to Upgrade Simple Shapes

Much of this chapter is devoted to stuff you can't do to rectangles, ovals, or symmetrical polygons. You can't move the nodes in a rectangle independently of each other, you can't adjust the curvature of a segment in an oval, and you can't drag a single node in a star independently of its symmetrical buddies.

Not, that is, until you convert the simple shapes to free-form paths. To make the conversion, select the shape with the arrow tool and press Ctrl+Q. That's all there is to it. By pressing Ctrl+Q or choosing Arrange➪Convert To Curves, you convert the selected shape to nodes, segments, and control points, just like a path drawn with the pencil tool. You can then edit the shape to any extent imaginable.

By converting a simple shape to a path, however, you ruin all semblance of the shape's original identity. You can no longer use the shape tool to add rounded corners to a rectangle, change an oval into a pie, or move all the points in a star together, as described in Chapter 4. The Convert To Curves command submits the shape to a state of complete anarchy.

Chapter 6
Celebrating Your Inner Draftsman

● ●

In This Chapter

▶ Disciplining yourself (and other sick ideas)

▶ Using the rulers

▶ Setting up the grid

▶ Positioning guidelines

▶ Creating guides at an angle

▶ Observing and modifying the status bar

▶ Moving objects incrementally and numerically

▶ Aligning and distributing objects

▶ Amassing objects into groups

▶ Changing the stacking order (whatever that is)

● ●

*D*o you have problems expressing your feelings? Are you critical of other people's driving? Do you insist on alphabetizing your guests at the dinner table? Do you distrust government, yet at the same time harbor suspicions that Ross Perot is a certifiable loony? If you said yes to any of these — except the bit about Perot — you may be a closet control freak. And you know what? That's okay. Because, doggone it, people like you. A couple of them, anyway. Well, maybe *like* is too strong of a word. Know, then. They scurry out of the room when you appear because, doggone it, people know you. Isn't that comforting?

This chapter is a call to arms for control freaks, a reawakening of the kindred spirit of the fussbudget. Together, we'll muck around with rulers, guidelines, and other tightly structured features in an attempt to precisely arrange minuscule details that no one notices but that you obsess about with a secret pride. I speak of the satisfaction that only a job well worried over can deliver.

I don't want to cure your perfectionism. I want you to rejoice in it! By the way, is that a grease stain on your shirt? Ha, made you look.

You Need to Be Disciplined

At least, that's what Madonna would tell you. But I'm talking about a different kind of discipline — namely, the kind provided by the big four CorelDraw
control functions:

- ✔ *Rulers,* which appear along the top and left sides of the drawing area,
serve as visual aids.

- ✔ The *grid* is a network of regularly spaced points or lines that attract
your cursor and prevent you from drawing slightly crooked lines and
other haphazard stuff.

- ✔ You can set up custom *guidelines* between grid increments to align
objects and generally ensure an orderly environment.

- ✔ The *status bar* shows you where your cursor is, the dimensions of
shapes, the distance and angle of movements, and a bunch of other
stuff I can't tell you right now or else I won't have anything to talk
about in the status bar section.

Rulers with no power

Unlike grids and guidelines, rulers don't constrain your mouse movements
or make you draw any better. In fact, they don't do much of anything. They
just sit there. But rulers can be nice to have around because they show you
how big objects are and how much distance is between them.

If you don't see any rulers on your screen, choose <u>V</u>iew⇨<u>R</u>ulers to display
them. As shown in Figure 6-1, one horizontal ruler and one vertical ruler
appear along the outskirts of the drawing area. With a little luck and a whole
lot of divine intervention, the rulers may even inspire you to create something as fantastic as the Roman Colosseum (Collos.CDR), found on the
second of the CorelDraw 8 CD-ROMs. (Open the Clipart folder, then the
Travel folder, and then the Landmark folder to find the Collos.CDR file.)

Here's how to exploit the rulers to their fullest:

- ✔ The rulers monitor the location of the cursor by using two *tracking lines.*
Meanwhile, the status bar displays the numerical coordinates of the
cursor, which correspond directly to the tracking lines. In Figure 6-1, for
example, the horizontal tracking line appears just to the right of the $4^1/4$
inch mark, whereas the status bar displays the coordinate 4.250.

- ✔ All measurements are made from the *zero point,* which is the point at
which both rulers display the value 0. You can change the location of
the zero point by dragging the ruler origin box, which appears at the
meeting of the two rulers, as shown in Figure 6-2. The point at which
you release the mouse button becomes the new zero point. (See

Rulers   Horizontal tracking line

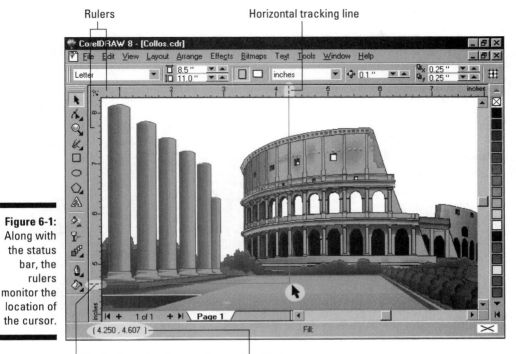

Figure 6-1:
Along with
the status
bar, the
rulers
monitor the
location of
the cursor.

Vertical tracking line   Cursor coordinates

Figure 6-3.) To return the zero point to its original position, double-click on the ruler origin box.

✔ Rulers generally display units in inches. But if you prefer to work in a different measurement system, you can change one or both rulers. To quickly change the unit of measurement for both rulers, select an option from the Units pop-up menu on the property bar, labeled in Figure 6-3.

✔ You also can change the unit of measurement for each ruler by right-clicking on a ruler and selecting Ruler Setup to display the Rulers panel of the Options dialog box, shown in Figure 6-4. If the Same Units for Horizontal and Vertical Rulers check box is selected, changing the horizontal value changes the unit of measurement for both rulers. If the check box is turned off, you can establish a different unit of measurement for each ruler.

✔ Use the Tick Divisions option on the Rulers panel of the Options dialog box to specify how many division marks appear between each major ruler increment.

✔ If the Show Fractions check box is selected, CorelDraw displays ruler measurements in fractions rather than decimals ($1\frac{1}{2}$ rather than 1.5, for example).

Ruler origin box

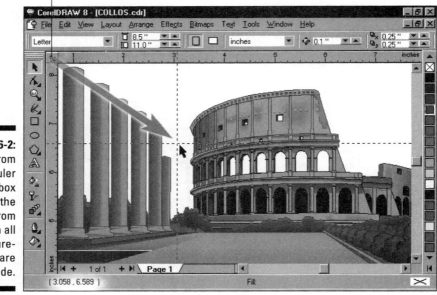

Figure 6-2:
Drag from the ruler origin box to move the point from which all measurements are made.

New zero points   Units pop-up window

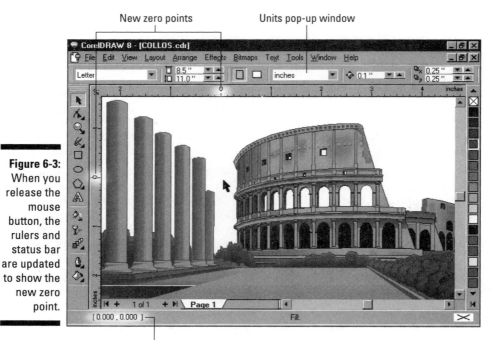

Figure 6-3:
When you release the mouse button, the rulers and status bar are updated to show the new zero point.

New cursor coordinates

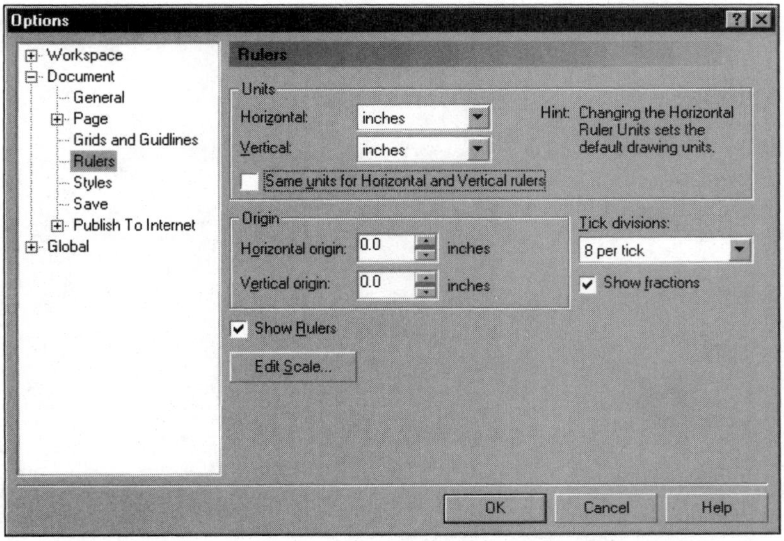

Figure 6-4:
The Rulers
panel of the
Options
dialog box
lets you
change
your unit of
measurement.

✔ The status bar coordinates always correspond to the units on the horizontal ruler (displayed on the ruler's far right side).

✔ To get rid of the rulers, choose View⟿Rulers.

Go downtown

Imagine a plan for the perfect city center, something like Washington, D.C. Every block measures $1/10$ mile by $1/10$ mile. No block has an alley. Exactly 11 east-west streets and 11 north-south avenues subdivide every square mile into 100 square blocks. Oh, sure, this layout is a little formal. It lacks spontaneity and joie de vivre, but you're supposed to be doing some work, not sitting around enjoying the scenery. Besides, your city plan is a grid, just like the one in CorelDraw.

In CorelDraw, the grid affects the placement of nodes, control points, handles, and so on. So although a free-form path can snake along wherever it pleases, its nodes are constrained to precise grid increments. The same goes for nodes in rectangles, ovals, and blocks of text. Here's how to set up a grid:

1. **Right-click on one of the rulers and select Grid Setup from the pop-up menu.**

   This displays the Grids and Guidelines panel of the Options dialog box, as shown in Figure 6-5.

2. **Select the Show Grid as Dots radio button.**

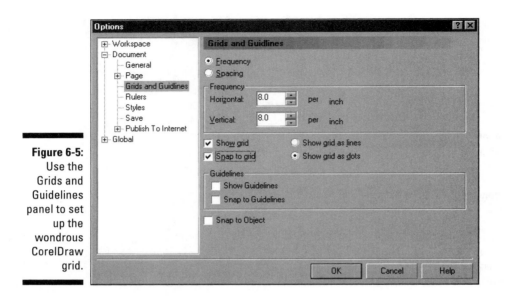

Figure 6-5:
Use the
Grids and
Guidelines
panel to set
up the
wondrous
CorelDraw
grid.

In CorelDraw 8, you can choose to display your grid as dots or lines. I suggest you choose dots, which is the default setting — they're much less intrusive on your drawing.

3. Define the distance between grid points by entering values in the Horizontal and Vertical option boxes.

The option boxes work differently depending on whether you select the Frequency or the Spacing radio button. If you select Frequency, the Horizontal and Vertical values specify how many grid points you want per unit of measure. For example, if you enter a value of 8 and you're using inches as your unit of measure, you get 8 grid dots per inch.

If you choose the Spacing radio button, you can place grid dots at specific increments across the drawing area. If you enter Horizontal and Vertical values of .25, CorelDraw places the grid dots one-quarter inch apart. This setting would be the same as choosing the Frequency option and choosing a Horizontal value of 4; the Spacing and Frequency options give you two different ways of looking at things.

The number of grid points per unit of measure is called the *grid frequency,* just in case you're even remotely interested.

4. Select the Show Grid check box.

This way, you can see the grid points on-screen.

5. Select the Snap to Grid check box.

When this option is active, nodes, control points, and handles gravitate — snap — to grid points. If you don't select this option, you can see the grid, but the grid has no effect on how you draw and edit paths. This step is the most important one. Don't skip it.

6. Press Enter.

Or click on OK. The grid points appear in the drawing area, as shown in Figure 6-6.

To try out the grid, draw a rectangle with the rectangle tool. Your cursor snaps from one grid point to the next, as in Figure 6-6. Incidentally, CorelDraw doesn't always display all grid points. Depending on the grid frequency and zoom ratio, the program may hide some grid points to cut down on-screen clutter (as is the case in the figure). But whether or not you can see a grid point, the snapping effect is still in force.

After you establish your grid, you can hide and display it by choosing View⇨Grid. You can turn its snapping powers on and off from the keyboard by pressing Ctrl+Y (or by choosing Layout⇨Snap to Grid).

You can also turn grid snapping on and off by selecting the arrow tool and then clicking on the Snap to Grid button on the property bar. (If you're using the 640-x-480 monitor display setting, you may not be able to see the Snap to Grid button. To reveal it, drag the property bar into the drawing area; the button is just to the right of the Duplicate Distance controls.)

Grid point

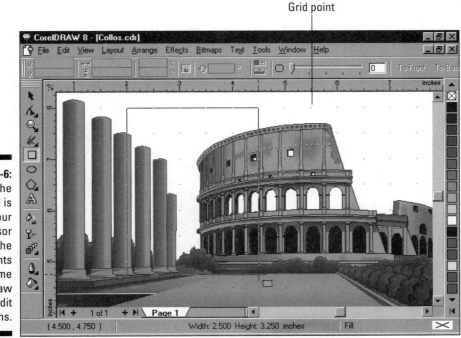

Figure 6-6:
When the grid is active, your cursor snaps to the grid points every time you draw and edit paths.

Let the lines be your guide

The CorelDraw grid is great for novices but loses some of its attraction after you become moderately familiar with the program.

That's where *guidelines* come in. Like the rulers, guidelines are available in horizontal and vertical varieties. Like the grid, they exude gravitational force. But guidelines differ from rulers and the grid in that you can create as many guidelines as you like and place them wherever you want. You can even draw a guide at an angle.

- ✔ To create a guideline, drag from a ruler into the drawing area, as demonstrated in Figure 6-7.

- ✔ Don't see a guideline when you drag? Choose Layout➪Guidelines Setup to display the Guidelines Setup dialog box, and then turn on the Show Guidelines check box and press Enter.

- ✔ Dragging down from the horizontal ruler produces a horizontal guideline; dragging right from the vertical ruler produces — everybody sing! — a bright red lobster in a green varsity sweater.

  Actually, that last action produces a vertical guideline. I just made up the bit about the lobster. No lobsters were made to wear sweaters in the making of this book. One was encouraged to wear a high-school

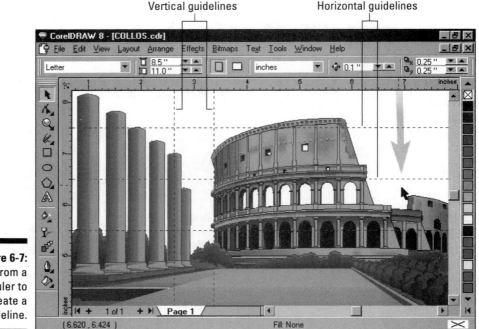

Figure 6-7:
Drag from a
ruler to
create a
guideline.

letter jacket, but only briefly. The lobster is now in a recovery program. (See Figure 6-8.) In fact, he and I are in the same ward.

✔ To move a guideline, click and hold on the guideline until the guideline turns red and the cursor changes to a cross with four arrows. Then drag. Be careful, though. It's easy to accidentally drag an object when you're trying to drag a guideline (and vice versa).

✔ In CorelDraw 8, guidelines are treated as objects, which means that you can select, move, nudge, and delete them just like any other object. For example, you can click on a guideline to select it and then press the arrow keys to nudge it (nudging is discussed later in this chapter) or the Delete key to delete it. Guidelines appear blue unless they are selected, in which case they're red.

✔ To change the angle of a guide, click once to select it and click again to display rotation handles on each end of the line. Then drag the rotation handles to reset the angle of the guide.

✔ To delete a horizontal, vertical, or angled guide, select it and press Delete.

If you have trouble deleting an angled guide, use this method instead: Double-click the guide to display the Guidelines Setup dialog box, and then select the Slanted tab. A list of angled guides appears on the left side of the dialog box, complete with techie coordinate data stating the location of some point on the guide and its angle. The guide on which you double-clicked should be selected. But you can also use the angle

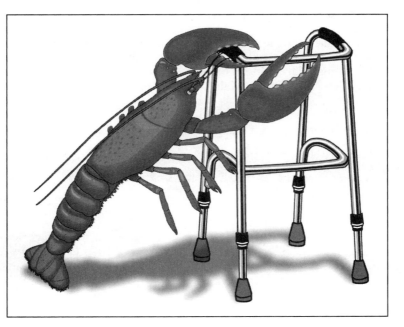

Figure 6-8:
The lobster demonstrates his indomitable will to survive.

data to figure out which guide is which. Guides with positive angle values slant up; guides with negative angles slant down. The larger the value, the more the guide slants. Select the guide you want to delete and click on the Delete button. If you deleted the wrong guide, press Esc and try again. Press Enter to make your change official.

✔ You can undo the movement of a guide — just as you can undo any other edit — by pressing Ctrl+Z (or Alt+Backspace).

✔ When the grid is active and the Snap to Grid option is enabled, the creation and movement of guidelines are constrained by the grid. There's no point to having a guideline that duplicates a line of grid points, so be sure to turn off the grid (Ctrl+Y).

✔ If guidelines and the grid are both active, a guideline takes precedence over either of its grid-point neighbors. The guideline has a stronger gravitational force, in other words.

✔ However, for guidelines to attract anything, the Snap to Guidelines option must be turned on. Choose Layout➪Snap to Guidelines to turn the guideline attraction on and off.

✔ You also can turn guideline snapping on and off by clicking on the Snap to Guidelines button on the property bar, which is just to the right of the Snap to Grid button. These buttons are cut off the right side of the screen if you're using the 640-x-480 monitor display setting. For more information on this topic, see Chapter 2.

The status bar tells all

Like the rulers, the status bar doesn't affect the movement of your cursor. Instead, it provides information on everything you do in CorelDraw. By default, this information is organized into five report regions, as illustrated in Figure 6-9 and explained in the following list:

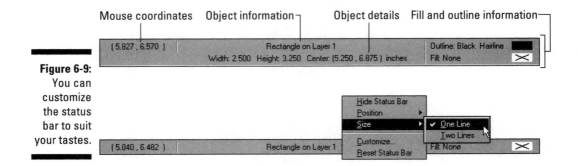

Figure 6-9:
You can customize the status bar to suit your tastes.

- When your cursor is inside the drawing area, the top-left corner of the status bar lists the horizontal and vertical coordinates of the cursor.

- The middle report region on the top line varies depending on the operation. If an object is selected, the status bar lists what kind of object it is. When you perform certain operations to the object, the status bar reports on the operation. When you drag a node in a path, for example, the status bar tells you the distance and angle of movement.

- The middle report region on the bottom line of the status bar displays additional details about the selected object. For example, if the selected object is a shape, it displays the shape's dimensions.

- The right corner of the status bar contains the last two report regions: outline and fill information. In addition to displaying color swatches showing the outline and fill colors, CorelDraw 8 displays the names of the outline and fill applied to the selected object. If the object is not filled or if an open path is selected, a big X appears in the fill swatch.

The middle report regions appear only when an object is selected. If you are using the 640-x-480 monitor display setting, the middle report regions do not appear by default because there isn't enough room to display them.

In Version 8, the default status bar occupies two lines. To free up more space for the drawing area, you may want to customize the status bar to display on one line the information you refer to most frequently . That's what I did in preparing the figures in this book. To change the size of the status bar, right-click on one of the report regions and select Size⇨One Line, as shown in the lower example in Figure 6-9. To customize the size or kind of report regions, right-click on one of the report regions and select Customize from the pop-up menu. This displays the Toolbars customization options in the Options dialog box. Click on the Status Bar folder to display a selection of report regions to choose from. You can alter the status bar so that it shows different information or additional report regions. You can also allocate more room to one report region or another by clicking on a report region and dragging the resulting gray box to the left or right.

- You can move the status bar to the top of the interface by right-clicking on the status bar and choosing Position⇨Top. And naturally, Bottom puts the status bar back at the bottom of the screen. (I know, I didn't have to tell you that, but my lawyer said I'd better.)

- You can also move the status bar to the top or bottom of the screen by simply dragging it with the regular old left mouse button.

- To return the status bar to its default setting, right-click on the status bar and choose Reset Status Bar.

Even something as useful as the status bar can get in your way. If you just want to get the thing out of your face, choose View⇨Status Bar. Choose the command again to redisplay the status bar.

Tell Your Objects Where They Can Go

In Chapters 4 and 5, I explain how to move whole objects and individual nodes by dragging them. But dragging isn't the only means for movement in CorelDraw. You can move objects in prescribed increments, by numerical distances, or in relation to each other.

Nudging with the arrow keys

The arrow keys put selected items in motion. Whether you want to move a few nodes selected with the shape tool or one or more objects selected with the arrow tool, pressing the arrow keys nudges the items incrementally in the direction of the arrow. If you press and hold the arrow key, the selected node or object scoots across the drawing area until you let up on the key.

By default, each arrow key moves a selected item $1/10$ inch. However, you can change this to any increment you want. Just do either of the following:

- Press Ctrl+J or choose Tools⇨Options to display the Options dialog box. Click on Edit and enter a value in the Nudge option box, spotlighted in Figure 6-10. If necessary, select a different unit of measure from the Units pop-up menu.
- With the arrow tool selected but with no objects selected, change the Nudge value on the property bar, spotlighted and labeled in Figure 6-10.

If you press Ctrl plus an arrow key, you perform a Super Nudge, which simply means you move the object a certain multiple of the regular Nudge value. For example, if the Nudge value is .10 and the Super Nudge value is 10, a Super Nudge moves your object .10 times 10, or a full inch. You can change the Super Nudge value in the Options dialog box.

Pressing Alt plus an arrow key scrolls your view of the drawing on-screen, as explained in Chapter 3.

Nudge value

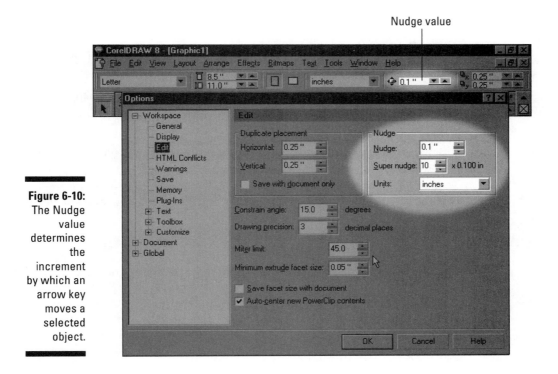

Figure 6-10:
The Nudge
value
determines
the
increment
by which an
arrow key
moves a
selected
object.

Moving by the numbers

To move an object a specific numerical distance, you can use either the property bar or the Position roll-up, which you display by pressing Alt+F7 or choosing Arrange⇨Transform⇨Position.

Moving an object by using the property bar controls, labeled in Figure 6-11, is a cinch. Just select the object with the arrow tool and then adjust the X and Y values. You can click on the up- and down-pointing arrows next to the X and Y option boxes, or you can double-click on an option box, enter a new value from the keyboard, and press Enter. The X value affects the object's horizontal position; the Y value affects its vertical position. Both values reflect the position of the center of the object.

The Position roll-up, also shown in Figure 6-11, is slightly more complicated but offers you more options than the property bar. You can approach moves made with this roll-up in two ways. You can move the object either relative to its current position or to an exact coordinate location.

To move the object a relative distance, enter values into the H and V option boxes. A negative value moves the object leftward or down. A positive value moves the object the other way.

Moving an object to a specific coordinate location is a little trickier:

1. **Select the object you want to move by clicking it with the arrow tool.**

2. **Click on the Expand button (labeled in Figure 6-11).**

   The roll-up grows to reveal eight check boxes surrounding a single radio button. These boxes are the reference point options.

3. **Turn off the Relative Position check box.**

4. **Select a check box or radio button from the reference point options.**

   The check boxes represent the eight handles around the selected object; the radio button represents the object's center. So, for example, if you want to position the upper-right corner of an object at a specific location, you would select the upper-right check box.

5. **Enter the coordinates in the H and V option boxes.**

   The coordinates are measured relative to the rulers' zero point. So, if you position the zero point smack dab in the middle of the page, all coordinates are measured from this center. By default, however, the zero point is at the lower-left corner of the page.

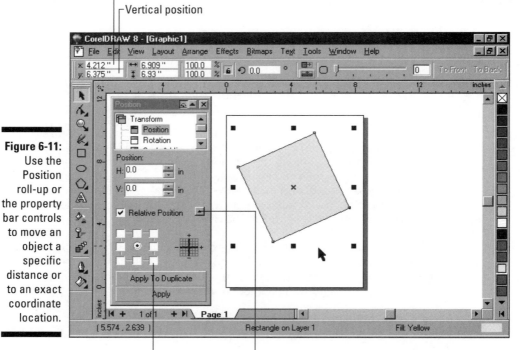

Horizontal position

Vertical position

Figure 6-11:
Use the
Position
roll-up or
the property
bar controls
to move an
object a
specific
distance or
to an exact
coordinate
location.

Reference point options   Expand button

If you're not sure what coordinates you want to use — gee whiz, who would know such a thing? — deselect the object, move your cursor to the desired destination, and note the mouse coordinate values in the status bar. Then select the object again and enter those very values in the H and V option boxes.

6. Click on the Apply button.

Oh, by the way, the Apply to Duplicate button creates a copy of the object at the new location. Duplication is one of the subjects of Chapter 8.

The X and Y controls on the property bar always move the object a relative distance, regardless of whether the Relative Position option box in the Position roll-up is turned on or off.

Aligning and distributing objects

The last way to move objects is to shift them in relation to each other. Suppose that you drew a series of silhouetted soldiers marching down the road. But you were so busy concentrating on making the shapes look like soldiers against an eerie twilight sky that you neglected to line them up. So, instead of marching on a flat road, the soldiers bob up and down. To align their feet along a perfectly horizontal surface, select all the soldier shapes and press Ctrl+A or choose Arrange⇨Align and Distribute. The Align and distribute dialog box appears, as shown in Figure 6-12, enabling you to evenly space objects by using various alignment and distribution options.

You also can open the Align and distribute dialog box by clicking on the property bar button labeled Align, which appears when you have multiple objects selected. Unfortunately, if you're using the 640-x-480 display setting for your monitor, you can't get to this button unless you drag the property bar into the drawing window as discussed in Chapter 2.

To align two or more selected objects vertically, choose the Top, Center, or Bottom check box from the Align tab of the dialog box. (The icon next to

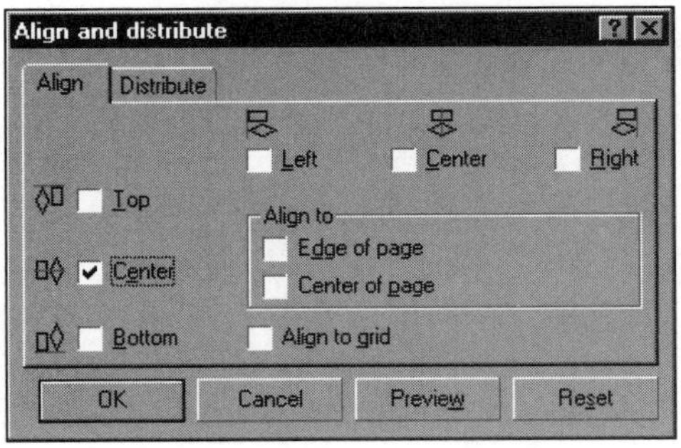

Figure 6-12:
Use these
options to
align
selected
objects.

each check box gives you an idea of how the objects will be aligned.) To align objects horizontally, choose the Left, Center, or Right check box. You can select only one check box at a time from the vertical alignment options and one from the horizontal alignment options. To preview the effects of your choices, click on the Preview button.

CorelDraw aligns objects by their selection handles, not by their actual edges. For example, if you choose left alignment, CorelDraw aligns the objects by the left selection handles rather than their left borders.

Figure 6-13 shows each of the vertical alignment options applied in tandem with each of their horizontal counterparts. (The arrows surrounding the Center labels show whether the centering was horizontal or vertical.)

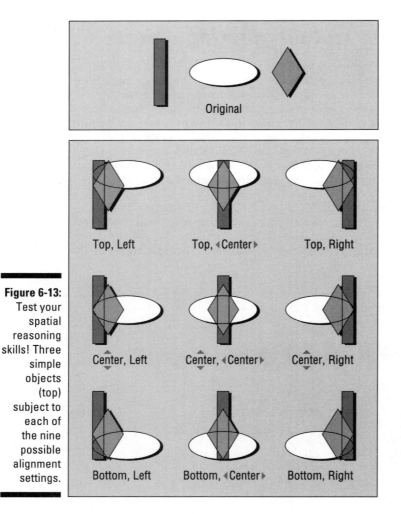

Figure 6-13: Test your spatial reasoning skills! Three simple objects (top) subject to each of the nine possible alignment settings.

You don't have to select an option from both the vertical and horizontal groups. To align the soldiers along the road, for example, you would select the Bottom check box without selecting any horizontal option. In fact, more often than not you will select only one alignment option. Otherwise, the shapes bunch up onto each other, as in Figure 6-13.

If you like what you see when you click on the Preview button, press Enter or click on OK to make the alignment official. If you select one of the vertical or horizontal options but then change your mind, you can deselect it by clicking on it again. Click on the Reset button to move your shapes back to the positions they held before you opened the dialog box.

The following information falls into the gee-whiz-that-certainly-is-interesting camp of Align and distribute dialog box knowledge:

✓ Select the Align to Grid check box to align objects to the nearest grid point according to the vertical and horizontal settings. For example, if you select the Top and Left alignment check boxes, CorelDraw aligns the top-left corner of each selected object to the nearest grid point.

✓ Select the Center of Page check box to align selected objects with respect to the center of the page. Select Edge of Page to align — that's right — to the edge of the page.

✓ If you don't select either check box, CorelDraw aligns the objects to the so-called *target object*. If you selected your objects by dragging around them with the arrow tool, the bottom object is the target object. If you Shift+clicked on the objects to select them, the last object you clicked is the target object.

✓ Use the options on the Distribute tab of the dialog box, shown in Figure 6-14, to evenly space three or more selected objects. You can choose one check box from the vertical distribution options (Top, Center, Spacing, and Bottom) and one check box from the horizontal distribution options (Left, Center, Spacing, and Right).

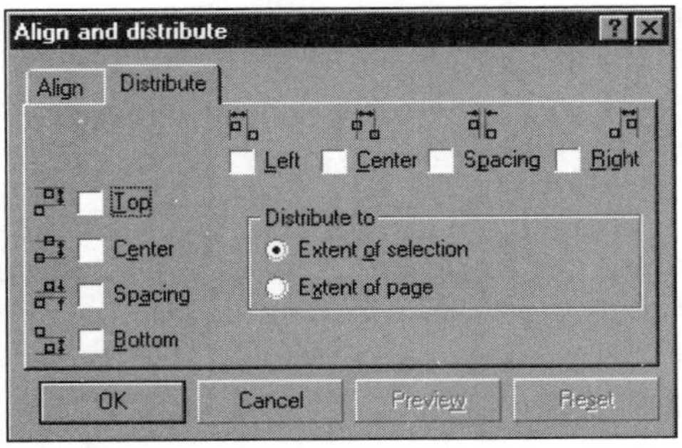

Figure 6-14:
The
distribution
options.

Align and distribute

Align · Distribute

☐ Left   ☐ Center   ☐ Spacing   ☐ Right

☐ Top
☐ Center
☐ Spacing
☐ Bottom

Distribute to
○ Extent of selection
○ Extent of page

OK   Cancel   Preview   Reset

✔ Choosing the Left option moves the objects so that equal spacing exists between the left edges of the objects. The Right and Center options space the objects according to their right edges and centers, respectively. And the Spacing option puts an equal amount of space between each object.

✔ The horizontal distribution options work similarly: The Top, Bottom, and Center options distribute objects relative to their top edges, bottom edges, and centers, respectively. The Spacing option places the objects an equal distance apart.

✔ Select the Extent of Selection option to keep the most extreme objects — leftmost and rightmost or topmost and bottommost — stationary and distribute the others between them. Or select Extent of Page to distribute the objects over the entire width or height of the page.

✔ As with the options on the Align tab of the dialog box, you can click on the Preview button to see how your chosen options move your objects. Click on Reset to put the objects back to the way they were before you started mucking around with things.

✔ The options in the Align and distribute dialog box work only on whole objects. To align nodes selected with the shape tool, double-click on the shape tool to display the Node Edit roll-up, and then click on the Align button. (See Chapter 5 for more information.) You can't distribute nodes.

Gang Behavior

In the preceding section, I asked you to imagine drawing silhouetted soldiers. You probably thought I was just trying to stimulate your interest by setting a mood. But there was a modicum of method behind my madness, something that's normally absent.

See, you can create a silhouette using a single shape. If, however, each of your soldiers comprise multiple shapes, the Align and Distribute options can present a problem. Figure 6-15, for example, shows a soldier made up of 18 shapes. When I aligned the shapes along the bottom, the soldier fell apart, as in the second example. This happened because CorelDraw aligns the bottom of each and every shape.

To prevent the problem, you need to make CorelDraw think of all 18 shapes as a single object. First select the shapes (Shift+click). Then press Ctrl+G, or choose Arrange⇨Group, or click on the Group button on the property bar. All shapes in the group now behave as a single, collective object.

✔ To align many soldiers that are each composed of many shapes, group the shapes in each soldier — each soldier is its own group, in other words — and then apply options from the Align and distribute dialog box, discussed in the preceding section.

Figure 6-15:
A soldier
crumbling
under
pressure is
a sad sight
indeed.

✔ To bust the group up into its individual shapes, press Ctrl+U (Arrange⊃Ungroup) or click on the Ungroup button on the property bar.

✔ You can include groups in other groups. For example, after grouping the shapes in each soldier, you can group all the soldiers together. To restore the original shapes, press Ctrl+U to ungroup the first group. Then select each group within the previous group and ungroup it separately. Or, to ungroup all grouped objects, choose Arrange⊃Ungroup All or click on the Ungroup All button on the property bar.

✔ Just because an object is part of a group doesn't mean that you can't edit it. To select a single object inside a group, Ctrl+click on it with the arrow tool. To adjust the location of nodes and the curvature of segments inside a grouped path, Ctrl+click on the path with the shape tool.

Your Drawing Is a Plate of Flapjacks

Once again, I speak metaphorically. Don't pour maple syrup on the screen or anything. Most condiments will damage your computer. My reference to flapjacks has to do with their typical arrangement in stacks. One flapjack is at the bottom of the stack, one flapjack is on top, and each additional flapjack is nestled between two others.

Now pretend that you're looking down at the flapjacks from an aerial view, like a hungry magpie. You can see the butter on the top, several flapjacks beneath that, and a plate at the bottom, as shown in Figure 6-16. Each flapjack obscures but does not completely hide the flapjack beneath it.

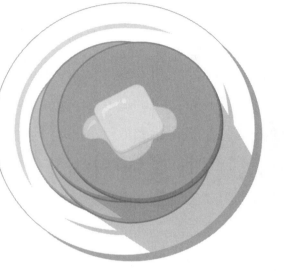

Figure 6-16: Viewing objects in CorelDraw is like looking down on a stack of flapjacks, except not as appetizing.

CorelDraw stacks objects in the drawing area in a similar fashion. Every object in your drawing is in front of or behind some other object. When displaying your artwork on-screen or when printing it, CorelDraw starts at the back of the drawing and works its way to the front, one object at a time. If two objects overlap, the frontmost of the two partially obscures the other. This hierarchy of objects is called the *stacking order*.

If you left objects to their own devices, the first object you drew would appear at the back of the drawing, and the most recent object would appear at the front. But you can change the order of any object by selecting it and choosing one of the seven commands in the Arrange➪Order submenu:

✔ Press Shift+Page Up (or choose the To Front command) to bring one or more selected objects to the front of the drawing. Figure 6-17 shows the result of selecting the face and hands of the soldier and pressing Shift+Page Up. Having moved to the front of the drawing, the face and hands conceal portions of the shapes that make up the cap and jacket. In the last example of the figure, I selected the jacket and pressed Shift+Page Up again, which covered up the buttons and medal.

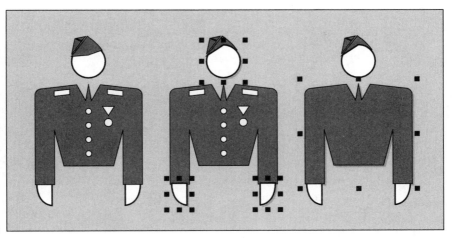

Figure 6-17:
The results of moving the face and hands (middle) and the jacket (right) to the front of the drawing.

✔ Press Shift+Page Down (or choose the To Back command) to send one or more selected objects to the back of the drawing.

✔ You can also use the property bar buttons labeled To Front and To Back to send an object to the front or back of the stack. Sadly, these buttons are obscured when you use the 640-x-480 monitor display setting; if you want to access them, drag your property bar into the drawing window.

✔ Press Ctrl+Page Up to nudge selected objects one step forward. Or, if you prefer, choose the Forward One command.

✔ Press Ctrl+Page Down to nudge selected objects one step backward. If you like choosing things, choose the Back One command.

✔ As your drawing becomes more complicated, you'll want to spend less of your time choosing the commands I've discussed so far, and more time using the In Front Of and Behind commands. These commands enable you to stack objects relative to other objects. If you want to place a rat in front of some cheese, for example, select the rat, choose Arrange➪Order➪In Front Of, and then click on the cheese. To place the cheese and rat behind a cat, select rodent and supper, choose Arrange➪Order➪Behind, and click on the cat.

✔ Last but not least is the Arrange➪Order➪Reverse Order command, which reverses the stacking order of selected objects, as demonstrated in Figure 6-18. You must have at least two objects selected to use this command.

✔ You can access the entire Order submenu of commands — as well as Group and Ungroup for that matter — by right-clicking on a selected object. Right-clicking is an especially convenient way to choose the In Front Of and Behind commands.

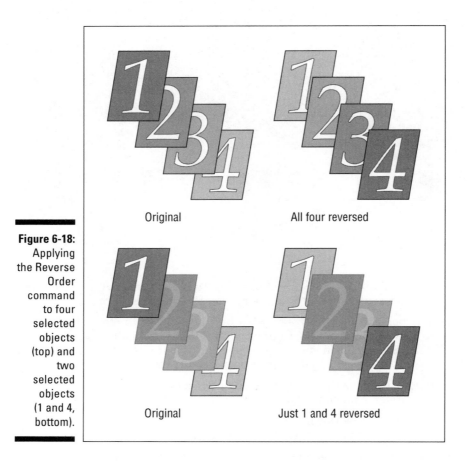

Original

All four reversed

Original

Just 1 and 4 reversed

Figure 6-18:
Applying
the Reverse
Order
command
to four
selected
objects
(top) and
two
selected
objects
(1 and 4,
bottom).

Chapter 7

Making Your Shapes Look Like Something

. . . .

In This Chapter

▶ Filling closed paths with solid colors

▶ Selecting and creating colors

▶ Creating custom color palettes

▶ Applying outlines to open and closed paths

▶ Assigning corners and caps

▶ Exploring advanced fill options

▶ Applying patterns and fills from the scrapbook

▶ Searching and replacing fills and outlines

. . . .

*I*t was an ashen morning on the blanched desert. The dusty earth was pallid, the cacti were bleached, even the lone coyote was a bit pasty. But worst of all, I myself was entirely without pigmentation.

Suddenly, I spied a flash of color on the horizon. Big, billowy clouds of green, yellow, and a sort of grapey purple were accompanied by the thunder of hoofbeats. It could mean only one thing — the Chromastazi tribe was on the warpath.

Moments later, the swiftest rider emerged from a poofy pink cloud and stopped dead in front of me. Fixing me with his terrible emerald gaze, he drew from his ceremonial paint bucket the biggest, most menacing brush I had ever seen. Before I had time to run, the warrior threw his weapon straight and true. The brush hit me full in the chest, releasing a fountain of colors. As I hit the ground, I couldn't help but notice the sky itself explode with fragments of deepest azure highlighted with streamers of pale blue and crystal white.

"Pale Shape is no more!" went up the savage cry.

Looking down at myself, I hardly believed my eyes. I was no longer transparent. Finally, I knew what it meant to be filled!

— excerpted from *Memoirs of a Pioneerin' Path*, 1875

Fills, Spills, and Chills

Wasn't that introduction thrilling? I remember when I first read that passage in art history class. The student body was so inspired, we spraypainted the professor.

Nowadays, what with these huge wads of computer experience under my belt, I can see the truth of the story. Regardless of how paths look or act, deep down inside, they want to be filled. It's in their nature. Take Figure 7-1, for example. On the left, you see an enhanced version of Shenbop, *primus inter amphibius.* Because all the lines and shapes are transparent, focusing on the picture is nearly impossible. The Shenbop on the right contains the same paths as its transparent neighbor, but the paths are filled, giving the frog form, substance, and a mighty big sense of self-worth.

Figure 7-1:
Several
paths
shown as
they appear
when
transparent
(left) and
filled (right).

Fill 'er up with color

To fill the interior of a path with a solid color, do the following:

1. **If a path that you want to fill is open, close it.**

   You can fill closed paths only. Open paths are inherently transparent. You can close a path by dragging from one node to the other with the pencil tool, as discussed in Chapter 5. Or select the two last nodes in the path and click on either of the join buttons in the Node Edit roll-up or property bar, as described in the "How to open, split, close, and join paths" section of Chapter 5.

2. Select one or more shapes you want to fill.

Using the arrow tool, draw a marquee around the shapes or click on one shape and then Shift+click on the others. To select all shapes in your drawing, double-click on the arrow tool icon in the toolbox.

3. Click on a color in the color palette.

The *color palette* is the strip of color swatches on the right side of the CorelDraw window, shown in Figure 7-2. The palette contains too many colors to display all at once in a single strip, so you can click on the up- and down-pointing arrows on either side of the palette to display additional colors. Or click on the left-pointing arrow at the bottom of the palette to display a pop-up menu that shows all the colors at once. (The next section explains more options for viewing the color palette.) Notice that as you move your cursor over a swatch in the color palette, the color name appears in the left corner of the status bar.

The first 11 options in the color palette are shades of gray, which are organized from black to white in 10 percent increments. For example, 50 percent black is midway between black and white. All 11 shades are ideal for creating black-and-white artwork.

No fill   Color palette

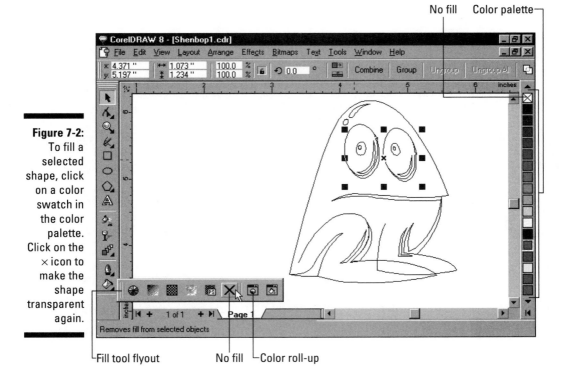

Figure 7-2:
To fill a selected shape, click on a color swatch in the color palette. Click on the × icon to make the shape transparent again.

Fill tool flyout   No fill   Color roll-up

You also can fill a closed path by selecting the arrow tool and then dragging a color swatch from the color palette onto the object you want to fill. The advantage of this method is that you don't have to select the object first. As you move your mouse, a little color swatch moves with your cursor. If you move the cursor over a shape that can be filled, the swatch appears as a solid square. Release the mouse button to fill the shape. If you see a hollow square, you're about to apply the color to the outline of the shape rather than to the interior.

If you see a little page icon next to the color swatch, your cursor isn't over any path. If you release the mouse button, you see a dialog box enabling you to set up default settings for your drawing tools. For more on this subject, see "I Don't Like the Default Setting!" later in this chapter.

Hasta la fillsta

If a shape has no fill, you can see through its interior to the objects behind it. To return a filled shape to absolute transparency, select the shape and click on the x icon at the end of the color palette (labeled in Figure 7-2). Or if you like doing things the hard way, click on the fill tool icon to display the fill tool flyout menu, and click on the x button in the flyout.

Make the color palette your own

In this modern world, you don't have to accept the color palette that CorelDraw gives you. You can change the colors, move the palette, and change the way the color swatches look in a variety of terrific ways:

✔ To scroll to the beginning or end of the colors in the palette, right-click in the gray area around the swatches — do not right-click on a color itself — to display a pop-up menu of options. Then choose Move to Start or Move to End.

✔ Click and hold on any color in the color palette to display a small pop-up palette of different hue variations of that color. You can then apply any color variation to a selected path by clicking on the hue you want in the mini-palette.

✔ To change the colors in the palette to one of CorelDraw's other pre-defined collections of colors, choose View➪Color Palette. This command displays a submenu of possible palettes, many of which come from professional color-production companies (if you can believe that such crazy things exists).

✔ Do not select the Pantone Matching System Colors or Pantone Hexachrome Colors option from the submenu unless you know exactly what you're doing and have a good reason for using spot colors. (If you don't know what I'm talking about, steer clear of this option.)

✔ To hide the color palette and free up still more screen space, choose View⇔Color Palette⇔None.

✔ Drag a gray area around the color swatches to make the palette float independently of the interface. When the palette is floating, resize it by dragging any edge. In Figure 7-3, for example, I dragged the bottom of the palette to stretch it vertically, which reveals more color swatches.

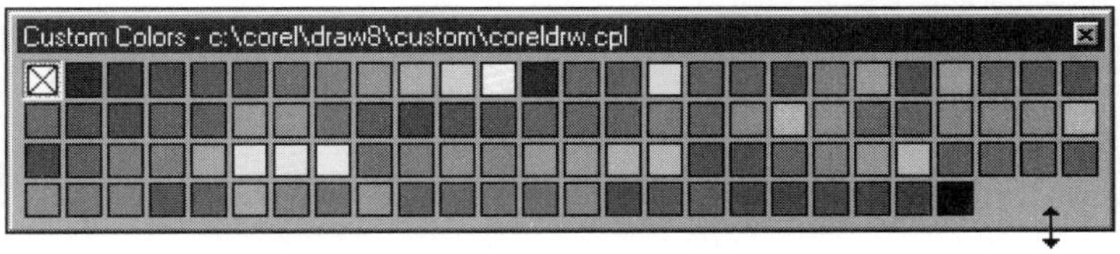

Figure 7-3: Stretch the floating palette to see more colors .

Custom Colors - c:\corel\draw8\custom\coreldrw.cpl

✔ To re-adhere the floating palette to the interface, double-click on the palette's title bar or in the gray area around the colors.

✔ Just because the palette isn't floating doesn't mean that you can't display more than one row of swatches at a time. To see two or more rows, right-click inside the gray area of the palette and select the Properties option from the resulting pop-up menu. Then, in the Maximum Number of Rows While Docked option box, enter the number of rows you want to see and press Enter.

Make New Colors in Your Spare Time

If you can't find the color you want in the color palette, you can create a color. But I warn you, the process is kind of messy. After selecting one or more shapes in your drawing, click on the fill tool and then click on the Color roll-up button (the second button from the right in the flyout menu, labeled back in Figure 7-2). Or, choose View⇔Roll-Ups⇔Color. In response, the Color roll-up, shown in Figure 7-4, graces your screen. The following two sections tell you what you need to know about this roll-up.

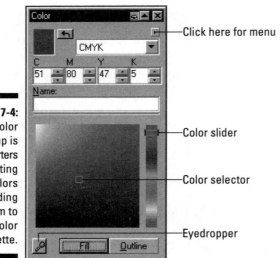

Click here for menu

Color slider

Color selector

Eyedropper

Figure 7-4:
The Color
roll-up is
headquarters
for creating
new colors
and adding
them to
your color
palette.

Choosing a color model

Before you can understand how the Color roll-up works, you need to know a little bit about how colors work. In elementary school, you learned how to mix colors using the three primary colors: blue, red, and yellow. Commercial printers also make colors by mixing primaries, but the primaries are different:

- ✔ Instead of blue, printers use a light green-blue color called *cyan.*

- ✔ In place of red, they use *magenta,* a pinkish purplish color.

- ✔ Instead of yellow . . . well, actually, they decided to hang onto yellow.

- ✔ And because the science of color printing is about as reliable as reading tea leaves, printers throw in black to ensure uniform dark colors.

So, there you have it: cyan, magenta, yellow, and black, better known as the CMYK (pronounced C-M-Y-K, not *simyk* or *kamick* or *ceemwac*) color model. (Incidentally, printers call black the *key* color, which is why its initial is K.) If you're printing your drawing, CMYK is the color model of choice. If, on the other hand, you're creating a drawing for distribution on the World Wide Web or for a multimedia presentation — in other words, if your drawing will be viewed on a monitor or other television-like thing — you should use another color model, RGB (for red, green, blue). The RGB color model mixes red, green, and blue light to display colors on-screen.

Mixing up a batch of color

Because too much color theory has been known to drive people stark raving mad, the following items seek to disseminate the abstractions of CMYK and RGB into the real world of the Color roll-up:

- ✔ Before you do anything, select either the CMYK or RGB color model from the pop-up menu in the upper-right corner of the roll-up. Remember, use CMYK if you plan to print your drawing, or RGB if your drawing will be viewed on-screen.

- ✔ To create a color, you can enter values in the C, M, Y, and K option boxes (or R, G, and B option boxes, if you're using that color model). With CMYK, the higher the values, the darker the color gets. For example, 100 percent cyan plus 100 percent magenta makes deep blue. If you add either yellow or black, you darken the color. Try entering a few random values to get a feel for things.

- ✔ When you use the RGB color model, things work a little differently. The higher the R, G, and B option box values, the lighter the colors. Entering 255 in all option boxes creates white; entering 0 in all the option boxes creates black.

- ✔ If you're working in the CMYK color model, you can create a custom shade of gray by entering 0 into the C, M, and Y option boxes, and then entering the shade of gray in the K option box. For example, 0 percent is white, 25 percent is light gray, 50 percent is medium gray, 75 percent is dark gray, and 100 percent is black. In the RGB color model, enter the same number in all three option boxes to create gray. The higher the number, the lighter the shade of gray.

- ✔ Instead of entering values into the option boxes, you can also use the color slider and color selector box, labeled in Figure 7-4, to create a color. Drag the color slider to choose the approximate color you want. CorelDraw displays variations on that color in the preview box next to the slider. To refine your color selection, drag the color selector square. Notice that any changes made with the color selector or color slider are reflected by the values in the option boxes.

- ✔ If you want to base your new color on a color that already exists in your drawing, click on the eyedropper icon at the bottom of the roll-up. Then click on the color in your drawing.

- ✔ To add the color to the color palette, enter a name into the Name option box. Then click on the little menu button above the pop-up menu (labeled *Click here for menu* in Figure 7-4) and select the Add Color to Palette option.

- ✔ To apply the color to the fill of one or more selected shapes, click on the Fill button. To apply the color to the outline of your selected shapes, click on the Outline button.

You also can add, remove, and replace colors in the color palette by using the new Palette Editor, which you can display by choosing Tools⊅Palette Editor. Use the C, M, Y, K (or R, G, B) option boxes, color slider, and color selector on the left side of the dialog box just like the ones in the Color roll-up. To replace an existing color with a custom color, click on the color you want to replace in the palette on the right side of the dialog box. Then click on the Replace button. Click on the Add button to add a new color to the palette. To delete a color from the palette, click on the color you want to delete and click on the Remove button.

You can create custom colors on the fly with CorelDraw's new interactive color mixing feature. Suppose that you have a shape with a blue fill and you want to give it a greenish hue. Just select your blue shape, Ctrl+click on the yellow swatch in the on-screen color palette, and continue Ctrl+clicking until you're satisfied with your new color mix.

Creating a palette of your own

You'll likely encounter times when you'll want to save the colors in a specific drawing for future use, especially if you've created custom colors by using one of the methods just described. Well, you're in luck. With CorelDraw's new Palette Editor, it's easy to create your own custom color palette, which you can load and reuse time and time again.

To save the colors in a drawing as a custom palette, follow these steps:

1. **Choose Tools⊅New Palette From Document.**

   The New Palette dialog box appears.

2. **In the File name option box, type a name for your palette and then press Enter.**

   Your palette is now saved and ready for duty.

Next time you want to use your custom color palette, select View⊅Color Palette⊅Load Palette. A dockable window appears, displaying all your color palettes. Click on the name of the palette you want to use, and it becomes your on-screen palette.

The Thick and Thin of Outlines

Although you can apply a fill to closed paths only, an outline can be assigned to any path, open or closed. Furthermore, whereas a fill has one property — color — an outline has two properties: color and thickness. Known as the *line width* (or in more gentrified circles, as the *line weight*), the thickness of an outline is traditionally measured in *points,* which are tiny increments equal to ¹/₇₂ inch. To put it in perspective, a penny is 4 points thick, a typical pencil is 20 points in diameter, a business card is 254 points wide, a football field measures 259,000 points from one end zone to the other, Mount Everest is 25 million points above sea level, light travels at 850 trillion points per second, presidential elections occur every leap year, and a dozen eggs contain 12 yolks.

Points are a useful system of measurement because most outlines tend to be pretty thin. Nearly all the figures in this book, for example, feature outlines with line widths of 1 point or thinner. Type is also typically measured in points.

Outlining a path

To assign an outline to a path — which is also referred to as *stroking the path* — follow these sweet and simple steps:

1. **Select the path or paths you want to outline.**

2. **Select a line width option.**

   Click on the pen tool — the one that looks like a pen nib — to display a flyout menu of six preset outline options. The last six options in the flyout, labeled in Figure 7-5, control the thickness of the outline.

   Note that when you pause your cursor over the pen tool icon, the little pop-up label says that the tool is called the outline tool. CorelDraw refers to the tool sometimes as the outline tool and sometimes as the pen tool (oops). Because the icon looks like a pen and, more importantly, because the roll-up for controlling the tool is called the Pen roll-up, I refer to this tool as the pen tool. And unlike Corel, I call the tool the same thing all the time. I'm just fussy about things like that, I guess.

   If a path drawn with the pencil or the natural pen tool is selected, a pop-up menu offering preset line widths appears on the far right end of the property bar. The menu also appears for shapes that were converted to curves, as discussed in Chapter 5. If you use the 640-x-480 display setting for your monitor, though, you have to drag the property bar into the drawing area to access the pop-up menu.

3. **Select a color for the outline.**

   Just right-click on a color in the color palette.

You can also change the outline color by dragging a swatch from the color palette. A little color swatch appears next to your cursor as you drag. When you see the swatch change to a hollow square, you know that you're over the area of the path that can accept the outline color. Release the mouse button to apply the color.

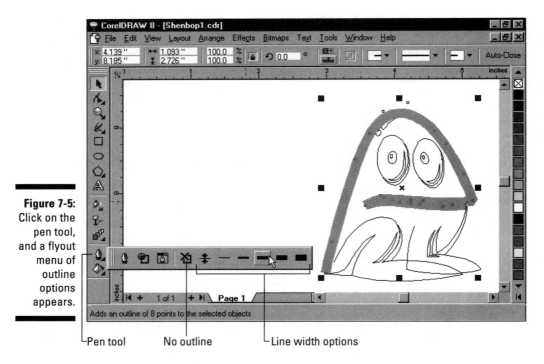

Figure 7-5:
Click on the
pen tool,
and a flyout
menu of
outline
options
appears.

└Pen tool   No outline   └Line width options

For a more sure-fire way to change the outline color, Alt+drag the color swatch from the palette. Now you can drop the color swatch anywhere on the shape to change the outline.

To define a custom color for your outline, use the Color roll-up or the interactive color mixing feature as described earlier in this chapter. To display the roll-up, choose View➪Roll-Ups➪Color or click on the Color roll-up icon in the fill tool flyout. To apply interactive color mixing to an outline, select the outline and Ctrl+right-click on the color you want to mix with the existing outline color.

Removing the outline

To remove the outline of a path, select the path and right-click on the No Color button — which looks like an x — at the end of the color palette. Or click on the No Outline button in the pen tool flyout, labeled in Figure 7-5.

Generally you want to delete the outline of only a filled shape. If you delete the outline from a transparent shape or an open path, you make it entirely invisible and run the risk of losing the path. (By the way, you can usually find a lost path by choosing View➪Wireframe to switch to wireframe mode.)

Avoiding embarrassing line widths

The pen tool flyout menu, shown in Figure 7-6, offers access to several predefined line widths and also to the more functional Pen roll-up.

Figure 7-6:
This menu provides predefined line widths.

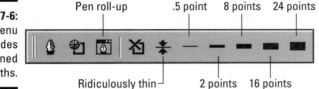

Pen roll-up   .5 point   8 points   24 points

Ridiculously thin ⎤   2 points   16 points

Each time you draw a line, the first line width option — appropriately labeled *Ridiculously thin* in Figure 7-6 — is in force. This option generally assigns the thinnest outline your printer can possibly print. On drawings printed on laser printers and cheaper printer models, the outline looks okay. But on professional-level typesetters, it can result in a nearly invisible outline that doesn't stand a chance of reproducing.

Figure 7-7 demonstrates three line-weight options from the pen tool flyout menu applied to Shenbop, resulting in a story much like the one about the three bears. The first example, which shows the CorelDraw default outline, is too thin. The last example is too fat. Only the middle example qualifies as acceptable.

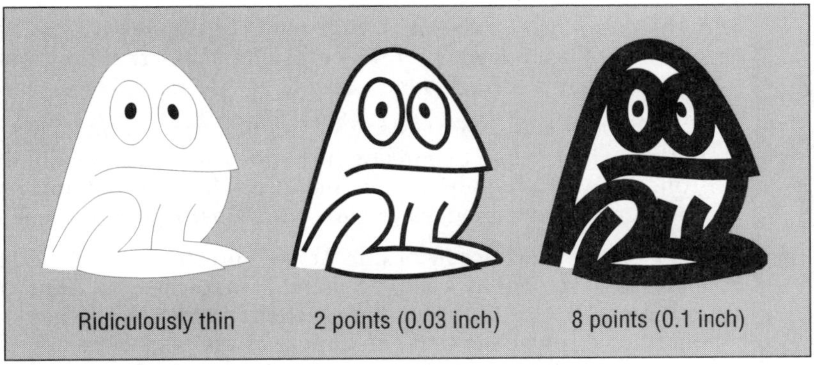

Figure 7-7:
Shenbop hates the predefined line weights in the Pen tool flyout and is highly embarrassed to appear in this figure.

Ridiculously thin   2 points (0.03 inch)   8 points (0.1 inch)

Setting better line widths

To access other line widths, select the Pen roll-up icon (labeled in Figure 7-6) to display the Pen roll-up shown in Figure 7-8. Alternatively, you can press Shift+F7 to display the roll-up. The Pen roll-up offers several options for changing the outline of a selected path:

✔ Click on the scroll arrows on the right side of the roll-up (labeled Thicker and Thinner in Figure 7-8) to increase or decrease the line width in $^1/_{100}$-inch increments. The area to the left of the scroll arrows displays the line width in inches.

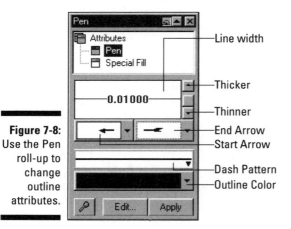

Figure 7-8:
Use the Pen roll-up to change outline attributes.

✔ If the line width is 0.003 inch (0.2 point) or thinner, a cross fills the line width area, as in Figure 7-9. The cross indicates that your outline is too thin and may not reproduce well.

✔ To change the line width display from inches to points, click on the Edit button. The Outline Pen dialog box appears. Select the Points option from the Width pop-up menu. Then press Enter. From now on, clicking on a scroll arrow changes the line width in 0.7-point increments.

✔ Click on the Start Arrow or End Arrow button (both labeled in Figure 7-8) to display a pop-up menu of arrowhead options, shown in Figure 7-9. Use the scroll bar on the right side of the menu to access different arrowheads that can appear at the beginning or end of an open path. (Arrowheads have no effect on closed paths.)

The left pop-up menu of arrowhead options establishes the arrowhead setting for the beginning of the path. The right pop-up menu controls the setting for the end of the path.

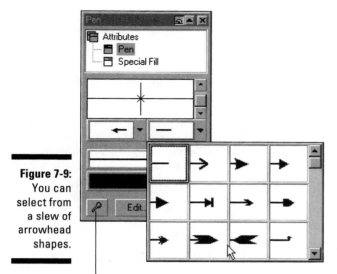

Figure 7-9:
You can
select from
a slew of
arrowhead
shapes.

└Eyedropper

✔ Click on the Dash Pattern button (just below the arrows) to display a pop-up menu of dotted line patterns you can assign to an open or a closed path.

✔ Click on the Outline Color button to select a color for the outline.

✔ Click on the Apply button to apply the settings in the Pen roll-up to the selected paths in the drawing area.

✔ If a path drawn with the pencil or natural pen tool (or a simple shape that's been converted to curves) is selected, you can also access the Start Arrow, End Arrow, and Dash Pattern pop-up menus from the property bar.

Lifting an outline from an existing shape

You can copy the outline from one path and assign it to another. Suppose you have two paths, Path A and Path B, known to their friends as Fred and Wilma. To make the outline of Fred look just like the one assigned to Wilma:

1. **Select Fred and click on the eyedropper icon in the bottom of the Pen roll-up.**

   The icon is labeled in Figure 7-9 in case you need help. When you click on the icon, your cursor changes to a big, fat arrow.

2. **Click on Wilma.**

   The Pen roll-up now displays the outline settings assigned to Wilma.

3. **Click on the Apply button.**

   Now Fred and Wilma look the same, like so many other married couples.

Alternatively, you can select Fred and then choose the Edit⇨Copy Properties From command or press Ctrl+Shift+A. This command displays a dialog box from which you can choose which of Wilma's attributes you want to copy onto Fred. After you click on OK, click on Wilma.

Creating custom line widths

As I mention earlier in this chapter, the Pen tool flyout menu offers six mostly useless line widths. The Pen roll-up offers an unlimited number of line widths, but only in 0.7-point increments. If you want to access an even wider array of line widths without any weird or artificial constraints, click on the Edit button in the Pen roll-up or press F12, which brings up the Outline Pen dialog box, shown in Figure 7-10.

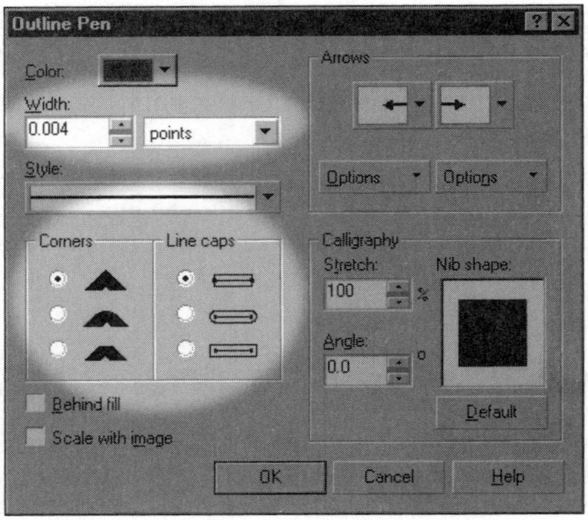

Figure 7-10:
Use the spotlighted options to change the thickness of an outline and the appearance of its corners.

▸ To set the line width, enter a value into the Width option box. The value is accurate to $^1/_{1000}$ point. That's mighty accurate.

▸ Don't go any thinner than 0.3 point or 0.004 inch. Line widths between 0.3 and 0.5 point are called *hairlines,* because they're about as thick as hairs, depending on how thick your hair is, of course.

Personally, my hair rivals cotton candy for fortitude and manageability. Hairlines look like Corinthian columns compared to my hair. I suspect that my hair wouldn't reproduce well. If I were to photocopy my face, I'd no doubt look like a cue ball.

✔ To change the system of measurement, select an option from the pop-up menu to the right of the Width option box. In addition to inches and points, the pop-up menu offers millimeters and ciceros for you worldly, metric types and picas for you newspaper and magazine types.

Changing line corners and caps

In addition to the Width option, the Outline Pen dialog box offers a few other interesting items, which also have the spotlight trained on them in Figure 7-10. These options fall into two categories: corners and caps.

Corners determine the appearance of the outline at corner nodes in the path:

✔ The miter corner option ensures sharp corners in a path.

✔ When curved segments slope into each other to form an acute angle, miter corners can produce weird spikes that make your path look like it's covered with bits of barbed wire. If you encounter this phenomenon, select one of the other two Corners options.

✔ The second option is the round corner option, which rounds off the corners in a path. I use this option a lot. It takes the edge off things.

✔ The last option is called the bevel corner because it lops off the end of the corner as if, well, as if the corner were beveled.

Figure 7-11 shows the three corners applied to mere fragments of Shenbop. The outlines appear black. I've represented the paths with thin white outlines so that you can see how path and outline relate. Pretty insightful, huh?

The Line Caps options determine how the outline looks at the beginning and end of an open path, as illustrated in Figure 7-11. Caps have no effect on closed paths.

✔ The first Line Caps option is the butt cap. Honest, that's what it's called. I'm not trying to be offensive to inspire controversy and sell books. Which is funny, because that's exactly what I was trying to do when I wanted to use the word *butt* in my last book and the editors wouldn't let me. Now they have to. After all, I didn't come up with the term *butt cap*. Huge corporate forces beyond my control decided on it. I'm sure they giggled while they were at it. They must have been feeling very immature that day.

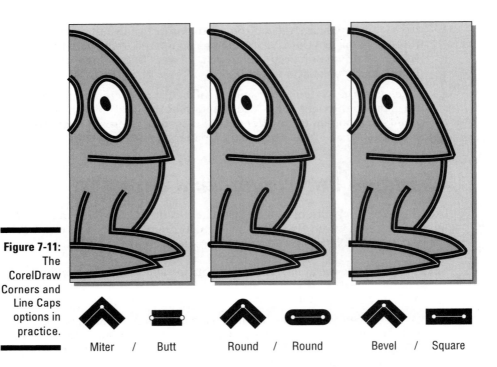

Figure 7-11:
The
CorelDraw
Corners and
Line Caps
options in
practice.

Miter / Butt   Round / Round   Bevel / Square

✔ Just in case you want to know what the butt (snigger) cap option does, it ends the outline exactly at the end of the path. The outline butts up (hee hee) against the node, as it were. (Guffaw!)

✔ The round cap does just that. It extends the outline slightly beyond the end of the path and rounds it off. Like the round corner, the round cap option gives a path a friendlier appearance.

✔ Like the round cap, the square cap extends the outline past the end of a path. But instead of rounding off the outline, it caps it off with a square. This option is useful when you want to prevent a gap between an open path and an adjacent object or when you're simply too embarrassed to use a butt cap, as when drawing for mixed company.

I Don't Like the Default Setting!

If you select an option from the fill or pen tool flyout menu or click on the Apply button in the Pen roll-up when no object is selected, CorelDraw assumes that you want to change the default attributes that will affect each and every future path you create. To confirm this assumption, the program displays a rather verbose message explaining that you are about to change default settings. You also see the message if you drag a color from the color palette and drop it into an empty area of your drawing window, as discussed earlier, in the section "Fills, Spills, and Chills." If you don't want to change the defaults, click on the Cancel button. If you want to change the default settings for all future paths, select the Graphic option and press Enter.

The Artistic Text and Paragraph Text options affect varieties of CorelDraw text discussed in Chapter 10.

Fill and Outline Join Forces

If you gave much attention to the fully filled and outlined version of Shenbop shown back in Figure 7-1, you may have noticed something unusual about it. Namely, a few open paths, such as the main body and the legs, appear to be filled. The interior of the body covers up the background behind it; the interior of the front leg covers part of the body; and the interior of the hind leg covers part of the front leg. There's no question about it; these paths are filled.

Well, how can that be? After all, I specifically said that you can't fill an open path. I wouldn't lie — my mom won't let me — so something else must be going on.

The answer is that the body and the legs are actually made up of two paths apiece: one closed path with a fill and no outline, and one open path with an outline and no fill. Figure 7-12 demonstrates how this works. The filled version of the path is stacked behind the outlined version of the path, creating what appears to the uninitiated viewer to be a single shape.

Figure 7-12:
A filled, closed path (first column) behind an outlined open path (second column) creates the appearance of a filled, open path (last column).

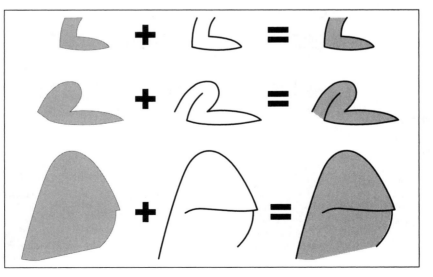

Just for laughs, Figure 7-13 shows the order of the paths used to create Shenbop from back to front. The paths that make up the body and legs are either strictly filled or strictly outlined, providing optimum flexibility. In fact, only the whites of the eyes are both filled and outlined. All outlines are 1-point thick. If you're really in the mood for trivia, you'll be interested to know that the border around the figure is 0.5-point thick.

The World of Wacky Fills

In CorelDraw, you can fill your shapes with more than simple, solid colors. You can apply to a shape a variety of special fill effects, including gradations, geometrics, and textures. You access these special fill effects through three avenues: the Special Fill roll-up, the Scrapbook, and the interactive fill tool.

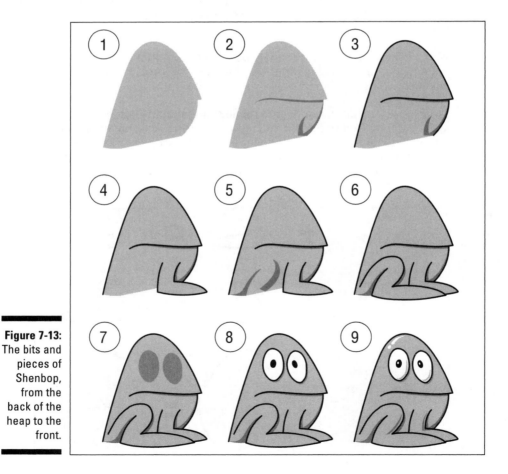

Figure 7-13: The bits and pieces of Shenbop, from the back of the heap to the front.

Using the Special Fill roll-up

Taken to their extremes, the fill effects available through the Special Fill roll-up can prove extremely complicated. So rather than delve into tiresome lists of options and obscure settings, I introduce each effect in the most basic terms possible.

To display the Special Fill roll-up, click on the fill tool icon to display the flyout menu, and then click on the Special Fill roll-up button, labeled in Figure 7-14. Each of the buttons along the top of the Special Fill roll-up duplicates a function in the fill tool flyout menu. The only exception is the last button, PostScript fill, which is available in the fill tool flyout menu but is missing from the Special Fill roll-up. The difference between the flyout icons and the roll-up icons is that the options in the roll-up are easier to use.

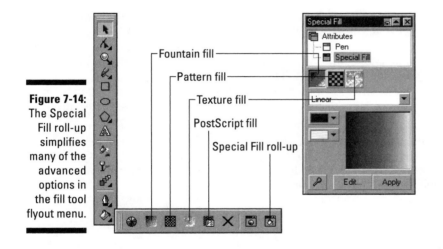

Figure 7-14:
The Special Fill roll-up simplifies many of the advanced options in the fill tool flyout menu.

The following list explains how to use the options in the Special Fill roll-up:

✔ Click on the Fountain fill button to fill a selected path with a gradual blend from one color to another, called a gradation or a gradient. Select a beginning color and an end color from the pop-up menus to the left of the gradient preview in the roll-up. Or, to lift a color from your drawing, click on the eyedropper icon and then click on the color in your drawing.

Specify the type of gradation by choosing an option from the pop-up menu directly above the gradient preview. You can create a linear, radial, square, or conical gradation. Finally, drag inside the gradient preview to determine the direction or center of the gradation. To apply the gradation to the selected shape, click on the Apply button.

✔ The Pattern fill button enables you to fill a shape with a pattern of pixels. You can apply a two-color pattern, a full-color pattern, or a bitmap pattern. Select the type of pattern you want to apply from the pop-up menu above the preview box. If you select the two-color pattern option, select the two colors from the pop-up menus next to the preview box. To change the pattern, click on the down-pointing arrow the right of the preview box to display a pop-up menu of options.

Similarly, the Full Color and Bitmap pattern options let you fill a shape with predefined full-color and bitmap patterns. Click on the down-pointing arrow on the right side of the preview box to display a pop-up menu of pattern choices. After you choose a pattern, click on Apply to fill your shape with the pattern.

 ✔ Textures are naturalistic patterns such as clouds and raindrops. To change the texture, first select a category of textures from the pop-up menu just above the texture preview. Then click on the down-pointing arrow on the right side of the preview, select the desired texture from the resulting pop-up menu, and click on Apply or press Enter.

 ✔ The PostScript fill button appears only in the fill tool flyout menu. It lets you apply special object-oriented patterns described in complex PostScript code. When you click on the PostScript fill button, a dialog box filled with a list of patterns appears. Select a pattern and click on the Preview Fill check box to see what it looks like. Press Enter after you find a fill you like.

PostScript fills have a couple of strikes against them. First, PostScript fill patterns don't look right on-screen. After you apply them, you don't see the pattern itself inside your shape; instead, CorelDraw displays the repeating letters *PS*. Second, you can print PostScript fills only with high-end laser printers and typesetters that understand PostScript.

Dragging special fills from the Scrapbook

You also can apply fills to your shapes by using the Scrapbook. To display the Favorite Fills and Outline tab of the Scrapbook, choose <u>V</u>iew⇨ Scrapbook⇨Favorite <u>F</u>ills and Outlines. Or, if you have your toolbar displayed, click on the Scrapbook icon, labeled in Figure 7-15. If you open the Scrapbook using the toolbar button, you may need to navigate to the Favorite Fills and Outlines tab by using the folder pop-up menu.

The special fills and outlines are stored in the Favorite Fills and Outlines folder, which should appear in the folder pop-up menu automatically if you open the Scrapbook through the View menu. Double-click on the folders that appear in the scrolling list to display thumbnail views of the available fills and outlines. To close a folder and display the contents of the folder that contains it, click on the Up One Level button, just as in the Open dialog box discussed in Chapter 3.

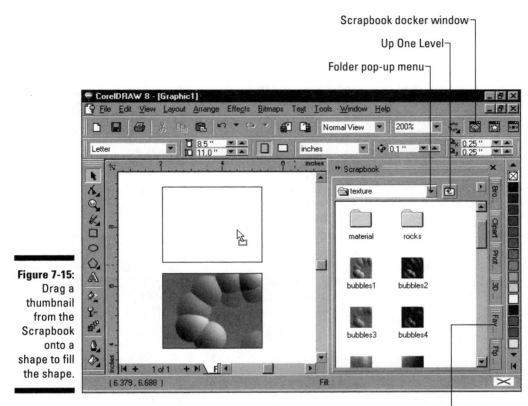

Scrapbook docker window

Up One Level

Folder pop-up menu

Figure 7-15:
Drag a
thumbnail
from the
Scrapbook
onto a
shape to fill
the shape.

Favorite Fills and Outlines tab

When you find a fill or outline you like, just drag it from the Scrapbook to
your shape, as shown in the top rectangle in Figure 7-15. CorelDraw fills your
shape with the effect, as shown in the lower rectangle in the figure. You
don't have to select the shape before you drag. To apply the fill or outline to
two or more shapes, select the shapes and then drag from the Scrapbook.

Filling on the fly

The interactive fill tool, labeled in Figure 7-16, gives you yet another way to
fill shapes. When this tool is selected, the property bar displays controls
that let you choose a fill type (pattern, fountain, texture, and so on) as well
as many of the same controls found in the Special Fill roll-up, discussed
earlier in the section "Using the Special Fill roll-up."

By far, the biggest advantage of the interactive fill tool is that it lets you gain
precise control over the position, direction, and colors of a fountain (gradient) fill. If one of CorelDraw's preset gradients doesn't suit your needs, you

can create a custom gradient by using the interactive fill tool. You can also edit existing gradients by using the tool.

To create a custom gradient with the interactive fill tool, first select a shape. Then select the interactive fill tool, choose Fountain Fill from the Fill Type menu on the property bar (labeled in Figure 7-16), and drag across your shape. The point at which you begin dragging sets the beginning of the gradient; the point at which you release your mouse button sets the end of the gradient. A fill arrow appears to show you the direction of the gradient, as shown in Figure 7-16. After you create a gradient, you can manipulate it as follows:

✔ To change the gradient type, click on one of the Gradient Type icons in the property bar. As in the Special Fill roll-up, you can choose from a linear, radial, conical, or square gradient.

✔ To change the color used for the beginning of the gradient, choose a color from the start point color pop-up menu in the property bar. Or drag a swatch from the color palette onto the small box at the beginning of the gradient (labeled *start point* in Figure 7-16). To change the other color in the gradient, drag a color to the end point box or choose

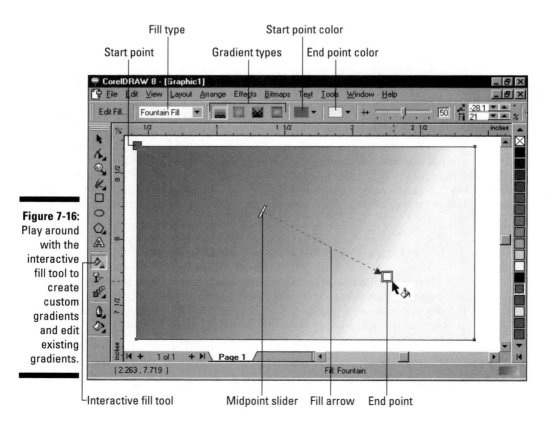

Figure 7-16: Play around with the interactive fill tool to create custom gradients and edit existing gradients.

a color from the end point color pop-up menu on the property bar. If you drag a color from the color palette, make sure that the cursor arrow, and not the color swatch, is on the start or end point box as you release the mouse button.

✔ For even more fun, you can add colors to your gradient. Just drag a color from the color palette to any spot along the dotted fill arrow line. When you see a small plus sign next to your cursor, release the mouse button to set the color in place. A hollow square appears at the point where you added the color. If you decide that you don't like your addition, right-click inside that hollow square. You can add as many colors to your gradient as you want.

✔ To change the position of colors in the gradient, drag the boxes along the fill arrow line. For example, drag the end point box to move the end of the gradient.

✔ Alternatively, you can reposition the colors in a two-color fountain fill by dragging the midpoint slider, labeled in Figure 7-16. Be careful to select the rectangular line slider and not the fill arrow line.

✔ You can also change the angle of the gradient by dragging the end point box. To constrain the angle to 15-degree intervals, press Ctrl as you drag.

✔ If you click outside your gradient or switch to another tool, the fill arrow disappears. But you can redisplay it and edit your gradient at any time by clicking on the shape with the interactive fill tool.

✔ You can also edit a preset gradient you applied by using the Special Fill roll-up or the Scrapbook. Just click on the gradient with the interactive fill tool.

✔ If you want to save a custom gradient so that you can use it again, select the shape and then click on the Fountain fill button in the fill tool flyout. When the Fountain Fill dialog box appears, enter a name for your gradient in the Presets box at the bottom of the dialog box, click on the plus sign next to the Presets box, and press Enter. When you want to apply the gradient to a new shape, select the shape, open the Fountain Fill dialog box, select the gradient from the Presets box, and press Enter.

✔ You can also store your gradient in the Scrapbook. Open the Scrapbook and open the folder where you want to store the gradient. (If the gradient is a radial gradient, for example, open the Radial folder in the Fountain folder.) Then select the shape that has the gradient applied and drag it into the appropriate folder in the Scrapbook. A dialog box appears asking you to identify the properties you would like to save. Select the appropriate check boxes and press Enter. To name the gradient, right-click on it in the Scrapbook and choose Rename. You can apply the gradient to a new shape by dragging the gradient from the Scrapbook, as discussed earlier in this chapter.

Save Time with Find and Replace

CorelDraw offers an additional tool you may find helpful for filling and outlining shapes. Using the Find and Replace commands, Edit⇨Find and Replace⇨Replace Objects, you can automatically replace all occurrences of a fill or outline color with another color. You can also replace one outline width with another. This command can come in handy if you want to make wholesale design changes to a drawing — for example, replace all your thin, black lines with fat, red ones.

When you choose the Replace Objects command, CorelDraw displays the Replace Wizard dialog box. If you want to replace a color, select the Replace a Color option and click on the Next button. You then see the second screen of the Replace Wizard dialog box. Choose the color you want to replace from the Find pop-up menu; choose the color you want to use instead from the Replace With pop-up menu. Select the Fills option to find and replace fills that match the color in the Find pop-up menu. Select the Outlines button to replace outlines that match the Find color.

The three check boxes at the bottom of the dialog box determine whether colors in fountain fills, two-color pattern fills, and monochrome (black-and-white) bitmap fills are replaced. If you don't want to replace colors in those fills, turn off the check boxes.

To replace an outline width, select the Replace Outline Pen Properties button in the first screen of the Replace Wizard dialog box and click on Next. (If you're currently looking at the color replacement screen of the wizard, you can return to the first screen by clicking on the Back button.) In the Find section of the resulting dialog box, enter the line width you want to replace. Enter the new line width in the Replace section of the dialog box.

After you specify what you want to find and replace, click on Finish. CorelDraw displays a miniature Find and Replace toolbar and selects the first object that matches the criteria you specified in the Replace Wizard dialog box. If you want to replace the color or outline for that object, click on Replace. To leave the object as-is and skip to the next object, click on Find Next. Click on Find Previous to go back to the previously selected object. To select all objects and replace the color or line width for the entire batch, click on Replace All.

When CorelDraw makes its way through all the objects that match your find and replace request, it displays a dialog box telling you that the search mission is complete. Click on OK to get rid of the dialog box, and then click on the Close button in the Find and Replace toolbar to remove the toolbar from your screen.

Chapter 8
The Fine Art of Cloning

*W*hat was the big deal with the movie *Jurassic Park?* Oh sure, lawyer-eating dinosaurs — obviously, I'm all for that. And if I were a poison-spitting Dilophosaurus, I can't imagine a tastier treat than a well-fed computer programmer. But the cloning bit, how hard can it be? CorelDraw has been able to clone things for years. You don't need any mosquito trapped in amber to clone in CorelDraw. You give me a Velociraptor, and I'll make as many duplicates as you like.

This chapter shares all my inside secrets on cloning so that you, too, can churn out as many duplicates of an object as you like. I also show you how to transfer your dinosaurs, er, objects, from one drawing to another.

Clipboard Mania: Cut, Copy, and Paste

One way to copy and transfer objects is to use the Windows 95 Clipboard. The Clipboard is a temporary storage tank for objects you want to copy or move from one spot to another. Three Edit menu commands — Cut, Copy, and Paste — provide access to the Clipboard:

✔ The Cut command (Ctrl+X) removes all selected objects from your drawing and places them on the Clipboard. In doing so, the command replaces the Clipboard's previous contents. So if you cut Object A and then cut Object B, Object B knocks Object A off the Clipboard into electronic oblivion.

- The Copy command (Ctrl+C) makes a copy of all selected objects in your drawing and places the copy on the Clipboard. Like Cut, the Copy command replaces the Clipboard's previous contents.

- The Paste command (Ctrl+V) makes a copy of the contents of the Clipboard and places them in your drawing. Unlike Cut and Copy, the Paste command leaves the contents of the Clipboard unaltered. You can choose the Paste command as many times as you want to make copy after copy after copy.

Novices generally have problems remembering the keyboard equivalents for the Clipboard commands. Granted, Ctrl+C makes sense for Copy. Ctrl+X is a stretch, but it sort of brings to mind Cut. But where did Ctrl+V for Paste come from? The answer resides at the bottom-left corner of your keyboard. The keys are Z, X, C, and V. That's Undo (the first command in the Edit menu), Cut, Copy, and Paste. Then again, if you think of the Paste command as regurgitating the contents of the Clipboard, Ctrl+V takes on new meaning. Just trying to help.

Snap, crackle, paste

Here's an example of how you can use the Clipboard to duplicate an object:

1. **Select one or more objects that you want to duplicate.**

   If you have a dinosaur handy, please select it now. (Incidentally, the drawing in Figure 8-1 comes from the file Tyranno2.CDR, found in the Prehist/Dinosaur folder on the second CorelDraw CD-ROM.)

2. **Choose Edit⇨Copy or press Ctrl+C.**

   Figure 8-1 shows this step in progress. CorelDraw makes a copy of each selected object and places it on the Clipboard. This process sometimes takes a long time.

3. **Toodle around.**

   Perform scads of operations. Work for hours and hours. Wait several weeks if you like. Time has no effect on the Clipboard. Just don't touch the Cut or Copy commands, don't exit CorelDraw or Windows 95, and don't turn off your computer.

4. **Choose Edit⇨Paste or press Ctrl+V.**

   Bazoing! (That's a sound effect, in case you didn't recognize it.) CorelDraw makes a copy of the objects on the Clipboard and places them in the drawing area at the exact location where they appeared when you chose the Copy command. (If the Paste command appears dimmed, by the way, the Clipboard is empty — go back to Step 2 and try again.)

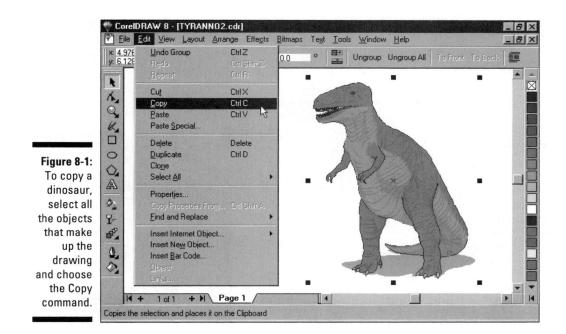

Figure 8-1:
To copy a
dinosaur,
select all
the objects
that make
up the
drawing
and choose
the Copy
command.

If you don't change the location of the original objects before you
choose Edit➪Paste, you won't notice any difference in your drawing
because the copied objects sit directly in front of the originals. Drag the
copied objects slightly off to the side to see that you do indeed have
two identical versions of your objects, as shown in Figure 8-2.

A few Clipboard facts

Here are a few random bits of information about the Clipboard to sock away
for future use:

✔ The most common purpose for using the Clipboard is to cut or copy
objects from one drawing and paste them into another. For example, to
create Figure 8-3, I copied the tyrannosaur objects, opened the stego-
saur drawing, and pasted the tyrannosaur. The two beasts should be
great friends; they have so much in common. One is a tasty, crunchy
dinosaur, and the other likes to snack on tasty, crunchy dinosaurs.

✔ The Clipboard isn't the only way to move objects from one drawing to
another, though. You can drag and drop selected objects, as described
in the section "Do the Drag and Drop" later in this chapter.

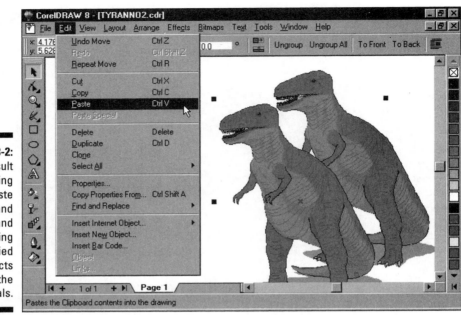

Figure 8-2:
The result of choosing the Paste command and offsetting the copied objects from the originals.

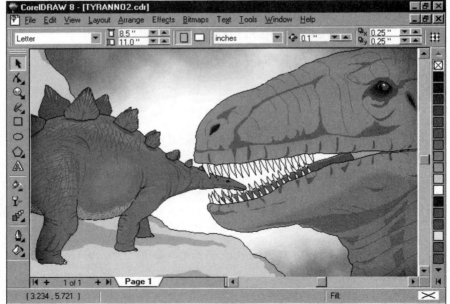

Figure 8-3:
The Clipboard enables you to combine objects from different drawings in cruel and unusual ways.

✔ If the current document contains more than one page — as discussed in Chapter 12 — you can use the Clipboard commands to transfer objects from one page to the next. If you plan on using the same object several times throughout your drawing, you may want to place a copy of the object on the pasteboard (that blank space that surrounds your drawing page). Objects on the pasteboard are available to you from all pages of your drawing.

✔ You can cut, copy, and paste objects also within a single-page drawing. But generally, duplicating the objects using the Duplicate or Clone command, as described later in this chapter, is easier.

Why I hate the Clipboard

Well, I don't really hate the Clipboard. It's a useful feature every once in a while. But the Cut, Copy, and Paste commands have three problems:

✔ Clipboard functions can be very slow, depending on the complexity of your drawing. Copying the tyrannosaur takes . . . well, let's just say that you probably have more than enough time to grab a cup of coffee — maybe even brew a new pot — while you wait. What a waste of time.

✔ You have to choose two commands to pull off Clipboard actions: first Cut or Copy and then Paste. What a waste of effort.

✔ Every time you choose the Cut or Copy command, the previous contents of the Clipboard go up in smoke. If you want to use the objects on the Clipboard over and over again, you can't go around upsetting them every time you want to duplicate something. What a waste of status quo.

The moral is, you should avoid Clipboard commands whenever possible, which is almost always. The following sections explain how.

The Gleaming Clipboard Bypass

The easiest way to bypass the Clipboard is to choose Edit➪Duplicate or just press Ctrl+D. CorelDraw creates a copy of all selected objects and offsets them a quarter inch up and to the right, as demonstrated in Figure 8-4.

Group before you duplicate

When you duplicate several paths at a time, CorelDraw places each duplicated object directly in front of the respective original object. This placement means that the paths weave in and out of each other, as demonstrated in Figure 8-5, creating an indecipherable mess.

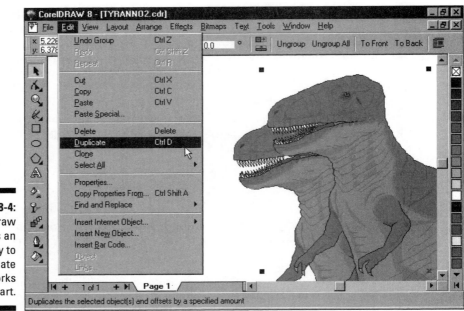

Figure 8-4:
CorelDraw
provides an
easy way to
duplicate
your works
of art.

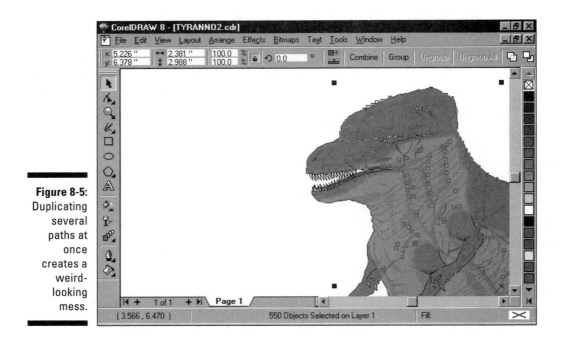

Figure 8-5:
Duplicating
several
paths at
once
creates a
weird-
looking
mess.

Oh sure, it's great if you're buzzing on caviar and aperitifs at a tony gallery and are willing to call anything you see the highest of all possible art — "Don't you just love it, Madge? It's like Dino Descending a Staircase!" — but hardly the thing for the strictly nine-to-five crowd.

To remedy this situation, press either of the following key sequences:

- ✔ Shift+PgUp
- ✔ Ctrl+Z, Ctrl+G, Ctrl+D

The first option brings the duplicated objects to the front, creating an effect like that shown in Figure 8-4 — assuming that in your panic, you haven't clicked randomly in the drawing area and deselected the paths before pressing Shift+PgUp. If you have, you're still okay. The second sequence of keyboard shortcuts steps undoes the damage, groups the original selected objects, and reapplies the Duplicate command.

The Group (Ctrl+G) command is an ideal prerequisite to the Duplicate command. By choosing the Group command, you ensure that all your objects stay together after they are duplicated. I recommend that anytime you want to duplicate five objects or more, you group them first. If you want to edit the objects, you can always ungroup them afterwards. For more on grouping and ungrouping objects, see Chapter 6.

Duplication distance

By default, the Duplicate command offsets the copied objects ¼ inch from the originals. You can change the offset by pressing Ctrl+J (or by choosing Tools⇨Options), clicking on Edit, and editing the values in the first two option boxes in the Options dialog box, spotlighted in Figure 8-6. Positive values offset the duplicate to the right or up; negative values move it to the left or down.

When the arrow tool is selected but no objects are selected, you can also use the X and Y option boxes near the right end of the property bar to change the duplicate offset values. The X option box controls the horizontal offset; the Y option box controls the vertical offset.

I recommend that you make these values an even multiple of the Nudge value. Better yet, make them the same. That way, if you want to line up the duplicated objects with the originals, all you have to do is press the down- and left-arrow keys.

Figure 8-6:
The
Horizontal
and Vertical
values
determine
the
increment
by which
the
Duplicate
command
offsets a
copied
object from
its original.

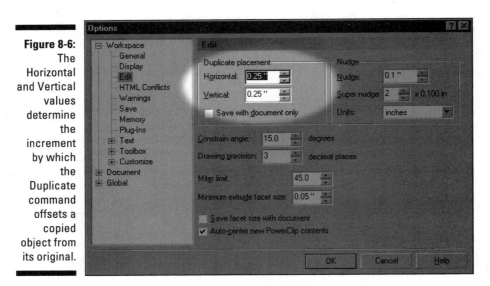

Duplicate in place

In addition to Ctrl+D, CorelDraw has another keyboard equivalent for the Duplicate command: the + key on the numeric keypad. That's right, just select your object and press the + key. Unlike Ctrl+D, however, the + key duplicates an object without offsetting it. You can drag the duplicate to a new location as desired. Pretty hot stuff, huh?

They Look Alike, They Act Alike, You Could Lose Your Mind

Imagine what would happen if every time Patty Duke changed her clothes, that identical cousin of hers changed her clothes, too. Or if every time Patty missed a question on a test, her cousin entered the same wrong answer. Or if every time Patty locked braces with her boyfriend . . . well, you get the idea. That's cloning.

If you're too young to remember *The Patty Duke Show,* substitute those identical twins from the newer show *Sister, Sister* for Patty and her identical cousin in the preceding analogy.

Allow me to elucidate. The Clone command creates a true twin of an object. Like the Duplicate command, Edit⇨Clone creates an immediate copy, bypasses the Clipboard, and offsets the copy by the amount specified in the Options dialog box or property bar. But unlike the Duplicate command, the

Clone command creates a link between copy and original. Most changes made to the original also affect the clone.

Suppose that I clone the group of objects that make up the T. Rex and move the cloned group over a little so that I can see what the heck I'm doing. Then I select the original T. Rex and drag one of its corner handles. Instead of scaling just the one tyrannosaur, CorelDraw scales them both. Let's see those hotshots in *Jurassic Park* do that!

You can't clone multiple objects of different types unless you group them first (press Ctrl+G, click on the Group button on the property bar, or choose Arrange⇔Group). You can, however, clone multiple selected objects that are all the same type of object. For example, you can clone two rectangles without grouping them, but you can't clone a rectangle and a path drawn with the pencil tool.

Links on the brink

The link between a clone and its original object works in only one direction. For example, if you select a clone and apply a new fill, CorelDraw fills the clone only, as demonstrated in Figure 8-7. But if you select the original and fill it, both original and clone change, as in Figure 8-8.

Original   Selected clone

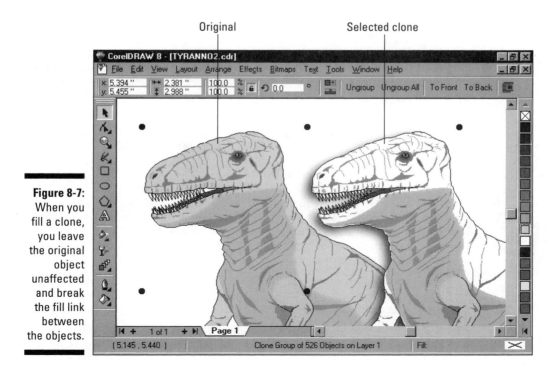

Figure 8-7: When you fill a clone, you leave the original object unaffected and break the fill link between the objects.

Selected original   Clone

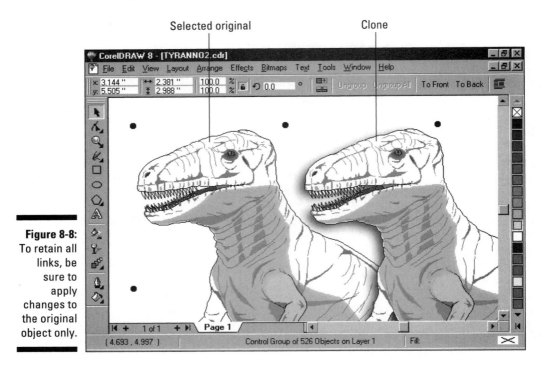

Figure 8-8:
To retain all links, be sure to apply changes to the original object only.

Furthermore, altering a clone damages the link between cloned and original objects. You can think of the Clone command as providing three links: one that governs the fill of the objects, another that controls the outline, and a third that covers transformations (scaling, rotating, and so on). Each link is independent of the other two. So even if you apply a different fill to the clone, CorelDraw retains the link between outline and transformations.

The care and feeding of your clones

Here's some more stuff to know about clones:

✔ You can tell whether you've selected the clone or the original by keeping an eye on the status bar. When you select a cloned path, for example, the status bar includes the word *Clone* (as in Figure 8-7). If you select the original path, the status bar says *Control* (as in Figure 8-8). In other words, *Control = original.*

✔ Any transformation applied to a clone severs the transformation link. If you scale the clone, for example, you prohibit rotating, skewing, and all other transformations described in Chapter 9.

✔ If you cut the original object, you cut the clone as well. But if you then choose the Paste command, you paste only the original — the clone is lost forever.

✔ Deleting an object is like cutting it. So if you delete the original, you delete the clone as well. If you delete the clone, the clone and all links go away but the original object stays.

✔ The Copy command doesn't affect the clone. In other words, copying the original doesn't copy the clone. Nor does copying the clone copy the original.

✔ You can't ungroup a cloned group of objects unless you sever all links between clone and original. Similarly, you can't ungroup the original object until after you sever all links between clone and original. To edit an individual object in a cloned or original group, Ctrl+click with the arrow tool on the object you want to change. (I followed this approach in Figures 8-7 and 8-8 to select the bottom object in the original T-Rex.)

✔ To sever all links between clone and original, select both objects and choose Arrange⇨Separate.

Some operations do not affect clones. For example, you don't select the clone when you select the original. If you move the original object, the clone remains stationary. And if you change the stacking order of an original object, the clone does nothing much in particular. The Extrude and Blend commands don't affect clones, either.

Unfortunately, I was unable to discover the answer to one nagging question: "If you scratch the original object's tummy, does the clone purr or does it bite your head off?" Experiment at your own risk.

Do the Drag and Drop

Although the Duplicate and Clone commands outclass the Clipboard in small ways, drag and drop really puts it to shame. If you have two drawings open at a time, you can move or copy selected objects by simply dragging them from one drawing and dropping them into the other. Here's how it works:

1. **Open two drawings.**

   Make sure that you can see portions of both drawings. You don't want one drawing entirely covering up the other, for example. You can choose Window⇨Tile Horizontally (or Window⇨Tile Vertically) to split the interface evenly between the two drawings.

2. **Select the objects you want to move or copy.**

   If you want to copy Object A in Drawing 1, for example, select the arrow tool, click anywhere in Drawing 1 to make it active, and then click on Object A.

3. **Drag the selected objects into the other drawing.**

   In other words, drag Object A out of Drawing 1 and into Drawing 2. Your cursor changes to an arrow with a dotted page outline.

4. **Release the mouse button.**

   When you release the mouse button, you drop the object into its new environment. Corel deletes the selected objects from the original drawing and moves them to the new drawing. It's just as if you had cut and pasted the objects, except the Clipboard remains unaffected.

To copy the objects instead of moving them, press and hold the Ctrl key after you start dragging but before you release the mouse button. A little plus sign appears next to the cursor, as shown in Figure 8-9. Release the mouse button to drop the objects and then release the Ctrl key.

Figure 8-9: By dragging and Ctrl+ dropping the tyrannosaur into the brontosaur paddock (top), I copy the carnivore (bottom) without upsetting the contents of the Clipboard.

Chapter 9

The Twisty, Stretchy, Bulgy World of Transformations

*I*n the movie *The Blues Brothers,* original *Saturday Night Live* cast member John Belushi does a series of back flips in a church. You think, "Wow, that's amazing! This guy is so gonzo that despite the fact that he's verging on obesity, high on nonprescription inhalants, and obviously completely out of shape (he spends half the movie breaking out in a sweat), he's capable of performing complex floor exercises when sufficiently inspired."

Well, at least that's what I thought when I saw the movie in high school. Later, I learned the sad truth that it wasn't really John Belushi, but instead a padded stunt man. That fateful day, I promised myself that I would somehow make John's dream of gymnastic excellence come true. (I didn't really do anything of the kind, of course, but stay with me on this one. The whole introduction to this chapter hinges on your temporary suspension of disbelief.)

Today, I make good on that promise. In this chapter, you don't just see John do flips, though he performs quite a nice one in Figure 9-1. You see him undergo a series of elaborate transformations that would cause rational Olympic athletes at the peak of their careers to shrink in terror. By the end of the chapter, you'll swear that the guy is some kind of inhuman shape-shifter who can assume any form at will. Either that, or he's a drawing I've subjected to CorelDraw's vast array of transformation functions.

Note: The Belushi caricature comes from a company called Image Club, which offers a huge variety of celebrity and historical caricatures, almost all of which are splendid.

Scaling, Flipping, Rotating, and Skewing

Scaling, flipping, rotating, and skewing are the big four transformations, the ones that have been available to CorelDraw users since our ancestors crafted the first version of the program out of twigs and iron-ore filings in the early fifth century. Just so you know what I'm talking about — in approximate terms, anyway — here are a few quick definitions:

- ✔ To *scale* (or stretch) an object is to make it bigger or smaller. You can scale an object vertically, horizontally, or both.

- ✔ To *flip* an object is to make a mirror image of it, which is why CorelDraw calls this process *mirroring* or *reflecting* (depending on which tool you're using, as you'll see shortly). In the second example of Figure 9-1,

Figure 9-1:
Belushi finally does his own stunts.

I flipped Mr. Belushi both vertically and horizontally, making the top the bottom, the left side the right side, and vice versa.

✔ To *rotate* an object is to spin it around a central point like a top. Rotations are measured in degrees. A 180-degree rotation turns the object upside-down. A 360-degree rotation turns it right back to where it started.

✔ To *skew* (or slant) an object is to incline it to a certain degree. Like rotations, skews are measured in degrees. Just to give you some perspective, a 45-degree skew applied to a rectangle slants the shape so that its sides are perfectly diagonal.

Grouping comes before transforming

I recommend that you group all objects before you transform them. To transform the Belushi cartoon, for example, I selected all the shapes that made up the drawing by choosing Edit⇨Select All⇨Objects and then pressing Ctrl+G. (You can also choose Arrange⇨Group or click on the Group button in the property bar.) After grouping, you can scale, flip, rotate, and skew with a clear conscience. Grouping prevents you from accidentally missing an object — such as an eye or an ear — while transforming its neighbors.

Scaling and flipping

If you read Chapter 4, you're already familiar with how to scale and flip an object using the arrow tool. But just in case you missed that chapter, here's a quick review:

1. **Select one or more objects that you want to scale or flip.**

   Eight square handles surround the selected objects.

2. **Drag one of the handles to scale the objects.**

   Drag a corner handle to scale the objects proportionately, so that the ratio between the horizontal and vertical dimensions of each object remains unchanged. Drag the left or right handle to scale the objects horizontally only, as in Figure 9-2. Drag the top or bottom handle to scale the objects in a vertical direction only.

   Shift+drag to scale the object with respect to its center. Ctrl+drag to scale the object by an even multiple of 100 percent, such as 200 percent, 300 percent, and so on.

   Alternatively, you can use the property bar object size or scale controls (labeled in Figure 9-2) to scale your objects. To change one of the property bar values, double-click on the option box, enter a new value

Horizontal scale

Vertical size   Vertical scale

Horizontal size   Proportional sizing

Stretch cursor

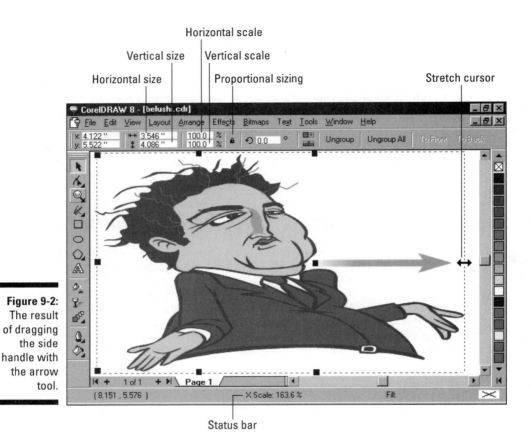

Figure 9-2:
The result
of dragging
the side
handle with
the arrow
tool.

Status bar

from the keyboard, and press Enter. To retain the object's original
proportions, click on the proportional sizing icon so that it appears to
be depressed. (That's depressed as in pushed in rather than as in
sitting around crying all day.)

3. Drag one handle past the opposite handle to flip the objects.

In Figure 9-3, for example, I dragged the right handle leftward past the
left handle to flip John B. horizontally, exactly as if he were rehearsing
an episode of "Samurai Pastry Chef" in front of a mirror . . . except he's
facing the wrong direction.

To create an exact mirrored version of the object that is the same size
as the original, Ctrl+drag a handle.

You can also create exact mirrored versions of objects by clicking on
the property bar's mirror buttons, labeled in Figure 9-3. Unlike dragging
the selection handles, clicking on the mirror buttons creates the
mirrored image in the same location as the original image.

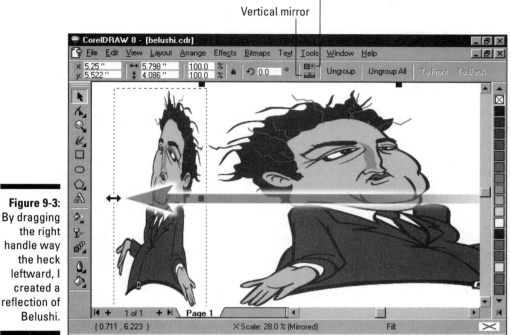

Figure 9-3: By dragging the right handle way the heck leftward, I created a reflection of Belushi.

Notice that in both Figures 9-2 and 9-3, the status bar measures the transformation in percentage points. A value below 100 percent indicates a reduction; a value above 100 percent indicates an enlargement. If the value is followed by the word *Mirrored* in parentheses, as in Figure 9-3, you flipped the graphic.

Using the provocative S&M roll-up

You can also scale or flip selected objects by entering numerical values in the Scale & Mirror roll-up. To do so, choose Arrange➪Transform➪Scale and Mirror or press Alt+F9. In response, the Scale & Mirror roll-up appears, as shown in Figure 9-4.

Most of the controls found in the Scale & Mirror roll-up are found also on the property bar, making the roll-up largely redundant if you display your property bar. But the roll-up does offer one key option that the property bar doesn't: the Apply to Duplicate button, which creates a duplicate of your selected object and applies the scaling or flipping to the duplicate. This option comes in handy if you want to play around to see what sort of effects you can create while still keeping your original object intact.

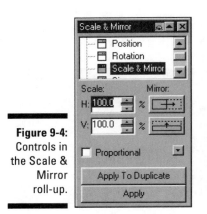

Figure 9-4:
Controls in
the Scale &
Mirror
roll-up.

The Scale & Mirror roll-up is part of a group of roll-ups that go by the combined name of Transform. Scroll to the top of the list just below the title bar and you see the name Transform above all the others. You can switch to a different roll-up in the group — such as Rotation or Skew — by clicking on its name in the list.

The options in the Scale & Mirror roll-up stretch your objects just as surely as if they were prisoners on a medieval rack, but without either the mess or the incessant groans of pain:

✔ Enter percentage values into one or both of the option boxes to scale the selection.

✔ To scale the selection by the same amount both horizontally and vertically, select the Proportional check box.

✔ Click on one of the Mirror buttons or enter a negative value in an option box to flip the objects horizontally or vertically.

✔ Click on the Apply button (or press Enter) to scale or flip the selection.

✔ Click on the Apply to Duplicate button to simultaneously duplicate the selected objects and scale or flip the duplicates. The original objects remain unchanged.

Rotating and skewing

To rotate or skew one or more objects, do this:

1. Select one or more objects that you want to rotate or skew.

As always, you see eight square handles.

2. Click on one of the selected objects a second time.

When you do, CorelDraw changes the square handles to a series of double-headed arrows, as shown in Figure 9-5. These arrows are the rotate and skew handles, or R&S handles for short. (The curved handles are the rotation handles, and the straight handles are the skew handles.) To return to the square stretch and mirror handles, click a third time on a selected object. Each time you click, you toggle between S&M and R&S.

3. Move the center of rotation marker as desired.

The circle in the middle of the selection is the center of rotation marker, which indicates the point about which the rotation takes place. Make sense? No? Think of the marker as a nail in a piece of cardboard. If you spin the cardboard, it whirls around the nail, right? In the same way, a selection rotates around the center of rotation marker. You can move the marker by dragging it.

4. Drag a rotation handle to rotate the selected objects.

Drag any of the four corner handles to rotate the selection around the center of rotation marker, as shown in Figure 9-6.

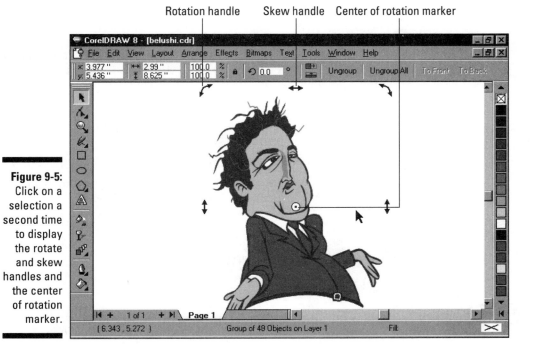

Figure 9-5:
Click on a selection a second time to display the rotate and skew handles and the center of rotation marker.

Rotation cursor   Rotation angle

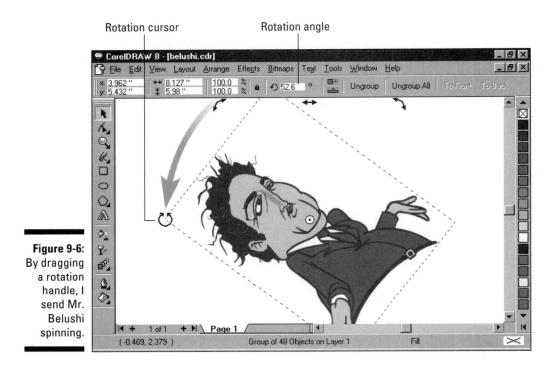

Figure 9-6:
By dragging
a rotation
handle, I
send Mr.
Belushi
spinning.

Notice that as you rotate your object, the angle of rotation is reflected in the rotation angle option box on the property bar, labeled in Figure 9-6. If you prefer, you can rotate a selected object by using the property bar rotation angle option box to rotate your object instead of dragging the rotation handles. Just enter a new value from the keyboard and press Enter. A positive value indicates a counterclockwise rotation, as in Figure 9-6; a negative value means the rotation is clockwise.

5. **Drag a skew handle to slant the selected objects.**

   Drag the top or bottom handle to slant the selected objects horizontally, as in Figure 9-7. To slant the objects vertically, drag one of the two side handles.

Transforming by degrees

Keep the following things in mind when you're rotating and skewing objects:

✔ I don't know how much you remember from geometry class, but here's a quick refresher. Think of degrees as being measured on a clock. A clock measures 60 seconds, and a geometric circle comprises 360

Skew handle

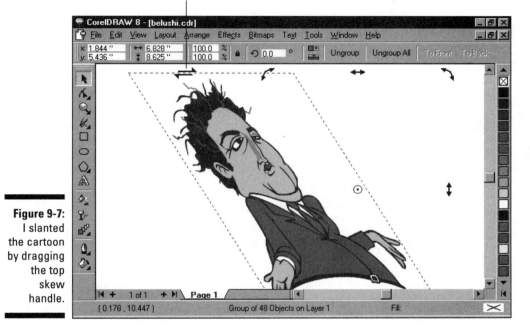

Figure 9-7:
I slanted the cartoon by dragging the top skew handle.

degrees. Each clock second is equal to 6 degrees, which means the hour markers on a clock are each 30 degrees apart. So a $^1/_4$ turn — the distance from 12 o'clock to 3 o'clock — is 90 degrees in CorelDraw.

✔ Ctrl+drag a handle to rotate or skew in 15-degree increments. For example, you can rotate a selection by 15 degrees, 30 degrees, 45 degrees, and so on. All major turns — $^1/_4$ turns, $^1/_8$ turns, all the way down to $^1/_{24}$ turns — are multiples of 15 degrees.

✔ If you don't like 15-degree increments, you can change the angle by pressing Ctrl+J (or choosing Tools➪Options). When the Options dialog box appears, click on General and enter a new value in the Constrain Angle option box. After you press the Enter key, Ctrl+drag a rotation handle to see the effect of your change.

✔ Ctrl+drag the center of rotation marker to align the center point with one of the eight handles. You can also Ctrl+drag to return the marker to the center of the selection.

Using the not-so-provocative R&S roll-ups

You can also rotate or skew a selection by entering values in the Rotation and Skew roll-ups, respectively. To rotate a selection, choose Arrange➪ Transform➪Rotate or press Alt+F8. To slant a selection by the numbers, choose <u>A</u>rrange⇨<u>T</u>ransform⇨<u>S</u>kew or press Alt+F11. Figure 9-8 shows the Rotation and Skew roll-ups, which are both part of the Transform group.

Here's how to use the options in the Rotation roll-up:

✔ Enter a degree value into the Angle option box to rotate the selection. Enter a positive value to rotate the objects in a counterclockwise direction; enter a negative value to rotate clockwise. Or, if you prefer, positive is left, negative is right.

✔ Enter values into the Center option boxes to position the center of the rotation. Select the Relative Center check box to position the center marker relative to the center of the selection; turn off the check box to position the marker with respect to the lower-left corner of the page.

✔ When in doubt, just select the Relative Center check box and enter 0 in both Center option boxes. That way, you rotate the selection about exact center. You can't go wrong.

And here's what to do with the options in the Skew roll-up:

✔ Enter values in the H and V option boxes to slant the selected objects. CorelDraw permits values between positive and negative 75.

✔ A positive value in the H option box slants the object backward; a negative value slants it forward.

✔ In the V option box, positive is up and negative is down.

✔ Ignore the Use Anchor Point check box. It enables you to position the center of the skew using some hidden options — you have to click on that down-pointing arrow to the right of the check box to get to them.

Click on the Apply to Duplicate button to duplicate the selected objects and rotate or skew the duplicates at the same time. To rotate or skew the originals, press Enter or click on Apply.

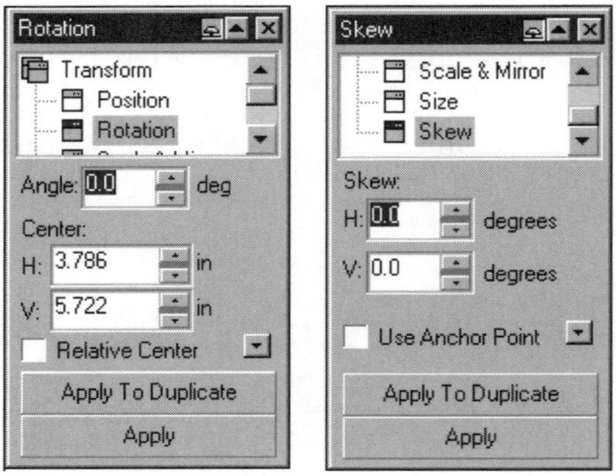

Figure 9-8:
The
Rotation
and Skew
roll-ups
make
objects
cartwheel
and slide.

Rotation		Skew	
Transform		Scale & Mirror	
Position		Size	
Rotation		Skew	
Angle: 0.0 deg		Skew:	
Center:		H: 0.0 degrees	
H: 3.786 in		V: 0.0 degrees	
V: 5.722 in			
Relative Center		Use Anchor Point	
Apply To Duplicate		Apply To Duplicate	
Apply		Apply	

Using the free transform tools

CorelDraw 8 offers yet another way to scale, mirror, rotate, and skew objects. The shape tool flyout menu houses the new free transform tool, labeled in Figure 9-9. Selecting the free transform tool adds four buttons to the property bar (also shown in Figure 9-9): the free rotation tool, the free angle reflection tool, the free scale tool, and the free skew tool.

Like the handles, property bar controls, and roll-ups, the free transform tools enable you to scale, flip, rotate, and skew objects. But unlike the handles, property bar controls, and roll-ups, the free transform tools let you do so in a freeform fashion by dragging from any point in the drawing window. Here's how these nifty little tools work.

- ✔ Drag with the free rotation tool to rotate objects with the selected point (the point at which you clicked to begin your drag) as the center of rotation. Ctrl+drag to rotate objects in 15-degree increments.

- ✔ Drag with the free angle reflection tool to reflect, or mirror, objects across a line. In the spirit of the word "free," you can also rotate your mirrored objects, with the selected point as the center of rotation, while dragging with the tool. Hey, it's like rotate and mirror in one tool.

- ✔ Drag with the free scale tool to scale objects horizontally and vertically in a single drag. Ctrl+drag to scale the objects proportionately.

- ✔ Drag with the free skew tool to skew objects horizontally and vertically around the selected point.

Figure 9-9 shows the free skew tool in action on an unsuspecting star. With the free transform tools, the possibilities are nearly endless. So go ahead, experiment.

Distortions on Parade

If scale, flip, rotate, and skew were the extent of CorelDraw's transformation capabilities, the program would be a real snoozer. It would be flexible, certainly, but hardly capable of inspiring the fanatic loyalty that follows this vast program. The next part of this chapter covers three amazing transformations you can perform with CorelDraw 8:

- ✔ Imagine a drawing printed on a sheet of rubber in a rectangular frame. If you were to grab a corner of that rubber and stretch it, the drawing would stretch in that direction. That's what it's like to distort objects in CorelDraw using the *Perspective* function. Corel calls the function Perspective because it simulates the effect of viewing a flat drawing in three-dimensional space.

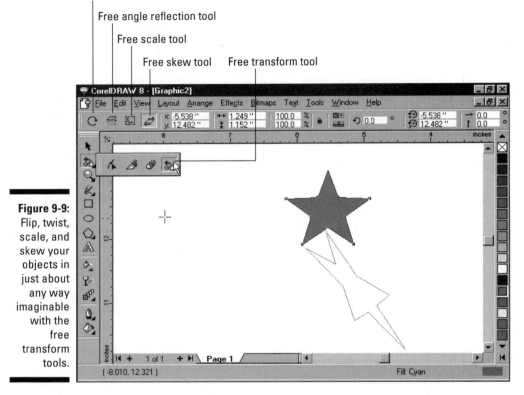

Free rotation tool
Free angle reflection tool
Free scale tool
Free skew tool   Free transform tool

Figure 9-9:
Flip, twist,
scale, and
skew your
objects in
just about
any way
imaginable
with the
free
transform
tools.

✔ *Enveloping* is like viewing a drawing's reflection in a fun-house mirror.
You can bow the edges of objects inward, outward, or even along the
edges of complex paths.

✔ *Extruding* an object gives it real depth by attaching sides to the shape. A
square turns into a cube; a circle turns into a cylinder. CorelDraw
accentuates the appearance of depth by automatically lighting the
extruded shape and rotating it in 3-D space.

A Lesson in Perspective

I want to caution you against thinking of CorelDraw as a three-dimensional
drawing program just because it provides a few wacky effects that simulate
3-D. In a true 3-D program — such as CorelDream 3D — you build a 3-D
structure called a *model* that you can walk around and view from any angle.
Then you wrap surface maps around the model, specify the reflectivity of
the surfaces, light the model, apply ray tracing, and perform a bunch of
other operations that very likely sound Greek to you.

TECHNICAL STUFF

Special effects you can ignore

If you take a look at your Effects menu, you'll notice that I ignore a few commands in this chapter, including Blend, Contour, Lens, and PowerClip. I wouldn't blame you if this fact cast a smidgen of doubt on my flawless wisdom. But the truth is, none of these commands are transformations. Here's my take on these features:

✔ The Blend command creates intermediate shapes between two selected paths. If you blend between a white square and a black circle, for example, CorelDraw creates a series of shapes that become increasingly circular as they progress from light gray to dark gray. The number-one use for the Blend function is to create custom gradations. It's a useful special effect but hardly eye-popping. To find out how to create a blend of your own, follow the steps in the "Morph between Two Shapes" section of Chapter 19.

✔ The Contour feature is the least useful of CorelDraw's special effects. It fills a path with concentric versions of itself. Theoretically, you can use the Contour function to create gradations that follow the contour of a path, but you generally end up with patterns that look for all the world like shooting targets.

✔ CorelDraw's Lens function blends the colors of a selected shape with the colors in the shapes below it. You can make an object appear translucent, you can make one shape invert the colors in another, and you can create magnifying-lens effects. These are cool effects, no doubt, but they come at a price. Lens effects almost always increase the time it takes to print a drawing, and they may make a drawing so complicated that you can't get it to print at all.

✔ PowerClip lets you create stencils. In other words, you can take a bunch of objects and stick them inside another object. The CorelDraw balloon, for example, is a bunch of stripes stuck inside a balloon shape. To use the feature, you select the objects you want to stick inside another shape, choose Effects⇨PowerClip⇨Place Inside Container, and then click on the shape you want to serve as a stencil. Bingo, in go your objects. But like the Lens function, PowerClip dramatically increases the complexity of a drawing. If you encounter printing errors after using this feature, don't come crying to me.

The point is, CorelDraw is solidly rooted in two dimensions. Its tiny supply of 3-D-like effects are pure mockery and flimflam. Something to do on a rainy night. If you want to get a taste for real 3-D, check out Chapter 18.

Viewing 2-D drawings in 3-D space (sorta)

Now that I've diplomatically sorted out that tender issue, allow me to show you how to distort one or more objects using the Add Perspective command.

1. **Select some random objects.**

2. **Press Ctrl+G, or choose Arrange⇨Group, or click on the Group button on the property bar.**

   If you don't group the objects, CorelDraw assumes that you want to distort each object individually.

3. **Choose Effects⇨Add Perspective.**

   CorelDraw converts the group to a perspective object and automatically selects the shape tool, as shown in Figure 9-10. Perspective objects are a unique kind of object in CorelDraw and require a special editing approach.

4. **Drag on any of the four corner handles.**

   CorelDraw stretches the selection to keep up with your moves.

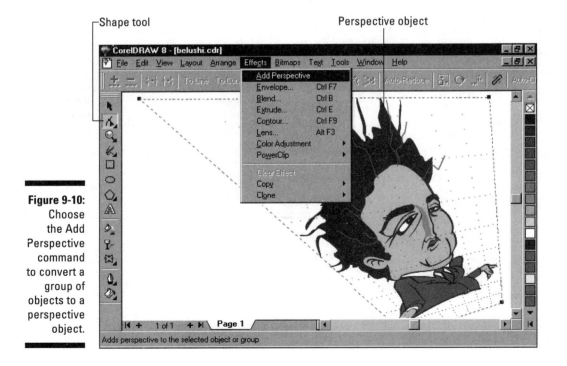

Figure 9-10:
Choose the Add Perspective command to convert a group of objects to a perspective object.

You can drag handles for as long as you want. Perspective objects are hard to predict at first, so be prepared to spend time editing. If dragging a handle produces an unwanted effect, drag the handle back. When you finish editing the selection, click on the arrow tool icon. CorelDraw exits the perspective mode and allows you to perform other operations.

Putting perspective in perspective

Editing a perspective object is straightforward stuff. But just in case you need a little guidance, the following list contains a few items to bear in mind along with a few suggested avenues for experimentation:

- ✔ Ctrl+drag a handle to drag it in a horizontal or vertical direction.

- ✔ Ctrl+Shift+drag a handle to move two handles at once. The handle that you drag moves either horizontally or vertically; a neighboring handle moves the same distance in the opposite direction. If you Ctrl+Shift+drag horizontally, the handle to the left or right of the handle that you drag also moves. If you Ctrl+Shift+drag vertically, the handle above or below the current handle moves.

- ✔ Imagine that the dotted outline that surrounds the perspective object extends forever in all directions. So instead of four straight sides, you have four straight lines extending across your screen. CorelDraw marks the two locations at which each pair of opposite imaginary lines meet — that is, the point at which the left side would meet the right side and the point at which the top side would meet the bottom — with Xs called vanishing points. Unless you're far away from your object, you probably can't see the vanishing points because they're off-screen. But if you zoom out (by pressing F3) or move two opposite sides at an extreme angle to one another (see Figure 9-11), one or both of the vanishing points will come into view. The reason I even brought up this complicated topic is that you can also drag a vanishing point to further distort the perspective object.

- ✔ To remove the most recent round of perspective edits from a selected object, choose Effects➪Clear Perspective.

- ✔ To edit an existing perspective object, just select the shape tool and click on the object. No need to choose the Add Perspective command.

- ✔ To edit the individual nodes and segments in a perspective object, you have to convert the object back to paths. First, press Ctrl+U (Arrange➪ Ungroup) to ungroup the object if necessary. Then, select the object you want to edit and choose Arrange➪Convert to Curves (Ctrl+Q).

Vanishing point

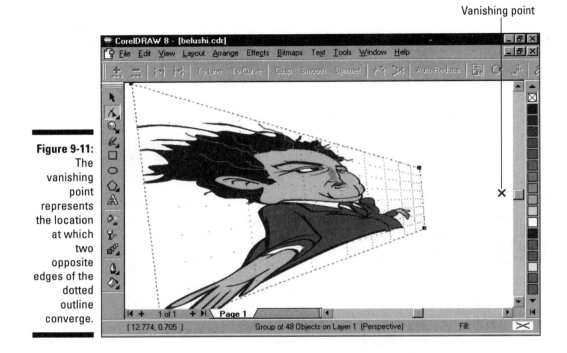

Figure 9-11:
The
vanishing
point
represents
the location
at which
two
opposite
edges of the
dotted
outline
converge.

Envelope of Wonders

With the CorelDraw Envelope feature, you can bend and twist objects as if they were imprinted on a piece of Silly Putty. The effect is sort of like when you used to smush a piece of Silly Putty on the comics page of the newspaper and then wrap it around your little brother's face.

If you've ever taken a look at the CorelDraw Envelope feature, you probably said something like, "What the . . . ?" or, perhaps more appropriately, "Duh." At least that's what I did. But have faith. If I — king of the short attention span — could figure it out, you can too. And believe me, it's worth the effort.

The ultimate distortion

To apply envelope effects, do this:

1. **Select those objects — any objects you want.**

   Click and Shift+click with the arrow tool until your mouse hand goes to sleep.

2. Group the objects.

The Envelope function works on only one object at a time. So if you want to distort several objects, you need to group them by choosing Arrange⇨Group, pressing Ctrl+G, or clicking on the Group button.

3. Press Ctrl+F7 or choose Effects⇨Envelope.

CorelDraw displays the Envelope roll-up, as shown in Figure 9-12.

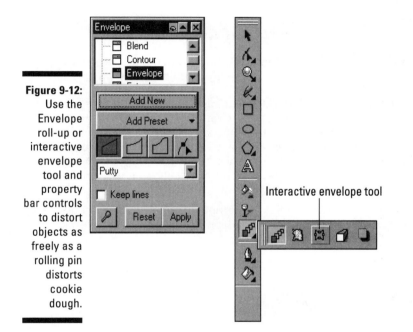

Figure 9-12:
Use the Envelope roll-up or interactive envelope tool and property bar controls to distort objects as freely as a rolling pin distorts cookie dough.

Interactive envelope tool

Alternatively, you can select the interactive envelope tool, which is the third tool on the interactive blend tool flyout menu shown in Figure 9-12. When this tool is selected, the property bar displays the same controls contained in the Envelope roll-up. If you select the interactive envelope tool, you can skip to Step 5.

4. Click on the Add New button.

CorelDraw automatically selects the shape tool and surrounds the selection with a dotted rectangle that has eight handles — four in the corners and four on the sides.

5. Select an editing mode.

The four icons in the middle of the roll-up and in the right-center of the property bar represent envelope editing modes. For now, it's not important which one you select. I explain how each one works in the next two sections.

6. Drag the handles to distort the object.

The object bends and stretches to keep up with your movements.

To exit the envelope editing mode, click on the arrow tool icon. To redisplay the envelope editing handles, click on the shape tool. Or, to begin a new transformation, select the object with the arrow tool and click on the Add New button in the Envelope roll-up or on the property bar.

The envelope editing modes

The envelope editing mode icons work like tools. Each one distorts the selected object in a unique and progressively more dramatic way:

✔ In the straight-line mode, CorelDraw maintains a straight side between each of the eight handles, as demonstrated in Figure 9-13. This mode is rather like the perspective distortion, except for two things: 1) You have some additional handles to play with, and 2) You can move the handles horizontally or vertically only. The left and right side handles move horizontally only; the top and bottom handles move vertically only. The corner handles move both ways.

✔ In the single-arc mode, CorelDraw permits a single arc to form between each pair of handles, as shown in Figure 9-14. Again, you can drag

Figure 9-13: Dragging a handle in the straight-line mode.

Straight-line mode

Single-arc mode

Figure 9-14:
The single-arc mode can produce a slenderizing effect.

handles horizontally and vertically only. The single-arc mode works best for distorting objects into hourglass and balloon shapes.

✔ The double-arc mode allows a wave to form between each handle. As demonstrated in Figure 9-15, you can create rippling distortions, as if you were viewing your object under water. Just as in the straight-line and single-arc modes, you can drag handles horizontally and vertically only.

✔ In the unconstrained mode, the sky's the limit. You can edit the outline exactly as if it were a free-form path drawn with the pencil tool. You can drag the handles — they're really nodes in this case — any way you please. To determine the curvature of the segments between handles, CorelDraw provides you with control points, as shown in Figure 9-16.

✔ You can add or subtract nodes by using the Node Edit roll-up, by using the property bar node editing buttons, or by simply double-clicking with the shape tool. (Double-click on the shape tool to make the roll-up appear.) You can even select multiple nodes at the same time. In short, if you can do it to a pencil path, you can do it to a shape in the unconstrained mode.

Push the envelope

Just in case you're hungry for more about enveloping, here are a few tricks you may find helpful:

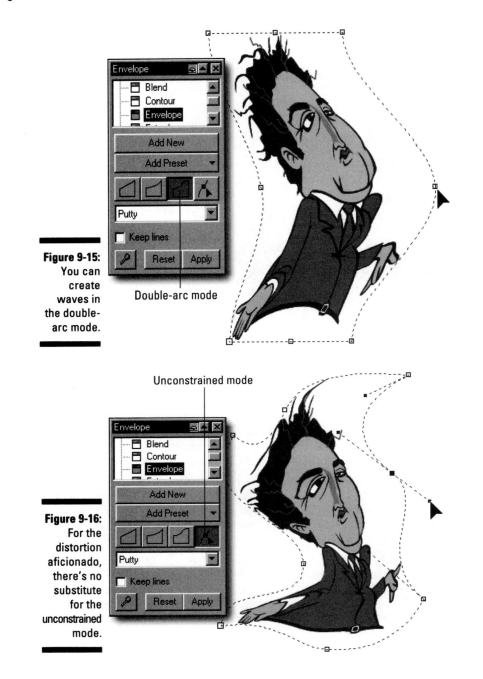

Figure 9-15: You can create waves in the double-arc mode.

Double-arc mode

Unconstrained mode

Figure 9-16: For the distortion aficionado, there's no substitute for the unconstrained mode.

✔ You can use envelope editing modes in tandem. For example, you can select the straight-line icon and drag one handle, and then select the double-arc icon and drag another handle.

- In the unconstrained mode, the Shift and Ctrl keys behave just as they do when you're editing a pencil path. Shift+click on a node to select it without deselecting other nodes. Ctrl+drag on a node to constrain the node to horizontal or vertical movements.

- In the other modes, Ctrl+drag a handle to move the opposite handle the same distance and direction as the handle you're dragging.

- Shift+drag to move the opposite handle the same distance but in the opposite direction as the handle you're dragging.

- Ctrl+Shift+drag a side handle to move all side handles the same distance but in the opposite directions. Ctrl+Shift+drag a corner handle to move all corner handles.

- If you don't feel up to editing the outline on your own, CorelDraw can help you out. Click on the Add Preset button in the Envelope roll-up or on the property bar to display a pop-up menu of outline shapes, as shown in Figure 9-17. Select the outline you want to apply. If you select an outline in the Envelope roll-up, you need to click on the Apply button. If you select an outline using the property bar controls, the outline is applied automatically.

- When using the Envelope roll-up, you can cancel an envelope distortion anytime before you click on the Apply button. Just click on the Reset button or select the arrow tool.

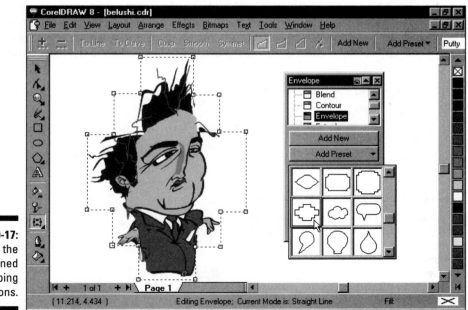

Figure 9-17:
Using the predefined enveloping options.

TIP

✔ After you apply a few distortions, the dotted outline may become prohibitively wiggly. To restore the dotted outline to a rectangle and take a new stab at enveloping an object, click again on the Add New button in the Envelope roll-up or on the property bar.

✔ To remove the most recent round of envelope edits from a selected object, choose Effects➪Clear Envelope.

Well, Extru-u-ude Me!

In future years, brilliant minds no doubt will argue the merit of discussing extruding — one of the most complex functions in CorelDraw — in a ...*For Dummies* book. (Yeah, right.) But I figure, what the heck, it's a fun feature, and with enough effort, you may even figure out how to do something useful with it. In the meantime, it's a great way to waste several hours being antisocial and playing with your computer.

Extruding in the real world

First, what is extruding? Simply put, *extrusion* is the act of assigning depth to a 2-D shape by extending its sides into the third dimension. Naturally, that explanation doesn't make any sense, so perhaps an example is in order. Did you ever play with one of those thingies that lets you crank Play-Doh through a stencil to create snaky geometric forms, as illustrated in Figure 9-18? You cut off the snaky bit with a plastic knife, and voilà — you have a 3-D star, polygon, or other useless piece of gook. If this is your idea of a fond childhood

Figure 9-18:
Play-Doh
oozing
through a
stencil is an
example
of an
extrusion.

memory, you are an extruder. Pasta machines extrude noodles. Sausage makers extrude columns of beef and pork by-products. Warts extrude out of your skin all by themselves. Life is filled with examples of extruding.

Extruding in the workplace

For time immemorial, the Extrude roll-up has served as the central head-quarters for CorelDraw's extruding functions. Ever since the Big Bang (or thereabouts), you've been able to access this roll-up by choosing Effects⇨Extrude or pressing Ctrl+E.

As with enveloping, CorelDraw can't extrude more than one object at a time. However, unlike enveloping, extruding is not applicable to groups. You can extrude a single path — open or closed — or a block of text. Sadly, I'm afraid that rules out any more transformations for John. To extrude an object:

1. **Press Ctrl+E to bring up the Extrude roll-up.**

   The roll-up appears in Figure 9-19. Your roll-up is probably part of the Effects roll-up group, which means that you see a bunch of stuff at the top of your roll-up that doesn't appear in mine. (I pulled my Extrude roll-up out of the Effects roll-up, as I explain in Chapter 2.)

2. **Select a path.**

   For now, keep it simple. Select some basic shape such as a circle or a star.

3. **Click on the Edit button in the Extrude roll-up.**

   A dotted extrusion outline representing the form of the extruded object appears, as shown in Figure 9-19.

   If the Edit button is dimmed, press Ctrl+Q (Arrange⇨Convert To Curves) to convert the object to a free-form path. Now the Edit button is ready to go. Also, if you select an object before pressing Ctrl+E — that is, you perform Step 2 before Step 1 — the Extrude roll-up automatically goes into the edit mode. This means you don't have to click on the Edit button. Just skip to Step 4.

   Note that after you click on the Edit button, the property bar displays controls related to extruding. But the buttons are dimmed until after you create the extrusion by clicking on Apply in the Extrude roll-up (which you do at the end of these steps). For now, just lick your lips at the thought of editing your extrusion using the property bar.

4. **Drag on the vanishing point to change the direction of the extrusion.**

   Labeled in Figure 9-19, the vanishing point represents the point from which the extrusion emanates. If the star were a bullet rushing toward you, the vanishing point would be the gun. An ugly analogy, I admit, but accurate. If you don't see a vanishing point, zoom out to reveal it.

Depth tab   Extrusion outline   Vanishing point

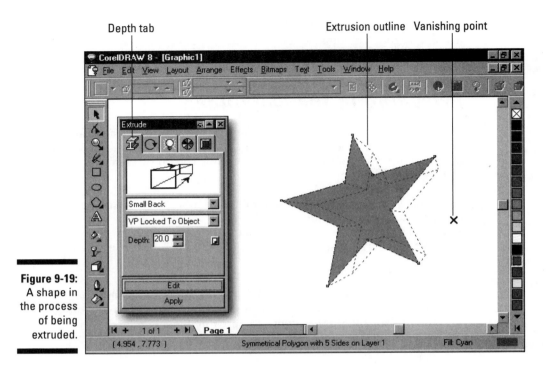

Figure 9-19:
A shape in the process of being extruded.

5. Enter a value in the Depth option box.

You find the option box on the Depth tab of the roll-up, as shown in Figure 9-19. If the Depth tab isn't showing, click on the tab.

The Depth value determines the length of the sides that stretch away from the object toward the vanishing point. If you enter the maximum value, 99, the extrusion outline touches the vanishing point. The minimum value, 1, creates a very shallow extrusion. Figure 9-20 shows some examples. Click on Apply to see the effects of your change.

6. Click on the 3-D rotation tab.

It's the second tab at the top of the Extrude roll-up, and it's labeled in Figure 9-21.

7. Drag the Corel C to spin the selected object in 3-D space.

Just drag around inside the roll-up, as demonstrated in Figure 9-21. Give it a try and see how easy it is. The front of the C is red and the back is blue, so you can see right away when you rotate the letter all the way around. Click on Apply to see what your rotation does to your object.

Ctrl+drag to rotate in 45-degree increments. If you want to unrotate the object, click on the X icon and then click on Apply.

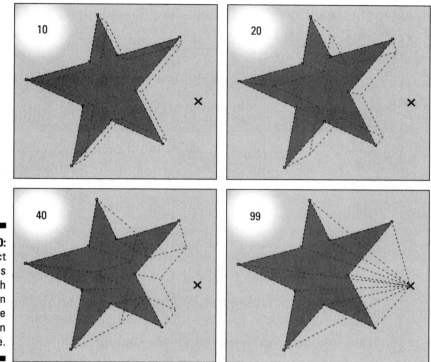

Figure 9-20:
The effect of various Depth values on the extrusion outline.

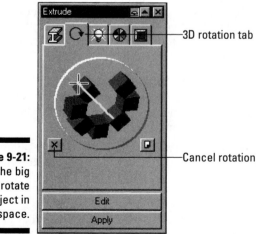

Figure 9-21:
Drag the big C to rotate an object in 3-D space.

3D rotation tab

Cancel rotation

8. Click on the Lighting tab.

This tab is labeled in Figure 9-22.

Light bulbs — Lighting tab

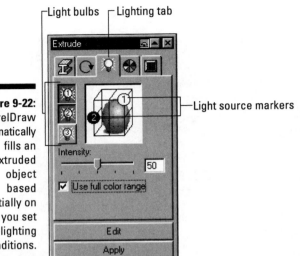

Light source markers

9. Click on the first light bulb to shine a light on the 3-D object.

You can shine up to three lights by selecting all three light bulbs.

10. Drag the light source markers in the cube.

A number in a circle indicates the location of the light source with respect to the object. Drag one of these markers to any spot in the cube where two gridlines intersect. (If you select more than one light source and it appears that each light source you select simply replaces the previous one, don't worry. The light source markers don't replace each other, but they do overlap sometimes. Simply drag the exposed marker to reveal the light source below it.)

11. Drag the Intensity slider to increase or decrease the amount of light.

Alternatively, you can enter a value between 0 and 100 into the option box. The lower the number, the dimmer the light. As before, click on Apply to see how your lights are affecting your object.

If you accidentally click outside the roll-up, the Apply button becomes dimmed. Simply reselect the object and click on the Edit button to reactivate the Apply button.

12. Click on the Bevel tab.

The Extrude roll-up contains a Bevel tab, shown in Figure 9-23. Using the options on this tab, you can create an extruded object whose edges appear beveled, as in the bottom-left object in Figure 9-23. To bevel your object's edges, select the Use Bevel check box. You can then set the angle and depth of the bevel using the check boxes in the roll-up or by dragging the bevel control box in the preview area above the check

Bevel control   Bevel tab   Beveled rectangled   No bevel   Bevel only

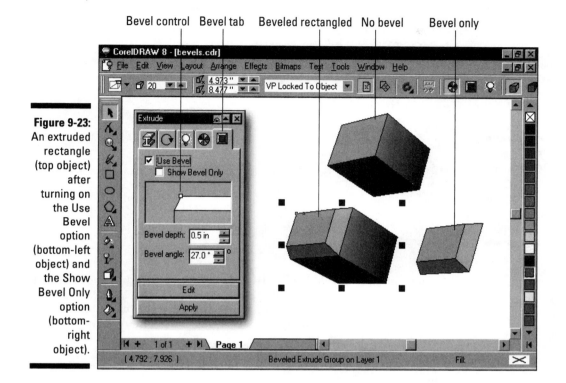

Figure 9-23:
An extruded rectangle (top object) after turning on the Use Bevel option (bottom-left object) and the Show Bevel Only option (bottom-right object).

boxes. Drag up or down to change the bevel depth; drag right or left to change the bevel angle.

If you select the Show Bevel Only check box, you wind up with only the beveled portion of your object, as shown in the bottom-right example in Figure 9-23. It's as if you took a knife and lopped off the rest of your object.

To preview how the object looks with the selected settings, click on Apply.

13. **Click on the Object Color tab, as shown in Figure 9-24.**

14. **Select the Shade radio button to fill the partially lighted portions of the object with continuous gradations.**

The other two radio buttons produce boring results.

15. **Select the desired colors from the pop-up menus.**

The first two pop-up menus set the colors for the main object fill. For best results, select a light and dark shade of the same color in the From and To pop-up menus. Click on Apply to check out your colors.

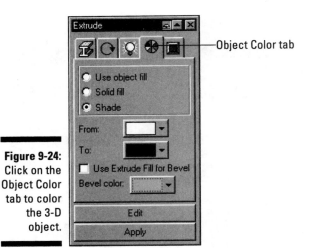

Object Color tab

Figure 9-24:
Click on the
Object Color
tab to color
the 3-D
object.

If you want your beveled edges to use a different color from your object fill, turn off the Use Extrude Fill for Bevel check box. (The option is unavailable unless you selected the Use Bevel check box in Step 12.) You can then choose a color from the Bevel Color pop-up menu.

16. Click outside the roll-up with the arrow tool.

CorelDraw automatically draws and fills the object to your specifications. Figure 9-25 shows the star from Figure 9-19 after I rotated it and lit it from the bottom-left corner. Note that this star does not use beveled edges. I like my stars sharp and pointy-like.

Remember that clicking on the Apply button simply displays a preview of your extrusion effects. To apply the extrusion for good and exit the edit mode, you must click with the arrow tool, as explained in Step 16.

Figure 9-25:
A three-
dimensional
star created
in a two-
dimensional
drawing
program.

Extruding is a long process, but not a particularly complicated one. Spend a little time playing around with the different controls to discover their effects, and you should become comfortable with extruding in no time. If you want to edit your extrusion, select the object with the arrow tool and then click on the Edit button in the Extrude roll-up. Or use the property bar controls, as explained in the next section.

Keep in mind that you can set the options on the various tabs of the Extrude roll-up in any order you like; you don't have to follow the preceding steps in the exact order I presented. If creating your beveled edges before you rotate the object is easier for you, for example, go ahead and do so.

Extruding interactively and with buttons

Ladies and gentleman, allow me to introduce the new interactive extrude tool. This tool allows you to extrude a selected object simply by dragging with the tool and using the property bar controls, which I discuss shortly. No roll-ups, no Apply buttons, just good old-fashioned mouse clicks and drags. Just follow these steps:

1. **Select the interactive extrude tool.**

2. **Click on the object and drag the vanishing point cursor to set the depth and direction of the extrusion.**

3. **Drag the midpoint slider to adjust the depth of the extrusion.**

   Alternatively, you can adjust the depth by using the property bar control labeled in Figure 9-26.

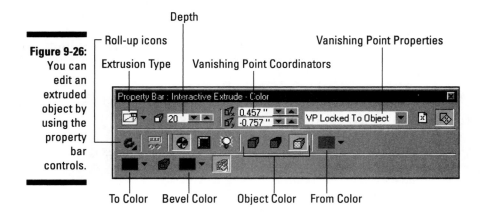

Figure 9-26: You can edit an extruded object by using the property bar controls.

Depth

Roll-up icons

Vanishing Point Properties

Extrusion Type   Vanishing Point Coordinators

To Color   Bevel Color   Object Color   From Color

As mentioned, the property bar displays controls you can use to edit an existing extruded object. These controls become available only after you click on the Apply button in the Extrude roll-up or create an extrusion using the interactive extrude tool; they're for editing the extrusion, not creating it. The buttons are displayed automatically when you select an extruded object with the arrow tool. (Note that you must select the extruded portion of the object for the buttons to be displayed.)

Also, as with other property bar controls, some buttons are hidden from view if you use the 640-x-480 display setting for your monitor. To access all the buttons, drag the property bar into the drawing window to create a free-floating palette of buttons, as in Figure 9-26. The pertinent controls are labeled in Figure 9-26 and work as follows:

✔ You can use the vanishing point controls to move the vanishing point to a specific numerical coordinate. Unless you're really persnickety about your work or you're trying to duplicate an earlier extrusion, though, dragging the vanishing point cursor as explained in the preceding steps is probably easier.

✔ The Depth option box sets the depth of the extrusion, just like the Depth option box in the Extrude roll-up. No mystery here.

✔ The three Object Color icons duplicate the three radio buttons on the Object Color tab of the Extrude roll-up. The rightmost icon in the group, the Shade button, is the option I recommend.

✔ The From Color and To Color pop-up menus set the colors of the extrusion for the main object. The Bevel Color pop-up menu sets the color for beveled edges.

✔ Click on one of the four roll-up icons to display the corresponding tab of the Extrude roll-up. There's no roll-up icon for the Depth tab because the controls on this tab are displayed separately on the property bar, as labeled in Figure 9-27. Come to think of it, you can probably suffer through without these buttons, which are the only ones hidden from view at the 640-x-480 monitor display setting. After all, you can always just press Ctrl+E to display the roll-up.

Ripping apart your new 3-D object

After you finish creating and lighting your object, you can break the 3-D object apart and fill it as you please. Just do the following:

1. **Select the extruded portion of the object.**

2. **Choose Arrange⇨Separate.**

   This step separates the original object from its extruded sides.

3. **Shift+click on the original object with the arrow tool.**

   This step deselects the object, leaving only the sides selected.

4. **Press Ctrl+U, or choose Arrange⇨Ungroup, or click on the Ungroup button on the property bar.**

   CorelDraw automatically creates the sides as a group, so you need to ungroup them before you can edit their fills.

After you separate the individual paths that make up the extruded object, you can fill each path independently to create a better-looking 3-D drawing.

Let's Get Funky Now

CorelDraw 8 offers a few new interactive distortions that I simply can't resist sharing with you. Along with the new interactive envelope and interactive extrude tools, a new interactive distortion tool (labeled in Figure 9-28) resides on the interactive blend tool flyout menu. When the interactive distortion tool is selected, the property bar offers three distortion options: push and pull, zipper, and twister. These options, which are labeled in Figure 9-27, are just plain fun and well worth experimenting with. I only explore the push and pull and twister distortions here. Okay, stop your bellyaching; I discuss the zipper distortion in Chapter 11.

Fortunately, our friend the star has volunteered to serve as guinea pig for yet another round of distortions. What a guy.

The push and pull distortion tool works just like you'd imagine it would. Depending on the direction of your drag, it either pushes the object's nodes away from or pulls the object's nodes in toward the center of the object. To apply a push and pull distortion to an object, do this:

1. **Select the interactive distortion tool from the interactive blend tool flyout menu and click on the Push and Pull Distortion button on the property bar.**

2. **Click on the object and drag to push or pull the object's nodes.**

   The point at which you click becomes the center of the distortion. Drag to the right to push the object's nodes away from its center or to the left to pull the object's nodes in toward its center. In Figure 9-28, I clicked on the center of the object and dragged to the left to turn the star into a purty flower.

After you apply a push and pull distortion, you can edit the effect by dragging the distortion arrow and end point or using the property bar controls (labeled in Figure 9-27):

✔ The Push and Pull Distortion Amplitude option box sets the amplitude of the distortion. A negative value results in a pull effect, and a positive value results in a push. Think of it this way: A negative value is equivalent to a left drag with the distortion arrow, and a positive value is equivalent to a right drag.

✔ The Center Distortion button simply positions the distortion on the center of your object.

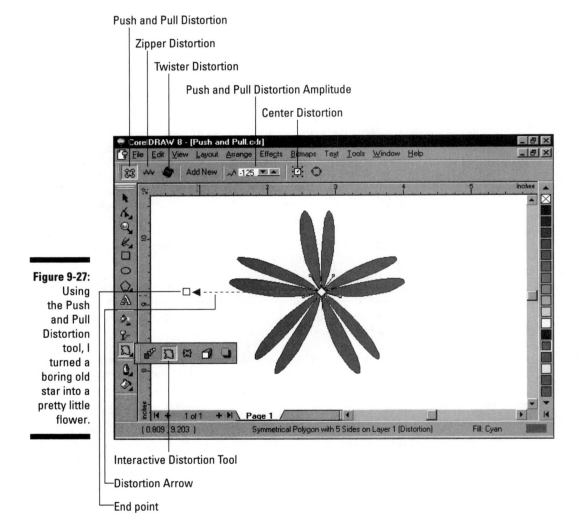

Push and Pull Distortion

Zipper Distortion

Twister Distortion

Push and Pull Distortion Amplitude

Center Distortion

Figure 9-27:
Using the Push and Pull Distortion tool, I turned a boring old star into a pretty little flower.

Interactive Distortion Tool

Distortion Arrow

End point

The twister distortion twists, or turns, nodes in a circular direction. To apply a twister distortion to an object, follow these steps:

1. **Select the interactive distortion tool from the interactive blend tool flyout menu and click on the Twister Distortion button on the property bar.**

2. **Click on the object and drag in a clockwise or counterclockwise direction to twist the object's nodes.**

   In Figure 9-28, I clicked on the center of the object and dragged in a clockwise direction to turn the star into a gentlemanly conehead inviting an unseen partner to dance.

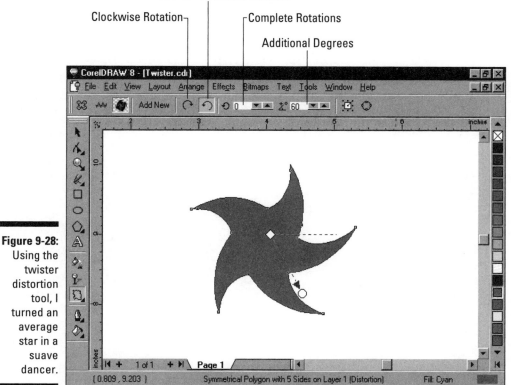

Counter Clockwise Rotation

Clockwise Rotation ┐   ┌Complete Rotations

Additional Degrees

Figure 9-28:
Using the twister distortion tool, I turned an average star in a suave dancer.

After you apply a twister distortion, the property bar displays the following controls, which are labeled in Figure 9-28.

- ✔ The Clockwise Rotation button twists the object clockwise.

- ✔ The Counterclockwise Rotation button twists the object in a counter-clockwise direction.

- ✔ The Complete Rotations option sets the number of complete 360-degree rotations applied to the object. For example, if you enter 2 in the option box, CorelDraw rotates the object 360 degrees two times.

- ✔ The Additional Degrees option box specifies the degree of rotation from 0 to 359 degrees.

Part III
Getting the Message Out There (Wherever "There" Is)

The 5th Wave   By Rich Tennant

"Your Elvis should appear bald and slightly hunched-nice Big Foot, Brad-Keep your two-headed animals in the shadows and your alien spacecrafts crisp and defined."

In this part . . .

1f all you could do with CorelDraw was draw, this book would be over by now. But as luck would have it, CorelDraw is equally adept at creating documents, such as fliers, newsletters, and those little wrappers that cover your hangers when they come back from the dry cleaners.

Like most desktop publishing programs, CorelDraw lets you enter and edit text, apply special formatting attributes, specify the size and orientation of a page, and print your document to paper. Unlike most publishing programs, however, it enables you to also drag letters independently of each other, create text on a circle, and actually edit the shape of characters of type. CorelDraw even lets you prepare documents that can be published on the World Wide Web. Few other pieces of software provide such a wide gamut of publishing capabilities.

At the risk of sounding like the crowned king of hyperbole, there hasn't been a tool like CorelDraw for slapping words on a bit of sliced timber since Johann Gensfleisch — who mostly went about using his mom's maiden name, Gutenberg — decided to smack some letters on a particularly abbreviated version of the Bible.

Chapter 10

The Care and Planting of Text

Creating text involves more than whacking your fingers in a hysterical frenzy against the keyboard. Remember all that stuff you learned in typing class? Forget it. Yesterday's news. I, for example, can't type — not a word — yet I write professionally, I format like a champ, and I don't have any wrist problems. Knock on wood . . . aaugh, I knocked too hard! I think my hand's going numb!

Ha! Not really! See? My hand's just fine. Seemed so real, though, didn't it? And do you know why? It's not because the text is lucid and gripping. Surely you've figured that out by now. It's because the text looks good. The pages in this book appear professional — granted, in a sort of goofy way — so you naturally assume that a professional is behind them, not some crackpot like me. That, my friend, is an example of the miracle of modern computer-book writing.

In the world of corporate communications, text is judged as much by its appearance as its content. Not to put too fine a point on it, but text is art. Simply typing in thoughtful and convincing text with a hint of Hippocrene genius is not enough. You also need to know what to do with text after you enter it. And that's what this chapter is all about. (You were beginning to wonder, huh?)

A Furst Luk at Tekst

Unless you already know a thing or two about word processing and desktop publishing, this chapter is going to seem like a trip through the dictionary. You're going to find out about so many terms that your brain will very likely swell up and pop. To prepare, you may want to tie a bandanna around your head and set a squeegee near your monitor.

For starters, text is made up of letters, numbers, and various symbols, such as &, %, $, and my favorite, §, which is meaningless to most of Earth's inhabitants. If § crops up in your documents, it's a sure sign that either a lawyer or an extraterrestrial has been using your machine.

Together, these little text elements are called *characters*. CorelDraw refers to a collection of characters as a *text block* or, in deference to its path cousins, a *text object*. A text block may contain a single word, a sentence, a paragraph, or an odd collection of §s arranged in the shape of a crop circle.

In CorelDraw, you work with two kinds of text blocks:

- Use *artistic text* for logos, headlines, labels, and other short passages of text that require special graphic treatment, such as blends, extrusions, and other effects.
- *Paragraph text* is suited to longer passages, such as full sentences, paragraphs, pithy quotes, encyclopedia entries, epic poems, works of modern fiction, and letters to Grandma. You can apply certain text formatting options, such as tabs and indents, to paragraph text that you can't apply to artistic text.

CorelDraw also offers access to specialized symbols, which — although they're technically not text — you can use as independent objects to highlight text objects or adorn your drawing. Symbols are organized thematically into categories such as animals, furniture, medicine, and semaphore. No smoke signals yet, but I've heard that's in the works.

Pick Up Your Text Tool

You create both artistic and paragraph text by using the same tool, the text tool. The text tool is the sixth from the bottom in the toolbox — the one that looks like a big letter *A*. The manner in which you use the tool determines whether you plop down a chunk of artistic text or paragraph text into your drawing.

Creating artistic text

To create artistic text, do this:

1. **Select the text tool.**

   Just click on the *A* icon in the toolbox. Better yet, just press F8.

2. **Click in the drawing area where you want the text to begin.**

   After you click, a vertical line called the *insertion marker* appears. The insertion marker indicates the location where new text will appear.

3. **Type away.**

   As you type, the corresponding characters appear on-screen. The insertion marker moves rightward with the addition of each character (see Figure 10-1), indicating the location at which the next character will appear.

4. **When you finish, select the arrow tool.**

   Eight square handles surround the text, as in the second example of Figure 10-1, to show that the text is selected.

   After you select the text tool, you can switch to the arrow tool quickly by pressing Ctrl+spacebar.

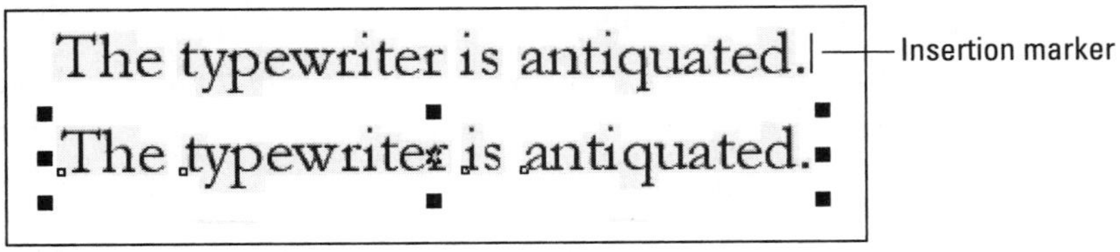

Figure 10-1: Artistic text as it appears when you're entering text (top) and after you select the arrow tool (bottom).

The typewriter is antiquated.| —— Insertion marker

The typewriter is antiquated.

Nearly every computer program in existence lets you change text after you create it, and CorelDraw is no exception. To add more characters, select the text tool and click inside the text block at the location where you want the new characters to appear. In Figure 10-2, for example, I first clicked in front of the *a* in *antiquated* and entered the word *an.* Next, I clicked between the *d* and the *period,* pressed Enter, and entered *piece of garbage.*

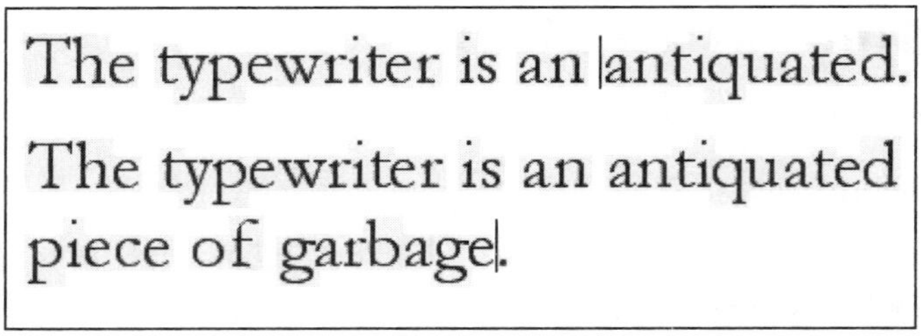

Figure 10-2:
Adding text
to an
existing
text block.

The typewriter is an |antiquated.

The typewriter is an antiquated

piece of garbage|.

Here are a few more things to know about entering and editing artistic text:

- ✔ Unlike text in a word processor, artistic text does not automatically wrap to the next line. In other words, when your text reaches the right edge of the text block, CorelDraw doesn't move the insertion point to the beginning of a new line. You have to manually insert line breaks by pressing the Enter key, just as you have to press the carriage-return key when using a typewriter.

- ✔ To move the text block to a new location in the drawing area, drag it with the arrow tool.

- ✔ The X and Y option boxes on the left end of the property bar give you another way to move the text block. The X value controls the text block's horizontal position, and the Y value controls its vertical position, just as with any other object. To display the controls, select the text block with the arrow tool. Remember that, as with regular objects, the X and Y values indicate the center of the text block. Also, if you enter an X or a Y value from the keyboard instead of using the up and down arrows next to the option boxes, you must press Enter before your changes take effect.

- ✔ You also can use the arrow keys to move a text block. Select the text block with the arrow tool and then press an arrow key to nudge the block to a new location.

- ✔ When you drag the handles of an artistic text block with the arrow tool, you change the size of the characters. Drag a corner handle to scale the characters proportionally.

- ✔ Drag the top or bottom handle to make the text tall and skinny, as in Figure 10-3. This kind of text is called *condensed*.

- ✔ Drag the left or right handle to make the text short and fat (called *expanded text*).

- ✔ In CorelDraw 8, you can move or scale text (artistic or paragraph) without leaving the text editing mode. If you pause a few seconds while typing, the bounding box appears, enabling you to move or scale your text block by using the selection handles and the center X marker. When you begin typing again, the bounding box disappears.

Figure 10-3:
I dragged
the bottom
handle with
the arrow
tool to
create
condensed
text.

✔ Click a second time on a text block to access the rotation and skew handles. These handles work just like those described in Chapter 9, enabling you to create rotated and slanted text.

✔ Alternatively, you can resize and rotate an artistic text block by using the property bar controls, just as you can any other object. For details, see Chapter 9.

Creating paragraph text

To create a block of paragraph text, follow these ingenious steps:

1. **Press F8 or click on the text tool icon.**

2. **Drag in the drawing area to create a text block.**

   You create a rectangular marquee, as shown in the first example in Figure 10-4.

3. **Bang those keys.**

   As you work out your aggressions, text fills up the text block. Unlike artistic text, paragraph text automatically wraps to the next line when it exceeds the right-hand boundary of the text block, as demonstrated in the second example of Figure 10-4.

4. **When you finish, select the arrow tool.**

   • You can switch from the text tool to the arrow tool quickly by pressing Ctrl+spacebar.

   • Eight square handles surround the text block, just as they do when you create artistic text. You also see little tabs on the top and bottom of the text block. The tabs are used to flow text between multiple text blocks, as discussed later in this chapter.

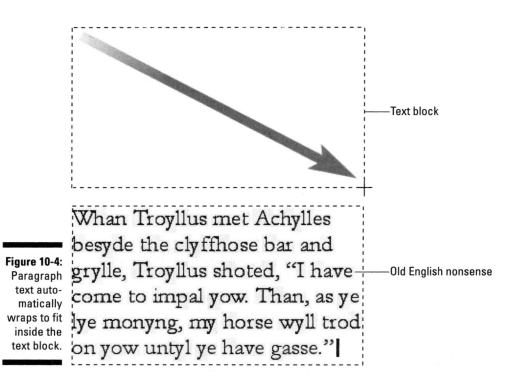

————Text block

Figure 10-4:
Paragraph
text auto-
matically
wraps to fit
inside the
text block.

Whan Troyllus met Achylles
besyde the clyffhose bar and
grylle, Troyllus shoted, "I have————Old English nonsense
come to impal yow. Than, as ye
lye monyng, my horse wyll trod
on yow untyl ye have gasse."

Some of the stuff that I say about artistic text applies to paragraph text as well. For example, you can add more characters to a block of paragraph text by clicking inside the text block with the text tool and then typing away. You can move a selected block of paragraph text to a new location by dragging it with the arrow tool, by pressing one or two arrow keys, or by using the property bar controls.

You can move or scale paragraph text by pausing while typing to display the bounding box. Then you can drag the selection handles or center X marker with the text tool.

But a few operations work differently:

 ✔ Dragging a corner handle scales the text block but not the text inside it. CorelDraw reflows the text to fit inside the new text block borders, as demonstrated in Figure 10-5. You can also use the property bar's size and scale controls to resize the text block.

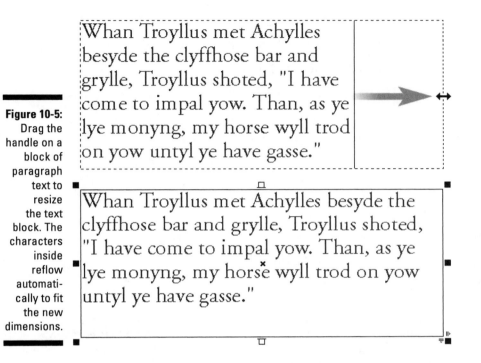

Figure 10-5:
Drag the handle on a block of paragraph text to resize the text block. The characters inside reflow automatically to fit the new dimensions.

✔ To resize the text block and also the text inside, Alt+drag a corner handle of the text block.

✔ Normally, the text block remains the same size regardless of how much text you type. If you type more characters than the text block can hold, CorelDraw hides the extra text from view. To display it, just enlarge the text block by dragging one of the handles with the arrow tool.

✔ If you want the text block to automatically grow or shrink to accommodate your text as you type, press Ctrl+J or choose Tools⇨Options to display the Options dialog box. Double-click on Text, click on Paragraph, and turn on the check box titled Expand and Shrink Paragraph Text Frames to Fit Text. Note that if you turn on the option, CorelDraw doesn't let you reduce the overall capacity of the text box. For example, if you drag a side handle to make the text box narrower, CorelDraw automatically increases the height of the text box so that all the characters still fit inside the box.

✔ Click on the text block with the arrow tool to display the rotate and skew handles, which work the same way for any object. You can also use the property bar's rotation angle control to rotate the text block.

✔ Rotating a paragraph text block rotates the characters inside, just as when you're rotating a block of artistic text. But skewing a paragraph text block slants the text block only, as shown in Figure 10-6. The characters remain upright and flow to fill the borders of the text block.

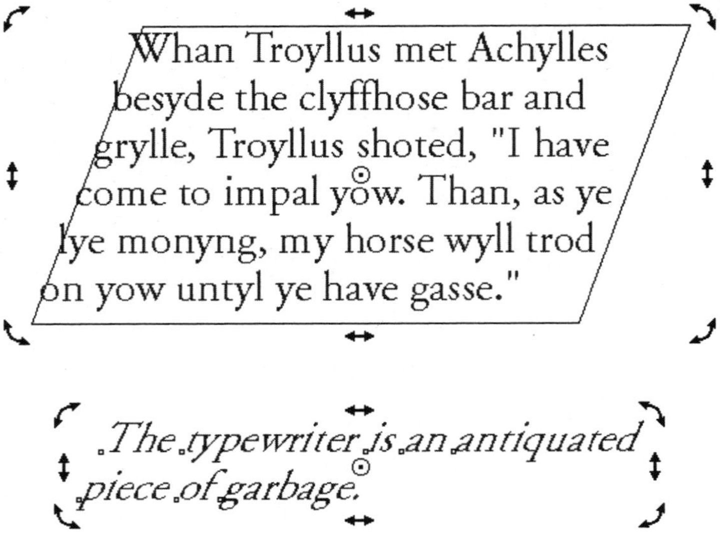

Whan Troyllus met Achylles besyde the clyffhose bar and grylle, Troyllus shoted, "I have come to impal yŏw. Than, as ye lye monyng, my horse wyll trod on yow untyl ye have gasse."

.The.typewriter.is.an.antiquated piece.of.garbage.

Figure 10-6:
Skewed
paragraph
text (top)
compared
with
skewed
artistic text
(bottom).

A single paragraph can contain no more than 4,000 characters, which is roughly the equivalent of two pages in this book with no figures. Okay, so maybe George Bernard Shaw would have had problems with this limitation. He and William Faulkner could have moaned about it endlessly in 10,000-character postcards to each other. But I don't think that you'll have any problems.

Press Ctrl+Shift+T or choose Text⇨Edit Text to edit your text in a separate text editing window. You may find this option helpful if you're working on a particularly long section of text, like that 4,000-character postcard you're sending to George and William. After you make your edits, click on OK to close the text editing window. Your changes are automatically reflected in the drawing window.

Navigating among the letters

Whether you're working with artistic or paragraph text, you can specify the location of the insertion marker inside the text by clicking in the text block with the text tool. After you position the insertion marker, you can move it around by using any of the following techniques:

✔ Press the left- or right-arrow key to move the insertion marker in one-character increments. Press the up- or down-arrow key to move from one line of type to the next.

✔ To move in whole-word increments, press Ctrl plus the left- or right-arrow key.

What's that red squiggly line?

When the text tool is selected, red squiggly lines appear underneath words that CorelDraw believes to be misspelled. The line is the CorelDraw way of saying, "Hey, bonehead, better think again!" You can either look up the word in the dictionary and correct it on your own, or right-click on the word to display a list of alternative spellings. Click on the alternate spelling you want to use or click on Ignore All to make CorelDraw leave you alone. The squiggly line changes from red to blue to show that you've inspected the word.

If you don't want CorelDraw to invade your text with its squiggly lines, press Ctrl+J or choose Tools⇨Options to open the Options dialog box. Double-click on Text, click on Spelling, and turn off the Perform Automatic Spell Checking option. Or, if you want CorelDraw to perform automatic spell checking but you don't want to see blue squiggly lines for words that you asked CorelDraw to ignore, leave the Perform Automatic Spell Checking option turned on but turn off the Show Errors Which Have Been Ignored option box.

✒ Press Ctrl and the up-arrow key to move to the beginning of the current paragraph. Press Ctrl and the down-arrow key to move to the end of the paragraph.

✒ Press the Home key to move the insertion marker to the beginning of the current line. Press End to move to the end of it.

✒ Ctrl+Home moves the insertion marker to the beginning of the current text block. Ctrl+End moves you to the end of the text block.

How to Flow Text between Blocks

As I discuss earlier in this chapter, when you enter long passages of paragraph text, the text may exceed the boundaries of the text block. Every character you enter still exists; you just can't see it. To view the hidden text, you can reduce the size of the characters so that they fit better, as I describe later in this chapter; enlarge the text block, as I describe earlier; or pour the text into a new text block.

That's right, you can pour excess text from one text block into another as if it were liquid. Here's how it works:

1. **Drag to create a paragraph text block with the text tool.**

2. **Enter far too much text.**

   Type in every page of *Beowulf.* This is your chance to bone up on classical literature.

REMEMBER

Make sure that the Expand and Shrink Paragraph Text Frames to Fit Text check box is turned off on the Paragraph panel of the Options dialog box (Ctrl+J). Otherwise, your text block grows as you add text, which prevents you from entering more text than your text block can hold.

3. Select the arrow tool.

Much of the text you entered should not be visible on-screen.

4. Click on the top or bottom handle of the text block.

These handles are called *tabs*. The top tab is empty, to show that the text starts here. The bottom tab has a little arrowhead in it to show that there's a bunch of overflow text that doesn't fit inside the text block. You can click on the top tab to pour lines from the beginning of the text block into a new text block. (Lines from the end of the text block shift up to fill the space left behind.) Or you can click on the bottom tab to pour the hidden lines of text into the new text block. In either case, after you click on a tab, your cursor changes to a page icon, as in Figure 10-7.

5. Drag to create a second text block.

Figure 10-7 demonstrates this process. CorelDraw then automatically pours lines of text originally entered into the first text block into this new text block, as shown in Figure 10-8.

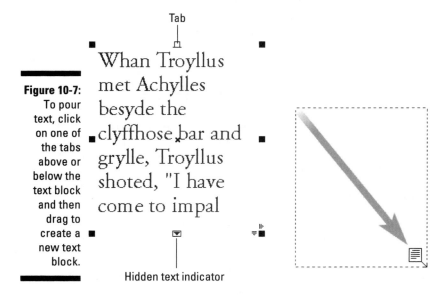

Figure 10-7: To pour text, click on one of the tabs above or below the text block and then drag to create a new text block.

Tab

Whan Troyllus met Achylles besyde the clyffhose bar and grylle, Troyllus shoted, "I have come to impal

Hidden text indicator

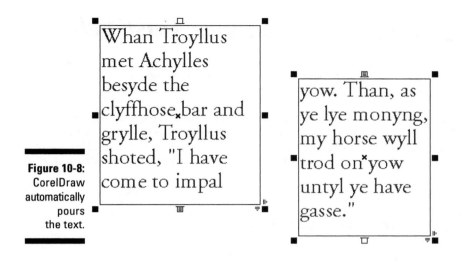

Notice that three tiny lines appear inside the bottom tab on the first text block and the top tab on the second. The lines indicate a link between the two text blocks.

To experiment with the link, keep stepping:

6. Drag up on the bottom tab on the first text block.

This step leaves less room in the first text block for the text. The overflow text automatically pours into the second text block.

7. Press Delete.

CorelDraw deletes the first text block (assuming that the first text block is still selected), but it does not delete the text inside the text block. Instead, the text pours into the second text block.

Pretty keen, huh? As long as at least one text block in the link remains in your drawing, the text remains intact. Now, if you were to delete the second text block, CorelDraw would indeed delete the text because there is no longer any place for the text to go.

When you click on a linked text block with the text tool, CorelDraw displays a dotted marquee around all the text blocks in the link and connects them with a skinny arrow. If you click on a linked text block with the arrow tool, you see the selection handles and tab around only the text block you click on.

You can pour text between as many text blocks as you like. Okay, I bet there's some maximum, such as 32 or 256, but who cares? You'd be a nut to want to pour between that many text blocks! You can pour your text even across multiple pages. (I discuss multiple-page documents in Chapter 12.)

Before You Can Format, You Must Select

To change the appearance of characters in a text block, you assign formatting attributes such as typeface, style, size, and a few others I get to later. But before you can do so, you have to select the text.

You can select text in two ways in CorelDraw. You can click on the text block with the arrow tool, in which case any formatting changes will affect all characters inside the text block. Or you can highlight individual characters and words with the text tool. Your changes then affect only the selected characters.

Selecting with the text tool

Using the text tool is the preferred method for selecting text because it enables you to make selective changes. For example, you can make a single word bold or a passage of text italic. By contrast, if you select text with the arrow tool, any formatting changes you make apply to the entire text block. The following items explain how to use the text tool to select type in any kind of text block:

✔ Drag over the characters you want to select. To show that the characters are selected, CorelDraw highlights the characters by setting them against a gray background. Generally, you use this technique to select type within a single text block. However, you can drag across type in linked text blocks, as demonstrated in Figure 10-9.

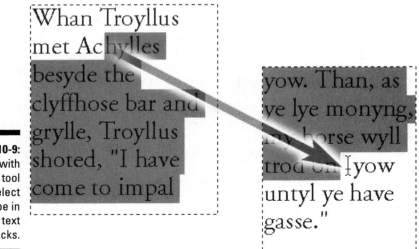

Figure 10-9: Drag with the text tool to select type in linked text blocks.

✔ Double-click on a word to select the word.

✔ Ctrl+click on a word to select the entire sentence.

✔ Click to set the insertion marker at one end of the text that you want to select. Then Shift+click at the other end of the desired selection. CorelDraw selects all text between the click and Shift+click. For example, to select the highlighted text in Figure 10-9, I could have clicked between the *c* and *h* in *Achylles* and then Shift+clicked between the words *on* and *yow* in the second text block.

✔ Press the Shift key in tandem with the left- or right-arrow key to select one character at a time. Press Shift key plus the up- or down-arrow key to select entire lines.

✔ Press Shift and Ctrl along with the left- or right-arrow key to select whole words at a time.

Converting from artistic to paragraph and vice versa

What do you do when you create a block of artistic or paragraph text, but then realize you made the wrong choice? No problem. You can easily convert one variety of text to the other.

An easy way to change from one text type to the other is to select the text block with the arrow tool and then click on the Convert Text button on the property bar, labeled in Figure 10-10. As with other controls on the right end of the property bar, the Convert Text button is hidden if you use the 640-x-480 display setting for your monitor. To reveal the button, drag the property bar into the drawing window, as in Figure 10-10.

CorelDraw 8 offers another quick and easy way to convert text. Simply right-click on the text you want to convert and choose Convert To Artistic Text or Convert To Paragraph Text from the pop-up menu that appears.

Figure 10-10:
Click on the
Convert
Text button
to toggle
between
artistic and
paragraph
text.

Convert Text button

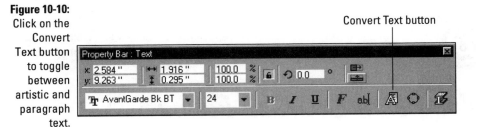

The Convert Text button is unavailable when a paragraph text block is too small for all your text to be displayed. To access the button, enlarge the text block to fit the text. Also, you can't use the Convert Text button to convert paragraph text that you poured into more than one text block. Nor can you convert multiple text blocks, artistic or paragraph, at a time.

If you prefer, you can convert your text by choosing Text⇨Convert to Artistic Text or Text⇨Convert to Paragraph Text. (The command name changes depending on the type of text block that's selected.) As with the Convert Text button, the command is unavailable if text isn't completely visible in the text block or is contained in multiple text blocks.

You can also use the Clipboard to convert paragraph text contained in multiple text blocks to artistic text. To convert paragraph text to artistic text, follow these steps:

1. **With the text tool, select the text you want to convert.**

2. **Press Ctrl+C (or choose Edit⇨Copy).**

   CorelDraw copies the text to the Clipboard.

3. **Click somewhere inside the drawing.**

   Just don't click inside a paragraph text block. CorelDraw creates a new artistic text block.

4. **Press Ctrl+V (or choose Edit⇨Paste).**

   CorelDraw pastes the text into the artistic text block. Now you can perform all those amazing special effects that are applicable only to artistic text, as I explain in Chapter 11.

   Notice that any line breaks that existed in your paragraph text remain in the new artistic text block. But you can remove them by clicking at the spot where the line break occurs and pressing Delete.

You say that you don't want artistic text? You want to be able to create long passages that flow between multiple, linked text blocks? Well then, to convert artistic text to paragraph text, take the same steps, but in Step 3, drag to create a paragraph text block or click inside an existing paragraph text block.

Not sure which type of text you're looking at? Select the text and then check the status bar, which indicates whether the text is artistic or paragraph text.

Okay, Now You Can Format

After you select some text, whether it be paragraph or artistic, you can assign formatting attributes. Now, a lot of folks change the typeface and other stuff by using the Format Text dialog box, which you get to by pressing Ctrl+T or choosing Text⇨Format Text. But for simple formatting chores, using the property bar or the Object Properties docker, both shown in Figure 10-11, is quicker. (Note that in Figure 10-11, I dragged the property bar into the drawing window to convert it to a floating window so that all the buttons are visible at the lowest monitor display resolution, 640 x 480.)

To display the Object Properties docker, select the text you want to format and press Alt+Enter. Or choose View⇨Dockers⇨Object Properties — or right-click on the text and select Properties from the pop-up menu that appears. The Text panel of the docker, shown in Figure 10-11, appears automatically.

If you select paragraph text, the Object Properties docker contains one additional option not shown in Figure 10-11: the Range pop-up menu. This option controls how formatting is applied to text in linked, paragraph text blocks. You can specify whether you want the formatting applied to all linked blocks, only the selected block, or the selected block and the subsequent linked block.

Using either the property bar or the Object Properties docker, you can change the typeface, type style, type size, and justification. I describe each of these formatting attributes in the following sections.

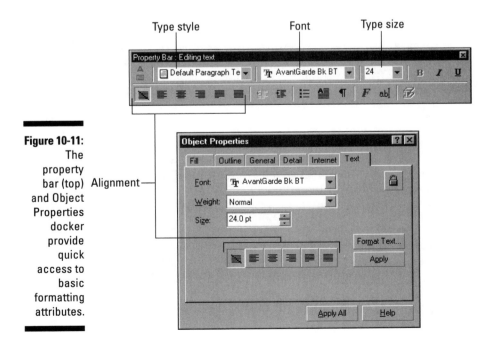

Figure 10-11:
The property bar (top) and Object Properties docker provide quick access to basic formatting attributes.

To display the property bar controls, shown in Figure 10-11, click inside the text block with the text tool. If you select the text block with the arrow tool, the property bar changes, but the font and size buttons are still available.

Remember that when you select the text block with the arrow tool, your changes affect all text in the text block. If you use the text tool, your changes affect the selected text in the text block only. The same holds true for changes that you make by using the Object Properties docker.

To change the default settings used by the text tool, make sure that no objects are selected and then press Ctrl+T or choose Te̲xt⇨F̲ormat Text. You then see the Format Text dialog box, where you can change the settings for everything from font to character spacing. After you change your settings, click on OK. CorelDraw asks you to specify whether you want the new settings to apply to paragraph or artistic text. Select the appropriate check box and press Enter.

Selecting a typeface

Changing the typeface is your number-one method for controlling the appearance of your text. Just in case you're wondering what I'm talking about, a *typeface* is a uniquely stylized alphabet. The idea is that the *letters* in one typeface look different from the *letters* in another typeface.

Some folks refer to typefaces as *fonts.* Back in the old days — up until as recently as 20 years ago — each letter was printed using a separate chunk of metal, and all the pieces of metal for one typeface were stored in a container called a *font.* (This use of the word, incidentally, is based on the French word *fonte,* which means a *casting,* as in type casting. It has nothing to do with the baptismal font — you know, one of those basins that holds holy water — which is based on the Latin word *fontis,* which means *spring.* Dang, this is interesting stuff!)

CorelDraw includes on CD-ROM about 50 quintillion fonts that you can install into Windows. You can also use any PostScript or TrueType font you've installed into Windows. If you don't know what PostScript and TrueType are, read the upcoming Technical Stuff sidebar, "The typface rivalry that isn't worth knowing about," or, better yet, don't worry about it.

To change the font of the selected text, select a typeface from the Font pop-up menu on the property bar or in the Object Properties docker. If you want to see what a typeface looks like before you apply it, do this:

Typeface preview box

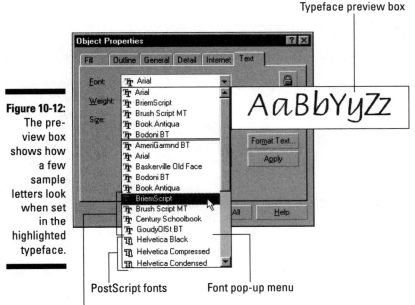

Figure 10-12: The preview box shows how a few sample letters look when set in the highlighted typeface.

TrueType fonts

PostScript fonts

Font pop-up menu

1. **Click on the name of the typeface in either the property bar or docker.**

   Or click on the down-pointing arrowhead to the right of the typeface name. The pop-up menu appears. CorelDraw also displays a preview box to the side of the pop-up menu, as shown in Figure 10-12.

2. **Move the cursor or press the down- and up-arrow keys to scroll through the list.**

   CorelDraw updates the preview box to show the selected typeface. If text is selected in your drawing, the actual text appears in the preview box.

Changing the type style

Most typefaces offer four type styles: plain, italic, bold, and bold italic. You can assign one of these styles by selecting the B or I button on the property bar. (You can also click on the U button to underline the text.) Or select an option from the Weight pop-up menu in the Object Properties docker and click on the Apply button.

The typeface rivalry that isn't worth knowing about

You may not associate something as fundamental as font technology with a brand name, but the truth is, everything has a brand name. *Billy Joel* is a registered trademark, for crying out loud. So if your last name is Joel, don't even *think* about naming your kid Billy.

Anyway, the two big brands in the world of digital typography are PostScript and TrueType. The PostScript font format was developed by Adobe Systems (the folks who created the well-known image-editing program Photoshop) and is the professional printing standard. Hewlett-Packard and several other printer manufacturers offer support for PostScript, as do all major brands of typesetters and other mega-expensive gadgets. Adobe also sells a Windows font manager called ATM (Adobe Type Manager) that lets you print PostScript fonts on non-PostScript printers.

Microsoft and Apple were sick of Adobe's having this monopoly in the font market. So they got together and codeveloped the TrueType font format. At the time, such a partnership seemed about as likely as the United States and Russia joining forces right after the Bay of Pigs to organize a worldwide polo tournament.

But they pulled it off, and Microsoft has amassed its 17th fortune selling TrueType fonts to eager consumers. Windows 95 offers built-in support for TrueType and can print TrueType fonts to nearly any model of printer. TrueType has been such a success, in fact, that Corel converted its entire 50-quintillion font library to the TrueType format.

Windows 95 even shows you which kind of font you're about to apply. Two *T*s before a typeface name in one of the font pop-up menus identify a TrueType font. An outlined T1 identifies a PostScript font. (T1 is short for Type 1, which is a PostScript font variation.) Take a look at Figure 10-12 to see these identifying marks.

Enlarging or reducing the type size

As I discuss in Chapter 7, line widths are measured in *points,* with one point equal to $1/72$ of an inch. Type is also measured in points. After all, type is generally pretty dinky. Even monster-big headlines in supermarket tabloids — you know, "Bigfoot Spotted Buying Cheezy-Poofs at a Wyoming 7-Eleven" or "Aliens Ate My Sweetheart, Then Complained about Taste" — don't get much bigger than an inch tall. For this reason, points are an ideal and time-honored unit of measure among typographers, layout artists, and others who do their best to try to attract your attention to the written word.

Type is measured from the bottommost point on a lowercase *g* to the tippy-topmost peak of a lowercase *b*. (Lowercase letters such as *b, d, k,* and others are generally taller than capital letters.) If you're familiar with type-writer terminology, it might help to know that elite type is 10 points tall — roughly the size of the type you're currently reading — whereas pica type is 12 points tall. You can adjust type sizes in the following ways:

✔ To change the type size, select an option from the type size pop-up menu on the property bar (labeled in Figure 10-11). Or double-click on the pop-up menu, enter any value between 0 (far too small) and 3,000 points (42 inches!) from the keyboard, and then press Enter.

✔ You can enter a value also in the Size option box in the Object Properties docker. Click on Apply to see how the text looks in its new size.

✔ If you prefer to use inches or some other nontraditional unit of measure for your type, you can choose a different unit from the Default Text Units pop-up menu on the Text panel of the Options dialog box. (Press Ctrl+J to open the dialog box.)

Mucking about with the justification

The row of buttons at the bottom of the Text panel of the Object Properties docker and the matching buttons on the property bar control the alignment of the lines of type in a text block. Text alignment is sometimes called *justification* — as in, "We need no justification to call this attribute what we please." Starting with the leftmost button in the dialog box and on the property bar and moving to the right, the alignment buttons (labeled in Figure 10-11) work as follows:

✔ The No Alignment button doesn't do much of anything. I know, that's a terrible thing to say, but it's true. Usually, this option produces the same effect as the Left Alignment button, discussed next. But when you get into the more complicated techniques described in the next chapter, the No Alignment option can wreak havoc on your text. The technical support guy I talked to claimed that he's never received a call about this option in his career. So not only does it not work, nobody cares about it. Good feature.

✔ The Left Alignment button aligns the left sides of all lines of text in a text block. The text in this book, for example, is left justified.

✔ The Center Alignment button centers all lines of type within the text block.

✔ The Right Alignment button aligns the right sides of all lines of text.

✔ The Full Alignment button aligns both the left and right sides of the text. As you can see in the last example of Figure 10-13, CorelDraw has to increase the horizontal space between characters and words to make this happen.

✔ Click on the Forced Full Alignment button to align the left and right edges of all lines of type, including the last line. This option is useful for stretching out a single line of text across the full width of a text block.

Figure 10-13 shows the results of applying the left, center, right, and full justification options. The gray areas in back of the text represent the text blocks.

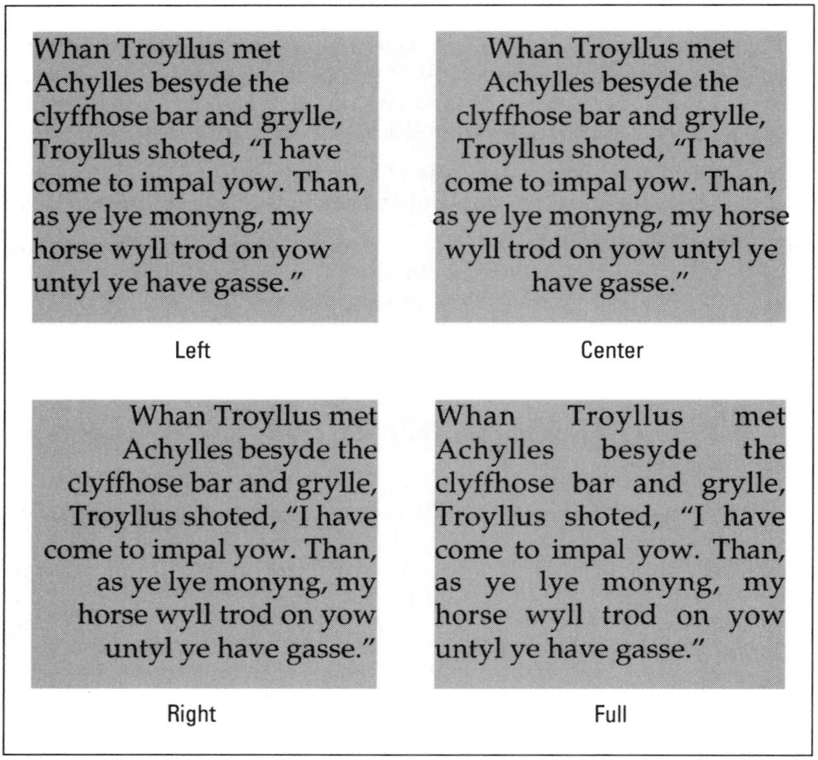

Whan Troyllus met Achylles besyde the clyffhose bar and grylle, Troyllus shoted, "I have come to impal yow. Than, as ye lye monyng, my horse wyll trod on yow untyl ye have gasse."

Left

Whan Troyllus met Achylles besyde the clyffhose bar and grylle, Troyllus shoted, "I have come to impal yow. Than, as ye lye monyng, my horse wyll trod on yow untyl ye have gasse."

Center

Whan Troyllus met Achylles besyde the clyffhose bar and grylle, Troyllus shoted, "I have come to impal yow. Than, as ye lye monyng, my horse wyll trod on yow untyl ye have gasse."

Right

Whan Troyllus met Achylles besyde the clyffhose bar and grylle, Troyllus shoted, "I have come to impal yow. Than, as ye lye monyng, my horse wyll trod on yow untyl ye have gasse."

Full

Figure 10-13: The primary justification buttons offered by CorelDraw.

When applied to artistic text, the justification options change the location of the text block on the page. If you select the Right Alignment button, for example, the right side of the text block scoots over to where the left side of the text block used to be.

Formatting options for rare occasions

In addition to those formatting attributes discussed earlier in this chapter, CorelDraw offers a mess of other formatting options that you may find interesting depending on, well, your level of interest. You can access these options by clicking on the Format Text button on the property bar (the button sports a big letter *F*), selecting the Format Text button in the Object Properties docker, or just pressing Ctrl+T. CorelDraw displays the Format Text dialog box, shown in Figure 10-14.

The dialog box changes depending on whether you select paragraph or artistic text. For artistic text, you see only the Font, Space, and Align tabs, and some Space options available for paragraph text run away and hide, too.

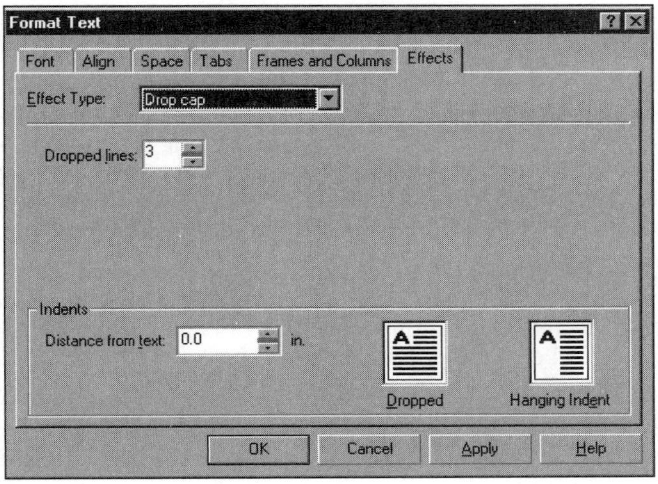

Figure 10-14:
Formatting
a drop
cap in
paragraph
text is
among the
formatting
tasks
you can
accomplish
in the
Format Text
dialog box.

Here are some options you may want to explore:

- ✔ In the Font tab of the dialog box, you can apply underlines and other kinds of lines to selected characters of text, create superscript or subscript type, or convert characters to all capital letters or small caps (capital letters).

- ✔ The Align tab offers alignment and indents options. The alignment options are the same as those available on the property bar and on the Text panel of the Object Properties docker. Use the indents options to position, that's right, indents.

- ✔ The Space tab contains options that enable you to change the amount of horizontal space between neighboring letters and words. You can also change the amount of vertical space between lines of type. Luckily, you can more conveniently change spacing by using the shape tool, as I discuss in the next chapter. As I mention earlier, you have more spacing options for paragraph text than for artistic text.

    The only unique option in the Space tab is the Use Automatic Hyphenation check box. Select this option, and CorelDraw automatically hyphenates long words so that they better fill the width of a text block.

- ✔ Switch to the Tabs panel to display an overwhelming assortment of options for positioning tabs. You can use these options in combination with indents (available on the Align tab) to create a table of information — for example, a price list.

- ✔ Click on the Frames and Columns tab to uncover options to divide the text in the active text block into multiple columns. Better yet, don't. Believe me, these options are more work than they're worth. Creating your own columns by drawing blocks of text is easier, as explained in the section "How to Flow Text between Blocks," earlier in this chapter.

(By the way, the term *frames* in this instance refers to good old paragraph text blocks, not the kind of page-dividing frames that some designers use in their World Wide Web pages.)

✔ One option on the Frames and Columns panel that may come in handy is the Vertical Justification pop-up menu. Using the options on the menu, you can center your text vertically in the text block, spread out all lines of text so that they fill up the text block (the Full option), or align your text to the top or the bottom of the text block.

✔ Switch to the Effects tab to add a symbol to the beginning of a paragraph, which is useful for adding fancy bullets to the beginning of paragraphs in lists (like this one). You can also format a character as a drop cap, as I explain in the next section.

Dropping your caps

Flip back to the first page of this chapter. Notice how the first character in the first paragraph is bigger than all the others and drops down into the second line of text? That oversized character is called a *drop cap,* and you can add one to your paragraph text in CorelDraw. Here's how:

1. **Select the letter you want to format as a drop cap.**

2. **Open the Format Text dialog box.**

   You can accomplish this feat of engineering in a snap by clicking on the blue italic *F* button on the property bar or by pressing Ctrl+T.

3. **Click on the Effects tab and select Drop Cap from the Effect Type pop-up menu.**

   The drop cap options reveal themselves, as shown in Figure 10-14.

4. **In the Dropped Lines option box, specify how many lines of text you want the drop cap to sink into.**

5. **In the Distance from Text option box, specify how far you want to shift the drop cap from the neighboring characters.**

   You'll probably need to play with this setting a bit to figure out the value that works best for the font and type size you're using.

6. **Under Placement, click on the icon for the design you want to use.**

   The two Placement options determine whether your drop cap appears within the normal paragraph margins or hangs out over the left margin all by itself, as shown in the two placement icons.

7. **Click on OK.**

   CorelDraw automatically resizes your selected character and formats the character according to the drop cap options you selected.

Think that drop cap looks silly? Your first instinct may be to simply select and delete the character to get rid of it. But when you do, CorelDraw just shoves the next character in the line of text over and formats that character as a drop cap. To temporarily turn off drop cap formatting, click on the Show/Hide Drop Cap button on the property bar, which looks just like the first drop cap placement icon in the Format Text dialog box. Click on the button again to bring the drop cap back.

To remove drop cap formatting from the text block entirely, select the character and then select (none) from the Effect Type pop-up menu on the Effects tab of the Format Text dialog box.

Please Check Your Spelling

Although CorelDraw isn't a word processor, it can help you correct your spelling. It knows you don't want to look stupid because you can't spell *leptodactylous* (which, by the way, means that you have slender toes). Okay, so it doesn't know how to spell leptodactylous any better than you do. But it does know several thousand common words, and you can teach it to spell leptodactylous if you so desire.

Here's how to check the spelling of your document:

1. **Choose Text⇨Writing Tools⇨Spell Check.**

   Or right-click on a text block with the text tool and select Spell Check from the pop-up menu. Or better still, just press Ctrl+F12.

   Whichever method you use, CorelDraw begins checking the words in your document. When it comes to the first bad word, it displays the Spell Checker dialog box, shown in Figure 10-15. The misspelled word appears selected inside the Not Found option box. The Replace With option box shows the best guess CorelDraw can make at the proper spelling. The Replacements scrolling list contains other alternatives. In Figure 10-15, Draw suggested such humorless replacements for *Whan* as *What* and *When,* along with such curious options as *Than, Tan,* and *Han.*

Figure 10-15: CorelDraw doesn't appreciate my Old English spelling.

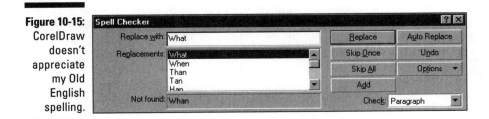

2. **Select an alternative spelling or enter a new one.**

   If the word in the Replace With option box doesn't strike your fancy, you can click on an alternative in the scrolling list. Or enter an entirely new spelling in the Replace With option box.

3. **Click on Replace.**

   CorelDraw replaces the misspelled word with the correct version and sets about searching for the next misspelling.

4. **Repeat Steps 2 and 3.**

   Keep checking words until CorelDraw announces that the spell check is complete. Click on the Yes button to close the Spell Checker dialog box.

If you're an alert reader, you may have noticed that the Spell Checker dialog box contains some buttons that I don't address in the previous steps. Not to worry — those options are described in the following list:

✔ What if CorelDraw flags a word as misspelled, but you want the word to appear just as it is? Take my Old English text, for example. It's 100 percent historically authentic, guaranteed by Lloyd's of London. Yet CorelDraw questions nearly every word. Just goes to show you how much things have changed since the 15th century, or whenever it was that I wrote the text. Sometimes, you have to teach CorelDraw how to spell. If your word is spelled correctly, you can add it to the dictionary by clicking on the Add button.

✔ If you don't want to correct a word and you don't want to add it to the dictionary — you just want CorelDraw to skip the word and continue checking the rest of the text — click on the Skip Once button.

✔ To make CorelDraw ignore all occurrences of a word throughout the current spelling session, click on the Skip All button.

✔ The Auto Replace button is a dangerous one. Click on this button, and you tell CorelDraw to replace the misspelled word automatically in this and all future documents you spell check — without notifying you. If you want to use this option, be sure to select the Prompt Before Auto Replacement option from the Options pop-up menu in the Spell Checker dialog box so that you can see all the changes that CorelDraw is making.

✔ Select the portion of your document that you want to spell check from the Check pop-up menu. Your choices vary depending on what type of text is selected, but in general, you can check a specific portion of your text — a paragraph, a sentence, a word, or selected text — or check the entire document.

Shortcut to Typographic Happiness

You can train CorelDraw to correct your most egregious errors as you make them — without ever once bringing up the Spell Checker dialog box. To use this feature, choose Te<u>x</u>t⇨<u>W</u>riting Tools⇨Typ<u>e</u> Assist, which displays the Type Assist panel of the Options dialog box, as shown in Figure 10-16. (Or press Ctrl+J, double-click on Text, and click on Type Assist.) The five significant options in this dialog box work as follows:

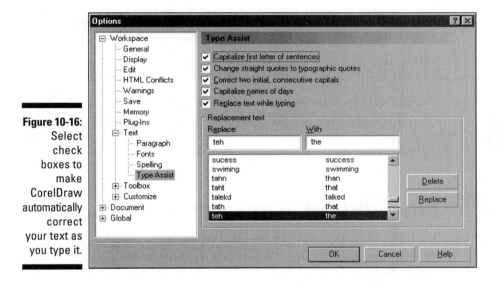

Figure 10-16: Select check boxes to make CorelDraw automatically correct your text as you type it.

✔ Select the first check box to automatically capitalize any word that follows a period, even if you enter the letter without pressing Shift. I heartily recommend this option.

✔ In the world of professional typography, quotation marks curl around the text. But when you enter a quotation mark from your keyboard, you get two boring, straight lines. Those lines aren't quotation marks, they're ditto marks. To turn your dreadful dittos into beautiful quotation marks, select the second check box.

✔ Select the third check box to correct any two capital letters in a row. For example, *THe* would become *The.*

✔ If you forget to capitalize the names of days, select the fourth option. Too bad it doesn't correct the names of months and other proper nouns as well.

✔ The last check box — Replace Text While Typing — replaces abbreviations with spelled-out words. If you type *cont.,* for example, CorelDraw replaces it with *continue.* If you type *3/4,* CorelDraw replaces it with the proper fraction symbol, $^3/_4$.

If you don't like the way CorelDraw replaces abbreviations — you may prefer that it swap *cont.* with *continued,* for example — select an abbreviation from the scrolling list, modify the word in the With option box, and click on the Replace button.

✔ You can remove entries from the scrolling list to make CorelDraw stop replacing certain words or characters you type. For example, if you find it annoying that CorelDraw changes *div.* to *division,* click on the *div.* entry in the scrolling list and click on Delete.

✔ You can also make Type Assist correct your spelling. Suppose that you constantly misspell the word *the* as *teh.* Just enter *teh* into the Replace option box, enter *the* into the With option box, and click on the Replace button. From then on, CorelDraw corrects your spelling of *teh* on the fly.

If you frequently type the same long string of text, use Type Assist to speed up text entry. For example, you can tell CorelDraw to replace the characters *CD8* with *CorelDRAW 8 For Dummies.*

A Different Kind of Alphabet

The only kind of text I haven't yet described is text consisting of symbols. Choose View➪Dockers➪Symbols or press Ctrl+F11 to display the Symbols docker shown in Figure 10-17. This roll-up offers access to a variety of simple pictures you can use to accent or enhance a drawing. You can even combine symbols to create drawings in and of themselves.

"Little pictures?" you're probably thinking. "Wait a minute. Pictures don't constitute text. What's going on here?" Hey, take it easy. Your problem is that you're used to a Western-style alphabet, in which abstract letters stand for sounds — the same way a dollar bill stands for a piece of gold approximately the size of a single-celled microorganism. Letters are merely metaphors for real communication.

But try thinking Eastern. Think hieroglyphics. Think kanji. These are bazillion-character alphabets in which each character represents a word or a phrase. Similarly, the CorelDraw symbol library is a big alphabet. If you want to say "chair," for example, show a chair.

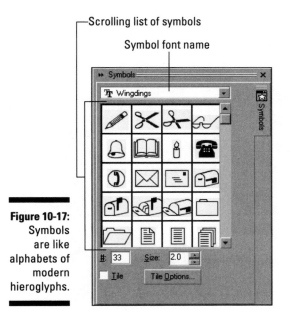

Scrolling list of symbols

Symbol font name

Figure 10-17:
Symbols
are like
alphabets of
modern
hieroglyphs.

To add a symbol from the Symbols docker to your drawing, do the following:

1. **Select a symbol category from the pop-up menu at the top of the docker.**

   The categories are actually fonts that CorelDraw recognizes as containing something other than standard letters, numbers, and punctuation.

2. **Select a symbol from the scrolling list.**

   CorelDraw shows you every single wacky character in the font.

3. **Enter the size of the symbol in the Size option box.**

   Or just use the default Size value. You can always resize the symbol later by dragging its selection handles, as you can any other object.

   Keep in mind that just as with letters in the alphabet, not all symbols in a font are the same height. The Size value is gauged by the tallest symbol in the category.

4. **Drag the symbol into the drawing area.**

   No need to mess around with the Tile option. It just repeats the symbol over and over inside a portion of your drawing, like some dreadful electronic wallpaper.

You can edit symbols in the same way that you edit free-form paths, as described in Chapter 5. You can also fill and outline symbols as described in Chapter 7, duplicate symbols as described in Chapter 8, and transform symbols as discussed in Chapter 9. Come to think of it, symbols may be drawings after all.

Chapter 11
Mr. Typographer's Wild Ride

● ●

In This Chapter

▶ Why CorelDraw is better than Disneyland

▶ Dragging characters to new locations

▶ Kerning special character combinations

▶ Changing the amount of space between characters and lines

▶ Fitting text to a path

▶ Changing character orientation and vertical and horizontal alignment

▶ Wrapping text around a circle

▶ Converting character outlines to editable paths

▶ Making characters zigzag

● ●

*1*magine that you're a character of text. An *H,* for example. Or a *P.* So far, your CorelDraw existence has been about as exciting as a traffic jam. Sometimes you wrap to the next line of type, and other times you get poured into a different text block. Characters are above and below you; you even have a few riding your rear end. It's no fun being a character in a standard text block.

But one day, you rub shoulders with a streetwise character, like an *E* or an *S* — you know, some character that really gets around — and it tells you about a world of possibilities you haven't yet explored. You can play bumper cars, ride loop-de-loop roller coasters, even stretch yourself into completely different shapes. It's one big amusement park for text!

This chapter is your golden admission ticket. Have a blast.

Learning the Rules of the Park

Before I stamp your hand and let you into the park, a word of caution is in order. Just as too many rides on the Tilt-a-Whirl can make you hurl, too many wild effects can leave a block of text looking bent out of shape. The trick is to apply text effects conservatively and creatively.

If you're not sure how an effect will go over, show it to a few friends. Ask them to read your text. If they read it easily and hand the page back to you, you know you hit the mark. If they say, "How did you make this?" the effect may be a little overly dramatic, but it's probably still acceptable. If they have trouble reading the text, or if they say "How did you *make* this?" — in the same way that they might say "What did I just *step* in?" — your effect very likely overwhelms the page and is therefore unacceptable.

Then again, I don't want to dampen your spirit of enthusiasm and exploration. Use moderation in all things, including moderation, right? So you make yourself sick on the Tilt-a-Whirl. It's part of growing up. So your first few pages look like run-amuck advertisements for furniture warehouses. It's part of learning the craft.

And if some blue-blood designer looks at your work and exclaims, "Gad, this page! Oh, how it frightens me!" you can retort, "Well, at least my text has more fun than yours." That's one way to get fired, anyway.

Playing Bumper Cars

As I explain in other chapters, you can drag an object's nodes and handles with the shape tool. Well, this basic functionality of the shape tool permeates all facets of CorelDraw, including text. If you select the shape tool (press F10) and click on a text block, you see three new varieties of nodes and handles, as shown in Figure 11-1. These nodes and handles appear whether you click on a block of artistic text or paragraph text. They enable you to change the location of individual characters and increase or decrease the amount of space between characters and lines of text.

Text nodes

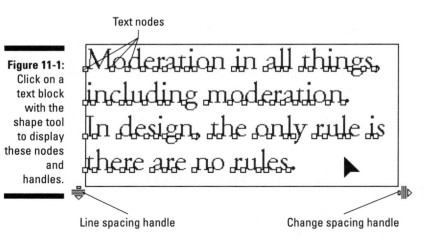

Figure 11-1:
Click on a
text block
with the
shape tool
to display
these nodes
and
handles.

Line spacing handle   Change spacing handle

Selecting and dragging text nodes

Text nodes enable you to change the locations of individual characters in a text block. You can slightly nudge the characters to adjust the amount of horizontal spacing, or you can drag a character several inches away from its text block just to show it who's boss. The following explains how text nodes work:

- ✔ Each text node is associated with the character directly on its right. Click on a node to select it and its character. Black nodes are selected; white nodes are not.

- ✔ To select multiple nodes at a time, drag with the Shape tool to draw a marquee (dotted outline) around the nodes. You can also Shift+click on a text node to add it to the selection.

- ✔ If you select a few too many nodes in the process of drawing the marquee, Shift+click on the ones you want to deselect.

- ✔ Drag a selected text node to reposition all selected characters. In Figure 11-2, for example, I selected every other letter in the word *Moderation* and dragged the selected node associated with the *n*.

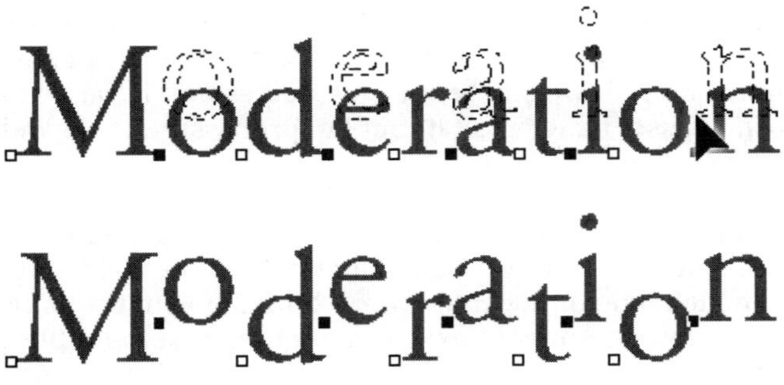

Figure 11-2:
Dragging
several
selected
characters
with the
shape tool
(top); the
outcome of
the drag
(bottom).

Moderation

Moderation

- ✔ You can also change the values in the X and Y option boxes on the property bar to move the selected text nodes and their corresponding characters. The X value shifts the characters horizontally; the Y value moves them vertically.

- ✔ Ctrl+drag nodes to move the letters along the current line of type.

- ✔ Use the arrow keys to nudge selected characters without fussing with your mouse. By default, each keystroke moves the selected characters $1/_{10}$ inch. You can change this distance by pressing Ctrl+J (Tools⇨Options) and changing the Nudge value (as explained in the "Nudging with the arrow keys" section of Chapter 6).

> ✔ Press Ctrl+arrow key to "super nudge" the characters — that is, to move them two times farther than a regular nudge.
>
> ✔ To return a single character to its original position, select its node and choose Text⇨Straighten Text. To undo all changes to an entire text block, select the text with the arrow tool and choose the Straighten Text command.

Kern, kern, the baffling term

You can drag entire lines to offset lines of type, drag whole words, or just create crazy text blocks by dragging individual characters six ways to Sunday, whatever that means. But the most practical reason for dragging nodes is to adjust the amount of horizontal space between individual characters, a process known as *kerning*.

In *Webster's Second Edition* — the sacred volume that editors swear by (or should it be "by which editors swear"?) — *kern* is defined as the portion of a letter such as *f* that sticks out from the stem. Those nutty lexicographers say that the term is based on the French word *carne,* which means a projecting angle.

Now, I don't know about you, but where I come from: A) we don't go around assigning words to projecting angles, and B) kern means to smush two letters closer together so that they look as snug as kernels of corn on the cob. Of course, I don't have any Ivy League degree and I don't wear any fancy hat with a tassel hanging off it, but I'm pretty sure them Webster fellers are full of beans.

Not like you care. You're still trying to figure out what I'm talking about. So here goes: Consider the character combination *AV.* The right side of the letter *A* and the left side of the character *V* both slope in the same direction. So when the two letters appear next to each other, a perceptible gap may form, as shown in Figure 11-3. Although the *A* and the *V* in *AVERY* aren't any farther away from each other than the *V* and the *E,* and the *E* and the *R,* and so on, they appear more spread out because of their similar slopes.

To tighten the spacing, I first chose Tools⇨Options, clicked on Edit, and reduced the Nudge value to 0.01 inch — a value that's significantly better to the art of fine-tuning text than the default .10 inch. After pressing Enter to return to the drawing area, I used the shape tool to select the *V*s as well as all the letters to the right of the *V*s. Then I pressed the left-arrow key a few times. (Selecting the letters to the right of the *V*s ensured that I didn't widen the spacing between any *V* and the letter that follows it.) Figure 11-4 shows the result of kerning the *A*s and *V*s. I also kerned a few other letters for good measure. (The nodes of these letters are selected in the figure.)

Figure 11-3: I wish I had a dime for every time we taunted Avery with this one.

Figure 11-4: Avery feels vindicated now that those who would malign him have kerned their ways.

As it turns out, CorelDraw is pretty darn good at kerning certain letter combinations automatically. It handles the classic *AV* combination with as little thought as you and I typically devote to blinking. Even so, I find myself kerning letters just about every time I create them, particularly in headlines and other prominent text blocks. You can trust CorelDraw to do a good job, but only you can make text picture perfect.

Changing overall spacing

Dragging text nodes changes the space between only selected characters. If you want to evenly adjust the spacing between all characters in a text block, you need to drag one of the two spacing handles, labeled back in Figure 11-1.

✔ Drag the character-spacing handle (located on the right side of the text block) to change the amount of horizontal space between all characters in the text block, as in the first example of Figure 11-5.

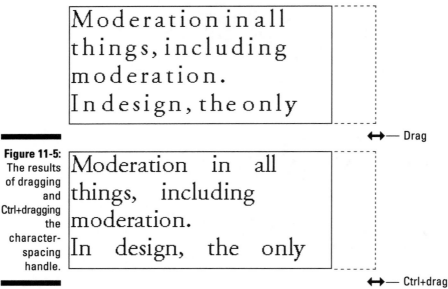

Moderation in all
things, including
moderation.
In design, the only

◄►— Drag

Figure 11-5:
The results
of dragging
and
Ctrl+dragging
the
character-
spacing
handle.

Moderation in all
things, including
moderation.
In design, the only

◄►— Ctrl+drag

Turn off the Snap to Grid function before dragging the spacing handles. (Choose Layout➪Snap to Grid, and if you see a check mark next to the command, click on the command to turn off the function.) With the grid off, you can drag the spacing handles anywhere you like.

✔ Ctrl+drag the character-spacing handle to change the size of the spaces between all words in the text block, as in the second example of Figure 11-5.

✔ Drag the line-spacing handle (located on the left side of the text block) to adjust the amount of vertical space between all lines of type, except those separated by a paragraph break (created when you press Enter while typing your text). In other words, lines in the same paragraph are affected, but neighboring lines in different paragraphs are not, as the first example in Figure 11-6 shows.

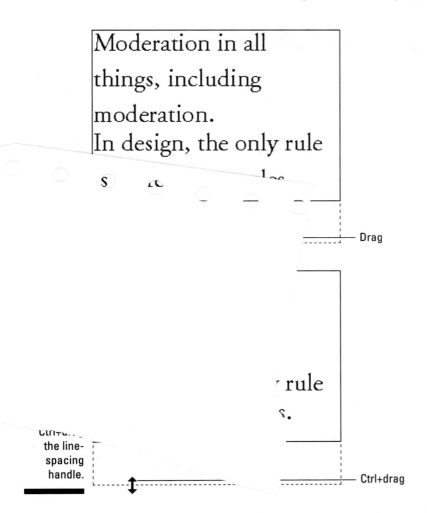

Moderation in all
things, including
moderation.
In design, the only rule

s   ꞇc   lꞔ⁓

Drag

rule

ꞔ.

Ctrl+d..
the line-
spacing
handle.

Ctrl+drag

> ✔ Ctrl+drag the line-spacing handle to change the amount of vertical space between different paragraphs, as in the second example of Figure 11-6. This tip doesn't work with artistic text because artistic text has no paragraphs.

Notice that dragging a spacing handle has no effect on the size of a block of paragraph text. The block itself remains the same size, and the newly spaced characters reflow to fit inside it.

Also, changes you make to a text block affect the characters in only that text block. If the text block is linked to another text block, some reformatted characters may flow into the linked text block, but the characters that originally occupied the linked text block remain unchanged.

Riding the Roller Coaster

CorelDraw calls the feature I'm about to discuss *fitting text to a path*. But I call it giving your text a ride on the roller coaster. After all, when your text is fit to a path, it has the time of its life, as Figure 11-7 clearly illustrates.

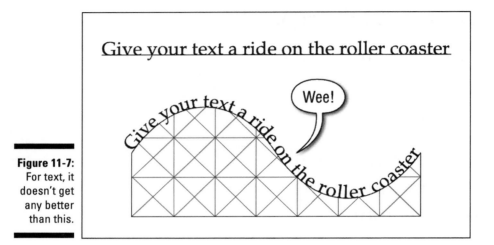

Figure 11-7: For text, it doesn't get any better than this.

As shown in the top example of Figure 11-7, text normally sits on an imaginary flat line called the *baseline*. You can substitute an oval or free-form path for the baseline in two ways in Version 8.

In previous versions of CorelDraw, only artistic text was mature enough to ride the roller coaster. But in Version 8, paragraph text has grown up a bit and can now be fit to a path using the second of the two methods I'm about to describe.

In Version 8, you can fit artistic text to a path quickly, like so:

1. **Select the text tool.**

2. **Move the text tool cursor near the path.**

   Circles, ovals, and gradually curving paths work best, by the way, but any path is acceptable.

3. **When the cursor changes to an insertion marker, click.**

   You should see a little *A* with a wavy line next to the insertion marker.

4. **Type your text.**

   CorelDraw automatically fits your text to the path, placing the text on top of the object. (You can change the position of the text after you create it, as I explain later in this chapter.)

5. Select the arrow tool and click in the drawing area.

This sets your text firmly in place.

If you want to fit existing artistic *or* paragraph text to a path, do this:

1. Select the text with the arrow tool.

2. Shift+click on the path.

CorelDraw adds the path to the selection.

3. Choose View➪Roll-Ups➪Fit Text To Path.

The Fit Text to Path roll-up appears. If the selected path is a free-form path, the roll-up looks like the left example in Figure 11-8. If the selected path is a rectangle, an oval, or a polygon, the roll-up appears as shown on the right side of the figure.

4. Select the desired options.

I describe them all momentarily. For now, you don't need to select anything. You can just accept the default settings and go on.

5. Click on the Apply button.

Watch the baseline adhere to that path. Those little characters are probably losing their lunches (in a good way, of course).

6. If the text doesn't attach to the path the way you had anticipated, select the Place on Other Side check box and click on Apply.

The text switches to the opposite side of the path and flows in the opposite direction. (Note that the Place on Other Side check box appears dimmed if you select the second or third options in the text orientation pop-up menu, labeled in Figure 11-8.)

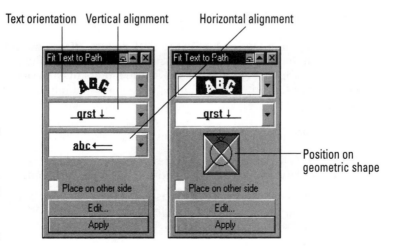

Figure 11-8:
Two variations on the Fit Text to Path roll-up.

The Fit Text to Path roll-up offers either three pop-up menus or two pop-up menus and a group of buttons, depending on the kind of path you're using. The options determine the orientation of characters on a path, the vertical alignment of the text, and the horizontal alignment. (The following sections explain how these options work.)

You can use the roll-up also to change the orientation and alignment of existing text fit to a path. Just click on the text with the arrow tool. Or, if you have more than one text block fit to the same path, Ctrl+click on the text block you want to change. The text and path become selected. You can then use the options in the Fit Text to Path roll-up to manipulate the text.

When you select text that's fit to a path, the property bar displays many of the same controls found in the Fit Text to Path roll-up, including the orientation and alignment pop-up menus and the Place Text on Other Side option. Happily, all the controls are accessible no matter what monitor display setting you use, as shown in Figure 11-9. (Okay, so the Place Text on Other Side button is partially cut off, but you can still click on it without any trouble.)

Figure 11-9:
Property
bar controls
for
adjusting
text to fit to
a path.

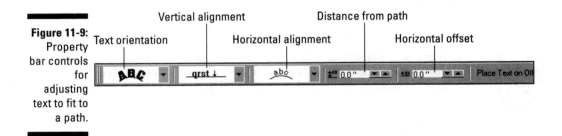

Orienting text on a path

The top pop-up menu in the Fit Text to Path roll-up offers you the choice of rotating characters along the path, skewing them horizontally or vertically, or none of the above. Figure 11-10 shows the effects of each option, in the same order that the options appear in the pop-up menu in both the roll-up and the property bar.

Want my opinion? All right, here goes:

- ✔ The rotate characters option is the most useful, which is probably why it's the default setting. When in doubt, stick with this option.

- ✔ The vertical skew option is also useful, as long as your path doesn't have any super-steep vertical inclines. Along the left and right sides of a circle, for example, characters skew into nothingness.

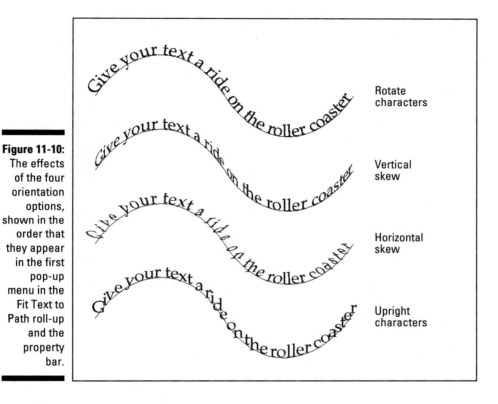

Rotate
characters

Vertical
skew

Horizontal
skew

Upright
characters

Figure 11-10:
The effects
of the four
orientation
options,
shown in the
order that
they appear
in the first
pop-up
menu in the
Fit Text to
Path roll-up
and the
property
bar.

✔ The horizontal skew option is set up backward so that letters skew
against the path instead of with it. The *G* at the beginning of the text in
Figure 11-10, for example, should skew to the right, into the path — not
to the left, away from it. Use this option only if you want to elicit
comments such as "Gee, this is weird" or "Maybe we should go back to
typewriters."

✔ The upright characters option is so ugly, it makes the horizontal skew
option look like a good idea.

To change the orientation of text by using the roll-up, select the option and
then click on Apply. If you select the option from the property bar pop-up
menu, CorelDraw automatically reorients the text.

Changing the vertical alignment

The vertical alignment pop-up menu enables you to change the vertical
positioning of characters with respect to the path. The options work as I
describe in the following list. (I list them in the order in which they appear
in the menu.)

✔ The first option adheres the baseline of the text to the path.

✔ The second option aligns the tops of the tallest characters, called ascenders (such as *b, d,* and, *k*), to the path. The text hangs from the path like a monkey hangs from a tree limb, except the text doesn't swing back and forth and scratch for ticks.

✔ The third option aligns the bottom of the hangy-down characters, called descenders (such as *g, j,* and *p*) to the path, so that the letters balance like little tightrope walkers.

✔ The fourth option causes the path to run smack dab through the middle of the text like a gold chain threaded through beaded pearls.

✔ Don't you just love these clever little analogies?

✔ The last option enables you to drag text anywhere you want with respect to the path. To use this option when you're fitting text to the path for the first time, select the option from the Fit Text to Path roll-up and click on Apply. After CorelDraw fits your text to the path, drag from the text to display a positioning line. The line indicates the distance between the path and the text. When you release the mouse button, CorelDraw redraws the text at its new location. To apply this option to existing text on a path, Ctrl+click on the text, select the option from the roll-up, click on Apply, and then drag the text. (If you want to use the property bar, click on the text, select the option from the pop-up menu, Ctrl+click on the text, and then drag the text.)

Generally, you should stick with the default setting, which adheres text by its baseline. The one time to change this option is when you're creating text on a circle, as I describe in the section after next.

Changing the horizontal alignment

When you're attaching text to a free-form path, you can use the third pop-up menu in the Fit Text to Path roll-up or the property bar to change the horizontal alignment of text:

✔ The first option aligns the first character of text with the first point in the path. This option works like the left-justification option in a normal text block.

✔ The second option centers the text on the path, just as the center-justification option centers text in a normal text block.

✔ Starting to get the idea?

✔ The last option aligns the last character of text with the last point in the path. It works like — you guessed it — the right-justification option in a normal text block.

Shifting text around a geometric object

When you attach text to a geometric object — a rectangle, an oval, or a polygon — CorelDraw replaces the third pop-up menu in the roll-up with a square that contains four inset triangular buttons. (See Figure 11-8.) The buttons work like radio buttons; that is, you can select only one button at a time. You can center the text along the top of the object, along the left or right side, or along the bottom. The third pop-up menu on the property bar offers you the same options.

Shifting text in specific increments

The property bar offers two controls that give you an easy way to fine-tune the placement of text on a path. Using the first option box on the property bar (labeled distance from path back in Figure 11-9), you can shift the text closer to or farther away from the path. Using the horizontal offset control (also labeled back in Figure 11-9), you can move the text horizontally along the path a specific distance.

To use the controls, just click on the up- or down-pointing arrows next to the option boxes. Or double-click on an option box, enter a new value from the keyboard, and press Enter. (Note that you can also access these two controls by clicking on the Edit button in the Fit Text to Path roll-up.)

Creating text on a circle

Want to see the vertical and horizontal alignment options put into use? Well, too bad, because I'm going to show you anyway.

I don't know why, but when folks want to fit text to a path, the path they usually have in mind is a circle. Ironically, however, text on a circle is the least intuitive kind of roller-coaster text you can create. If you simply attach a single text block around the entire circle, half of the text will be upside down. So, you have to attach two text blocks to a single circle, one along the top of the circle and another along the bottom, as I explain in the following steps.

Note that the steps instruct you to create your text first and then use the Fit Text to Path roll-up to fit the text to the path. Here's how it works:

1. **Draw a circle.**

   If you need help, see Chapter 4.

2. **Create two separate blocks of text.**

Remember, in Version 8 you can fit both artistic and paragraph text to a path.

Click with the text tool and enter text for the top of the circle. Then click at another spot and enter some more text for the bottom. Oh, and keep your text short.

3. Select the circle and the first block of text.

Using the arrow tool, click on the circle and Shift+click on the text you want to appear along the top of the circle. Or drag around both text and circle to enclose them in a selection marquee. (From here on, do everything with the arrow tool.)

4. Choose View⇨Roll-Ups⇨Fit Text To Path to bring up the Fit Text to Path roll-up.

If the roll-up is already displayed, skip this step.

5. Click on the Apply button.

The default settings are fine for now. The text adheres to the top of the circle, as in Figure 11-11. (If the text doesn't appear on the top of the circle, click the top triangle in the position square in the Fit Text to Path roll-up and then click Apply.)

6. Click in an empty portion of the drawing area with the arrow tool.

This step deselects everything. You have to do this so that you can select the circle independently in the next step.

7. Select the circle and the second block of text.

Click somewhere along the bottom of the circle to make sure that you select the circle only. (If you click along the top of the circle, you might select the text as well.) Then Shift+click on the second block of text.

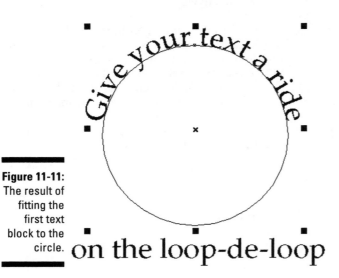

Figure 11-11:
The result of fitting the first text block to the circle.

8. **Click on the bottom triangular button in the Fit Text to Path roll-up.**

   See the location of the arrow cursor in Figure 11-12.

9. **Click on the Apply button.**

   The second block of text wraps around the bottom of the circle, as shown in Figure 11-12. Unfortunately, the text is upside down.

10. **Select the Place on Other Side check box and click on Apply.**

    Or just click on the Place Text on Other Side button on the property bar. The text now appears as shown in Figure 11-13 — right-side-up, but scrunched. To loosen the text up a bit, do Step 11.

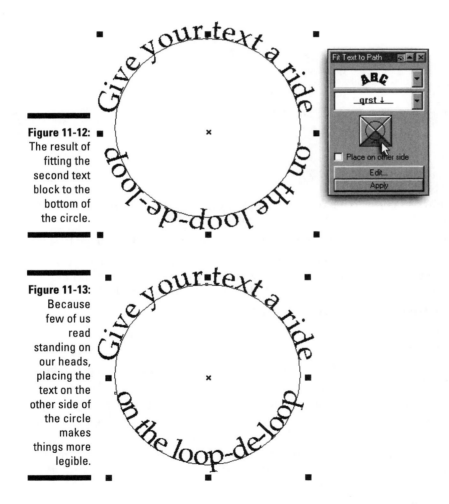

Figure 11-12:
The result of fitting the second text block to the bottom of the circle.

Figure 11-13:
Because few of us read standing on our heads, placing the text on the other side of the circle makes things more legible.

11. **Select the second option from the vertical alignment pop-up menu and click on Apply.**

   Figure 11-14 shows me in the process of selecting this option, which, as you may remember, aligns the ascenders of the characters to the circle so that the text hangs down.

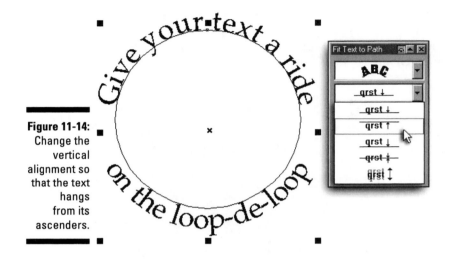

Figure 11-14: Change the vertical alignment so that the text hangs from its ascenders.

   You can choose this option from the property bar, too. Either way, the resulting text looks something along the lines of Figure 11-14.

12. **Click in an empty portion of the drawing area with the arrow tool.**

   Notice that the top row of type doesn't look like it's quite aligned with the bottom row. To correct this, you need to select the top text block independently of the other text. But first, you must deselect everything.

13. **Ctrl+click on a character in the top text block.**

   By Ctrl+clicking, you select the top text block along with the circle but independently of the bottom text block.

14. **Select the third option from the vertical alignment pop-up menu and click on Apply.**

   In Figure 11-15, you can see me selecting this option, which aligns the descenders of the characters to the circle, causing the text to walk the tightrope.

   As with other alignment options, this one is available from the property bar menu as well as in the roll-up.

   The top text block now aligns correctly with the bottom text block. Figure 11-15 shows text on a circle as it was meant to be.

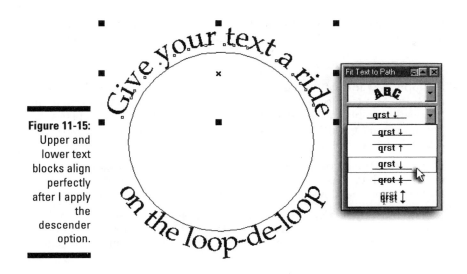

Figure 11-15:
Upper and
lower text
blocks align
perfectly
after I apply
the
descender
option.

If you want to create text on a circle on-the-fly — that is, by typing directly on the path instead of creating the text, selecting text and circle, and then clicking on the Apply button in the roll-up — you need to use artistic text and approach these steps in a different order. Create the text for the bottom of the circle *first*. Place the text on the bottom of the circle by using the property bar or the roll-up, and then create the text for the top of the circle.

Remember that to change the position of a text block when you have more than one text block fit to the same path, you need to Ctrl+click on the text block to select it.

Editing text on a path

After you fit a block of text to a path, you may find it difficult to edit the text with the text tools. You can do it by moving the text tool cursor around the letters until the cursor changes to an I-beam and then dragging across the text. But this technique requires dexterity and patience. The easier method is to select the text independently of the path. I touch on this technique in Step 14 of the previous section, but it bears probing in a little more depth.

✔ Ctrl+click *on the text* — not on the path — with the arrow tool to select the text independently of the path. If you fit two text blocks to a path, as in the previous example, Ctrl+click on the text twice in a row. (That's twice in a row on the same text.) Ctrl+clicking once on the text selects text and path together and enables you to change the orientation and alignment of the text by using the roll-up or the property bar.

✔ To edit the content of the text, Ctrl+click on the text to select it and then choose Text⇨Edit Text or press Ctrl+Shift+T. CorelDraw displays a separate text editing window in which you can edit characters or words and even change the typeface, style, and size. Click on the OK button when you're finished. (Don't press Enter; that just inserts a carriage return.)

- ✔ To apply new formatting, use the property bar controls or right-click (with the text tool for paragraph text) on a letter of text and choose the Properties command to display the Object Properties docker, just as you do when formatting normal text. (I discuss both property bar and dialog box in Chapter 10.)

- ✔ Click inside the color palette to apply color to the text. Right-click on a color swatch to apply a color outline around each letter of text. Click or right-click on the X swatch to delete the fill or outline, respectively.

- ✔ Kern the text by selecting text nodes with the shape tool and by then dragging them or using the arrow keys to nudge them. CorelDraw automatically constrains the movement of the text to the contour of the path.

Editing the path

You can change the fill and outline of the path to which the text is attached by selecting the object and using the Fill and Pen options described back in Chapter 7. It's straightforward — no special tricks involved. In many cases, you'll want to hide the path by selecting the object and right-clicking on the X icon at the top of the Color Palette.

If you prefer, you can delete the path entirely, leaving just your text behind. To do so, click on the path with the arrow tool and press Delete. Be careful not to select the text instead — if you delete the text, both path and text disappear.

You can also edit the shape of the path by using the shape tool. Again, just be sure that you click on the path and not the text. For laughs, try dragging the top node of the circle back in Figure 11-15 to cut out a pie wedge. Without missing a beat, CorelDraw fits the text along the contours of the wedge.

Breaking it up

To detach text from a path and return it to the straight and narrow, do the following:

1. **Select the path and the text.**

   Using the arrow tool, just click on the text or on the marquee around the text and the path.

2. **Choose** <u>A</u>**rrange**⇨<u>S</u>**eparate.**

This step separates the text from the path. If your text is paragraph text, CorelDraw straightens it automatically. Artistic text remains all twisty-curly, however, so you must proceed to Step 3.

3. **Choose Te**<u>x</u>**t**⇨<u>S</u>**traighten Text.**

The text returns to its plain old self.

Meddling with Type

If you're interested in creating logos or other special text, you should know about another command that's applicable to artistic text. After selecting a block of artistic text with the arrow tool, the shape tool, or one of the text tools, choose <u>A</u>rrange⇨Con<u>v</u>ert To Curves or press Ctrl+Q. CorelDraw converts the outlines of every single character in the text block to free-form paths. An *A,* for example, ceases to be a letter of text and becomes a triangular path with a bar across it.

After you convert the characters to paths, you can edit the paths by using the arrow and shape tools (described in Chapter 5) exactly as if you drew the characters with the pencil tool. The top example in Figure 11-16 shows a block of everyday, mild-mannered text. The second example is the same block of text after I converted it to paths and edited the heck out of it.

Figure 11-16:
A line of artistic text as it appears before (top) and after (bottom) converting it to paths and editing the paths with the shape tool.

Try this technique out a few times and you'll soon find that converted characters are as easy to integrate and edit as symbols and other pieces of clip art. Converted text serves as a great jumping-off point for creating custom logos and other exciting effects.

Creating Creepy Text

If you're a fan of B-grade horror movies and your favorite holiday is Halloween, you'll want to get acquainted with the new zipper distortion feature, labeled in Figure 11-17. The zipper distortion is one of three distortions you can apply by using the interactive distortion tool, which I introduce in Chapter 9. You can apply a zipper distortion to any CorelDraw object, including lines, shapes, and curves, but you may find it most intriguing for creating creepy (and not so creepy) text effects. Try this:

1. **Create some artistic text.**

   This effect doesn't work with paragraph text. Sorry.

2. **Select the interactive distortion tool and click on the Zipper Distortion button on the property bar.**

   The interactive distortion tool is the second tool on the interactive blend tool flyout menu. The Zipper Distortion button is labeled in Figure 11-17.

3. **Click on the text and drag in any direction to apply the distortion.**

   The edges of your text become a series of zigzags. The point at which you click becomes the center of the distortion, and the direction you drag determines the direction of the distortion. Figure 11-17, for example, shows the result of clicking in the center of the text and dragging slightly to the left.

You can edit the effect by dragging the distortion arrow and end point or using the property bar controls (labeled in Figure 11-17):

✔ The Zipper Distortion Amplitude option box controls the size of the zigzag applied to the object. You can enter a value between 0 and 100. Higher values produce a more pronounced zigzag effect.

✔ The Zipper Distortion Frequency option box controls the number of zigzags per segment. Higher values result in more zigzags.

✔ The Random Distortion button randomizes the distortion effect. In other words, clicking on this button applies a haphazard array of amplitudes and frequencies to every portion of the selected object.

✔ The Smooth Distortion button smooths the points of the zigzags.

✔ The Local Distortion button enables you to emphasize the existing distortion in a specific area of the object. After you click on the Local Distortion button, drag the start point to reposition it on the object.

✔ The Center Distortion button is used to position the distortion on the center of the object.

You can apply the other interactive distortions — push and pull and twister — to your artistic text as well. See Chapter 9 for the lowdown on these distortions.

Figure 11-17:
Spice up your text by using the new zipper distortion feature.

Chapter 12

The Corner of Page and Publish

Desktop publishing has revolutionized the way folks churn up and spit out bits of Oregon forestry, thereby remedying the grossly inefficient way we were churning up the forests back in the 1970s. Happily, we now have more open space in which to park our cars and receive computer-created fliers we never wanted stuck under our windshield wipers. And now you can be a part of this ever-expanding field.

Okay, that's an overstated bit of sarcasm. With the proliferation of CD-ROMs and World Wide Web pages, computers will very likely lessen our reliance on paper over time. But for now, the printed page is usually the medium of choice. Furthermore, although I'd love to warn you about the evils of printing, I'm in no position to lecture, having myself wasted more pieces of paper than you will probably use in a lifetime. Don't get me wrong — I'm a dedicated recycler. Ecocycle loves me. I use only the cheapest bond paper available, and I print only when I absolutely have to. Hey, you want to get off my case?

Now that I've insulted folks on both sides of the spotted owl debate, let's get down to business. This chapter and the next are devoted to output. This chapter explains how to set up your pages; Chapter 13 explains how to print them. After you finish these chapters, you'll be fully prepared to create fliers and stick them under windshield wipers with the best of them.

And remember, always use bright pink or yellow paper. That way, folks can spot your fliers nine miles from their cars and mentally prepare themselves to snatch the fliers up and wad them into balls at their earliest convenience.

Pages upon Pages

Unless you've read some outside sources or scoped out the Layout menu, you may assume that CorelDraw is good for creating only single page documents.

Not so. Although primarily a drawing program, CorelDraw lets you add as many pages to a document as you like. (As usual, I'm sure there's a maximum number of pages, but I'll be darned if I care what it is. I mean, if you're trying to lay out an issue of *National Geographic,* you need a different piece of software. If you have in mind a newsletter, a report, or maybe a short catalog, CorelDraw will suffice.)

Adding new pages

When you create a new drawing (choose File⇨New or press Ctrl+N), CorelDraw gives you a one-page document. To make the document a multipager, you have to add pages manually, like so:

1. **Choose Layout⇨Insert Page.**

   Or simply press either the PgUp or PgDn key. The dialog box shown in Figure 12-1 appears.

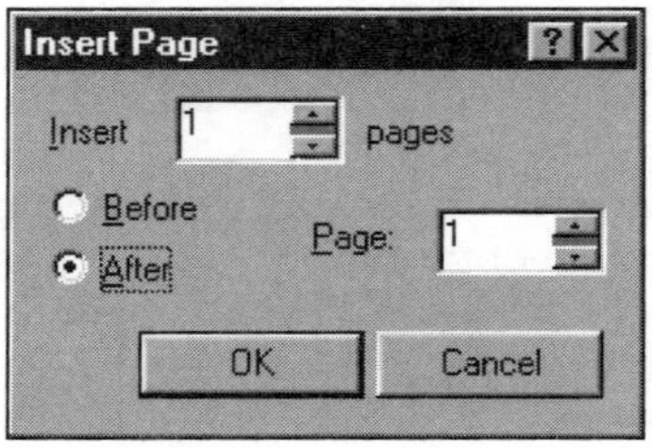

Figure 12-1:
Add pages
using this
dialog box.

2. **In the Insert option box, type the number of pages you want to add.**

3. **Press Enter.**

   CorelDraw adds the specified number of pages to your document.

Adding pages bit by bit

The rest of the options in the Insert Page dialog box enable you to add pages sporadically rather than in one fell swoop. Suppose that you set up a four-page document and then discover that you need six pages to hold all your wonderful drawings and ideas. Using the Before and After options together with the Page option, you can tell CorelDraw exactly where to insert the pages. If you want to insert pages between pages 3 and 4, for example, you could do either of the following:

- 🖋 Type 3 in the Page option and select the After radio button.
- 🖋 Type 4 in the Page option and select the Before radio button.

Rocket science it ain't. If the pages you want to enter aren't sequential, you have to use the Layout➪Insert Page command more than once. For example, to insert one page between pages 2 and 3 and two others between pages 3 and 4, choose the Insert Page command twice, once for each sequence.

Version 8 offers an easy way to add pages on the fly. Right-click on a page tab (labeled in Figure 12-2) and select Insert Page After or Insert Page Before.

Thumbing through your pages

After you add pages to your previously single-page drawing, CorelDraw displays a series of page controls near the lower-left corner of the screen, as shown in Figure 12-2. Here's how they work:

- 🖋 Click on the first icon — the left-pointing arrow with a line next to it — to go to the first page in your document.
- 🖋 Click on the left-pointing Page Back button to back up one page (for example, from page 3 to page 2).

Figure 12-2:
These page controls appear in the lower-left corner of the drawing window.

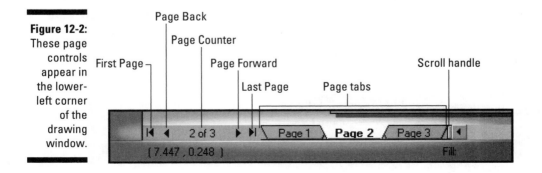

Page Back

Page Counter

First Page

Page Forward

Last Page

Page tabs

Scroll handle

- ✔ Click on the right-pointing Page Forward button to advance one page (for example, from page 2 to page 3).

- ✔ You can change pages by pressing the PgUp and PgDn keys. PgUp backs up a page, and PgDn advances one page. "But wait a minute," you think. "Didn't you say that the PgUp and PgDn buttons bring up the Insert Page dialog box?" Yes — you're not losing your mind. If you're on page 1 and press the PgUp key, or if you're on the last page in your document and press the PgDn key, the dialog box appears.

- ✔ Click on the Last Page button — the right-pointing arrow with a line next to it — to advance to the last page in the document.

- ✔ When you're on the first page in your document, the Page Back button changes to a + sign. The same thing happens to the Page Forward button when you're on the last page. Click on the + sign to add pages automatically before the first page or after the last page in your document.

- ✔ Click on the Page Counter button to display the Go To Page dialog box, which enables you to turn to any page you like. Just enter the page number and press Enter, and off you go. (You can also access this dialog box by choosing Layout⇨Go To Page.)

- ✔ A series of page tabs appears to the right of the Last Page button. You can click on the tab for any page to go to that page.

- ✔ To increase or decrease the amount of space allotted to the page tabs, drag the scroll handle between the tabs and the scroll bar (the handle is labeled in Figure 12-2).

Removing the excess

If you add too many pages, you can delete a few by choosing Layout⇨ Delete Page. A dialog box, shown in Figure 12-3, asks which pages you want to delete. You can delete the single page you're viewing by pressing Enter. Or you can delete another page by entering the page number in the Delete Page option box. To delete a sequential range of pages, select the Through to Page check box and enter a page number in the option box to the right.

You can also delete a single page by right-clicking on its page tab and selecting Delete Page from the resulting pop-up menu.

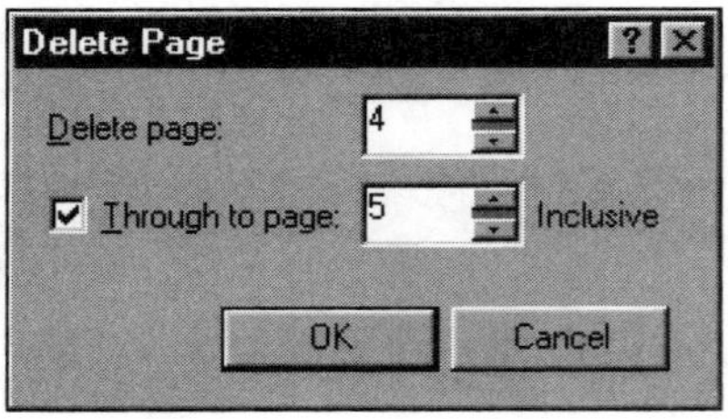

Figure 12-3:
Use this dialog box to kiss pages good-bye.

Delete Page

Delete page: 4

☑ Through to page: 5 Inclusive

OK   Cancel

You cannot delete all pages in the document. That would leave you with no pages at all, and CorelDraw will have none of that.

Flowing text between pages

As I mention in Chapter 10, you can pour text across multiple pages. The following steps reveal the secret to accomplishing this little trick:

1. **Drag with the text tool to create a block of paragraph text.**

2. **Type too much text for the text block.**

   Be sure that the Expand and Shrink Paragraph Frames to Fit Text option in the Paragraph panel of the Options dialog box (Ctrl+J) is turned off. (To access the Paragraph panel of the Options dialog box, double-click on Text and click on Paragraph.) Otherwise, your text block keeps growing as you type, and that defeats the purpose of this merry exercise.

3. **Select the arrow tool and click on the bottom tab in the text block.**

   You get the page cursor.

4. **Go to the page where you want to flow the text.**

   Use the page tabs or page arrows to navigate to the correct page.

5. **Drag with the page cursor on your new page.**

   Your overflow text appears in the new text block.

Isn't that a trip? Despite the fact that the two text blocks are on separate pages, they're linked.

When the text tool is selected, a dotted blue line extends from the text blocks to indicate that they're linked. A little box next to the line indicates the page number where the next linked block is located.

If you drag up on the tab in the text block on page 1, excess text flows into the text block on page 2. Incidentally, linked text blocks don't have to be on sequential pages; they can be several pages apart. You can start a story on page 5 and continue it on page 44. You can even make a separate text block that tells readers, "Continued on page 44." These are professional page-layout capabilities!

Your Logo on Every Page

If you're serious about creating multipage docs, I have another prescription for you. It's called the *master layer*. This function enables you to put special text and graphic objects on every page of your document without having to place them all individually. For example, suppose you are creating a company newsletter and want to show the name of the newsletter at the bottom of each page and the company logo in the upper-right corner. CorelDraw can handle the chore of inserting the name and logo on every page automatically.

Establishing a master layer

If you want CorelDraw to automatically place certain elements on every page of your document, you have to create a master layer and then place the elements on it. The following steps explain how:

1. **Choose Layout⇨Object Manager.**

   The Object Manager docker appears, as shown in Figure 12-4.

2. **Choose the New Layer button at the top of the docker.**

   This button is labeled in Figure 12-4. CorelDraw adds a new layer — presumably named Layer 2 — to the list in the Object Manager docker.

Figure 12-4:
Use the Object Manager docker to create a master page.

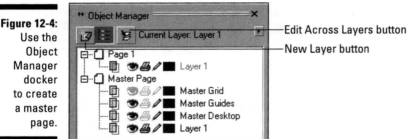

Edit Across Layers button
New Layer button

3. **Enter a name for the master page layer.**

   Immediately after you create a layer, its name is active, so you can just enter a name from the keyboard. Press Enter when you're finished.

4. **Right-click on the name of your new layer, and then select Master from the pop-up menu that appears.**

   This tells CorelDraw to specify this layer as the master layer. Figure 12-5 shows this step in action.

5. **Add text and graphics to taste.**

   Create those logos, add those newsletter names, draw those boxes. Add everything you want to repeat throughout your document. (Incidentally, it doesn't matter what page you're on. A master layer is a master layer throughout every page of the document.)

Figure 12-5:
Right-click
on a layer
name in the
Object
Manager
docker to
specify a
layer as
a master
layer.

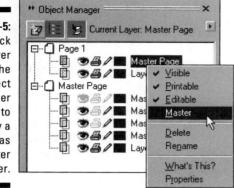

6. **Click on Layer 1 in the Object Manager docker.**

   This step makes the original layer active again.

7. **Drag Layer 1 up a level so that it appears above the Master Page layer.**

   In all likelihood, you want the text and graphics on the master page to appear in back of the text and graphics you add to a page. By dragging the Layer 1 name up one notch in the list — or, alternatively, dragging the Master Page layer to the bottom — you change the order of the layers so that the master page rests in back of the active layer.

8. **Click on the Edit Across Layers button at the top of the Object Manager docker.**

   This step turns the option off so that you can manipulate objects on the current layer only, thus protecting the master layer objects. Make sure the button appears unpressed, as it's shown in Figure 12-4.

To see how the master page you just created works, try this: First, draw an oval or some other simple shape on one page of your document. Then, go to another page in your document. When you turn to the other page, you see all the objects you added to the master layer, but you don't see the oval you drew on the standard layer.

In most cases, you need only two layers in a document: one for the master page and one for your main document pages. The only reason for having more than two layers is to segregate objects in extremely complex drawings. People who go around drawing human anatomies and blowouts of car engines — we're talking about folks with the patience of saints — use layers. However, typical novice and intermediate users have little reason to explore layers — except for creating a master page, of course — and they're all the merrier for it. I almost never use layers, and I'm an expert. At least, that's what my wife tells me every time I take the trash out to the curb. And she's not just saying it, either; you can sense she really means it.

In any case, to find out a little more about layers — not much, mind you, but a little — see Chapter 20.

Hiding master layer objects on page 1

As a general rule, you don't display master layer objects on the first page of a multipage document. For example, what's the point of listing the name of the newsletter at the bottom of the first page? The name is already listed at the top of that page in big bold type. Very likely, the company logo is a part of the newsletter title, so there's no reason to repeat it, either.

To hide master layer objects on one page only, do this:

1. **Turn to the first page.**

   Or, if you don't want to see the master layer objects on some other page, turn to that page.

2. **Right-click on the name of your master layer in the Object Manager docker, and then select the Properties command.**

   The Master Page Properties dialog box, shown in Figure 12-6, appears.

3. **Click on the Visible check box to remove the check mark.**

   This step hides the master layer objects.

4. **Click on the Apply Layer Changes to the Current Page Only check box to add a check mark.**

   This step enables you to change the settings for the current page only.

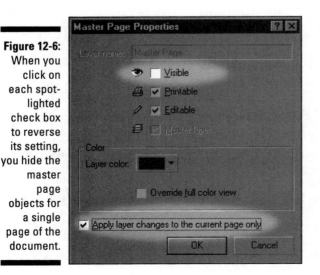

Figure 12-6: When you click on each spotlighted check box to reverse its setting, you hide the master page objects for a single page of the document.

5. Press Enter.

CorelDraw closes the dialog box and returns you to the drawing area. All master layer objects have now disappeared from view, but remain visible on all other pages.

To get rid of a master layer entirely, right-click on the Master Layer name and choose Delete from the resulting pop-up menu.

If you want to hide the master layer for printing, click on the little printer icon next to the master layer name in the Object Manager docker or deselect the Printable check box in the Master Page Properties dialog box.

I Need a Bigger Page!

In the United States, most folks use letter-sized paper (8^1/$_2$ inches wide by 11 inches tall). In other countries, page sizes vary. But no matter what — at least, I don't know of any exceptions — CorelDraw is set up for the most likely scenario. If you're using the most common page size in your neck of the woods and you like your pages upright, you don't have to worry about the command I'm about to describe.

But what if you're doing something slightly different? Maybe you're creating a document that will be printed on legal-sized paper. Or maybe you're planning to print on letter-sized paper, but you want to flip the page on its side. No problem. Changing the page size and orientation is simple.

You can make most changes to your page setup by simply using the property bar controls labeled in Figure 12-7. A few more-advanced controls reside on the Size and Layout panels of the Options dialog box. The Size panel appears in Figure 12-7, too. To display the Size panel of the Options dialog box, choose Layout➪Page Setup or right-click on the page border or on the shaded area around the right and bottom edges of the page and select Page Setup from the resulting pop-up menu.

Use the property bar options and the Page settings in the Options dialog box as follows:

✔ To change the size of the pages in the document, select a predefined page size option from the Paper pop-up menu in the dialog box or on the property bar.

✔ If you're unsure how large one of the predefined page sizes is, just select it. CorelDraw automatically displays the dimensions of the selected page size in the Width and Height option boxes, both in the dialog box and on the property bar.

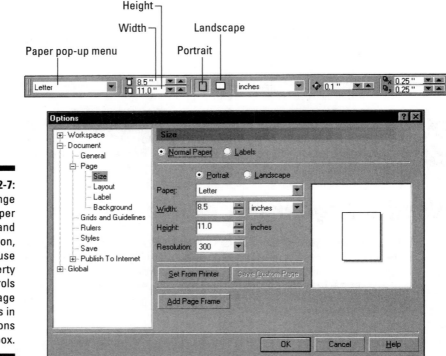

Figure 12-7:
To change
your paper
size and
orientation,
you can use
the property
bar controls
or Page
settings in
the Options
dialog box.

✔ If you just want to set the page size to match the size of the paper loaded into your printer, click on the Set From Printer button in the dialog box.

✔ If none of these page sizes strikes your fancy, enter your own dimensions into either set of Width and Height option boxes. You can change the unit of measurement by making a selection from the Units pop-up menu on the property bar or from the pop-up menu to the right of the Width option box in the dialog box.

✔ Select the Landscape button to lay the page on its side. Select the Portrait button to stand it up again. You can access this option using the dialog box or the property bar.

✔ Click on Layout in the Options dialog box and select the Facing Pages check box to display two facing pages in the drawing area at once. For example, when you open up a four-page newsletter, page 2 and page 3 face each other. The even-numbered page (page 2) is on the left, and the odd-numbered page (page 3) is on the right. To see these pages as your reader will see them, select the Facing Pages option.

✔ Don't even bother with the rest of the options. Unless you're creating three-fold flyers on bright pink paper with ugly borders around each page, they're a waste of time.

Chapter 13

Those Poor, Helpless Trees

● ●

In This Chapter

▶ Preparing your drawing to be printed

▶ Orienting your drawing on the printed page

▶ Selecting a paper size

▶ Printing every page of a document

▶ Printing multiple copies

▶ Printing a specific range of pages

▶ Scaling the drawing on the printed page

▶ Tiling poster-sized artwork onto several pages

▶ Using the page preview options

▶ Creating color separations

● ●

*A*dvising a perfect stranger like you how to use your printer is like trying to diagnose a car problem without ever seeing the car, without knowing the make and model, without having driven more than, say, ten models in my entire life, and without even knowing what sort of symptoms your car is exhibiting. Printers come in so many different types and present so many potential printing hazards that I can't possibly give information designed specifically for your machine.

In other words, I'm completely in the dark. Sure, I can tell you how to print from CorelDraw — in fact, that's exactly what I'm going to do in this chapter — but every word I write assumes that

✔ Your printer is plugged in.

✔ Your printer is turned on and in working order.

✔ The printer is properly connected to your computer.

✔ Windows 95 is aware of your printer's existence.

✔ Your printer is stocked with ribbon, ink, toner, paper, film, or whatever else is required in the way of raw materials.

If you barely know the location of the printer, let alone anything else about the God-forsaken thing, assume for now that everything is A-OK and follow along with the text in this chapter. If you run into a snag, something is probably awry with your printer or its connection to your computer. As a friend of mine likes to tell me, "When in danger or in doubt, run in circles, scream and shout." If you shout loudly enough, someone may come to your rescue and fix your problem. (A helpful reader advised me that the "scream and shout" quote originates "from none other than the greatest science fiction writer of all time, Robert Anson Heinlein." I'll take his word for it.)

Reviewing the Basic Steps

The overall printing process includes these steps:

1. **Turn on your printer.**

2. **Press Ctrl+S or choose File⇨Save.**

   Although this step is only a precaution, it's always a good idea to save your document immediately before you print it, because the print process is one of those ideal opportunities for your computer to crash.

3. **Press Ctrl+P or choose File⇨Print.**

   A dialog box appears, enabling you to specify the pages you want to print, request multiple copies, scale the size of the printed drawing, and mess around with a horde of other options. (I explain the various options throughout the rest of this chapter.)

4. **Click on the Properties button.**

   Up comes another dialog box that lets you make sure that you're printing to the correct printer and that the page doesn't print on its side. (Again, the options are explained later in this chapter.)

5. **Press Enter and click on the Print button at the bottom of the Print dialog box.**

   And they're off! The page or pages start spewing out of your printer faster than you can recite the first 17 pages of *Beowulf.*

It's magic, really. Through the modern miracle of computing, you've taken what is for all practical purposes a completely imaginary drawing — a dream known to only you and your machine — and converted it into a tangible sheet of hard copy.

Making Sure Everything's Ready to Go

Before you tell CorelDraw to print your drawing, you should check to see whether all applicable print settings are in order. This process is like checking to see that you have your keys as you exit your house. Just as you probably have your keys, your print settings are probably fine. But double-checking things may help you avoid some grief later.

Selecting a printer

When you press Ctrl+P (or choose File⇨Print), CorelDraw displays the Print dialog box. The dialog box offers lots of options, but for now, the only ones you need to care about are the Name pop-up menu and the Properties button, which I zoom in on in Figure 13-1. (The entire Print dialog box appears in Figure 13-3.)

Figure 13-1:
Select a
printer and
then click
on the
Properties
button.

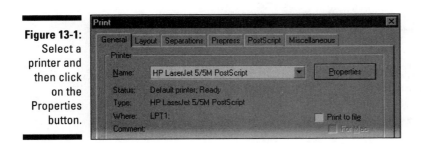

From the Name pop-up menu, select the type of printer connected to your PC. If you generally print all your documents from the same printer, the proper printer should already be displayed.

Changing paper size and orientation

After you choose a printer, click on the Properties button in the Print dialog box to display a printer properties dialog box like the one shown in Figure 13-2. Although your dialog box may look different from the one pictured in the figure, it should provide three or four areas of interest:

✔ Select the correct paper size from the Paper Size list at the top of the dialog box. Ideally, the paper size should match the page size you selected for your drawing using the Page Setup dialog box or property bar (described just pages ago, in Chapter 12). Unless you have a special kind of paper loaded in the paper tray, you probably want to select letter-sized paper.

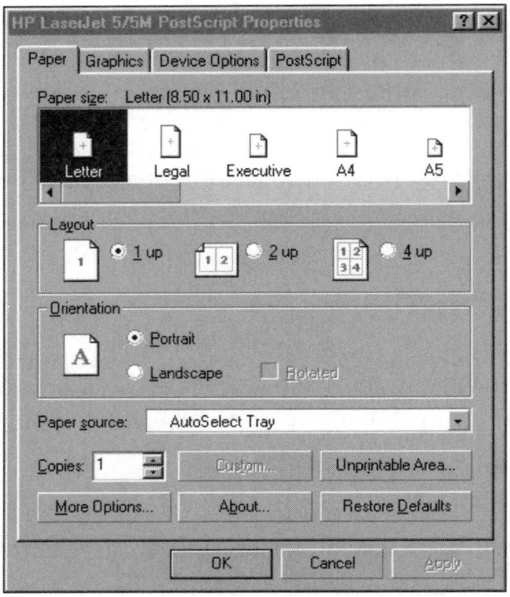

HP LaserJet 5/5M PostScript Properties [?][X]

Paper | Graphics | Device Options | PostScript

Paper size: Letter (8.50 x 11.00 in)

Letter | Legal | Executive | A4 | A5

Layout
○ 1 up ○ 2 up ○ 4 up

Orientation
A ● Portrait
○ Landscape ☐ Rotated

Paper source: AutoSelect Tray ▼

Copies: 1   Custom...   Unprintable Area...

More Options...   About...   Restore Defaults

OK   Cancel   Apply

Figure 13-2: Check this dialog box to make sure everything's in order.

✔ Not available for some printers, the Layout options let you group multiple pages from your drawing onto a single printed page. For example, you could select the 4 Up radio button to print four pages from your drawing on a single page, each reduced $1/4$ its normal size. This option is useful for getting a sense of what your pages look like without wasting a lot of paper and printing time.

✔ Select a radio button in the Orientation area to make sure your drawing lines up correctly on the printed page. If your drawing is taller than it is wide, select Portrait. If not, select Landscape.

✔ Some printers offer a Paper Source pop-up menu that enables you to specify where the paper is coming from. Most office printers have more than one paper tray. If you want to print on letterhead or some other kind of special paper, select the Manual Feed option. Then shout to the printer guy, "Shove a piece of letterhead into the manual feed slot, would you?"

You might also find a Copies option box, which lets you print more than one copy of each page in your drawing. Ignore this option for now. An identical, more convenient version of the option resides in the standard Print dialog box, as I explain in the upcoming "Printing multiple copies" section.

After making your selections, press Enter to return to the Print dialog box, which I discuss further in the next section.

Printing Those Pages

The Print dialog box is displayed in its entirety in Figure 13-3. Naturally, I could tell you how every single one of these options works. But for the moment, I assume that you're more interested in accomplishing a job than in finding out about printing on an option-by-option basis. To this end, the following sections outline some common printing scenarios. Later, I describe a few of the most important printing options on their own.

Figure 13-3:
The Print dialog box lets you specify which pages you want to print and how many copies of each page you want.

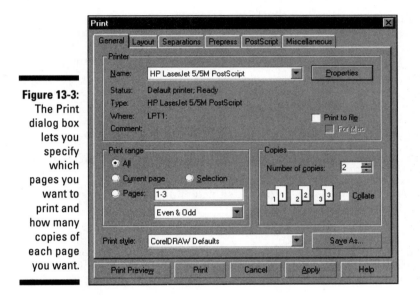

Printing the entire document

To print your entire document — whether it's a single-page drawing or a multipage document — do the following:

1. **Press Ctrl+P or choose File⇨Print.**

   The Print dialog box appears.

2. **Press Enter or click on OK.**

   CorelDraw initiates the printing process.

As CorelDraw works on printing your drawing, the progress bar in the right corner of the status bar shows how close the printer is to printing your artwork. If you think of something you missed — for example, "Aagh, I forgot to draw in the toenails!" — and you're interested in saving a bit of tree, press Esc to halt the print job and return to your drawing.

Printing multiple copies

The tried-and-true method for producing multiple copies of a drawing, newsletter, or other document is to print a single copy and then photocopy it or trundle it off to a commercial printer. The latter option offers the benefit of a variety of paper stocks and the satisfaction of truly solid inks, compared with the malaise of toner and spotty ink cartridges supplied by computer printers. Even a fly-by-night, cut-rate commercial printer delivers better results than a photocopier.

If you don't have time for a commercial printer and the office photocopier is out of whack, you can print multiple copies directly from CorelDraw:

1. **Make sure that the printer is turned on and stocked with enough paper.**

   A full paper tray is a happy paper tray.

2. **Press Ctrl+P or choose File⇨Print.**

   There's that Print dialog box again.

3. **In the Number of Copies option box, type the number of copies you want to print.**

   You can go as high as 999 copies, a sufficient number of copies to send most printers to the repair shop.

4. **Select the Collate check box to group all pages in a document.**

   When Collate is turned off, CorelDraw prints all copies of page 1, followed by all copies of page 2, and so on. When the option is checked, CorelDraw prints the first copy of each page in the document, then the second copy, then the third, and so on. The helpful little graphic to the left of the check box changes to demonstrate what you can expect.

5. **Press Enter.**

Printing a few pages here and there

When working on a multipage document, you won't always want to print every single page. One time, you might just want to see what page 2 looks like. The next, you'll want to reprint page 6 after correcting a typo. Still another time, you'll have to print a new copy of page 3 after the first one jams in the printer. To print certain pages only, follow these steps:

1. **Press Ctrl+P.**

   You've been through this enough times to use the keyboard equivalent and quit relying on the Print command.

2. **Click on the Current Page radio button to print the single page displayed on-screen.**

   If you want to print a range of pages, double-click on the value in the Pages option box (or press Tab until the box is highlighted). Then type in the pages separated by a hyphen. For example, to print pages 1, 2, and 3, enter **1–3** into the Pages option box.

   You can also print nonsequential pages separated by commas. To print pages 1, 2, 3, 5, 7, 8, and 9, for example, you enter **1–3,5,7–9**.

3. **Press Enter.**

Still More Printing Options

If you want to store up some extra printing knowledge for a rainy day, you might like to know what the following options do:

- ✔ Click on the Selection radio button to print only those objects in the drawing that are selected. (If no object was selected when you chose the Print command, this option is dimmed.)

- ✔ The Print dialog box also contains a Layout tab that provides options you can use to change the size of the drawing with respect to the printed page, as shown in Figure 13-4. (These options don't affect the actual size of the objects in the drawing area, mind you; they affect output only.)

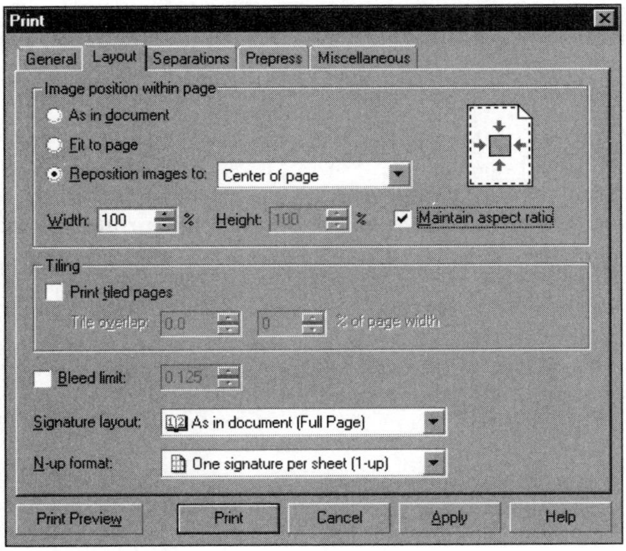

Figure 13-4:
Use the options on the Layout tab to change the size at which your drawing prints.

Print

General | Layout | Separations | Prepress | Miscellaneous

Image position within page

- As in document
- Fit to page
- Reposition images to: Center of page

Width: 100 % Height: 100 % ☑ Maintain aspect ratio

Tiling

☐ Print tiled pages

Tile overlap: 0.0   0   % of page width

☐ Bleed limit: 0.125

Signature layout: As in document (Full Page)

N-up format: One signature per sheet (1-up)

Print Preview | Print | Cancel | Apply | Help

If you access any tabs in the Print dialog box from print preview mode (discussed in the next section), the Print dialog box appears renamed as the Print Options dialog box. This seemingly weird renaming occurs probably because previous versions of CorelDraw housed the Print dialog box options in a separate dialog box named Print Options. I guess the folks at Corel just didn't want to confuse us.

✔ Select the As in Document radio button to print your drawing in the position it appears in your document.

✔ Select the Fit to Page check box to reduce the size of the drawing so that it just fits onto a sheet of printed paper. This option is especially useful when you're printing poster-sized drawings on printers that handle only letter-sized paper.

✔ Select an option from the Reposition Images To pop-up menu to specify the location of the drawing on the printed page. CorelDraw kindly provides a little picture to the right of the pop-up menu so that you can preview the result of your selection.

✔ Enter a value into the Width option box to change the width of the drawing by a percentage. By default, CorelDraw resizes the drawing proportionally, automatically adjusting the Height value according to your changes to the Width value. This is why the Height value is dimmed.

✔ To resize the drawing disproportionately, turn off the Maintain Aspect Ratio check box. The Height value becomes available so that you can edit it independently of the Width value.

✔ If you want to print a large drawing on small paper without reducing the drawing, you can cut it up into paper-sized chunks by selecting the Print Tiled Pages check box. For example, when printing an 11-x-17-inch drawing on a standard laser printer, the Print Tiled Pages option divides the drawing into four pieces and prints each piece on a separate page.

✔ Like the Layout options in the Properties area of the Print dialog box (see "Changing paper size and orientation" earlier in this chapter), the N-up Format pop-up menu offers options that enable you to group multiple pages from your drawing onto a single printed page.

✔ Man, is this stuff dry or what? Reading about printing options is like having sand in your mouth. Makes you want to spit. Ptui, ptui.

✔ Luckily, changing the printed size of a drawing by using the page preview window is much easier than messing around with many of the options mentioned so far. Read on to find out how.

Using the page preview area

CorelDraw's page preview options are located inside the print preview window, as shown in Figure 13-5. (Note that the default print preview window displays the property bar. But you may want to turn off the property bar, as in Figure 13-5, to display more of the print preview window as the toolbar offers the more useful controls.) To display your drawing in the preview window, you can either choose File⇔Print Preview or click on the Print Preview button in the Print dialog box. The various parts of the print preview window work as follows:

✔ To increase or decrease the size of the drawing, click on the arrow tool icon and then click on your drawing. The entire drawing becomes selected. You can then drag one of the corner selection handles to proportionally increase or decrease the printed size of the drawing. As you drag, the status bar shows you the current width and height of the drawing.

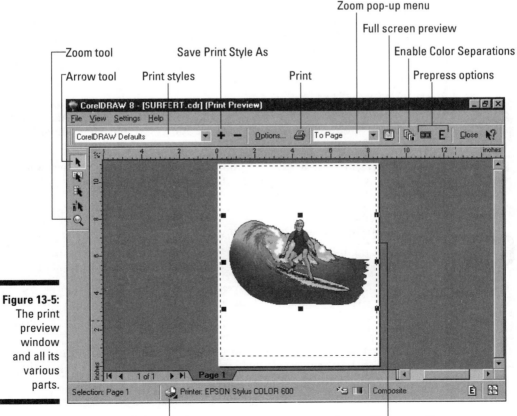

Zoom pop-up menu

Full screen preview

Enable Color Separations

Prepress options

Zoom tool

Arrow tool   Save Print Style As   Print

Print styles

Figure 13-5:
The print preview window and all its various parts.

Selected printer   Imageable area guide

✔ If the Maintain Aspect Ratio check box in the Print dialog box is turned off, you can drag a side, top, or bottom handle to stretch the drawing without regard for the original proportions.

✔ The Undo function doesn't work inside the print preview window. If you stretch your drawing beyond recognition and want to return to the original dimensions, just click on Close to close the preview window. Then, reopen the window to display your drawing at its original size.

✔ Click on the Options button to return to the Print dialog box (which appears renamed as the Print Options dialog box, as I mention earlier), and change any settings therein.

✔ Drag inside the area enclosed by the selection handles to change the placement of the drawing on the printed page.

✔ To zoom in on an area of your drawing, click on the zoom tool icon and click on the area that you want to inspect. To zoom out, Shift+click or right-click with the zoom tool. Alternatively, choose a zoom ratio from the Zoom pop-up menu or enter a custom zoom ratio in the pop-up menu.

✔ The *imageable area guide* outlines the area in which your printer can print objects. Except for typesetters and other fabulously expensive high-end printers, most printers have a dead zone around the outside of the page on which they cannot print. (Fax machines and old-style dot-matrix printers can print all the way from the top of the page to the bottom, but have dead zones along the sides.)

✔ If you select the Print Tiled Pages check box in the Print Options dialog box, you can enlarge the drawing to take up multiple pages. As you drag to make the drawing larger, CorelDraw adds more pages. If you make the drawing smaller, the program automatically deletes pages.

✔ The rulers provide additional points of reference when you're scaling your drawing. They even display tracking lines so that you can monitor the location of your cursor.

✔ Use the page navigation buttons and page tabs to view different pages, just as in the regular drawing window.

✔ Click on the full-screen preview icon to the right of the Zoom pop-up menu to fill the entire screen. Press Esc to return to the normal page preview window.

✔ Click on the status bar area labeled Selected printer in Figure 13-5 to display a pop-up menu, where you can choose a different printer for this print job.

✔ Press Ctrl+E to display the Separations tab of the Print Options dialog box, where you can specify whether you want to print color separations.

✔ Press Ctrl+M to display the Prepress tab of the Print Options dialog box. This contains options that enable you to add certain elements that may be required if you're sending your drawing to a service bureau for professional printing. Two of these options are available also as buttons on the print preview toolbar, as labeled in Figure 13-5. Check with your service bureau to see which, if any, of these elements you should include. If you're not sending your drawing out for high-end printing, you don't need to bother with these options.

✔ Click on the Print icon to send your drawing on its merry way to the printer. Or click on Close to return to the drawing window and play with your drawing some more.

If you find yourself using the same print settings repeatedly, you can save the settings as a *print style* by choosing File⇨Save Print Style As or by pressing the + button on the toolbar in the print preview window. CorelDraw displays a dialog box in which you can give the print style a name and select which print options you want to save. After you press Enter, your print style appears on the print styles pop-up menu in the print preview window as well as on the General tab of the Print dialog box. To apply the same print settings to another drawing, just select the style from the pop-up menu.

Printing full-color artwork

So far, I've covered and ignored roughly equal halves of CorelDraw's printing options. For reasons already discussed, I intend to leave it that way. But you should know about one other option, especially if you intend to print color drawings: the Enable Color Separations button.

Before I go any further, some background information is in order. You can print a color drawing in two ways: on a color printer or by separating the colors in a drawing onto individual pages. Each method has its benefits and its drawbacks:

✔ Printing on a color printer is easy, and you get what you expect. The colors on the printed page more or less match the colors on-screen. Unfortunately, a commercial printer can't reproduce from a color printout. Oh sure, you can make color photocopies, but professional printing presses can print only one color at a time.

✔ If you want to commercially reproduce your artwork, you have to tell CorelDraw to print color separations, one for each of the primaries: cyan, magenta, yellow, and black (introduced in Chapter 7).

To print color separations in CorelDraw 8, do the following:

1. **Click on the Enable Color Separations button in the print preview toolbar.**

   This button is labeled in Figure 13-5.

   Alternatively, you can select the Print Separations check box on the Separations tab of the Print Options dialog box, which you can access by pressing Ctrl+E from the print preview window.

2. **Press Ctrl+P.**

   CorelDraw automatically prints a separate page for each of the four primary colors.

Each page looks like a standard black-and-white printout, but don't let that worry you. When you take the pages to your commercial printer, a technician will photographically transfer your printouts to sheets of metal called *plates*. Each plate is inked with cyan, magenta, yellow, or black ink.

The technician prints all the pages with the cyan plate first and then runs the pages by the magenta plate, then the yellow plate, and finally the black plate. The inks mix together to form a rainbow of greens, violets, oranges, and other colors. For example, the four separations shown in Figure 13-6 combine to create a green Shenbop sitting on a royal purple lily pad. (Use your imagination — this is, after all, a black-and-white book.)

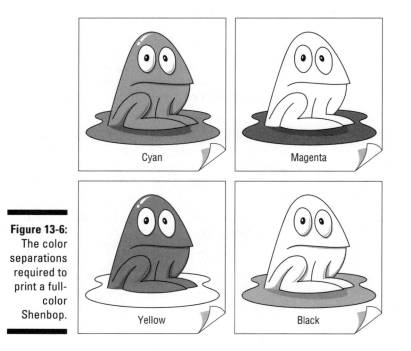

Figure 13-6: The color separations required to print a full-color Shenbop.

Chapter 14

Taking It to the Wide Web World

· ·

In This Chapter

▶ What you can and can't do with CorelDraw

▶ Preparing to create a document for the Web

▶ Creating a document for the Web

▶ Checking a document for HTML compatibility

▶ Saving a document as an HTML file

▶ Viewing an HTML file in a Web browser

· ·

*T*he World Wide Web is huge, exciting, and often downright frustrating, but it appears to be here to stay. No graphics software worth its salt would ignore the need to support the creation of Web-ready graphics. Fortunately, CorelDraw is worth its salt, and Version 8 includes new features to help make creating simple Web pages quick and easy work. In this chapter, I take you through the basics of creating a simple Web page and saving it for use on the Web.

CorelDraw and the Web

First, I should tell you that CorelDraw is not a full-fledged Web page design program and there are plenty of things CorelDraw can't do. However, CorelDraw can create Web-ready graphics and simple documents consisting of backgrounds, text, graphics, and clickable objects called *hyperlinks*. For the scoop on hyperlinks and other Web-related terms, check out the sidebar "Weird Web words."

Setting Up for the Web

Before you begin creating a document for the Web, do the following:

  ✔ Plan your Web page. Think about what you're trying to achieve. Decide how you are going to set up the graphics and text. You may want to sketch your page on paper before you begin creating it in CorelDraw.

✔ Choose Layout⇨Page Setup and change the unit of measurement to pixels. Consider how big you want your Web page to be. If you don't want people to have to scroll to view your entire page, set the Width and Height values to no more than 600 and 420, respectively.

✔ Choose View⇨Color Palette and select Netscape Navigator. This loads an 8-bit palette of 256 colors optimized for displaying graphics on the Web.

✔ Keep your Web page small and simple. On the Web, smaller is better. Large file sizes mean long download times, and no one wants to wait several minutes or more to download a page. Keep the design simple. Too many objects, busy or complicated backgrounds, or too much text makes for a confusing visual experience. You don't want visitors to your Web page to flee with aching heads, do you?

You need a Web browser, such as Netscape Navigator or Microsoft Internet Explorer, to view your finished Web page. You can download Navigator from Netscape's Web site at www.netscape.com or Internet Explorer from Microsoft's site at www.microsoft.com.

Creating a Web Document

To create a document for display on the Web, follow these steps:

1. **Create a background for the document.**

   To select a background color, press Ctrl+J to display the Options dialog box. Double-click on Document, double-click on Page, and click on Background. Then select the Solid radio button, choose a color for your page background from the color pop-up menu, and click on OK. In Figure 14-1, I chose a sea blue to suit my aquatic theme.

2. **Add objects and text to taste.**

   As I explain in Chapter 10, use artistic text for logos, headlines, and other text that requires special graphic treatment, such as blends, extrusions, and other effects. Use paragraph text for longer passages, such as full sentences and paragraphs, and for any text you want to be able to edit after you save your Web-ready file.

3. **Select an object you want to make a clickable hyperlink, and display the Internet Objects toolbar.**

   Select the object with the arrow tool. Right-click on the property bar and select Internet Objects from the resulting pop-up menu to display the Internet Objects toolbar, labeled in Figure 14-1. This toolbar enables you to assign a URL to the object, thus making it clickable.

Internet Objects toolbar Internet Bookmark Use Object Shape to Define Hotspot

Internet Address Use Bounding Box to Define Hotspot

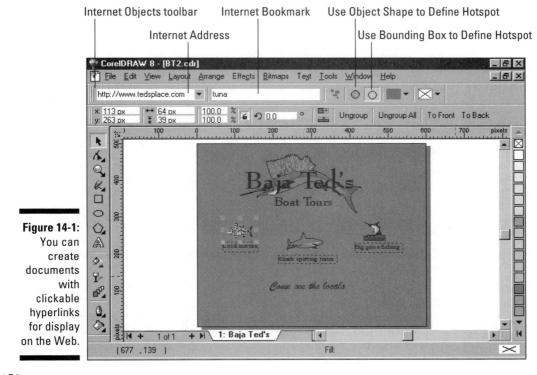

Figure 14-1:
You can create documents with clickable hyperlinks for display on the Web.

Weird Web words

Every hobby, occupation, and area of interest has its own vocabulary, and the Web is no exception. Here's a quick rundown on several basic Web terms you encounter in this chapter.

✔ **Uniform Resource Locator (URL):** The address of a Web page or other resource on the Internet. URLs usually begin with `http://www`.

✔ **Hyperlinks:** Objects that, when clicked, transport the clicker to another page on the Web via a URL.

✔ **Hypertext Markup Language (HTML):** The authoring language used to create documents on the Web. It consists of a set of tags used to add elements such as italics, images, and hyperlinks to Web pages.

✔ **Image map:** A graphic that consists of clickable areas containing links to other documents.

4. Assign a URL and bookmark to the selected object.

Enter a URL in the Internet Address pop-up menu on the Internet Objects toolbar to specify the address to which visitors will be linked when they click on the object. You may want to link visitors to another page on your Web site or to another Web site that may be of interest. In Figure 14-1, for example, I selected the tuna and typed in the URL for Baja Ted's other lucrative business, a restaurant called Ted's Place. Be sure to enter the complete URL (for example, `http://www.tedsplace.com`) or else the link won't work. After you assign a URL to the object, it becomes what CorelDraw refers to as an *internet object.* (By the way, Baja Ted and all other persons, places, and URLs in this chapter are fictional. Any resemblance to actual persons, places, or URLs is mere coincidence.)

Make sure that no internet objects overlap.

5. Assign a bookmark to the selected object.

Enter a name for your internet object in the Internet Bookmark option box. This creates a bookmark for the object, which helps you keep track of the hyperlinks you've created in your document.

To see a list of all bookmarks in your document, choose View⇨Dockers⇨ Internet Bookmark Manager. This displays the Internet Bookmark Manager docker, which offers options for selecting and removing bookmarks in your document. You can also link objects in your document to existing bookmarks; simply select an object, click on the bookmark that you want to link it to, and click on the Link button at the bottom of the docker window.

6. Assign properties to your internet object.

You need to define the boundaries of the clickable area of your internet object. This clickable area is called a *hotspot.* To set the object's shape as the hotspot, click on the Use Object Shape to Define Hotspot button on the Internet Objects toolbar. To set the object's bounding box as the hotspot, click on the Use Bounding Box to Define Hotspot button. Both of these buttons are labeled in Figure 14-1.

Using an object's shape to define a hotspot has its benefits. It enables you to position hyperlinks close together without running the risk of your objects' bounding boxes, and thus hotspots, overlapping. A major drawback, however, is that using an object's shape to define a hotspot can increase the size of your final file dramatically. If file size is a concern, you may want to define hotspots using bounding boxes.

7. Make paragraph text HTML compatible.

Select all paragraph text with the arrow tool and choose Text⇨Make HTML Compatible. The Make HTML Compatible command is available only when paragraph text is selected. This command converts paragraph text to HTML text so that you can edit your document's text directly in a Web browser after it's saved as an HTML file. Note that you can't apply transformations or other effects to HTML-compatible text.

If you don't make your paragraph text HTML compatible, it is converted to a bitmap (which is an image composed of pixels, as I explain in Chapter 1) when published to the Internet and cannot be edited in a Web browser. Artistic text, by the way, cannot be converted to HTML and is always treated as a bitmap.

8. Press Ctrl+S to save your document.

Checking Out Your Web Document

CorelDraw 8 offers a new feature that enables you to perform a search for any elements that may cause problems when you save your document as an HTML file, such as overlapping internet objects or text that is not HTML compatible. To search your document for potential conflicts, choose View➪Dockers➪HTML Object Conflict to display the HTML Conflict Analyzer docker. Select the Rescan the Document button, labeled in Figure 14-2. CorelDraw searches your document and displays warning messages in the docker window identifying any potential conflicts. Double-click on a warning message to select the object in your document to which the warning corresponds. Then you can correct the object causing the conflict.

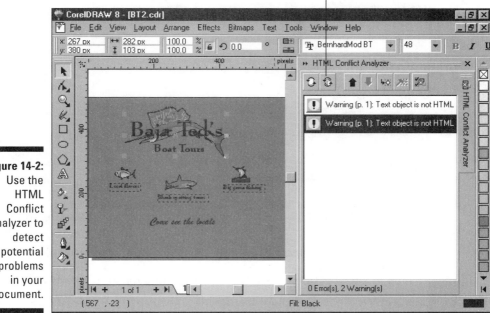

Figure 14-2:
Use the HTML Conflict Analyzer to detect potential problems in your document.

The HTML Conflict Analyzer has an annoying habit. It recognizes artistic text as not HTML compatible and displays warnings for every occurrence of artistic text in your document. In Figure 14-2, for example, it detected that "Baja Ted's Boat Tours," which I created as artistic text, was not HTML compatible. You can safely ignore warnings related to artistic text and rest assured that your text will be saved as an image file in your HTML document.

Saving Your Document as an HTML File

After you create your Web document, the next step is to save it as an HTML file. Fortunately, CorelDraw 8 walks you through the process with the Publish To Internet Wizard:

1. Choose File⇨Publish To Internet.

The Publish To Internet Wizard welcome screen appears.

2. Select the HTML radio button and click on Next to display the dialog box shown in Figure 14-3.

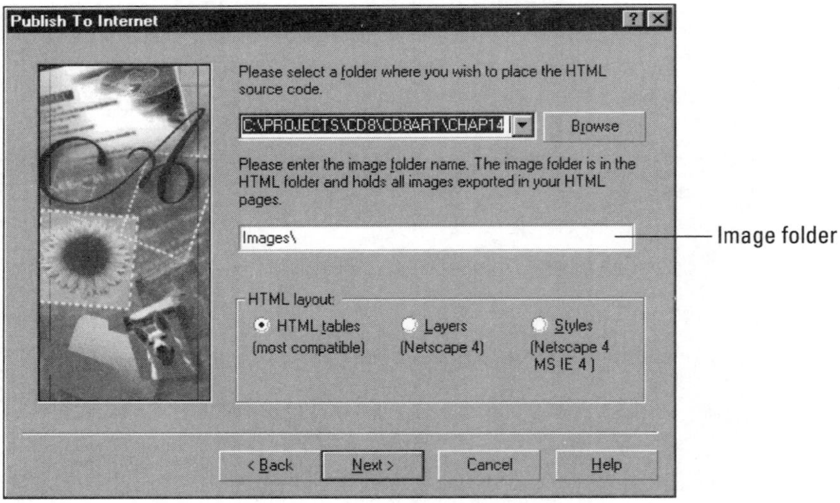

Figure 14-3:
Enter the names of the folders in which you want to save your HTML and graphics files in this dialog box.

> **Publish To Internet**
>
> Please select a folder where you wish to place the HTML source code.
>
> `C:\PROJECTS\CD8\CD8ART\CHAP14` [▼] [Browse]
>
> Please enter the image folder name. The image folder is in the HTML folder and holds all images exported in your HTML pages.
>
> `Images\` ————— Image folder
>
> HTML layout:
> ⦿ HTML tables (most compatible) ○ Layers (Netscape 4) ○ Styles (Netscape 4 MS IE 4)
>
> [< Back] [Next >] [Cancel] [Help]

3. Specify the folders in which you want to save the HTML file and image files.

In the pop-up menu at the top of the dialog box, select the folder in which you want to save the HTML file you are about to create. Click on the Browse button to navigate to an existing folder or to create a new folder. Then, in the Image Folder option box, which is labeled in Figure 14-3, type the name of the folder in which you want to save the graphics files for your document. By default, CorelDraw creates a folder named Images in the folder you specified as your HTML folder.

4. **Be sure that the HTML <u>T</u>ables radio button is selected, and click on <u>N</u>ext.**

5. **Select a file format for your images.**

The Publish To Internet Wizard, like Photo-Paint, saves your CorelDraw graphics as image files. (See Chapter 15 for details.) Your options are JPEG and GIF, as shown in Figure 14-4. JPEG is the better format for photographic and scanned images because it decreases file size by using lossy compression (a compression scheme that eliminates data with minimal impact on image quality), resulting in high-quality images with small file sizes. GIF is a suitable choice for high-contrast artwork and text but results in some color loss.

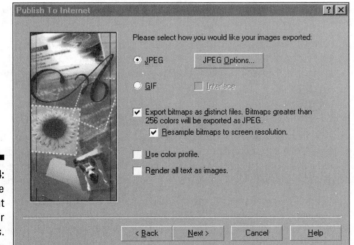

Figure 14-4: Select a file format for your images.

If you select JPEG, click on the JPEG Options button to display the JPEG Export dialog box, shown in Figure 14-5. This dialog box enables you to set the amount of compression, specify an encoding method, and preview the results of applying the settings to your image. See the sidebar "Setting JPEG export options" for details on using the options in the dialog box.

If you select GIF, you can choose to save your image so that it displays gradually on-screen (similar to the progressive option for JPEG files) by selecting the Interlace checkbox.

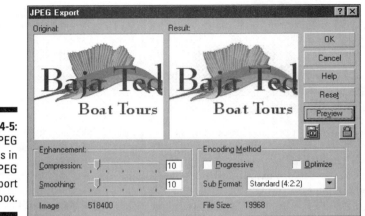

Figure 14-5:
Set JPEG
options in
the JPEG
Export
dialog box.

6. Set the remaining options in the dialog box.

Select the Export Bitmaps as Distinct Files check box. This tells
CorelDraw to export each graphic as its own file.

Select the Resample Bitmaps to Screen Resolution check box. This
ensures that any high-resolution files you may have imported into your
document will be resized to display properly on your Web page.

Click on Next to continue.

7. Select and name your document for export.

If your document is more than one page, select the pages you want to
export in the Page column of the Publish to Internet Wizard dialog box.
(See Figure 14-6.) If you want to export all pages in your document,
click on the Export All Pages button near the bottom of the dialog box.

In the Title (Page Name) column, type a title for your page. Finally,
enter a name for the new HTML file that CorelDraw is about to produce
in the File Name column. By default, CorelDraw retains the name of
your CDR file and simply replaces the cdr extension with htm. For
example, my file BT2.cdr is renamed BT2.htm.

8. Click on Finish to exit the Publish To Internet Wizard.

CorelDraw chugs away for several seconds and saves your document as
an HTML file.

CorelDraw automatically runs the HTML Conflict Analyzer before saving
a file to HTML. If it finds any potential conflicts in your document, it
displays a dialog box warning you that there are potential errors and
asking whether you want to correct them. If you have artistic text in your
document and you ran the HTML Conflict Analyzer before saving your
document (as I recommend earlier in this chapter), you can click on the
No button to proceed with saving your document as an HTML file.

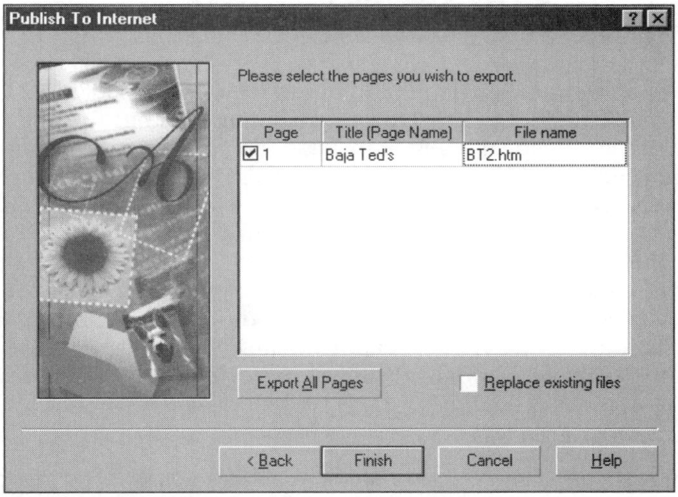

Figure 14-6:
Select and name the document for export as an HTML file in this dialog box.

Setting JPEG export options

The JPEG Export dialog box, shown in Figure 14-5, offers options for saving your images as JPEG files. Here's how it works.

✔ Use the Compression slider to set the amount of compression applied to your image. Lower values mean less compression and larger file sizes, and higher values mean more compression and smaller file sizes. Setting the compression to a value higher than 10 results in substantial damage to your image, so make sure that the Compression value is 10 or smaller. You can see the effect of your compression setting by clicking on the Preview button and comparing the original image to the compressed image in the Original and Result preview windows. Drag inside the Original preview window to preview different portions of the image.

✔ Use the Smoothing slider to tone down differences between adjacent pixels in your image. This process results in some loss of detail, so again, use a value of 10 or smaller. You can preview the result of your Smoothing setting by clicking on the Preview button.

✔ Set the encoding method by selecting either the Progressive or Optimize check box. The Progressive option saves the image so that it will gradually appear on-screen in multiple passes, thus enabling your Web page's visitors to get an idea of what the image looks like without having to wait for the entire image to load. The Optimize option saves the image so that it will appear on-screen in line-by-line passes, from left to right and top to bottom.

When you're happy with the settings you've specified, click on OK.

Viewing Your HTML File

To view your Web page, open the folder in which you instructed CorelDraw to save the HTML file in Step 3 in the preceding section. You see a new file with the name you specified in Step 7. My file, for example, is called BT2.htm. Open the HTML file in your favorite Web browser. Figure 14-7 shows Baja Ted's page when the HTML file is viewed in Microsoft Internet Explorer at a 640-x-480 monitor display setting.

You may recall that I designated the tuna as a hyperlink to the Web site for Ted's Place. So when I pass my cursor over the tuna, the bottom of the browser window displays the URL for the link, as shown in Figure 14-7. If I click on the tuna, my computer will be connected to the Web site for Ted's Place at www.tedsplace.com.

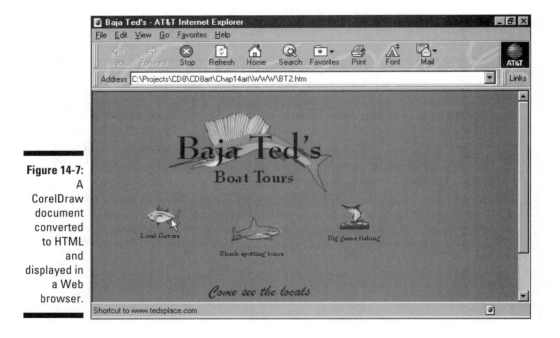

Figure 14-7:
A CorelDraw document converted to HTML and displayed in a Web browser.

Part IV
Corel's Other Amazing Programs

GUS & LILY'S
DOG GROOMING
NOW USING CorelDRAW

In this part . . .

As I mention in the introduction to this book, the CorelDraw 8 package contains more programs than you can shake a stick at, whatever that means. And as I discuss in Chapter 1, I consider several of those programs of marginal value at best.

But the two programs that I discuss in this part — Photo-Paint and Dream 3D — are a different matter entirely. Photo-Paint is a highly capable program for editing photographs on a computer, which is why I devote three chapters to the subject. After introducing the Photo-Paint interface, I move on to such topics as opening images; painting inside images using traditional tools, such as pencils and airbrushes; erasing mistakes; applying effects; and cloning portions of the image to cover up blemishes and add stuff that wasn't there in the first place. I also cover the Photo-Paint selection tools in alarming detail and explain the best way to sharpen the focus of an image and correct contrast and brightness.

Dream 3D takes you to the next frontier in computer graphics: three-dimensional drawing. Unfortunately, the frontier is pretty intimidating — Dream 3D is undoubtedly one of Corel's most complex programs. Chapter 18 eases you into the third dimension by providing a brief and gentle tour of Dream 3D. You find out how to import 3-D objects, how to move and rotate them in 3-D space, how to apply surface textures, and how to save the finished drawing as a photographic image. With remarkably little effort, you'll be rendering 3-D artwork, a practice so rarefied that fewer than 10 percent of all computer artists have ever attempted it.

Chapter 15

Everyone Say Hello to Corel Photo-Paint

*I*n the world of print advertising, nearly everything you see is a distortion of reality. Food products are lacquered with hair spray, the performance of major appliances is simulated, prefab clothing is custom tailored to fit the actors. As your mom warned you, you can believe only half of what you see, none of what you hear, and the exact opposite of what you see and hear in ads.

But what goes on in front of the camera is nothing compared with what happens after the film enters the mind of the computer. Rumor has it, for example, that every major movie poster is a veritable collage of body parts and other elements. The body you see almost never belongs to the actor whose head is pasted on top of it. In most cases, there's nothing wrong with the actor's body; it's simply more convenient to have an extra strike some poster pose and later slap one of the hundred or so head shots of the actor onto the body.

Corel Photo-Paint is the sort of program you might use to slap well-known heads on obscure bodies. Although it's not necessarily as capable as the mega-expensive image-editing systems used by professionals, Photo-Paint performs more than adequately for the price. You can open an image stored on disk and edit it in your computer. Draw a mustache on Aunt Patty, put Grandma Ida's eyebrows on Grandpa Neil's face, or distort little baby Melvin until he looks like Mighty Joe Young. The possibilities are absolutely limitless.

Blasting off with Photo-Paint

You start Photo-Paint by choosing Start⇨Programs⇨CorelDraw 8⇨Corel Photo-Paint 8. The first thing you see is a welcome screen similar to the one you see when you start CorelDraw. You can click on an icon to start a new image, open an existing image, scan an image using the CorelScan wizard (if you installed that option and you have a scanner), view the Photo-Paint tutorial, or view an introduction to the new features in Version 8. And if you never want to be bothered with the welcome screen again, deselect the Show This Welcome Screen at Startup check box.

After you open an image (as I explain later in this chapter), the Photo-Paint interface looks something like the one shown in Figure 15-1. Don't worry if your interface doesn't look exactly like mine. For one thing, Photo-Paint doesn't automatically open an image of a scary monster. And if you're using a monitor resolution of greater than 640 x 480, you should see a few more property bar and toolbar buttons on your screen than you see in Figure 15-1. But the interface shown in the figure is more or less what you can expect to see.

Here's paint in yer eye!

With luck, you recognize a few old friends from CorelDraw when you look at Figure 15-1. Photo-Paint offers a title bar, a menu bar, a property bar, a whole bunch of tools, a color palette, and a status bar, all of which perform like their counterparts in CorelDraw.

But just to make sure that you don't lose anything in the translation — or perhaps more appropriately, to ensure that the translation doesn't lose you — the following list should help jog your memory:

✓ You choose commands from menus by clicking on a name in the menu bar and then clicking on a command name in the ensuing menu. Alternatively, you can press the Alt key followed by the underlined letters in both the menu and command names.

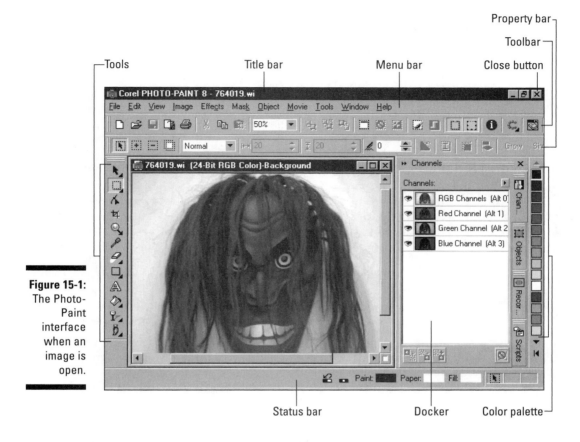

Figure 15-1:
The Photo-
Paint
interface
when an
image is
open.

Property bar
Toolbar
Close button

Tools   Title bar   Menu bar

Status bar   Docker   Color palette

✔ Or feel free to try out the keyboard shortcuts listed to the right of the command names in the menus. Common commands — such as File⇨Open and Edit⇨Copy — have the same shortcuts as they do in CorelDraw — in this case, Ctrl+O and Ctrl+C, respectively.

✔ The buttons on the property bar and toolbar duplicate functions found in the menus. To find out what a button does, pause your cursor over the button. Photo-Paint responds by displaying a little yellow label and providing a description of the tool in the status bar. The property bar buttons change depending on the tool that's currently selected in the toolbox.

✔ Any tool icon that has a small triangle in its lower-right corner offers a flyout menu of alternative tools. Press and hold the mouse button on the tool icon to display the flyout menu. Then click on an icon in the flyout to switch to a related tool.

✔ You can move the toolbox to a different location by dragging the gray area around the tools. You can move the property bar and toolbar in the same way. To return the toolbox, toolbar, or property bar to its original position, double-click on its title bar or in a gray area around the tools.

✔ As I mention in Chapter 2, some toolbar and property bar buttons are hidden if you use a monitor resolution of 640 x 480. To bring the buttons into view, drag the bar into the image editing area, as just discussed. Another alternative is to remove buttons you don't use; just Alt+drag the buttons off the bar. The remaining buttons scoot over to fill the empty space.

✔ Photo-Paint 8 displays a docker window on the right side of the document window by default at startup. It's actually a group of four dockers: Recorder, Scripts, Channels, and Objects. To tuck the docker away on the right side of the document window, click on the right-pointing double arrow in the top-left corner of the docker. Click on the left-pointing double arrow to redisplay the docker. To close the docker, click on the close button (the one with the X on it) in the upper-right corner.

The roll-ups in Photo-Paint work just like those in CorelDraw; for a refresher of all the ways to manipulate a roll-up, see Chapter 2.

✔ When in doubt, right-click on something to display a pop-up menu. You can uncover all kinds of useful Photo-Paint functions by right-clicking on tools, roll-ups, dockers, or the image itself. Generally, the functions in the pop-up menus duplicate commands found in the standard menus, but they can still come in handy.

Turn off the toolbar!

As I mention in Chapter 2, I'm not a big fan of toolbars. They take up space, their icons are scrunched and unrecognizable, and they duplicate commands already readily available in the menus. If you disagree — you prefer clicking on the little suckers to choosing commands or pressing keyboard shortcuts — then by all means leave the toolbar on-screen. But if you want to free up screen space, you can hide the toolbar by simply right-clicking on the gray space around the tools and clicking on the Standard option in the pop-up menu that appears.

To bring the toolbar back, choose View➪Toolbars, select Standard in the Options dialog box, and press Enter.

The toolbars are hidden in figures from here on. That way, I can show you more of the important stuff you need to see.

Opening Existing Images

Although you can create an image from scratch in Photo-Paint, you'll more likely be using the program to edit existing images, such as a photograph on disk or on CD-ROM. To open an image file, choose File⇨Open or press Ctrl+O. Photo-Paint displays the Open an Image dialog box, as shown in Figure 15-2. The dialog box works just like the CorelDraw Open Drawing dialog box, discussed in Chapter 3. After you select an image and press Enter or click on Open, the image opens up inside its own independent window, as shown back in Figure 15-1. Now you can edit that image till you're blue in the face.

Here are a few additional tidbits about opening images:

✔ The third CD-ROM included with your CorelDraw 8 package contains a sampling of photographic images. The images are stored inside the Photos folder on the CD.

✔ Unfortunately, the image files on the CD have unintelligible names such as 764019. (These images were originally scanned as special Kodak Photo CD files, which accounts for the random naming system.) If you turn on the Preview check box in the Open an Image dialog box, though, Photo-Paint shows you a tiny preview of what the photograph looks like when you click on the image file. If you want to play around with the frightening creature pictured in Figure 15-1, open the Objctvii folder and select file 764019.WI, as in Figure 15-2.

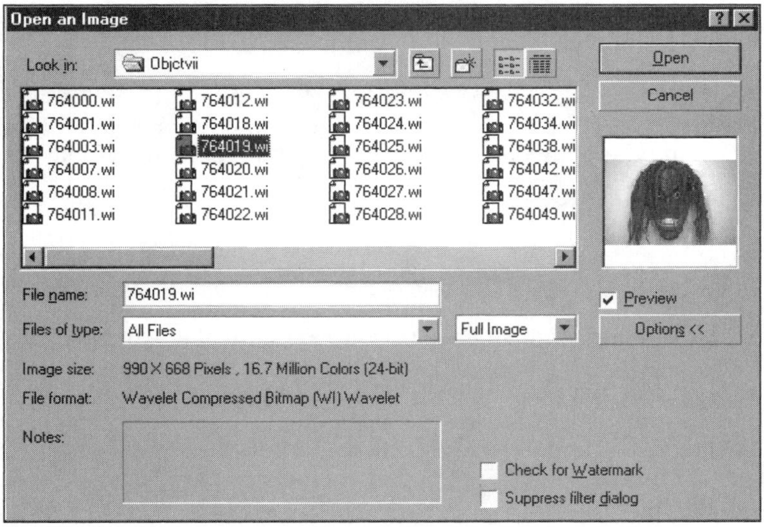

Figure 15-2:
Although Corel's image files have nonsense numerical names, you can take a peek at them by turning on the Preview check box.

Open an Image				? ☒
Look in: 🗀 Objctvii				Open
				Cancel

📄 764000.wi	📄 764012.wi	📄 764023.wi	📄 764032.wi
📄 764001.wi	📄 764018.wi	📄 764024.wi	📄 764034.wi
📄 764003.wi	📄 764019.wi	📄 764025.wi	📄 764038.wi
📄 764007.wi	📄 764020.wi	📄 764026.wi	📄 764042.wi
📄 764008.wi	📄 764021.wi	📄 764027.wi	📄 764047.wi
📄 764011.wi	📄 764022.wi	📄 764028.wi	📄 764049.wi

File name: 764019.wi

Files of type: All Files   Full Image   ✔ Preview   Options <<

Image size: 990 X 668 Pixels , 16.7 Million Colors (24-bit)

File format: Wavelet Compressed Bitmap (WI) Wavelet

Notes:

☐ Check for Watermark
☐ Suppress filter dialog

✔ The images provided in the CorelDraw 8 package are *huge*. If you're using a slower computer, Photo-Paint may take a long time — several minutes, actually — to open these images. So, if the little hourglass cursor (you know, the one that your computer displays to tell you to hurry up and wait) seems to be permanently affixed to your screen, don't panic and think that your system has crashed. Just go get a cup of coffee, walk the dog, or change the oil in your car. When you return, the image should be open.

✔ Photo-Paint can open images saved in any of the most popular image formats, including TIFF, PCX, JPEG, and Photo CD. For the lowdown on file formats, read Chapter 21.

✔ When you open an image from a CD-ROM, Photo-Paint displays a message telling you that the Save command is disabled. Because you can't save to a CD, Photo-Paint doesn't let you use the Save command at all. Instead, you have to use File➪Save As. Just press Enter to hide the message and get on with your life.

You also can open images by dragging them from the Scrapbook, shown in Figure 15-3. To display the Scrapbook, choose View➪Scrapbook➪Photos. Assuming that the CD is in your CD-ROM drive, the Photos tab of the Scrapbook appears on-screen. Use the Folder pop-up menu and Up One Level button to locate the folder that contains the image you want to open. Then, just drag the image thumbnail out of the Scrapbook and into the Photo-Paint editing window.

You can find a file using the Scrapbook's Find feature. Select Find from the pop-up menu labeled in Figure 15-3, and enter the name of the file you want to find in the Named pop-up menu in the Find: All Files dialog box that appears. In the Look In pop-up menu, specify the drive you want to search to find the file. Press Enter or click on the Find Now button to launch the search. The Find: All Files dialog box expands and, when Photo-Paint finds the file, it displays the name of the file, the folder in which it was found, the size and type of the file, and the date and time the file was last modified.

Viewing Your Image

When you first open an image, Photo-Paint displays the image as large as it can while still showing the entire image on-screen. But that doesn't necessarily mean that you can see every single pixel in the image. If you want to see one image pixel for every on-screen pixel, select the zoom tool, labeled in Figure 15-4, and choose the Zoom 100% icon on the property bar or select 100% from the Zoom Level pop-up menu, also found on the property bar.

Folder pop-up menu

Up One Level

Pop-up menu

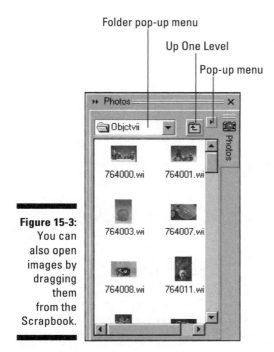

Figure 15-3:
You can
also open
images by
dragging
them
from the
Scrapbook.

The most accurate way to see an image is pixel for pixel. Otherwise, Photo-Paint has to redraw the image slightly to make the image pixels match the screen pixels. This redrawing is only temporary — Photo-Paint doesn't change any pixel in the actual file unless you tell it to — but the screen image may give you a slightly wrong impression of how the image will print. Of course, you have to view the image at smaller sizes sometimes, but it's good to return to the 100 percent view whenever possible.

To make the image fill the screen, click on the Maximize button, labeled in Figure 15-4. Photo-Paint hides all other open images so that you can concentrate on the one you're editing. You can still view another open image by choosing its name from the bottom of the Window menu. To return an image to an independent floating window, click on the Restore button, which takes the place of the Maximize button when the window is maximized.

Here are a few other ways to zoom and scroll around inside an image:

✔ Select the zoom tool, labeled in Figure 15-4, and click in the image to magnify the image. Or click on the Zoom In button on the property bar. Each click magnifies the image to the next preset zoom factor in the Zoom Level pop-up menu, found both on the property bar and the toolbar.

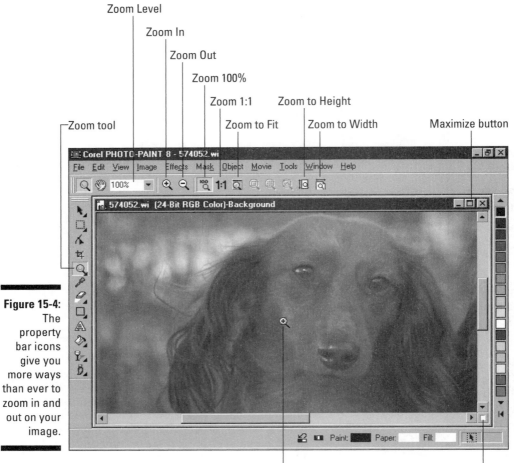

Figure 15-4:
The property bar icons give you more ways than ever to zoom in and out on your image.

Zoom Level

Zoom In

Zoom Out

Zoom 100%

Zoom 1:1

Zoom to Fit

Zoom to Height

Zoom to Width

Zoom tool

Maximize button

Zoom cursor

Navigator pop-up button

✔ Right-click or Shift+click with the zoom tool to reduce the image to the next lowest preset zoom level. (For right-clicking to work, the Use Right Mouse Button for Zoom Out option in the Tool Settings roll-up must be selected. Press Ctrl+F8 to display the roll-up.) Alternatively, you can click on the Zoom Out button on the property bar.

✔ Or use the same shortcut keys you use in CorelDraw: Press F2 to magnify the image; press F3 to reduce it.

✔ To fit the image on-screen so that you can see the entire photograph at once, press F4 or click on the Zoom to Fit button on the property bar.

✔ You can also choose specific view sizes — anything from 2 to 1600 percent — from the Zoom Level pop-up menu on the property bar.

✔ If you want to zoom to a custom view size — that is, a size not found on a menu — double-click on the Zoom Level pop-up menu, enter the view size from the keyboard, and press Enter. (Be sure to double-click on the pop-up menu's option box, not the arrow.)

✔ To view the image at the same resolution that it prints, choose the Zoom 1:1 button on the property bar. This view gives you an approximation of the printed size of your image. (Keep in mind that this setting is different than Zoom 100%, which shows one image pixel for every screen pixel, generally making the image appear larger than it will print.)

✔ To get a close-up look at a specific area of your image, drag with the zoom tool to create a marquee. Photo-Paint then magnifies the area inside the marquee to fill the entire window.

✔ By default, Photo-Paint does not change the size of the window when you zoom in or out of the image. You have to manually resize the window.

✔ To resize the window, just drag any corner of the image window.

✔ To make Photo-Paint automatically resize the window as you magnify or reduce the image, do this: Press Ctrl+J (or choose Tools➪Options) to display the Options dialog box. Click on General, select the Automatic View Resize check box, and press Enter. Now press F3 a few times. Photo-Paint reduces the window as it reduces your photograph. Notice that this feature doesn't work if the image window is maximized.

✔ If the image is bigger than the window, you can drag the scroll boxes in the scroll bars to reveal hidden portions of the photograph. Or you can click on the scroll arrows.

✔ But better yet, select the hand tool from the zoom tool flyout menu (or from the property bar if the zoom tool is selected) and then drag in the image to reveal the area you want to view.

✔ If you select the hand tool, you can also scroll the image by pressing the arrow keys.

If you don't care for the commands and tools I've mentioned so far, check out the next section, which explains the Navigator, another handy option for moving around your image.

Using the Navigator

In addition to using the scroll arrows and hand tool to display different portions of your image, you can take advantage of the pop-up Navigator window. Try this: Zoom in on your image until you see both the horizontal and vertical scroll bars appear. Now press and hold your mouse button on the little white box in the bottom-right corner of the image window (labeled "Navigator pop-up button" in Figure 15-4). The Navigator window appears, as shown in Figure 15-5. Without releasing the mouse button, drag the mouse to reposition the rectangle in the Navigator window. Photo-Paint scrolls your image to show the area surrounded by the rectangle. When you release the mouse button, the Navigator window disappears.

The Navigator pop-up button doesn't appear unless both the horizontal and vertical scroll bars are visible. In other words, if the entire width of your image or the entire length of the image is visible, you can't access the Navigator.

Figure 15-5: Drag the rectangle in the Navigator window to reveal a different portion of your image.

Dividing up Your Screen

Photo-Paint offers a grid, guides, and rulers, just like CorelDraw. You may not have much use for these tools, but they can come in handy on occasion. For the most part, the grid, guides, and rulers work just like the ones in CorelDraw, explained in Chapter 6. The major difference is that the commands for customizing the appearance of the grid and guidelines, which appear under the Layout menu in CorelDraw, appear under the Tools menu in Photo-Paint. Also, you can't create angled guidelines in Photo-Paint as you can in CorelDraw.

Creating a Brand Spanking New Image

If you'd rather not work from an existing image — as you do every time you press Ctrl+O — you can create an empty canvas and paint a new image from scratch. If the thought of doing so appeals to you, I can only assume that you're the type who's willing to forge ahead into the barren wasteland of the blank page. You're a pioneer — perhaps a little short on common sense, but full of confidence and bravery.

To create a new image, press Ctrl+N or choose File⇨New. Photo-Paint displays the dialog box shown in Figure 15-6. I darkened the two lowest check boxes in the dialog box to show how completely irrelevant they are to creating a new image. The remaining options require you to make three decisions:

- ✔ How large an image do you want to create?
- ✔ What is the image resolution?
- ✔ How many colors do you want to play with?

You don't need any help with image size; just enter the desired width and height of the image into the Width and Height option boxes.

Resolution and color open up whole new cans of worms, however, which is why I take a little extra time to explain them in the following sections.

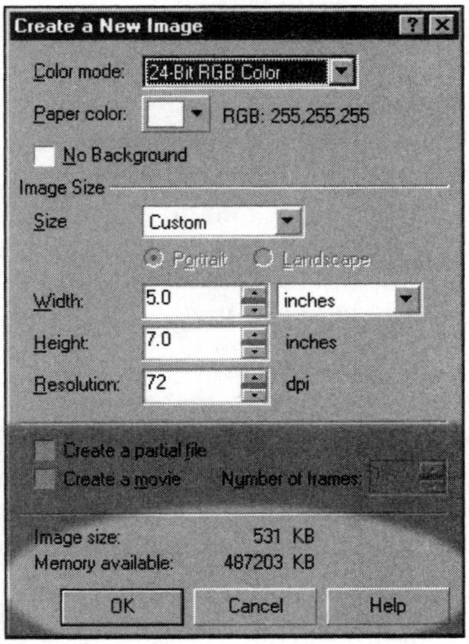

Figure 15-6:
In this dialog box, you can specify the size, resolution, and number of colors in a new image.

Dots per inch

The "Corel Photo-Paint" section in Chapter 1 tells about acquiring images and covers a few other items you may have found yourself wondering about — not the least of which is how images work. You may want to take a moment now and read that section.

To quickly recap: Unlike CorelDraw drawings, in which objects are defined by using complex mathematical equations, Photo-Paint images are made up of tiny colored dots called *pixels*. The number of pixels in an inch is called the *resolution*. So, if you create an image that measures 4 inches by 5 inches with a resolution of 72 dots per inch — or dpi (pronounced *d-p-i*) for short — Photo-Paint creates an image that's 288 pixels wide ($4 \times 72 = 288$) by 360 pixels tall ($5 \times 72 = 360$).

You specify a resolution by entering a new value in the Resolution option box.

Select your crayons

The first option in the Create a New Image dialog box, Color Mode, requires you to specify the number of colors you want to be able to display on-screen simultaneously. It's as if your mom required you to select a box of crayons before you sat down to color. The Photo-Paint Color Mode pop-up menu lets you select one of six boxes of crayons.

- ✔ The first option, 1-Bit Black and White, provides only two crayons, a black one and a white one. That's all you get.

- ✔ The second option is 1-Bit Grayscale, which offers 256 shades of gray, ranging from white to black.

- ✔ The next option, 8-Bit Paletted, contains 256 crayons. The interesting thing about this box is that you can swap crayons in the box for other colors. When you choose the option, Photo-Paint displays the Color Table dialog box, which shows you all the default crayons. If you don't like the default shade of a color, click on the color swatch, adjust the color as desired, and click on the Replace button. Click on OK to close the dialog box and open the new image window.

- ✔ The 24-Bit RGB Color option gives you access to 16 million colors. This option provides the most versatility, but it comes at a price. A 16-million-color image takes up three times as much room on disk as the same image in 256 colors. (All the photographs on the third CorelDraw CD-ROM are 24-Bit Color images.)

- ✔ The 24-Bit Lab Color mode is used by some high-end photo-editing folks. Trust me, you don't need to worry about this color mode.

- ✔ Neither do you need to worry about the 32-Bit CMYK option. It's specifically designed for painting CMYK images that you want to print to color separations (as described in the "Printing full-color artwork" section of Chapter 13). But you can print any color image to color separations, so the 32-Bit CMYK option makes your image more complicated without any real benefit.

For the best results, select the 8-Bit Grayscale option to create images that you want to print on a black-and-white printer, or select 24-Bit RGB Color to create full-color artwork. And if you're creating images for distribution on

What resolution do I use?

I wish that I could just tell you the perfect resolution to use and send you on your way. But even professionals who create images day in and day out can't agree on a perfect setting. Although I can't tell you exactly what resolution to use, I can give you some guidelines.

First, a little background: Higher resolutions result in better-looking images because they have more pixels to fool your eyes into thinking that they're seeing a regular photograph. Lower resolutions result in less focused images with occasionally jagged outlines.

High-resolution images also take up more space on disk, however, and make Photo-Paint work harder and print slower. Low-resolution images are speedy to edit and print.

Therefore, use the lowest resolution value you can get away with:

✔ If you're creating images for distribution on the World Wide Web or for display in a multimedia presentation, use 72 dpi, which is the resolution used by most computer monitors.

✔ If you just want to print the image on a laser or inkjet printer and tack it up on your wall, a value between 90 and 120 should suffice.

✔ If you're creating an image to include in a company newsletter, bump the resolution up to somewhere between 120 and 180. All the images printed in this book are in this range. All the full-screen images — such as Figure 15-1 — were printed at 140 dpi.

✔ If you plan on printing a full-color image for the cover of a catalog or some other spiffy publication, try a value between 180 and 300.

Try printing some test images between the aforementioned extremes and see how they look. You may even want to consult with a commercial printer whose opinion you trust. A lot of confusion exists in this area — and you'll very likely get different answers depending on whom you ask — so let me close with the only hard-and-fast rule: There's no wrong resolution value. What works for you is what counts.

the World Wide Web, you may want to use 8-Bit Paletted color mode; limiting your image to 256 colors results in smaller image files, and smaller image files require less time to send over the Internet, particularly when saved in the industry-standard GIF file format. The other color mode options aren't particularly useful.

Oh, and by the way, you can also change the color of the new canvas by selecting a color from the Paper Color pop-up menu. In general, however, I recommend that you leave the canvas white. After all, a white background ensures bright and vivid colors; any other background will mix with and therefore dim colors that you apply with some of the painting tools. Call me crazy, but I usually prefer to apply color with the painting tools as I go along instead of imposing a color on my artwork right from the start.

Taxing your memory

In the lower-left corner of the Create a New Image dialog box, spotlighted in Figure 15-6, Photo-Paint shows you how much memory is available to Photo-Paint. If the number is low, you may have trouble opening large images.

If Photo-Paint complains that it doesn't have enough available memory to create the image size you specify, try lowering the Resolution values. If that doesn't work, change the Color Mode option from 24-Bit Color to 8-Bit Grayscale or 8-Bit Paletted Color. And if the problem persists, lower the Width and Height values. (Note that the Image Size value in the Create a New Image dialog box refers to the amount of space the image consumes on disk, not in memory.)

Changing the Resolution and Color of Photographs

Resolution and color don't merely affect new images; they also affect photographs you open from CD-ROM or disk. For example, if you open an image from the third CorelDraw CD, its resolution is 96 dpi, and it contains millions of colors. To change the resolution of an open image, do the following:

1. **Choose Image⇨Resample.**

   Up comes the Resample dialog box, which lists the width and height of the image, along with two resolution values, much the same as the Create a New Image dialog box.

2. **Select the Maintain Original Size check box.**

   This step is extremely important! If you do not turn this option on, you run the risk of adding or deleting pixels, which you most certainly do not want to do.

3. **Make sure that Maintain Aspect Ratio is checked.**

   This option is probably already selected, but it's worth a quick look.

4. **Change the Horizontal value.**

   Thanks to Step 3, you don't have to worry about the Vertical value. Photo-Paint changes that automatically. (Similarly, if you change the Vertical value, Photo-Paint changes the Horizontal value automatically.)

5. **Press Enter or click on OK.**

To change the number of colors in an image, choose a command from the Image⇨Convert To submenu. For example, if you want to prepare one of the

Corel photographs for inclusion in a black-and-white publication, you remove the colors from the photograph by choosing Image⇨Convert To⇨ Grayscale (8-bit). In fact, that is exactly what I did to the photographs in this chapter.

Saving, Printing, and Closing

In general, saving, printing, and closing an image are very much like saving, printing, and closing a CorelDraw drawing, but you will find a few differences. Just for the record, here's how to perform these basic operations:

✔ To save an image, press Ctrl+S or choose File⇨Save. Remember, if you save early and save often, the brain you save could be your own.

✔ To save an image opened from a CD-ROM, you have to choose File⇨Save As. Photo-Paint displays the Save an Image to Disk dialog box. Here you can decide where to save the image on disk and what name you'd like to use. Because you're using Windows 95, your filenames can be virtually as long as you want (up to 256 characters).

✔ You may also want to change the file format by choosing an option from the Save as Type pop-up menu. By far the best option is TIFF Bitmap. TIFF is a standard among standards, supported by more programs than just about any other image format.

If you want to work repeatedly with an image from the third CD-ROM in the CorelDraw 8 package and your computer takes a long time to open the image, save the image as a TIFF file after you open it the first time in Photo-Paint. Then work with the TIFF version rather than the version on CD-ROM. Photo-Paint can open the TIFF version much more quickly than the CD-ROM version.

The second best format is JPEG Bitmaps, which alters the pixels in the image to save disk space. After you press Enter, a second dialog box appears, proffering a preview and some technical-looking options. Ignore all the options except the Enhancement slider bars. Make sure that the values to the right of the sliders are 10 or smaller. I'll say that again — 10 or *smaller.* (Higher values do major damage to the image — much more than I consider acceptable.) If the values are larger than 10, enter 10 in the option boxes and press Enter. Otherwise, just press Enter.

For more info on file formats, read Chapter 21.

✔ Just to be extra protected, turn on Photo-Paint's auto-save feature. Press Ctrl+J or choose Tools⇨Options to display the Options dialog box, and then click on Save. Check the Auto-Save Every option box and then specify how frequently you want Photo-Paint to save your image. If you want Photo-Paint to alert you before it saves the image, turn on the Warn Me Before Saving check box.

✔ If you want to print an image, press Ctrl+P or choose File➪Print to display the Print dialog box. For the most part, the options in the Print dialog box work similarly to those described in Chapter 13, which covers all the printing news that's fit to print. If you have more than one image open, the Documents to Print section of the Print dialog box offers check boxes for each image; select the check box(es) for the image(s) you want to print.

✔ Just as in CorelDraw, you can now preview your image before you print it by choosing File➪Print Preview. The Print Preview window works just like the CorelDraw preview window, also discussed in Chapter 13.

✔ To close the image in the foreground window, press Ctrl+F4, choose File➪Close, or click on the Close button in the upper-right corner of the image window (the one with an x on it). If you haven't saved your most recent round of changes, Photo-Paint asks whether you'd like to save the changes or chalk them up as a waste of time.

✔ Press Alt+F4, choose File➪Exit, or click on the Close button above the menu bar to get out of Dodge. If you've modified any open image since it was last saved, Photo-Paint asks you whether you might like to save the image to disk. After you answer this question for each and every altered image, you exit the Photo-Paint program and return to the Windows 95 desktop (or some other program you may be running).

Chapter 16
Spare the Tool, Spoil the Pixel

· ·

In This Chapter

▶ The Photo-Paint 8 toolbox

▶ Specifying foreground, background, and fill colors

▶ Erasing and undoing mistakes

▶ Creating rectangles and other basic shapes

▶ Filling areas with colors, gradients, textures, and patterns

▶ Using Photo-Paint's amazing paint tool brushes

▶ Applying special effects

▶ Cloning little bits and pieces of your photograph

▶ Erasing back to the saved version of an image

▶ Using the image sprayer tool

· ·

Chapter 15 kicks off your Photo-Paint adventure by explaining how to open and view images. But simply viewing an image is right up there with watching the grass grow. The real fun doesn't begin until you pick up the painting and effect tools, which I explain in this chapter.

Pawing through Your Toolbox

Figure 16-1 offers a field guide to the Version 8 painting and effect tools. If you're upgrading from Version 7, you'll notice a few changes to the toolbox. Most notably, the image sprayer, effect, and clone tools are now part of the paint tool flyout instead of having their own slots in the toolbox.

The key to controlling your tools is the Tool Settings roll-up, which you display by pressing Ctrl+F8 or choosing View➪Roll-Ups➪Tool Settings. The roll-up options enable you to customize a tool's performance with an astounding and sometimes excessive amount of precision, as illustrated by Figure 16-1, which shows how the roll-up appears when the paint tool is selected.

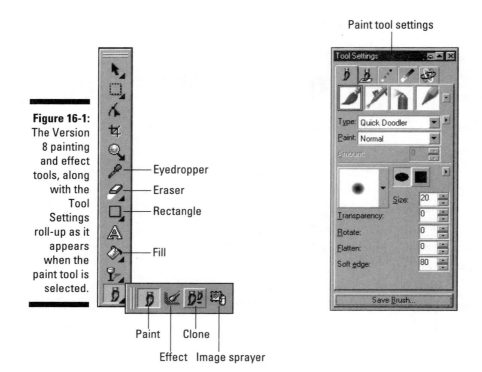

Figure 16-1:
The Version 8 painting and effect tools, along with the Tool Settings roll-up as it appears when the paint tool is selected.

Paint tool settings

Eyedropper
Eraser
Rectangle
Fill

Paint | Clone
Effect | Image sprayer

Many of the options in the Tool Settings roll-up are available also on the property bar. The important options are discussed along with their respective tools in the sections that follow.

Loading Your Tools with Color

Before you can apply color to your image, you have to specify which color you want to use. As you do in CorelDraw, you select colors from the color palette on the right side of the screen. Photo-Paint keeps track of three colors at a time: the foreground color, the background color, and the fill color. All three are displayed in the right portion of the status bar, as labeled in Figure 16-2. Here's the deal on the foreground, background, and fill colors:

✔ The line and paint tools draw in the foreground color (which Corel calls the paint color). Photo-Paint applies the foreground color also to the outlines of simple shapes — such as those drawn with the rectangle tool — and to characters created with the text tool.

You can select a new foreground color by clicking on one of the swatches in the color palette.

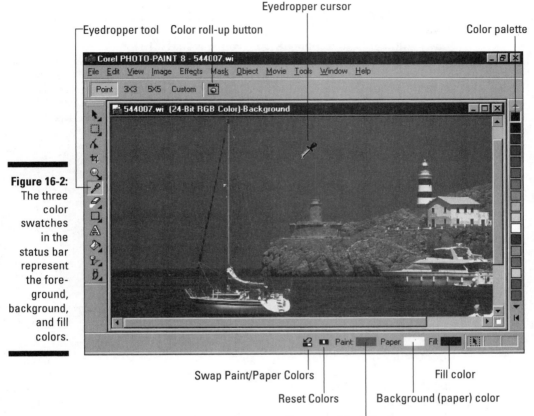

Eyedropper cursor

Eyedropper tool   Color roll-up button

Color palette

Figure 16-2:
The three
color
swatches
in the
status bar
represent
the fore-
ground,
background,
and fill
colors.

Swap Paint/Paper Colors

Fill color

Reset Colors

Background (paper) color

Foreground (paint) color

✔ The background color (which Corel calls the paper color) is used by the eraser tool. Also, if you select an area and press Delete, Photo-Paint fills the selection with the background color.

To switch to a different background color, Ctrl+click on a swatch in the color palette.

✔ The fill tool uses the fill color. Photo-Paint uses this color also to fill simple shapes created with the rectangle, ellipse, and polygon tools.

Change the fill color by right-clicking or Shift+clicking on a swatch in the color palette.

To swap the current foreground and background colors, click on the Swap Paint/Paper Colors button on the status bar. To return the background, foreground, and fill colors to their default colors — white, black, and black, respectively — click on the Reset Colors button on the status bar.

Lifting Colors Right Off the Canvas

When editing photographic images, you may find it helpful to match the foreground, background, or fill color to an exact color in the image. Doing so helps to hide your edits by maintaining color consistency with the original image. Sometimes, you want your effects to scream, "Look at me, I'm an electronic manipulation created in Photo-Paint!" But other times, you'd just as soon they didn't. When you're looking for subtlety, look to the eyedropper tool.

The eyedropper tool enables you to select colors from the image itself, and then turn around and apply these colors by using other tools. It's as if you're siphoning color out of your photograph by using a turkey baster or some other extracting device. Well, it's kind of like that anyway. The only difference is that you don't delete any color from the photograph. Oh, and unlike a turkey baster, the top of the eyedropper won't fall off in the dishwasher and melt on the heating unit. Here's how this savory tool works:

- ✔ After arming yourself with the eyedropper, labeled in Figure 16-2, click on a color in the image to select a new foreground color.
- ✔ Ctrl+click on a color in the photograph to replace the background color.
- ✔ Right-click or Shift+click on a color to replace the fill color.

Double-click on the eyedropper icon in the toolbox, press Ctrl+F2, or click on the Color roll-up button on the property bar (labeled in Figure 16-2) to display the Color roll-up, shown in Figure 16-3, which lets you define a custom foreground or background color. This roll-up works essentially like its counterpart in CorelDraw, which I describe in the "Make New Colors in Your Spare Time" section of Chapter 7. But a few items work differently:

- ✔ The two colored icons in the upper-left corner of the roll-up represent the foreground and background colors. Click on the icon for the color you want to change. It becomes surrounded by a black outline to show that it's selected. Then use the color slider and color selector box to define your custom color.
- ✔ Click on the swap colors icon to make the foreground color the background color and vice versa.
- ✔ Click on the default colors icon to return to the default foreground (black) and background (white) colors.
- ✔ To add your custom color to the color palette, choose Add Color from the roll-up's pop-up menu.

- ✔ To create a custom fill color, use the Color roll-up to establish your color, and then add the color to the color palette as just described. You can then assign your custom color as the fill color by right-clicking on the custom color's swatch in the color palette.

Background color

Foreground color

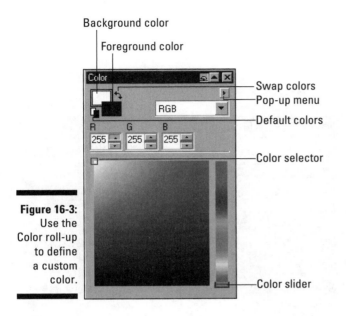

Swap colors
Pop-up menu

Default colors

Color selector

Figure 16-3:
Use the
Color roll-up
to define
a custom
color.

Color slider

You can create custom colors also by using the new Palette Editor (which you can display by choosing Tools➪Palette Editor). This works essentially like the Palette Editor in CorelDraw. See Chapter 7 for details.

Erasing and Undoing Your Way Back to the Good Old Days

In real life, an eraser gives you the opportunity to retract a pencil stroke. But it doesn't do a comprehensive job — you can still see some pencil remnants — and you can't use the eraser to undo other kinds of strokes, such as pen strokes, paint strokes, and big globs of black tar.

Photo-Paint 8 handily addresses this problem by offering not one but three erasers that erase everything under the sun, plus an Undo command that enables you to undo multiple operations. If necessary, you can even restore your image to the way it appeared when you last saved it to disk.

Scrubbing away those stubborn stains

Photo-Paint provides three different erasers — one that's very useful, another that's moderately so, and another that you can probably do without. The eraser flyout menu and its assortment of erasers are shown in Figure 16-4.

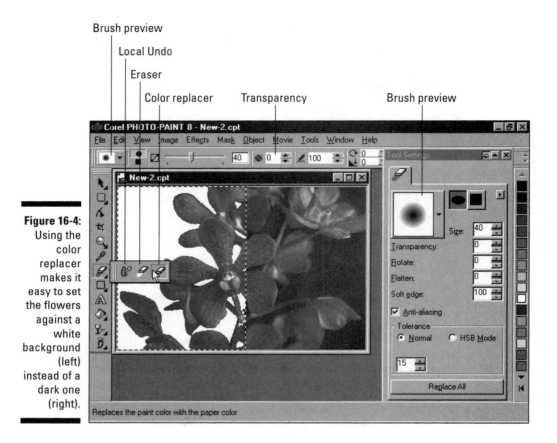

Figure 16-4:
Using the
color
replacer
makes it
easy to set
the flowers
against a
white
background
(left)
instead of a
dark one
(right).

Here's the lowdown on the three erasers:

✔ Drag with the Local Undo tool to selectively undo the effects of the most recent operation. Unlike Edit⇨Undo, which undoes the entire operation, the Local Undo tool restores only the portion of the image you drag over. This tool is especially useful for erasing small portions of a line you just finished drawing. I rate this tool as very useful.

Be sure to set the Transparency value (either in the roll-up or on the property bar) to 0 to completely erase to the saved image.

✔ If you double-click on any of the eraser icons, you apply that tool's effect to the selected portion of the image. (I explain how to select stuff in the next chapter.) If nothing is selected, Photo-Paint applies the effect to the entire image.

The tool icon must be visible in the toolbox for you to double-click on it. You can't double-click on a flyout icon.

✔ The standard eraser tool paints a line in the background color. But if you want to paint in white (the default background color), you're better off simply changing the foreground color to white and using the paint tool, which is infinitely more versatile. If you do decide to use the eraser tool, be sure to turn on Anti-aliasing, which softens the eraser's edges. To turn on Anti-aliasing, select the option in the Tool Settings roll-up or click on the Anti-aliasing button on the property bar. (If the option is turned on, the button appears depressed.)

Double-click on the eraser tool to fill your image or selection with the background color. (Selections are explained in Chapter 17.)

✔ As you drag with the color replacer tool, Photo-Paint replaces all occurrences of the foreground color (and colors similar to it) with the background color. This tool can be moderately useful.

For example, in Figure 16-4, the flowers in the left half of the image window were originally set against a black background, just like the flowers in the right half of the window. To change the background from black to white, I simply selected the left half of the window (as I explain in the next chapter), set the foreground color to black and the background color to white, and double-clicked on the color eraser icon. If I had tried instead to use the paint tool or regular eraser, changing the background would have been a tedious chore. The color replacer makes quick work of the job.

✔ Options in the Tool Settings roll-up and on the property bar let you change the size and shape of the eraser. Click on the brush preview (labeled in Figure 16-4) to display a pop-up menu of preset eraser shapes. You can also edit the Size, Rotate, and Flatten values to create a custom brush, but Photo-Paint provides you with so many presets that you probably won't need to bother.

✔ Raise the Transparency value to mix the background color with the existing colors in the image. Higher values — up to 99 — make the background color more translucent.

✔ When using the color replacer tool, you can control how many colors in the image get changed to the background color. The value in the Tolerance option box determines how close a color has to be to the foreground color to be replaced. Higher values cause more colors to be replaced; lower values replace fewer colors. (The Tolerance option box is at the bottom of the roll-up and just to the right of the HSB button on the property bar.)

Strangely enough, the best eraser tool isn't an eraser tool at all. It's a special function of the clone tool called the eraser brush. Read the "Painting One Portion of an Image onto Another" section to find out all about it.

Reviewing the history of your image

As long as I'm on the subject of undoing things, I should mention that the Undo command in Photo-Paint 8 works just like the one in CorelDraw. You can undo a whole series of operations. Just keep choosing Edit⇨Undo or pressing Ctrl+Z.

To do so, however, you need to change a setting in the Options dialog box. (Choose Tools⇨Options or press Ctrl+J.) Double-click on Workspace, click on Memory, and look for the Undo Levels option box. The default setting is 1, which limits you to undoing only one operation. Raising the value enables you to undo more operations. But keep in mind that the higher you set the value, the more you tax your computer's brain. I recommend that you set the Photo-Paint Undo Levels value no higher than 3 or 4 unless your computer has tons of memory. After you enter a new value in the Undo Levels option box and press Enter, Photo-Paint displays a message telling you that you must restart Photo-Paint for your new setting to take effect. Click on the Yes button to restart the program. Photo-Paint will ask whether you want to save changes to any open documents. I recommend that you accept this kind offer.

If you change your mind after choosing Edit⇨Undo, choose Edit⇨Redo. Photo-Paint redoes all those operations that you just undid.

Going back to square one

Suppose that you create and save an image. Then, in a creative fit, you paint all over your image, apply a half dozen special effects, and otherwise completely muck things up. After further reflection, you decide that you absolutely hate everything. No problem. Just choose File⇨Revert. Photo-Paint restores your image to the way it appeared the last time you saved it. All evidence of your embarrassing artistic flailings magically disappears.

Drawing Lines

If you simply want to draw straight lines, you have two options:

- ✔ Ctrl+drag with the paint tool. Using this method, you can create horizontal and vertical lines only.

- ✔ Pick up the line tool, which appears on the rectangle tool flyout. (The line tool icon looks like a pencil drawing a line, and it's labeled in Figure 16-5.) With this tool, you can create straight lines in any direction.

My biggest complaint with the line tool is that you can't assign arrowheads to the ends of the lines as you can in CorelDraw. Still, I guess you may occasionally find a use for this tool, so here's how to use it:

✔ Drag with the line tool to draw a straight line between two points. Click with the tool and then keep clicking at different locations to draw a free-form outline with straight sides. Each time you click, you set a corner in the shape. Double-click to end the line.

✔ Be sure to turn on the Anti-aliasing option (found both on the property bar and in the Tool Settings roll-up). Hard-edged lines have no business populating your photographs. After all, hard edges interrupt the seamless blend between pixels that is the hallmark of computer images.

✔ Using the controls on the property bar or Tool Settings roll-up, you can also adjust the transparency, width, and type of joint used to join two lines. In addition, you can tell Photo-Paint to automatically turn your line into an object after you finish drawing it. (Use the Render to Object option.) For more on turning stuff into objects, see Chapter 17.

✔ The options in the Paint Mode pop-up menu determine how the line color mixes with the colors in the image. For more on paint modes, see the upcoming section "Painting with a Tackle Box Full of Brushes."

Drawing Geometric Shapes

Photo-Paint provides three simple shape tools: the rectangle, polygon, and ellipse tools, which you access by clicking and holding on the rectangle tool icon, as illustrated in Figure 16-5. Here's how these tools work:

✔ The rectangle tool lets you draw rectangles. Ctrl+drag to draw squares; Shift+drag to draw the shape outward from the center. You can select the rectangle tool by pressing F6.

✔ The ellipse tool draws. . . . I think you can guess the ending to that sentence. Ctrl+drag to draw circles; Shift+drag to draw from the center out. Press F7 to select the ellipse tool. (Yet another waste of a keyboard shortcut.)

✔ The polygon tool draws orange hamsters dressed in festive German drinking costumes.

No, sorry, my mistake. After reviewing my notes, I find that the polygon tool actually draws free-form shapes with straight sides. This role means that it's less like the polygon tool in CorelDraw and more like the line tool in Photo-Paint. You click to add corners and double-click when you're finished.

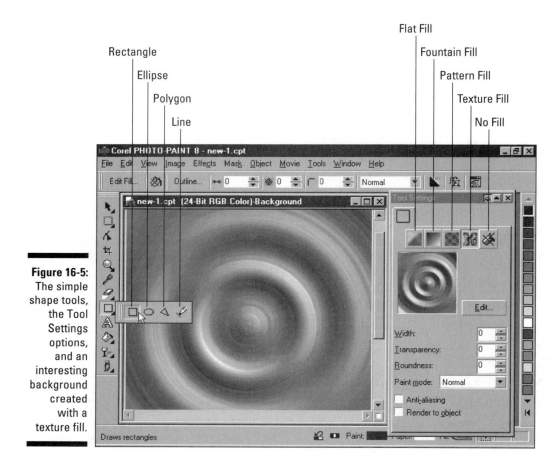

Figure 16-5:
The simple shape tools, the Tool Settings options, and an interesting background created with a texture fill.

By default, Photo-Paint fills the shapes with the fill color. But you can also request no fill or some special fill by using the options in the Tool Settings roll-up. Click on the Fountain Fill icon in the roll-up, for example, to fill the shape with a gradation. Click on the Edit button to choose a pattern or texture for your fill. Click on the No Fill icon to make the fill transparent. Each one of these icons, labeled in Figure 16-5, directly corresponds to a special fill function in CorelDraw, as described in "The World of Wacky Fills" section of Chapter 7. To return a solid fill, click the Flat Fill icon.

The Tool Settings roll-up contains a Render to Object option that enables you to convert a shape to an object immediately after you draw it. For more about converting images to objects, see Chapter 17.

You can access the various fill alternatives also by clicking on the Edit Fill button on the property bar. Photo-Paint displays a dialog box that contains some of the same options found in the Tool Settings roll-up. (The other options are presented as individual buttons on the property bar.)

Although the special fill options are certainly attractive, they can't gloss over the simple fact that geometric shapes lend themselves to image editing about as well as vampire bats lend themselves to deep-sea diving. Their harsh corners and high-contrast curves interrupt the naturalistic appearance of just about any image.

So if you don't want people to be able to see from several miles off that you've been mucking about in an image, don't use the simple shape tools. The only exception is the rectangle tool, which has one beneficial application: You can use it to draw an outline around your image. Select the No Fill icon, enter a Width value to set the outline to the desired thickness, and then draw a rectangle around the entire image.

In previous versions of Photo-Paint, the rectangle tool also came in handy for creating custom backgrounds like the one in Figure 16-5. You can still use the rectangle for this purpose: Set the Width value to 0 to turn off the outline, choose your fill, and then drag across the image. But an easier option is to use the Fill command, described next.

Filling Your Entire Image

The Fill command enables you to quickly fill your entire image or a selected area with a color, a gradient, a texture, or a pattern. This command can come in handy if you want to create a custom background like the one shown in Figure 16-5, or cover your image with a partially transparent fill.

To use the command, choose Edit⇨Fill to display the Edit Fill & Transparency dialog box, shown in Figure 16-6. The various options work as follows:

- ✔ The Fill Color tab contains options that enable you to choose whether you want to fill the image with the foreground color, background color, fill color, gradient, texture, or pattern.

- ✔ Click on the Edit button to select a different texture, pattern, or gradient or to define a custom color.

- ✔ To change the fill color to a color in your image, click on the eyedropper icon and then click on the color in your image.

- ✔ The Transparency panel enables you to fade the fill so that some of your underlying image shows through. To cover your entire image with a transparent fill, choose Flat from the Type menu. Then adjust the transparency level by using the Start Transparency value. Higher values make the fill more transparent.

Transparency control arrows

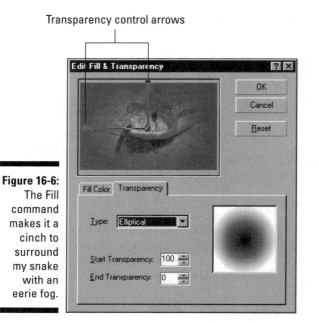

Figure 16-6:
The Fill
command
makes it a
cinch to
surround
my snake
with an
eerie fog.

✔ To create a gradient fill that fades from one level of transparency to another across your image, choose any other Type option except None. Photo-Paint displays transparency control arrows as in Figure 16-6. Drag the arrows to reposition the start and end points of the gradient. To adjust the amount of transparency at the beginning and end of the gradient, use the Start Transparency and End Transparency options.

To create the snake-peeking-out-of-the-fog look shown in Figure 16-6, for example, I lifted a fill color from my image with the eyedropper tool and selected the Current Fill option on the Fill Color tab. Then, on the Transparency panel, I selected the Elliptical option, set the Start Transparency value to 100, and set the End Transparency value to 0. Ooh, scary.

✔ If you want to fill only a portion of your image, select the area before choosing the Fill command. Selecting stuff is the subject of Chapter 17.

✔ As I mention earlier, double-clicking on the eraser icon in the toolbox fills the selected area or image with the background color.

Plunking Down the Paint

The next tool on our hit parade is the fill tool, which looks like a tipped bucket with paint dribbling out of it. Whereas the Fill command covers your entire image with a fill, the fill tool replaces an area of continuous color with the fill color.

In Figure 16-7, I set the fill color to white and clicked with the fill tool inside the archway. Photo-Paint replaced the previously black pixels with white, making the archway look like it goes right through the page — if you use your imagination, that is.

To control the range of colors affected by the fill tool, enter a value into the Tolerance option box, found in the bottom-left corner of the Tool Settings roll-up and just to the right of the HSB button on the property bar. Lower values affect fewer colors. You can also select the Anti-aliasing check box or property bar button to soften the edges of the filled area. (In Figure 16-7, the Tolerance value was 10, and Anti-aliasing was turned on.)

Fill tool cursor

Figure 16-7:
An area of black before (left) and after (right) clicking on it with the fill tool.

You can change the fill color from a flat fill to a gradation or texture by clicking on the icons along the top of the Tool Settings roll-up. These are the same icons labeled back in Figure 16-5. The No Fill icon is absent; after all, replacing an area with a transparent fill doesn't make any sense. I mean, what is there to see behind the image? The Windows 95 desktop? The motherboard and other yucky computer innards? The center of the Earth? Without the No Fill icon, we'll never know.

Creating Custom Gradients

Just like CorelDraw 8, Photo-Paint 8 offers an interactive fill tool (formerly known as the interactive gradient fill tool), labeled in Figure 16-8, which you can use to create custom gradients.

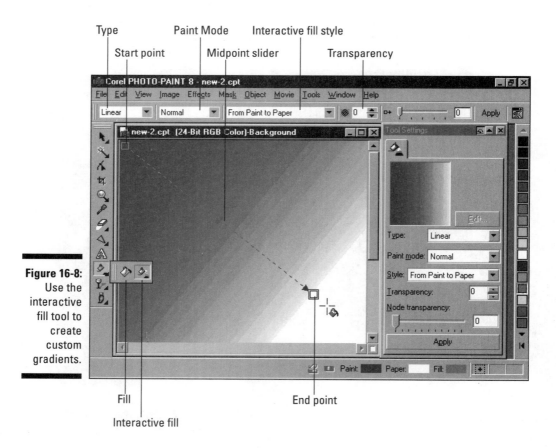

Figure 16-8: Use the interactive fill tool to create custom gradients.

To create a custom gradient, select the interactive fill tool and select a gradient type from the Type pop-up menu in the roll-up or from the property bar. (Don't choose Flat or None; these options don't create a gradient; rather, they enable you to replace a gradient-in-progress with a flat fill or no fill, as I explain a little later.) Photo-Paint automatically fills the image or the selected area with a gradient and displays the gradient start and end point controls and the midpoint slider shown in the figure.

Drag the start or end point controls to reposition the start and end colors in the gradient, or change the angle of the gradient. Or drag the midpoint slider to adjust the position of colors. Use the controls on the property bar or in the Tool Settings roll-up to change the gradient type, style, and transparency. If you want to return to having no fill or a solid fill, choose None or Flat, respectively, from the Type pop-up menu. For some really fun effects, play around with the different options in the Paint Mode pop-up menu, which control how the pixels in your gradient blend with the underlying image pixels.

When you're satisfied with your gradient, click on the Apply button on the property bar or in the roll-up. Your gradient is now set in stone; you can't edit it further as you can in CorelDraw. (Note that if you choose None from the Type pop-up menu, the Apply button is dimmed because Photo-Paint has nothing to apply.)

Painting with a Tackle Box Full of Brushes

Using the paint tool — the one that looks like a little paint brush — is simplicity itself. You merely click or drag around inside the image to lay down strokes of foreground color.

Adjusting the properties of the paint tool in the Tool Settings roll-up can be a nightmare, however. Quite simply, the roll-up offers far more options than you will ever exploit — assuming, of course, that you have a life.

So, rather than explain every available option, I limit my discussions to the handful of options that matter most:

✔ Shown in Figure 16-9, five tab icons appear along the top of the Tool Settings roll-up. You can click on one of these tabs to switch between the five panels of paint tool options. But don't. The second, third, fourth, and fifth panels are filled with goofy options that you'll never use in a billion years. The one exception is the Anti-aliasing option found on the fourth panel. This option is turned on by default, which is how you should leave it.

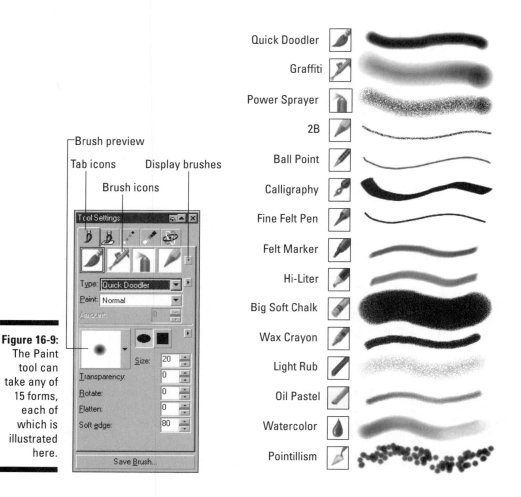

Figure 16-9:
The Paint tool can take any of 15 forms, each of which is illustrated here.

✔ Beneath the row of tab icons is a row of four slightly larger icons. These icons represent the predefined brushes. Although you can see only 4 brushes at a time, Photo-Paint 8 offers a total of 15 brushes. To display all the brushes, click on the down-pointing arrow to the right of the icons.

Instead of explaining how each of the 15 brushes works, I show lines painted with the brushes in Figure 16-9. Each brush is pictured and labeled next to its line. The paint tool always paints in the foreground color, except when you use the Watercolor brush (second from the bottom). This brush smears existing colors in the image as if the colors were wet. (When painting on a brand new image, the brush lays down watercolor-like strokes in the foreground color.)

✔ Below the brush icons is a Type pop-up menu. If you're looking for a slightly different effect than what is offered by the 15 brushes, you can select a different effect from this menu.

✔ To mix the foreground color with the existing colors in an image in wacky and unusual ways, select an option from the Paint pop-up menu. To explain how all these options work would take five more books. But I do want to call your attention to three fun options: Add, Subtract, and Color.

Select the Add option to lighten the colors in an image as you paint over them. This option works especially well with the Hi-Liter brush and a dark foreground color. Select Subtract to darken colors — great for use with the Felt Marker and a light foreground color. And select Color — much farther down the menu — to colorize an image with any brush. (By *colorize,* I mean to add color to a black-and-white image or replace the color without affecting the detail in a color image.)

✔ To change the size and shape of the brush, click on the brush preview (labeled in Figure 16-9) to display a pop-up menu of alternatives. You can also adjust the values in the five option boxes below and to the right of the preview, but you can generally rest assured that the pop-up menu offers every brush size and shape you'd ever want.

✔ Folks who are serious about painting generally prefer to work with a cursor that represents the brush size and shape. To swap the silly paintbrush cursor for a size and shape cursor, press Ctrl+J (or choose Tools➪Options), double-click on Workspace, click on General, select the Shape Cursor for Brush Tools check box, and press Enter. This option affects the cursors used by the tools that have adjustable brushes — namely, the paint, effect, clone, and eraser tools.

If you prefer a simple crosshair cursor, choose Crosshair from the Cursor Type pop-up menu and turn off the Shape Cursor for Brush Tools check box. With this option, all tools except the arrow tool and path node edit tools use the crosshair cursor. If you choose Shape from the pop-up menu, you get a size and shape cursor for the paint, effect, clone, and eraser tools, a crosshair for some other tools, and a cursor that resembles the tool icon for the remaining tools. Whew, that was a lot of work!

Almost all the options found on the first panel of the Tool Settings roll-up are also available on the property bar. If you're not sure what a property bar control does, pause your cursor over the control to display an identifying label.

Smudging, Lightening, Colorizing, and Blurring

The second tool on the paint tool flyout is the effect tool. As you do with the paint tool, you use the effect tool by dragging across your image. And as with the paint tool, you can adjust the way the effect tool works by selecting different brushes from the Tool Settings roll-up or property bar.

Altogether, the Version 8 effect tool supplies 12 brushes, displayed and labeled in Figure 16-10. Because many of the brushes work only in color, I can't show you how they work as I did for the paint tool brushes back in Figure 16-9. So you'll have to experiment and rely on the following descriptions:

✔ The first thing I should mention is that you can change how each brush behaves by selecting an option from the Type pop-up menu. I can't tell you how every single option works — we'd be here till next Saturday (whenever that is) — but I can tell you how the brushes function in general, regardless of which Type option is active.

✔ The Smear brush smears colors in the image. Sometimes, it smears colors as if they were wet; other times, it takes the pixels at the beginning of your drag and repeats them over and over throughout the drag.

✔ The Smudge brush mixes pixels from one area into another. It does this rather randomly, creating a rough, gritty effect. Try dragging two or three times in the same direction for the best results.

✔ Use the Brightness brush to brighten the area you drag over. Change the Amount value under the Paint pop-up menu to increase or decrease the lightening effect. You can also darken pixels by selecting Darken from the Type pop-up menu or entering a negative value into the Amount option box.

✔ Select the Contrast brush and the Increase Contrast option in the Type pop-up menu, or enter a positive Amount value to increase the contrast between light and dark pixels. Choose the Decrease Contrast option or enter a negative Amount value to, well, decrease the contrast. Again, raise or lower the Amount value to increase or decrease the effect. In fact, that goes for all the other effect tool brushes that have Amount values.

✔ The Hue brush is really dumb. It changes every color you drag over to a different color. Red changes to green, green to blue, blue to red, and everything else to other colors in between. Now that'll come in handy.

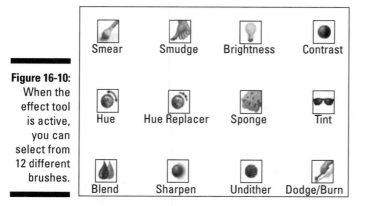

Figure 16-10: When the effect tool is active, you can select from 12 different brushes.

Smear   Smudge   Brightness   Contrast

Hue   Hue Replacer   Sponge   Tint

Blend   Sharpen   Undither   Dodge/Burn

- ✔ The Hue Replacer brush replaces every color in the image with the foreground color. This brush may sound even dumber than the Hue brush, but it's actually useful. It's just the thing for colorizing a color image. For example, you could change a blue dress to orange without otherwise changing the way the dress looks.

- ✔ If the colors in your image are too vivid or too faded and drab, you can downplay or bolster them by dragging over them with the Sponge brush. Choose Sponge Add from the Type pop-up menu or enter a positive value in the Amount option to put color into the image; choose Sponge Remove or enter a negative Amount value to suck color out.

- ✔ The Tint brush is the perfect tool for colorizing a grayscale photograph. After converting the image to color — by choosing Image⇨Convert To⇨ RGB Color (24-bit) — you can select a foreground color and paint with the Tint brush. But be sure to decrease the Amount value to 50 or lower to allow the highlights and shadows to show through.

- ✔ Paint with the Blend brush to blur the pixels in an image, giving the photograph a softer quality. It's just the thing for getting that Vaseline-on-the-lens effect that was so popular in the Sixties.

- ✔ You could use the Sharpen brush to sharpen the focus of an image. But it doesn't work worth a hill of beans. The much better way to enhance the focus of a photograph is to choose Effects⇨Sharpen⇨Adaptive Unsharp, as described in the "Bringing an image into sharper focus" section of Chapter 17. (I know that the process sounds hard, but it's not.)

- ✔ The Undither brush smooths the transition between differently colored pixels, especially in bad scans and GIF graphics from the Web. I don't think that you'll find this tool terribly effective, but it may come in handy for removing dust and scratches in a scanned photograph or for smoothing jagged edges.

- ✔ Version 8 offers a new effects brush, Dodge/Burn. This brush enables you to lighten or darken a specific portion of an image by dragging over it, much like a photographer might underexpose (lighten) or overexpose (darken) certain areas of a photograph while developing a print. Choose one of the Dodge brush options from the Type pop-up menu to lighten an area, or choose one of the Burn brush options to darken it.

Painting One Portion of an Image onto Another

Next to the effects tool on the paint tool flyout is the clone tool. It looks like two paint brushes, one big one and one little one with a line under it. The clone tool lets you copy one portion of an image onto another just by dragging. You can use the tool to duplicate portions of the image — take one cow and turn it into a herd, for example. Or you can cover up scratches and bits of dust that sometimes get scanned along with an image.

To use the tool, click to specify the portion of the image you want to clone. A blinking cross appears in this spot. Then move your cursor to a different spot and drag to clone the image. The cross moves with your cursor to show what is being cloned. You can change the clone spot any time by right-clicking.

When you select the clone tool, the Tool Settings roll-up and property bar offer four brushes, shown in Figure 16-11. They work as follows:

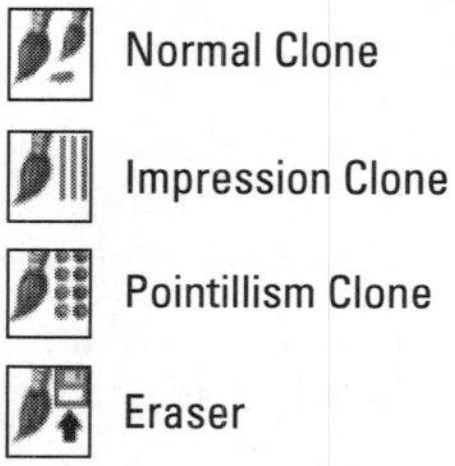

Normal Clone

Impression Clone

Figure 16-11:
The four
clone tool
brushes.

Pointillism Clone

Eraser

- ✔ The Normal Clone brush clones the image normally. No surprises here.

- ✔ The Impressionism Clone brush paints multiple lines at a time in different colors. The lines weave back and forth, so I guess you're supposed to think that Van Gogh may have used this brush. But come on, just because the guy cut off his ear doesn't mean he was totally insane. This brush is too goofy.

- ✔ If the Impressionism Clone brush captures the spirit of Van Gogh, the Pointillism Clone brush embodies Georges Seurat. The brush lays down a bunch of differently colored dots. If you're painting a Hawaiian lei or a DNA molecule, it'll come in quite handy. Otherwise, it won't.

- ✔ In fact, the only clone tool brush you're likely to use is the Eraser brush, which erases pixels back to the way they looked when you last saved the image to disk. This is an exceedingly useful brush. Set the Transparency value to 0 to completely erase the pixels.

Spray Painting with Images

For a fun afternoon of creative play, check out the image sprayer tool, which "sprays" existing objects onto your image. Try this:

1. **Open a new image and select the image sprayer tool, which is the last tool on the paint tool flyout and is labeled in Figure 16-12.**

2. **Click on the Load Image Sprayer List button on the property bar (or choose the command from the Tool Settings roll-up pop-up menu).**

   After the Load Image List dialog box appears, double-click on the file SUNFLOWR.CPT. (If the filename already appears on the property bar next to the Load Image Sprayer List button, you can skip this step.)

   An image list, by the way, is simply a file that contains the objects you want the image sprayer tool to apply.

3. **Drag across your image.**

   You should get a line of sunflowers. Keep dragging to spray more sunflowers. Using the settings in the property bar or Tool Settings roll-up, you can adjust the transparency and size of the sunflowers, as well as how many flowers appear each time you drag. (Change the Number of Dabs value.)

Cool, right? Except how often are you going to need to create a bed of sunflowers? Fortunately, you have other options. In addition to the sunflowers image list, Photo-Paint provides other sample image lists in the Load Image List dialog box. You can also create your own image list:

Load Image Sprayer List   Pop-up menu

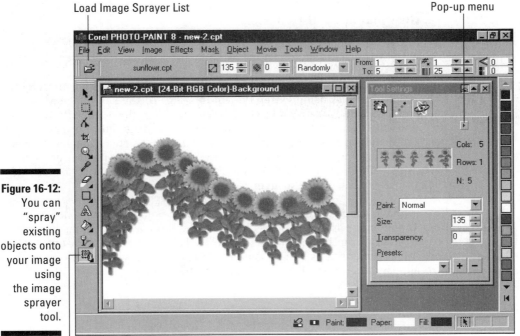

Figure 16-12:
You can "spray" existing objects onto your image using the image sprayer tool.

Image sprayer

1. **Convert the images you want to spray to objects, as described in Chapter 17.**

   You can also spray entire images, as I describe later, but objects work best with this tool.

2. **Select the objects and then select the image sprayer tool.**

   Just click on the first object with the arrow tool and then Shift+click on the others.

3. **Choose Save Qbjects as Image List from the roll-up pop-up menu or the property bar.**

   If you're turning a single object into an image list, Photo-Paint asks whether you want to create a directional image list. With a directional image list, each time you drag with the image sprayer tool, you lay down a series of slightly rotated variations of your original object. If you click Yes when asked whether you want a directional image list, you're then asked to specify how many different variations you want Photo-Paint to create.

   If you don't want a directional image list, click on No. In this case, dragging with the image sprayer tool simply lays down identical copies of your original object.

   If you're saving multiple objects as an image list, you don't need to worry about this issue.

4. **Give your image list a name.**

   Photo-Paint displays the standard Save an Image to Disk dialog box, with the IMGLISTS folder open. Name your image list and press Enter.

You can create an image list also from a whole image rather than an object, although the results usually aren't as interesting. To save an image as an image list, choose Save Document as Image List from the Tool Settings pop-up menu. You then get the option of dividing your image into horizontal and vertical tiles. If you use only one horizontal and one vertical tile, each click or drag of the image sprayer tool lays down your image in its entirety. If you enter a value higher than 1, Photo-Paint divides your image into tiles. Each click or drag of the image sprayer tool lays down a different tile.

If your image list contains more than one object, you can control how many objects the image sprayer applies by using the From and To values on the property bar or on the second tab of the Tool Settings roll-up. For example, if your image list contains 5 objects and you want to spray out only objects 1 through 3, enter **1** in the From box and **3** in the To box.

Chapter 17

Twisting Reality around Your Little Finger

· ·

In This Chapter

▶ Using the Photo-Paint mask tools

▶ Softening the edges of a selection

▶ Changing the sensitivity of the lasso, magic wand, and scissors mask tools

▶ Adjusting the outline of a selection

▶ Moving and cloning selections

▶ Cropping an image

▶ Combining images in creative and entertaining ways

▶ Sharpening focus

▶ Making colors bright and perky

▶ Converting selections to objects

▶ Transforming an object

▶ Creating and editing text in Photo-Paint

· ·

*W*hen you were young, authority figures no doubt told you that the more effort you put into something, the more you get out of it. (You didn't believe them at the time, of course, having figured out that you could just as easily get an A by peeking at your neighbor's paper as you could by spending hours studying.)

But with Photo-Paint, the time-honored motto holds true: expend a little more effort and you enjoy greater results. Take the tools discussed in this chapter, for example. They're a little harder to use than those discussed in Chapters 15 and 16, but they can deliver amazing results. You can isolate portions of the image you want to edit, change the focus, balance the colors, and even slap colors onto different backgrounds. Pretty soon, you'll be performing the kind of image-editing feats that would make those folks at the supermarket tabloids drool with envy.

(Just in case anybody's lawyer decides to take offense at that last statement, I want to state emphatically that I'm only joking. Of course supermarket tabloids don't print altered photographs. If you see a picture of a two-headed alien baby on the pages of one of these fine publications, that's a real, honest-to-goodness alien baby.)

Specifying Which Part of the Image You Want to Edit

The first three slots in the Photo-Paint toolbox contain tools that enable you to select and manipulate portions of your image. Altogether, these tools — labeled in Figure 17-1 — represent the most important collection of tools that Photo-Paint has to offer.

Rectangular mask

Arrow | Freehand mask

Scissors mask

Figure 17-1:
These tools
enable you
to select
and
manipulate
portions of
your image.

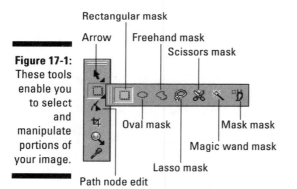

Oval mask | Mask mask

Magic wand mask

Lasso mask

Path node edit

These tools fall into three categories:

✔ With the arrow tool — which Corel calls the pick tool — you can manipulate selections that you've converted into objects. Very likely, you have no idea what I'm talking about, which is why I examine this tool in the "Setting Your Selections Free" section toward the end of this chapter.

✔ The arrow tool now shares its slot in the toolbox with the mask transform tool, which used to reside on the rectangular mask tool flyout. Its new location makes sense because the mask transform tool manipulates, rather than creates, selections. I discuss this tool in the "Fine-tuning your selection outline" section later in this chapter.

To switch from any selected tool to the arrow tool, press the O (that's the letter *O*, not a zero) key. To switch back to the previous tool, press the spacebar.

✔ Use the seven mask tools — all available from the flyout menu shown in Figure 17-1 — to select portions of the image. (A *mask* is Corel's fancy word for a selection outline.) I discuss these indispensable tools in the very next section.

✔ The path node edit tool is twice as complicated as its name makes it sound. You draw a CorelDraw-like path one node at a time. Then you fuss around with the nodes and control points using a collection of buttons straight out of CorelDraw's Node Edit roll-up. And finally, you convert the path to a selection outline that you could have more easily drawn with one of the mask tools. If you don't mind a little advice, I suggest that you run fast, run far, and avoid this tool like the plague.

In Version 7, the path node edit tool housed a repeat brush stroke tool on its flyout menu. In Version 8, the repeat brush stroke tool has been removed, but its functionality remains as the Edit⇨Stroke⇨Repeat Stroke command. This command lets you save a brush stroke and then repeat that same brush stroke over and over again.

Carving out a bit of imagery with the wondrous mask tools

As in CorelDraw, you have to select a portion of an image in Photo-Paint if you want to manipulate it. But instead of selecting discrete objects — such as rectangles, polygons, and letters of text — you select free-form areas of the image, much as if you were cutting patterns out of a bolt of fabric.

Photo-Paint provides seven types of scissors to cut with; they come in the form of the seven mask tools labeled in Figure 17-1. Here's how these seven slick scissors stack up:

✔ Drag with the rectangular mask tool to select a rectangular portion of the image. (Corel calls this the rectangle mask tool, but rectangular mask is more accurate. Small point, but I just didn't want you to get confused by my nit-picking.) Drag with the tool and press the Ctrl key to create a square selection. Drag and press the Shift key to draw the selection outward from the center. Drag and press Ctrl+Shift to draw a square selection from the center out.

Note that I say "drag and press" the Ctrl or Shift key rather than Ctrl+drag or Shift+drag. This is not a subtle change in semantics. In Photo-Paint 8, you must begin to drag *before* pressing the Shift or Ctrl keys. Ctrl+dragging and Shift+dragging with the rectangular and oval mask tools has a different function in Version 8, as I discuss later in this chapter.

✔ Drag with the oval mask tool to select an oval area. (Corel calls this tool the circle mask tool, but it draws circles only if you press the Ctrl key as you drag.) Shift+drag to draw the selection from the center out. (Ctrl+Shift+drag to draw a circular selection from the center out.)

✔ Use the freehand mask tool to create a free-form selection outline with straight or curved sides. To draw straight sides, click to set the first point and then continue clicking to add corners to the polygon. To draw curved sides, just drag with the tool. When you finish drawing your outline, double-click to convert it to a selection.

Before you double-click to convert the outline to a selection, you can delete the last corner or node in the outline by pressing Delete. You can even press Delete several times in a row to delete the last few corners or nodes. This is a good way to fix portions of the selection outline you don't like. Try it with curved or straight-sided outlines.

✔ The lasso mask tool works similarly to the freehand mask tool: You click to add corners or drag to create a curved outline, and then you double-click to convert the outline to a selection. The difference is that when you double-click, the lasso mask tool tightens the selection around a specified background color. In other words, it adjusts your selection to home in on a specific portion of the image.

Perhaps an example will help to clarify: Suppose that you want to rope a calf set against an alfalfa-green background. If you begin dragging on the alfalfa, Photo-Paint sets green as the background color and tightens around the calf. If you begin dragging on the calf, Photo-Paint sets calf brown as the background and tightens on the alfalfa.

✔ The scissors mask tool is a souped-up freehand mask tool. This tool helps you create intricate selections by finding *edges* — areas of high contrast — and automatically placing the selection marquee along those edges. This tool takes some getting used to.

To get a feel for how the tool works, open an image that has areas of high contrast like the lizard image in Figure 17-2. Click on a spot where two colors meet. For example, I clicked on the outer edge of the lizard's snout. Now move your mouse along the edge where the two colors converge. Photo-Paint automatically creates a selection outline along the edge between the two colors. The pixel that you clicked serves as Photo-Paint's reference point – that is, the program detects an edge when it finds pixels that contrast with the pixel you clicked.

✔ When you get a section of the selection outline the way you want it, click to set it in place. Then keep moving your mouse along the edge where the colors meet, clicking to set down new sections of the selection outline. Each time you click, Photo-Paint sets a new reference point, so be careful where you click. For best results, don't try to create too large a portion of your outline all at once. (The tool's reach extends only a limited distance from the point at which you click anyway, as explained in the next section.) Double-click to close the selection outline.

Scissors mask tool   Radius square

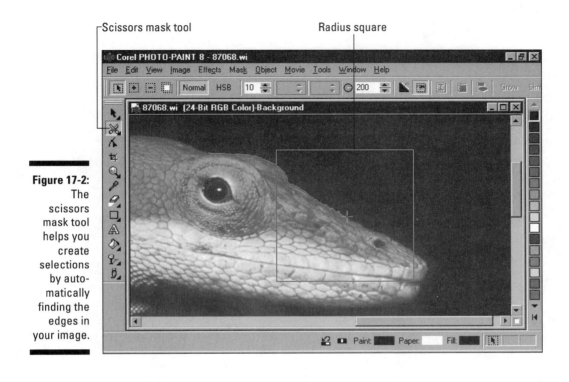

Figure 17-2:
The scissors mask tool helps you create selections by automatically finding the edges in your image.

At any point while you're creating your selection, you can simply drag to draw a selection outline as you would with the freehand mask tool.

The scissors mask tool is most useful when you want to separate a complex subject from a busy, multicolored background. For an image like the one in the figure, where the background is more or less a solid color, you'd probably find it easier to use the magic wand, described next, to create your selection. But I wanted to give you a simple example so that you can clearly see how the scissors mask tool works.

✔ Click with the magic wand mask tool to select an area of continuous color. In the first example in Figure 17-3, I clicked in the center of the kid's forehead, at the location shown by the cursor in the second example in the figure. Photo-Paint selected a range of colors in the kid's face, extending all the way from the top of his cranium down to the base of his chin. Just to make the selected area more obvious, I pressed Delete to fill it with white.

✔ To create a selection outline with the mask brush tool, just drag as if you were painting with the paint tool. In the first example in Figure 17-4, I dragged around the perimeter of the kid's head. Photo-Paint traced the selection around the brushstroke. To more clearly demonstrate the selection, I pressed Delete to get the second example in the figure.

Magic wand
mask cursor

Figure 17-3:
After
opening an
image (top),
I selected
an area of
continuous
color with
the magic
wand and
pressed
Delete
(bottom).

Regardless of which tool you use to select your image, Photo-Paint displays around the selected area an animated conga line of dots, known far and wide as *marching ants.* Everyone thinks that computer jargon has to be obscure and intimidating, but sometimes it's just plain silly.

If the marching ants annoy you or prevent you from seeing some part of the image you want to scrutinize, choose Mask⇨Marquee Visible or press Ctrl+H to turn the command off and hide the ants. The selection is there — you just can't see it anymore. To bring the ants back so you know where the selection is, choose the Marquee Visible command or press Ctrl+H again.

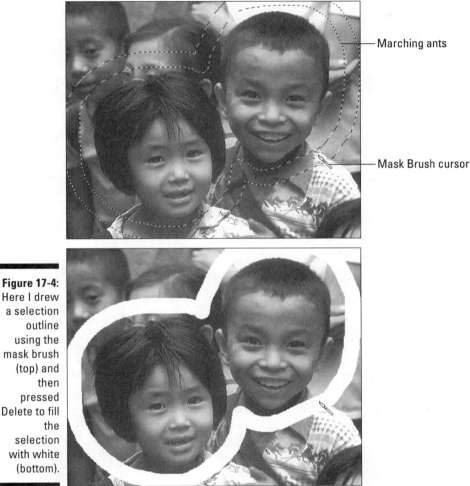

— Marching ants

— Mask Brush cursor

Figure 17-4:
Here I drew
a selection
outline
using the
mask brush
(top) and
then
pressed
Delete to fill
the
selection
with white
(bottom).

You can change the color of the mask marquee by choosing a different color from the Mask Marquee pop-up menu on the Display panel of the Options dialog box (press Ctrl+J to open the dialog box, and click on Display).

Fine-tuning your selection outline

If the methods just described were your only means of creating selection outlines, Photo-Paint would be a pretty poor excuse for an image-editing program. After all, it's not as if you can expect to draw a selection outline and get it just right on the first try. Suppose that you wanted to select that kid's head in Figure 17-4 and then plop it onto a baby fur seal, as I did in

Figure 17-5. Creating a selection this perfect requires a little effort. You have to spend a lot of time refining the selection until you get every hair, ear, and whisker just the way you want it.

That's where the Photo-Paint Tool Settings roll-up, property bar, mask transform tool, and Mask menu come in. These items enable you to modify selection outlines in ways too numerous to mention. I wanted to take a stab at mentioning a few of them anyway:

✔ When you use any mask tool except the rectangular mask tool, the Tool Settings roll-up includes an Anti-aliasing check box. (This control is found also on the property bar; the icon looks like a big black triangle.) Anti-aliasing is one of the most cherished terms in all of computer-dweebdom because it sounds really technical and it means something very simple: soft edges. Unless you want jagged edges around your selection, turn anti-aliasing on for each and every tool.

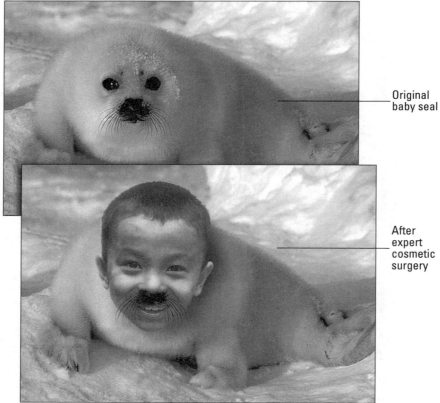

Original baby seal

After expert cosmetic surgery

Figure 17-5: Before I could plaster the kid's face onto this innocent arctic critter, I had to spend lots of time perfecting the selection outline.

✔ If you draw a selection with anti-aliasing turned off, you can't go back and apply anti-aliasing after the fact. You can, however, blur the selection outline after creating it. (Figure 17-6 demonstrates the difference between softening and blurring.) Choose Mask⇨Shape⇨Feather or click on the Feather Mask button on the property bar to display the Feather dialog box. (The Feather Mask button is the second button to the right of the Anti-aliasing button.) Then enter a value between 1 and 200 in the Width option box. Larger values produce blurrier selections. To get the effect in the right-hand image in Figure 17-6, I entered a value of 12.

Figure 17-6: Softened and blurred selections placed against a white background.

Softened (Anti-aliasing)   Blurred (Mask⇨Shape⇨Feather)

✔ The Direction pop-up menu determines whether Photo-Paint blurs outward away from the selection outline or inward toward the center. When in doubt, select the Middle option. And always select Curved from the Edges pop-up menu. The Linear option creates harsh edges inside the blur, a singularly unattractive effect.

✔ You can also turn on feathering before you create a selection with the rectangular, oval, or freehand mask tools by entering a value in the Feather option box in the Tool Settings roll-up or on the property bar.

✔ When you select the lasso, magic wand, or scissors mask tool, the Tool Settings roll-up and property bar also include a Tolerance setting. (On the property bar, the control is just to the right of the HSB button. The pop-up label for the control reads "Color Similarity or Hue Levels" just to confuse you.) A high Tolerance value for the lasso causes the selection outline to shrink farther and avoid more background colors. In the case of the magic wand, a higher Tolerance value causes Photo-Paint to select a wider range of related colors. And for the scissors, the higher the Tolerance value, the more contrast is required for Photo-Paint to find an edge. Try raising and lowering the value while using each tool to get a sense of how this option works.

✔ While we're on the subject of the scissors: Each time you click with the scissors, Photo-Paint draws a square boundary around the spot you click. This boundary is called a Radius square and is labeled in Figure 17-2. If you move your cursor outside the Radius square, the tool loses its automatic edge detection powers. The Radius value, found both in the Tool Settings roll-up and on the property bar, sets the size of the Radius square. The higher the Radius value, the greater the size of the Radius square and the reach of the scissors. If you're not happy with how the tool is functioning, try adjusting this value.

✔ When you use the mask brush tool, the Tool Settings roll-up and property bar controls enable you to change the size and shape of the brush. Fatter brushes result in fatter selection outlines. Although Photo-Paint provides quite a few options for creating a customized brush, I recommend that you click on the brush preview on the property bar or in the roll-up and select an alternative brush from the pop-up menu. Unless you get seriously interested in this tool — which is unlikely — the predefined brushes should prove more than adequate.

✔ After you create a selection outline, you can move, scale, rotate, skew, or distort it independently of the image by using the mask transform tool on the arrow tool flyout menu. Drag the selection with the tool to move it. Drag one of the handles around the selection to scale it.

Click on the selection with the mask transform tool to switch to the rotate and skew mode. Then you can drag a corner handle to rotate the selection outline or drag a top, bottom, or side handle to slant it.

Click again to display the distort arrows; drag an arrow to distort the marquee. Click yet again to display hollow circular handles, which you can drag to create perspective effects. When you finish manipulating the selection outline, double-click inside the outline. Or to cancel all changes, click outside the outline.

You can use the options in the Tool Settings roll-up to move, scale, rotate, and skew the outline numerically. These options work like their counterparts in CorelDraw, which I explain in Chapter 9. The property bar also contains controls that enable you to manipulate your selection outline when the mask transform tool is selected. To switch between the various modes — scale, rotate, skew, and so on — click on the first button on the left end of the property bar to display a flyout menu containing buttons for each mode.

✔ To select all colors throughout the image that are similar to the selected colors, choose Mask⇨Shape⇨Similar or click on the Similar button on the property bar. This command is a great way to expand the colors selected with the magic wand. Suppose that you're working on a map in which all the water is blue and the land is green. If you click with the magic wand inside a lake, you select just the lake. But if you then choose the Similar command, you select all the water on the map, whether it's surrounded by land or not.

✔ The Grow command (Mask⇨Shape⇨Grow, or click on the Grow button on the property bar) is a cousin of the Similar command. Grow expands the selection to include adjacent pixels that are similar in color to those along the edges of the selection outline. Photo-Paint selects pixels according to the Tolerance value set for the magic wand tool. Raise the value to select more pixels.

✔ You can increase the size of a selection by choosing Mask⇨Shape⇨Expand and entering a value in the ensuing dialog box. Larger values increase the selection by larger amounts. To similarly decrease the size of the selection, choose Mask⇨Shape⇨Reduce.

✔ To reposition a selection relative to the center of the document, to one or more objects, or to a grid, choose Mask⇨Align or click on the Align Mask button (just to the left of the Grow button) on the property bar. The Mask Align dialog box that appears works just like the Align panel in the Align and distribute dialog box in CorelDraw, which is discussed in Chapter 6. Choose from the horizontal and vertical alignment options to reposition a selection. Click on the preview button (the one that looks like an eyeball) in the bottom-left corner of the dialog box to preview the results of the alignment you specify.

✔ To select everything that's not selected and deselect everything that is — in other words, to invert the selection — choose Mask⇨Invert.

✔ To deselect everything, choose Mask⇨Remove, press Ctrl+Shift+R, or click outside the selection with any of the mask tools except the magic wand or scissors. You can use the last method — clicking outside the selection — only when working in the Normal selection mode (explained in the next section).

✔ To select every last pixel in the image, choose Mask⇨Select All, press Ctrl+Shift+A, or double-click on a mask tool icon in the toolbox.

Making manual adjustments

All the selection modifications I've mentioned in the preceding sections are automatic. You tell Photo-Paint what to do, and it does it. But what if you want to make more precise adjustments manually? Suppose that you select a kid's head, but you miss his ears. Sadly, Photo-Paint does not offer Mask⇨Add Ears. So how do you add the ears to the selection?

The answer lies in the Mask⇨Mode submenu. Choosing one of these four commands turns the others off. Also, each command remains in effect until you choose a different one:

✔ By default, the Normal mode is active. In this mode, every time you create a new selection outline, you deselect the rest of the image.

✔ If you want to increase the size of the selection, choose the Additive mode. To select the kid's ears without deselecting the head, for example, choose this mode, drag around one ear, and then drag around the other.

✔ To decrease the size of the selection, choose the Subtractive mode. Now you can carve areas out of the selection outline using a mask tool.

✔ The last command — XOR Mask — is kind of weird. It lets you find the intersection of two selection outlines. In other words, any pixels inside both selection outlines become selected; any other pixels do not. For example, if you draw an oval selection, choose XOR Mask, and then draw an oval selection inside the first oval, you get a donut-shaped selection. (The donut is selected but the donut hole isn't.)

You can also choose a mask mode with the first four buttons on the left end of the property bar. From left to right, the buttons are: Normal, Additive, Subtractive, and XOR Mask. Or if you prefer, you can access the mode commands by pressing shortcuts on the keypad (the right-hand portion of the keyboard with the numbers on it). Press Ctrl+plus (+) to choose the Additive command; Ctrl+minus (–) for Subtractive; Ctrl+asterisk (*) for XOR Mask; and Ctrl+period (.) to return to the Normal mode.

Just in case the property bar options and keyboard shortcuts simply don't do it for you, Version 8 offers yet another way to enable the various mask modes. Pressing and holding the Ctrl and Shift keys before you begin dragging enables you to switch modes on the fly. Ctrl+drag to draw a selection in the Additive mode; Shift+drag to draw in the Subtractive mode; and Ctrl+Shift+drag to draw in the XOR Mask mode. When you complete your drag, Photo-Paint returns to the default Normal mode.

Remember, Ctrl and Shift+dragging with the rectangular and oval mask tools in Photo-Paint 8 works differently than Ctrl and Shift+dragging with the rectangle and ellipse tools in Photo-Paint or CorelDraw. In Photo-Paint, you press the Ctrl or Shift key *after* you begin dragging with the rectangular or oval mask tools to create a square or circle or to draw a selection from the center out. Pressing the Ctrl or Shift key before you begin dragging changes the mask mode, as I just described.

Things to Do with a Selected Image

After you select a handful of pixels, you can manipulate them with absolute impunity. Not only can you do things to Photo-Paint pixels that would make CorelDraw objects stare with wonder, you can perform these edits with relatively little effort. For starters, the following list describes a few of the minor modifications you can make to images:

✔ Drag the selection with any mask tool other than the mask brush or mask transform tool to move it to a new location. Photo-Paint leaves a background-colored hole in the wake of the moved selection, as demonstrated in Figure 17-7. (In the figure, white is the background color.) You must be working in the Normal mask mode for this technique to work.

✔ You can also nudge a selected area when one of the mask tools is selected by pressing an arrow key. Remember, you must have a mask tool selected if you want to nudge.

✔ As in CorelDraw, pressing Shift+arrow performs a super nudge, which nudges the selection ten times as far as a regular nudge by default. You can set the nudge and super nudge distances on the General panel of the Options dialog box (Tools⇨Options or Ctrl+J).

✔ To clone the selected area and leave the image unchanged in the background, Alt+drag the selection using a mask tool. The bottom image in Figure 17-7 illustrates what I mean.

✔ When you clone a selected area as just described, you create a floating selection. The floating selection hovers above the rest of the image on its own plane, which means you can manipulate the selection without harming the underlying image. You can float a selection in place (that is, without dragging it from its original position) by choosing Mask⇨Float.

If you click outside the selection outline, choose the mask transform or mask brush tool, or use any other mask tool outside the selection, you defloat the selection. Defloating glues the selection back onto the underlying image. You can also defloat a selection by choosing Mask⇨Defloat.

✔ You can paint inside a selection with one of the painting or effect tools described in Chapter 16. The selection acts as a stencil, preventing you from painting outside the lines. (Artists also call such stencils *masks,* which is why Corel calls the selection tools mask tools.) Try painting inside a selection, and you'll quickly see how it works.

✔ To trace the masked selection outline with the paint, eraser, color replacer, effect, or image sprayer tool, select the tool you want to use to apply the stroke and choose Edit⇨Stroke⇨Stroke Mask. Photo-Paint asks you to specify whether you want to place the stroke along the outside, inside, or center of the selection outline. Choose an option and click OK to apply the stroke.

✔ To get rid of all the stuff outside the selection outline, choose Image⇨Crop⇨To Mask. This technique allows you to focus on a detail in the image. All the images in this chapter, for example, have been cropped to some extent.

White hole   Moved selection   Cloned selection

Figure 17-7:
Drag with a
mask tool to
move a
selection
(top);
Alt+drag to
clone the
selection
(bottom).

You can crop an image also using the crop tool — located between the path node edit and zoom tools. Drag with the tool to surround the portion of the photograph you want to retain. You can adjust the size of the cropping boundary after drawing it by dragging the square handles around the boundary. You can drag inside the boundary to move it. When you're finished, double-click inside the boundary to crop away excess pixels.

Combining Images

As soon as you see the half-boy, half-seal image in Figure 17-5, you no doubt begin imagining all sorts of fun things you can do with your own images, including putting your head on some buff athlete's body. By selecting something in one image and then plopping the selection into another image, you can wreak all sorts of havoc on reality.

The easiest way to clone a selection and place the clone into another image is to use the mouse to drag the selection from one image window to the other. Here's how:

1. **Open both images.**

2. **Choose Window⇨Tile Vertically to place the image windows side by side.**

3. **Select the area you want to clone.**

4. **Choose Mask⇨Float.**

   This step creates a clone of your selection. The clone floats above your image, so you can move it without harming the underlying image.

5. **Drag the floating clone to the other image window.**

   First, make sure the Normal mask mode is active. Then use any mask tool except the mask transform or mask brush tool to drag the selection. Your cursor changes to the mask transform cursor when you drag inside the original image window. When you cross over into the other image window, you see a regular arrow cursor with a little box attached.

   When you release the mouse button at the end of your drag, Photo-Paint places the clone into the image window as an object. (Objects are explained later in this chapter.) Change the clone into a floating selection by choosing Mask⇨Create From Object(s) or by pressing Ctrl+M. (You first need to click on the title bar of the image window to make that window the active window.) You can then drag the selection to reposition it if need be.

6. **To defloat the clone, click outside the selection outline or choose Mask⇨Defloat.**

   The clone is now permanently settled in its new home.

An alternative method of transferring selections between images is to use the Windows Clipboard. By using the Clipboard, you can cut or copy a selection and paste it into another image. Here's what you need to know:

   ✔ To remove a selection from one image and paste it into another image, choose Edit⇨Cut or press Ctrl+X. Then, inside the destination image (the one into which you want to place the selection), choose Edit⇨Paste⇨As New Selection. Photo-Paint pastes the selection as a floating selection.

   ✔ To copy a selection and paste the copy into another image, choose Edit⇨Copy or press Ctrl+C instead of using the Cut command.

✔ Ctrl+V, the universal shortcut for the Paste command, pastes the selection as a new object rather than as a floating selection. For more on this subject, see the upcoming section "Making an object."

Correcting Focus and Contrast

Not all images are born perfect. In fact, most images can benefit from an application of the Level Equalization and Adaptive Unsharp commands, which you can use to adjust the contrast and focus of an image.

Level Equalization is found on the Image menu. Adaptive Unsharp resides on the Effects menu, along with nearly 70 other commands that apply special effects to an image. Most of the other Effects commands create the kinds of effects that you can have a lot of fun playing around with but that serve little practical purpose. (For examples of a few of the more interesting effects, read Chapter 19.) Not so with Adaptive Unsharp; this effect can make your image look better instead of weirder.

Bringing an image into sharper focus

The Effects➪Sharpen➪Adaptive Unsharp command sharpens the focus of an image. That's right, you can actually sharpen the focus after the photo comes back from the developer. You can't bring out details where none exist — if the camera was way out of focus when you shot the picture, there's not much you can do — but you can sharpen photos that are slightly soft. In fact, you'll probably want to sharpen every photograph you open in Photo-Paint. Although Photo-Paint provides many sharpening commands, Adaptive Unsharp does the best job of combining ease of use and good results.

When you choose the Adaptive Unsharp command, Photo-Paint displays the Adaptive Unsharp dialog box. Click on the preview mode toggle button in the bottom-left corner to display the dialog box as shown in Figure 17-8. Here you find two previews — before and after — plus a Percentage slider bar.

In Version 8 you can elect to preview the results of your sharpness settings on-screen. The first time you open the Adaptive Unsharp dialog box, the on-screen preview mode is the default. In other words, you won't see the Original and Result previews shown in Figure 17-8. Click on the preview mode toggle button labeled in Figure 17-8 to switch between the on-screen and in-dialog preview modes. The benefit of the in-dialog preview is that it allows you to see the before-and-after effect.

Before   After

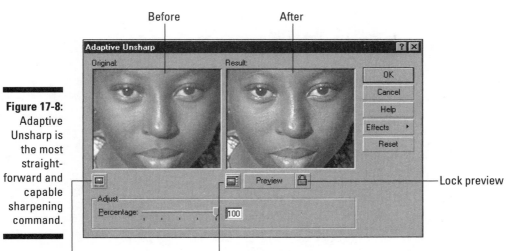

Figure 17-8:
Adaptive
Unsharp is
the most
straight-
forward and
capable
sharpening
command.

Lock preview

Preview mode toggle   Expand preview window

The dialog box options work like so:

✔ Drag the Percentage slider handle to decide how much you want to sharpen the image. Or enter a value between 1 and 100 into the option box to the right of the slider bar. The higher the value, the sharper your image gets.

For reference, Figure 17-9 features an image at several different Percentage values. The top picture shows the original image, which is surprisingly soft. The left examples show the results of applying Percentage values of 50 percent and 100 percent.

Because 100 percent is the highest value permitted, you may have to apply the command more than once. The right examples in the figure show the results of applying the command two and three times in a row. If you start seeing jagged pixels, as in the last example, you know that you've gone too far.

✔ To preview the effect, click on the Preview button. The right preview shows the sharpened image; the left preview shows the soft one.

✔ If you want Photo-Paint to automatically update the preview every time you change the Percentage value, click on that little lock icon to the right of the Preview button. This locks the preview function on so that you never need to click on the Preview button again.

✔ Only so much of the image fits into the preview windows. To preview a different portion of the photograph, position the cursor inside the left preview window to display the hand tool. Drag with the hand tool to reposition the image in the preview window.

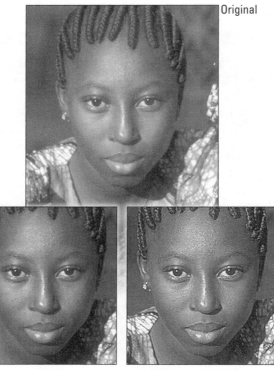

Original

50% once

100% twice

Figure 17-9:
This image, like many, benefits from sharpening. But be careful that you don't oversharpen, as in the bottom-right image.

100% once

100% three times

✔ To see more of the image at a time, right-click with the hand tool in the left preview to zoom out. To magnify the preview, just click with the hand tool.

✔ Although you use the hand tool in the left preview, Photo-Paint automatically updates the right preview as well.

✔ If you click on the expand preview window button, labeled in Figure 17-8, the left original view disappears and the right preview is enlarged, enabling you to see an even greater portion of your image. To return to the two-preview setup, click again on the expand preview button. (The button scoots to the right side of the dialog box when you enlarge the preview.)

✔ To close the dialog box and apply the sharpening effect, press Enter or click on OK.

Reapplying an Effects command

At this point, I feel obliged to share one tidbit about the Effects menu: After you apply any one of the menu commands, Photo-Paint displays that effect as the first command in the Effects menu. This way, you can easily reapply the effect by choosing the first command or simply pressing Ctrl+F.

Just about every Effects command brings up a dialog box so that you can mess around with a few settings. If you simply choose the command at the top of the Effects menu or press Ctrl+F, Photo-Paint reapplies the effect using the last settings that were in force.

Making an image less dark and murky

Most photographs look bright and perky on-screen. But when you print them, they typically darken up and fill in, which can lead to muddy colors and murky detail. That's where the Level Equalization command comes in handy.

Photo-Paint offers other commands under the Adjust submenu, but they are either monumentally complicated or grossly inept. Level Equalization is the exception.

Choose Image⇨Adjust⇨Level Equalization or press Ctrl+E to display the dialog box shown in Figure 17-10. When you see a dialog box as complicated as this one, your inclination is to sweat, wring your hands, and wail. This dialog box was big and scary looking in Version 7, and it's just as intimidating in Version 8. In fact, the dialog box is so big that the whole thing doesn't fit on-screen if you use a monitor resolution lower than 800 x 600.

Thankfully, you can accomplish what you need to accomplish without worrying about a good majority of the controls in the dialog box. I took the liberty of shading all the parts of the dialog box that you can safely ignore. The following list tells you what you need to know to correct your image:

✔ That mountain of spiky lines in the lower-right corner of the dialog box is called a *histogram*. A histogram is a graph of the colors in the image, with the darkest blacks on the left side of the graph and the lightest

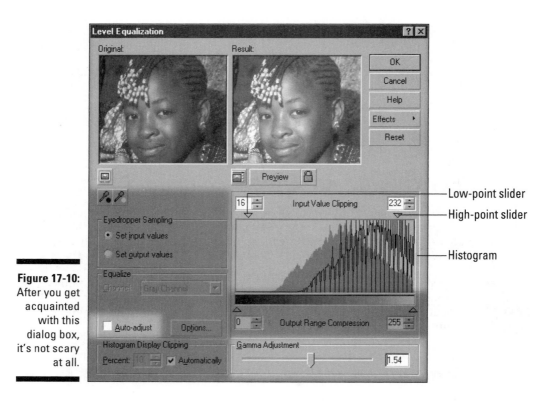

Figure 17-10:
After you get acquainted with this dialog box, it's not scary at all.

Low-point slider

High-point slider

Histogram

whites on the right. In Version 8, you get two histograms: a solid gray one representing your original image, and a black one representing your image with the adjustments you select in the dialog box.

✔ Before you do anything else in the Level Equalization dialog box, turn off the Auto-adjust option. When this option is turned on, Photo-Paint tries to even out all the colors in the image from light to dark, which results in some pretty drastic color modifications and unrealistic effects. When the option is turned off, Photo-Paint just goes ahead and does what you tell it to do without making any bad guesses of its own.

Likewise, don't try to avoid the Level Equalization dialog box by choosing the Auto Equalize command on the Image➪Adjust submenu. This command does the same thing as the Auto-adjust option.

✔ See those two triangles above the histogram — the ones labeled low-point slider and high-point slider in Figure 17-10? These two controls enable you to darken the dark colors and lighten the light colors in your image. To make the darkest colors in the image black — not some wishy-washy gray — drag the low-point slider to the right so that it lines up with the left edge of the big histogram mountain. Then, drag the high-point slider to the left until it meets with the right end of the histogram. This step makes the lightest colors in the image white. It's just the thing for whitening eyes and for whitening teeth to make it appear as though the folks in the photograph brush regularly.

✔ To alter the lightness or darkness of the medium color — the color smack dab between black and white — drag the Gamma Adjustment slider at the bottom of the dialog box. Drag to the right to lighten the image and drag to the left to darken the image.

Keep in mind that the image looks brighter on-screen than it will when it's printed. Monitors project light, but the printed page reflects it. So generally, an image that looks a little too light on-screen prints just right. Make a few test prints to be sure.

✔ Use the Preview button, lock icon, expand preview window button, and the hand tool as explained in the preceding section. These options just help you get an idea of how your correction will look before you apply the command.

The top example in Figure 17-11 shows an image as it appeared when I first opened and converted it to a grayscale image by choosing Image➪ConvertTo➪Grayscale (8-Bit). The image is dark, it has bad contrast, and it's soft. The second image shows the results of applying the Level Equalization and Adaptive Unsharp commands. I wouldn't dream of printing an image without these helpful commands.

Setting Your Selections Free

There comes a time in every selection's life when it yearns for independence. You can grant this independence by turning the selection into a free-floating object. You can then select and manipulate the Photo-Paint object by clicking on it with the arrow tool, just as you can with an object in CorelDraw.

For example, after putting all that time into selecting the kid's head in Figure 17-5, I don't want to have to go through all that effort again if I decide to plop the head on the body of some other unwitting creature. By converting the head to an object, I make sure that I don't have to. As an object, the head remains intact and independent forever.

Making an object

To convert a selected area into an object, do any one of the following:

✔ Choose Object➪Create➪Object: Cut Selection or press Ctrl+Shift+up-arrow key to convert a selection to an object without cloning it. This command leaves a background-colored hole underneath the object, just as when you drag a selection.

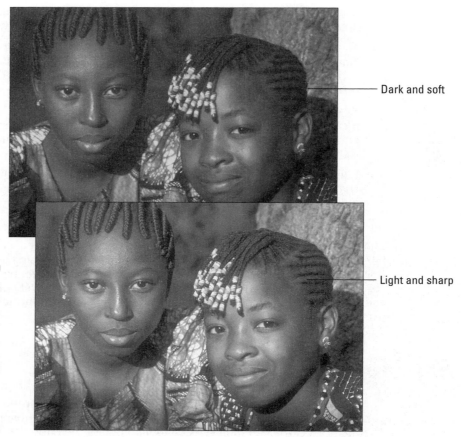

Dark and soft

Light and sharp

Figure 17-11:
If you do nothing else to your photograph, make sure you correct the colors and sharpen the focus.

✔ Choose Object➪Create➪Object: Copy Selection or press Ctrl+up-arrow key. Photo-Paint clones your selection, leaving the original image intact, and surrounds the selection with eight handles, just like an object in CorelDraw. It even automatically selects the arrow tool, which is the primary tool for editing objects.

✔ If all that stuff is too complicated, just copy the selection by pressing Ctrl+C, and then paste it by pressing Ctrl+V. (Or choose Edit➪Copy and then choose Edit➪Paste➪As New Object.) Photo-Paint pastes the new object right in place and automatically selects the arrow tool so that you can play with the object.

✔ Photo-Paint can automatically turn a shape you draw with the rectangle, polygon, or oval tool into an object after you draw the shape. Just turn on the Render to Object option in the Tool Settings roll-up or click on the Render to Object button on the property bar. You can do the same thing for lines drawn with the line tool.

✔ To turn an object back into a selection mask, select the object by clicking on it with the arrow tool. Then choose Mask⇨Create From Object(s) or press Ctrl+M.

✔ By default, text created with the text tool is also created as an object, as explained in the section "Adding and modifying text."

Manipulating an object

After you create an object, you can scale it, rotate it, skew it, distort it, and add perspective effects. These transformations are different from those you perform with the mask transform tool (described in the earlier section, "Fine-tuning your selection outline"). Instead of affecting the selection outline without changing the image inside the selection — as is the case with the mask transform tool — these transformations affect the object itself.

In fact, before you can scale or rotate part of an image in Photo-Paint, you must first convert it to an object.

Of course, before you transform an object, you have to select it. If you just created the object, it's already selected. If you have multiple objects floating around inside your image and you want to select a different object, just click on the object with the arrow tool.

As in CorelDraw, you can select multiple objects by clicking on one and Shift+clicking on the others. Or you can drag around the objects with the arrow tool to surround them with a marquee.

To hide those distracting marching ants around the boundaries of your objects, choose Object⇨Marquee Visible. (If marching ants remain on-screen, they surround areas selected with the mask tools.) To bring the marching ants back, choose the command again.

To change the object marquee color, select a new color from the Object Marquee pop-up menu on the Display panel of the Options dialog box.

After you select the objects you want to modify, you can change them as outlined in the following sections.

Moving, cloning, and deleting objects

You can move and clone a selected object in several different ways:

✔ Move the object by dragging it with the arrow tool. Ctrl+drag to constrain the movement to a horizontal or vertical drag. (Remember, you can select the arrow tool by pressing the O key.) Because the object floats above the background image, the background remains unaffected.

✔ When the arrow tool is selected, press the arrow keys to nudge the selected object in 1-pixel increments. Press Shift plus an arrow key to super nudge in 10-pixel increments. To change the nudge or super nudge distance, go to the General panel of the Options dialog box. (Press Ctrl+J to open the dialog box.)

✔ You can also use the Object Position option boxes on the property bar and in the Tool Settings roll-up to precisely place the object. After you enter horizontal and vertical coordinates for the object, click on the Transform button.

✔ To clone the object in place, choose Object⇨Duplicate or press Ctrl+D.

✔ You can make objects snap to guidelines and grid points, just as in CorelDraw. Turn on the Snap to Grid and Snap to Guidelines commands in the View menu. For more on snapping, the grid, and guidelines, see Chapter 6.

✔ To delete a selected object, just press Delete.

If you want to see a copy of the object as you drag instead of just the object's outline, press and hold on the object a few seconds before you begin your drag.

Scaling, rotating, and other effects

You can also apply a bunch of transformations to objects, just as in CorelDraw.

✔ To scale an object, select it with the arrow tool. Drag a corner handle to scale the object proportionally. Drag a side handle to scale horizontally; drag the top or bottom handle to scale vertically.

✔ Click again on the selected object to display the rotate and skew handles. Drag a corner handle to rotate the object; drag a top, bottom, or side handle to slant the object.

Keep in mind that pixels are always square and upright. So when you rotate or skew an object, you don't actually rotate or skew the individual pixels. Rather, you force Photo-Paint to recolor the pixels to best represent the rotated or skewed image.

The practical upshot of this is that each and every rotation or skew causes a tiny bit of damage to the image. The recolored pixels don't look quite as good as the original ones did. If you rotate or skew the object many times in a row, it starts to look blurry and jagged.

Figure 17-12 compares an image rotated three times to an image rotated the same amount once.

✔ Click a third time on the object to display the distortion handles. Drag one of these handles to stretch the image any which way. Figure 17-13 shows the results of stretching the image from Figure 17-12.

✔ Click yet a fourth time to display little round handles on each corner of the image. Drag these handles to create perspective effects.

✔ Click a fifth time to return to the scale handles.

✔ When the arrow tool is selected, the Tool Settings roll-up includes five panels of options that let you move, scale, rotate, and slant the object numerically. (Sorry, no numerical distortions or perspective effects.) These options work similarly to those in CorelDraw (see Chapters 6 and 9).

You can also access the various transformation modes and options with the property bar. To switch from one transformation mode to the next,

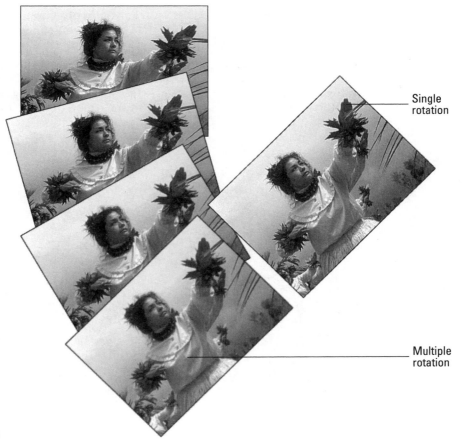

Figure 17-12:
An image rotated three times (left) becomes blurry and jagged, whereas the same image rotated just once (right) looks more focused.

Single rotation

Multiple rotation

press and hold on the first button on the left end of the property bar, which displays a flyout menu of transformation icons. Click on the icon for the transformation you want to apply.

✔ If you transform an object by dragging its handles, Photo-Paint immediately displays the results of the transformation. But if you transform the object using the property bar or roll-up, you need to click on the Transform button to see the results of your changes. (Note that the Tranform button is not available for the Distort and Perspective modes.) The Transform button temporarily applies the transformation. You can cancel the transformation by double-clicking outside the object or by right-clicking on the object and choosing Reset from the pop-up menu that appears.

✔ To permanently apply a transformation, click on the Apply button, double-click inside the object, or choose another tool.

✔ You can clone the object and apply the transformation to the clone by clicking on the Apply to Duplicate button on the property bar or in the roll-up rather than clicking on the Apply button.

✔ To undo a transformation after you click on Apply, choose Edit⇨Undo or press Ctrl+Z.

✔ You can flip an object horizontally or vertically by dragging a side handle past the opposite side handle, just as in CorelDraw. Ctrl+drag to keep the original object size as you flip. Alternatively, you can click on the Flip buttons on the Object Scale tab of the Tool Settings roll-up or on the property bar. (Select the object scale icon from the flyout menu

Figure 17-13:
I dragged the distortion handles to create this effect.

on the left end of the property bar to display the Flip buttons.) All these methods both flip and move the object, though. To flip an object in place, choose one of the commands from the Object➪Flip submenu. (You have to cancel or apply any transformations in progress to access these commands.)

✔ As if all those options aren't enough, you can also rotate an object in 90-degree increments by choosing a command from the Object➪Rotate submenu. (Choosing Object➪Rotate➪Free just displays the rotate and skew handles, as if you had clicked twice on the object.) When the rotate transformation mode is active, the property bar also offers buttons that rotate your object 90 degrees. As with the Flip commands, you have to cancel or apply any current transformations to access these property bar buttons and Rotate commands.

✔ Using the Opacity and Merge mode controls in the Objects docker or the property bar, along with the new object transparency brush tool and object transparency tool, you can adjust the transparency of a selected object. For an example of how to use these features, see Chapter 19.

Stamping Some Text into Your Image

The text tool — the one that looks like an A in the toolbox — lets you add text to your image. Because type in Photo-Paint is made up of pixels, you should use the text tool only to create large letters that you want to embellish in ways that CorelDraw doesn't permit. (In Photo-Paint, small text comes out jagged and illegible because there aren't enough pixels to adequately represent the letters.) For example, after creating text in Photo-Paint, you can paint inside the letters to add stripes. You can also apply special effects from the Effects menu.

If you want to label an image, create a caption, or add other commonplace text, do it in CorelDraw. For best results, drag and drop the image as an object into CorelDraw.

Adding and modifying text

If you decide, after thoughtful consideration, to go ahead and create your text in Photo-Paint, you can select the text tool by pressing F8 (the same shortcut used in CorelDraw to select the text tool). Then click with the tool in the image and enter text from the keyboard. Photo-Paint colors the text in the current foreground color.

As shown in Figure 17-14, both the Tool Settings roll-up and the property bar contain formatting options when the text tool is selected, so you can change

Figure 17-14:
You can
create some
cool text
effects in
Photo-Paint.

the typeface, size, justification, and spacing of type after you enter it from the keyboard. Be sure to turn on anti-aliasing, also available both from the property bar and roll-up, to soften the edges of the letters.

At this point, you may be wondering why I'm discussing text in a chapter about selections and objects. Well, I'm doing it because text in Photo-Paint is created as an object by default, and if you choose, you can create text as a selection mask. When you select the arrow tool, Photo-Paint automatically surrounds each letter of text with marching ants (assuming that Object⇨ Marquee Visible is turned on). Click on the text with the arrow tool to select it and display the standard object handles. You can then move the text, scale it, rotate it, and so on.

If you ever want to edit the characters or change the formatting or color of the text, click on the text object with the text tool. (You know that you've properly activated the text when the marching ants disappear and a big rectangle surrounds the letters.) You can't drag across letters to highlight them as you can in CorelDraw, but you can move the insertion marker around using the left- and right-arrow keys, as well as add and delete characters from the keyboard. Click on a swatch in the color palette to change the color of the text, and adjust the formatting options in the Tool Settings roll-up or on the property bar to change the font and size.

If you turn on the Render to Mask option in the roll-up or on the property bar, Photo-Paint creates your text as a selection mask rather than an object. You can then manipulate and edit the selection as you would any other selection. However, you can't edit or format the text with the text tool as you can a text object. To turn a text object into a selection mask after you create the text, choose Mask⇨Create From Object(s) or press Ctrl+M.

Painting inside text

The following is a little exercise that demonstrates something fun you can do with text in Photo-Paint. The steps explain how to paint inside text and then apply a drop shadow to the text.

1. **Create a few characters of text.**

   Format and color the text as desired. Be sure to make the text really big by entering a Size value of 200 or more. That may sound excessive, but 200 is the size of the type in Figure 17-14. You may also want to click on the B icon to make the text bold. And for a nice effect, select red from the color palette.

   Be sure that the Render to Mask option in the Tool Settings roll-up is turned off. For this effect, you need to create your text first as an object.

2. **Select the arrow tool.**

   Photo-Paint selects the text object.

3. **Convert the text to a mask selection.**

   As mentioned earlier, you can convert an object to a selection by choosing Mask⇨Create From Object(s) or by pressing Ctrl+M.

4. **Change the foreground color.**

   Click on a swatch in the color palette. Make sure that the new foreground color contrasts well with the text color. May I suggest yellow?

5. **Select the paint tool.**

6. **Paint stripes inside the text.**

   The yellow stays entirely inside the selection boundaries. If you followed my color recommendations, you now have red text with yellow stripes, similar to the second example in Figure 17-14.

7. **Click on the text with the arrow tool.**

   Photo-Paint selects your original text object, which exists behind the stripes you just painted.

8. **Choose Object⇨Drop Shadow.**

   Photo-Paint displays the Drop Shadow dialog box, shown in Figure 17-15, which gives you an easy way to create a drop shadow.

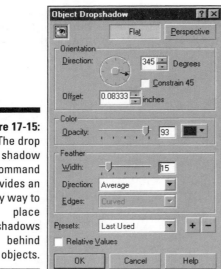

Figure 17-15:
The drop
shadow
command
provides an
easy way to
place
shadows
behind
objects.

Use the options in the dialog box to specify the position (offset), color, opacity, and softness (feathering) of the shadow. The Direction option in the Feather section of the dialog box controls the direction of the feathering. The Direction option in the Orientation section of the dialog box controls the angle of the shadow in degree increments. The Flat button applies a standard drop shadow as shown in the bottom example in Figure 17-14. The Perspective button applies a shadow you can manipulate almost as if you were able to change the position of the sun in the sky. You can preview your drop shadow on-screen as you set the options in the dialog box.

9. Click on OK.

Photo-Paint places the drop shadow behind your text, as in the bottom example in Figure 17-14. Note that what you wind up with is a text selection mask on top of a text object. If you click on the text with the arrow tool, you select the text object. You can then adjust the drop shadow. If you choose a painting or editing tool, the text mask becomes selected, and you can then apply the tool inside the bounds of the mask. And if you delete the text object, the text selection mask remains.

If you want to gain more control over your shadow, you can paint a shadow in by hand. In that case, follow Steps 1 through 6, but choose Mask⇨Invert in Step 7. This selects the area outside the letters. Then use the paintbrush, with black as the paint color, to trace around the edges of the letters.

Chapter 18

Do Dogs Dream in Three Dimensions?

*A*s mentioned a few hundred pages ago in Chapter 1, CorelDream 3D is a three-dimensional drawing program that enables you to create astoundingly realistic graphics. You draw and arrange shapes in 3-D space, assign textures to the shapes, and capture the final scene as an image file that you can then turn around and edit in Photo-Paint.

Sound exciting? You bet. Sound complicated? And how. It takes much longer to get to first base with Dream 3D than either CorelDraw or Photo-Paint, and it takes weeks or even months to master the program. Three-dimensional drawing programs are among the hardest pieces of software in the universe to use. Occasionally, they have the distressing habit of baffling long-time computer artists like me.

In this chapter, I concentrate on getting you midway to first base by walking you through the process of assembling a 3-D scene. Don't get discouraged if you have to experiment to figure out how a feature works. And don't expect to understand it all overnight. By the time you finish this brief introduction, you should have a pretty sound idea of how the program works and whether or not you want to integrate it into your artistic regimen.

The Dream That Starts Like a Nightmare

Now that I've nearly frightened you into swearing off Dream 3D forever, I'd like to scare you a little further by having you start the program. Just choose Programs➪CorelDraw 8➪CorelDream 3D 8 from the Windows 95 Start menu. After a few moments, the Dream 3D interface takes over your screen. As in CorelDraw and Photo-Paint, Dream 3D begins your encounter by asking whether you want to start an empty scene, open an existing scene, or use the Scene wizard, which offers an assortment of ready-made backgrounds for your scene. (For more about the Scene wizard, see "Adding a Prefab Backdrop" later in this chapter.)

After you open an empty scene, your screen appears something like the one shown in Figure 18-1. The layout of your screen may be a little different, depending on your monitor resolution and the option you select from the Windows➪Workspace submenu, which enables you to choose from several different layouts. (The different layouts are designed to work with different monitor resolutions.) Some portions of the screen are familiar. Dream 3D offers a bunch of menus, a toolbar, a toolbox, and a status bar, just like Corel's other programs. But the four windows in the middle of the screen herald a decidedly different artistic approach. Sure, they're weird, but you have to get used to them:

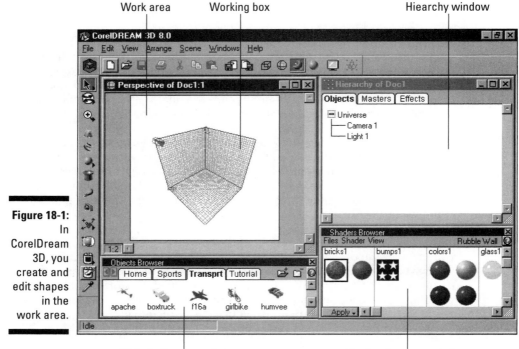

Figure 18-1:
In CorelDream 3D, you create and edit shapes in the work area.

✔ The *work area* is where you create your drawing. It's like the drawing area in CorelDraw, except this one shows your objects in perspective.

✔ To demonstrate the perspective scene, Dream 3D throws in something it calls a *working box,* which looks like a chicken-wire cage that's missing a top and two sides. The remaining two sides and bottom represent the three planes of 3-D space. The edges where the planes meet are known as *axes.*

✔ The window to the right of the work area shows the hierarchy of the objects in the work area. (Now let's try that sentence again, but in English.) See, it's easy to lose items in a complex 3-D drawing. The Hierarchy window lists the names of objects and other items so that you can easily locate and select them without having to waste time searching for them in the work area.

✔ The Objects Browser window, below the work area, contains an assortment of predrawn 3-D objects, called *models.* Each tab (Home, Sports, Tranprt, and Tutorial) in the Object Browser window represents a different folder of objects. To display the objects in a particular folder, just click on the folder's tab. You can add additional folders and objects, as explained in the next section. To use one of the 3-D objects, just drag the object out of the window and drop it into the work area.

✔ The Shaders Browser window includes colors, patterns, and textures. Click on a shader and then click on the Apply button in the bottom-left corner of the Shaders Browser window to apply the shader to the selected shape in the work area. Or drag the shader and drop it right onto the object.

✔ As in CorelDraw and Photo-Paint, you can reposition your toolbar and toolbox by dragging the gray area around the buttons. And you can hide or display the various toolbars and the status bar by right-clicking the gray area surrounding the toolbar or toolbox and clicking the name of the element you want to turn on or off.

✔ You may want to resize both Browser windows and move them into the upper-right corner of the screen to get them out of the way of the scroll bar. (Check out Figure 18-2, which appears later in this chapter, if you want to see how I did it.)

In all likelihood, you have no immediate need for the Hierarchy window. You can cut down on the screen clutter by clicking on the Maximize button in the top-right corner of the work area window. The work area expands to fill the entire screen. The Hierarchy window is covered up, but the Objects Browser and Shaders Browser windows remain visible. If you ever need to get to the Hierarchy window later, just choose the Hierarchy command from the Windows menu.

Three planes of pure drawing pleasure

Dream 3D's working box is really an average, everyday dimensional grid. You know how a bar graph has a horizontal X axis and a vertical Y axis? Well, the only difference between that bar graph and the working box — besides a complete absence of bars — is the addition of a third axis, called the Z axis. The X axis points to the right, the Y axis goes straight up and down, and the Z axis shoots off to the left.

Each plane is connected to two of the axes. The right plane borders the X and Y axes, for example. As a result, it's called the X,Y plane.

(Uninspired, but accurate.) Similarly, the left plane is called the Y,Z plane, and the bottom one is called the X,Z plane.

In CorelDraw, you have two dimensions: width (X) and height (Y). Therefore, you have just one plane, the X,Y plane. By adding a third dimension — depth (Z) — you add two additional planes — X,Z and Y,Z — to your drawing area. This third dimension is why Dream 3D presents you with the 3-D working box rather than the flat drawing area you see in CorelDraw.

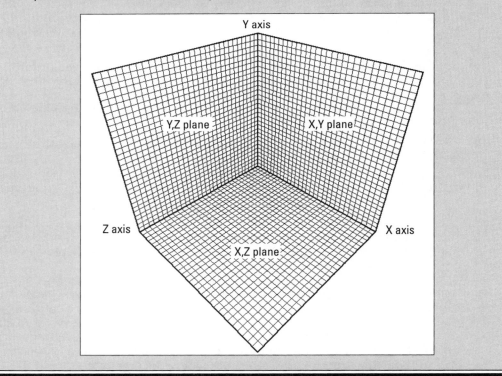

A Beginner's Guide to 3-D Objects

Dream 3D provides two ways to add objects to a drawing. You can either draw the objects from scratch or select from the hundreds of predrawn objects that Corel includes on CD-ROM.

To import a predrawn object, you can drag it from the Objects Browser and drop it into the work area. But the Objects Browser contains only a limited selection of models. More models are included on the second CD-ROM in your CorelDraw 8 box. You can add as many folders of models to the Objects Browser as you want.

To add a folder from the CD-ROM to the Objects Browser window, click on the Add Folder button in the upper-right corner of the window, labeled in Figure 18-2. A tiny Directory Selection dialog box appears. Open up the 3dmodels folder on the CD-ROM. Then double-click on a folder name that looks interesting — such as Aircraft or Fashion — and press Enter or click on the Select button. Dream 3D displays the folder and its objects in the Objects Browser window. (This process may take a few minutes, so be patient.)

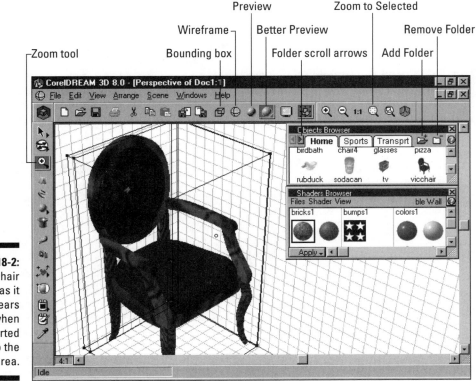

Figure 18-2: The vicchair object as it appears when imported into the work area.

If all the folder tabs aren't visible in the Objects Browser, you can scroll through the various tabs by using the folder scroll arrows in the upper-left corner of the window, labeled in Figure 18-2. To remove a folder from the Objects Browser window, click on the folder tab and then click on the Remove Folder button, also labeled in the figure.

Importing and magnifying an object

For an example of how to use Dream 3D, drag the vicchair item from the Home tab in the Objects Browser window and drop it into the work area. A 3-D chair appears in the work area, surrounded by a box shape with handles in each corner. The box and handles show that the chair is selected.

To get a closer look, press Shift+F2 to magnify the selected portion of the drawing. This keyboard shortcut is the same one used in CorelDraw. You can also press F2 to zoom in and F3 to zoom out.

If you don't like shortcuts, click on the Zoom to Selected icon on the toolbar, labeled in Figure 18-2. (To display the zoom icons on the toolbar, right-click on an empty area of the toolbar and click on the Zoom item.) You can also click with the zoom tool or drag around the object you want to magnify. To zoom out, Alt+click with the zoom tool.

The little black arrow at the bottom of the zoom tool icon indicates a flyout menu containing additional tools, just as in CorelDraw and Photo-Paint. Press and hold on the zoom tool flyout to access the zoom out tool and a hand tool. (Drag with the hand tool to display a different portion of your work area.) Click on the tool you want to use. Or just keep clicking on the tool icon to cycle through the different tools.

Changing how the object looks on-screen

You can also change the way Dream 3D displays the model on-screen:

✔ The default view mode is the preview mode, which shows the object in color but does not accurately show textures and other realistic stuff. You can return to this mode at any time by clicking on the preview icon in the toolbar (labeled in Figure 18-2). You can also choose View⇨Default Quality⇨Preview or press Ctrl+Alt+Shift+Y.

✔ If things seem to be happening too slowly, you can speed them up by switching to the wireframe mode. This mode displays coarse, chicken-wire versions of the objects without any color. Although it's not terribly accurate, this mode is much faster. To make the switch, click on the wireframe icon on the toolbar, choose View⇨Default Quality⇨ Wireframe, or press Ctrl+Shift+Y.

> ✔ Bounding box quality shows you just the object's selection box. You may find this mode helpful for quickly positioning objects in a complex drawing. Turn on Bounding box mode by pressing Ctrl+Y or choosing <u>V</u>iew➪Default <u>Q</u>uality➪<u>B</u>ounding Box.

> ✔ If you own a powerful computer or you simply want to see more detailed versions of your objects, click on the Better Preview icon on the toolbar. When you work in this mode, you can see surface textures and shadows, as demonstrated in Figure 18-2. You can also turn on this mode by choosing <u>V</u>iew➪Default <u>Q</u>uality➪Be<u>t</u>ter Preview or pressing Ctrl+Alt+Y.

Moving an object in 3-D space

To move an object, click on it with the arrow tool — the one at the top of the toolbox — to select it. Then drag it just as in CorelDraw or Photo-Paint. You can also nudge the object by pressing the arrow keys. The nudge distance is determined by the Spacing setting in the Grid dialog box, which you display by choosing <u>V</u>iew➪<u>G</u>rid or pressing Ctrl+J.

The only trick to moving an object is figuring out where the heck you're dragging it. I mean, how do you move an object side to side, forward and backward, and up and down when the only directions you can move your mouse are side to side and forward and backward? Sadly, you can't lift your mouse and expect the object to levitate in 3-D space.

Based on the way other programs work, you may think that up and down motions would be a breeze; but if you do, you're not thinking in 3-D. Granted, when you move your mouse forward and backward on the mouse pad, your cursor moves up and down on-screen. So, over time, you've come to associate forward and backward mouse movement with up and down object movement.

Not so in Dream 3D. In this program, you have to imagine that the mouse pad is sitting on the bottom plane (X,Z). When you drag the object, it doesn't move up and down; it moves back and forth. The object never moves off the ground when you drag it.

In Figure 18-3, for example, I dragged the object down. But the object moved toward me, just as my mouse moved toward me. How can I tell? By watching the tracking boxes on the two other planes (as labeled in the figure). The tracking boxes move along with the object to show how it aligns with the planes, much as the tracking lines in CorelDraw's rulers move with an object. Because the tracking boxes remain firmly fastened to the X and Z axes, I know that the chair does not move upward.

Arrow tool   Tracking boxes

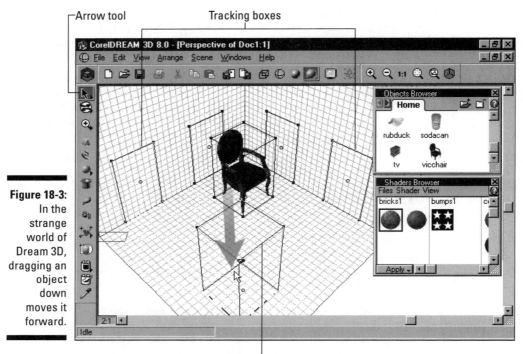

Figure 18-3:
In the
strange
world of
Dream 3D,
dragging an
object
down
moves it
forward.

Selection box

TIP

So, how do you move an object up and down? Well, it turns out that you can drag a tracking box directly. When you drag a tracking box, the corresponding object follows along with your move — on the same plane as the tracking box. In Figure 18-4, for example, when I dragged the right tracking box up, the chair moved upward into 3-D space. Because a tracking box always adheres to its plane, you can move it in only two directions: up and down or left and right.

Moving an object by dragging a tracking box is frequently easier than dragging the object directly, because you don't have to translate your 2-D mouse movements into 3-D space. So when in doubt, drag a tracking box.

Scaling and spinning the object

You can also scale and rotate objects inside Dream 3D. To scale an object, drag the corner handles around the selection box. You can also drag the corner handles of one of the tracking boxes.

To rotate an object, use the virtual trackball tool, the one below the arrow tool. Although the tool has a ridiculous name, it can be very useful. Drag the selected object to spin it around in 3-D space, as shown in Figure 18-5.

Tracking box

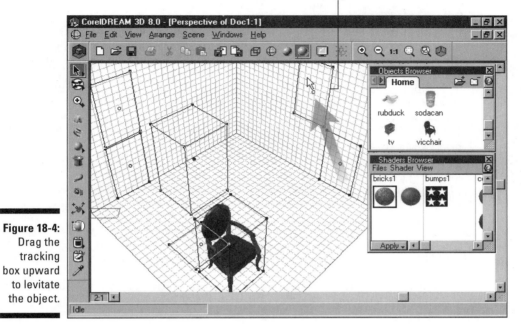

Figure 18-4:
Drag the
tracking
box upward
to levitate
the object.

Virtual trackball

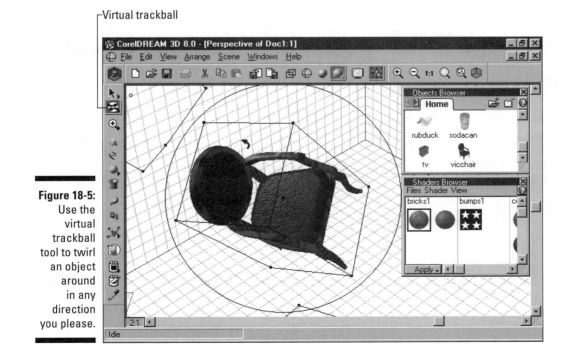

Figure 18-5:
Use the
virtual
trackball
tool to twirl
an object
around
in any
direction
you please.

Every Object Needs a Look

As I mentioned earlier, you assign colors and textures to objects using the options in the Shaders Browser window. Dream 3D calls these items *shaders* because they affect not only the color and texture of an object, but also the translucency, reflectivity, and all kinds of other properties. (Okay, so *shader* doesn't necessarily conjure up colors, textures, and all that other stuff in your mind, but it did to some daffy program manager at Corel. Unfortunately, the industry-standard term, *texture maps,* doesn't make much more sense.) Using shaders, you can make an object appear as if it were made out of glass, wrapped in burlap, or covered with mud.

Corel's predrawn objects comprise many separate objects, each of which you can color separately. The chair, for example, has plush blue fabric applied to the cushions and wood grain applied to the legs and trim.

In Figure 18-6, I changed the bottom cushion to stone by dragging the first shader from the Tutorial column in the Shaders Browser and dropping it onto the cushion. This step colored only the bottom cushion; I had to drag the stone shader and drop it onto the back cushion separately. To change the wood grain trim and legs to the striped pattern, I had to drag and drop the same shader onto ten different sections of the chair.

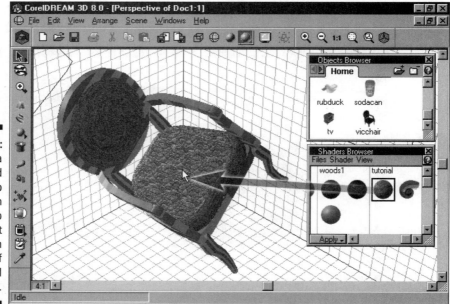

Figure 18-6:
Drag a shader and drop it onto a shape in the model to change that shape from one type of material to another.

Adding a Prefab Backdrop

Creating and spinning a single object in 3-D space is a little complicated but nothing compared with the difficulties of putting together an entire 3-D scene. That's why Dream 3D is equipped with a Scene wizard you can use to add to your scene a ready-made backdrop, complete with lighting and other effects, as I did in Figure 18-7. In many cases, you can move, shade, and otherwise edit the background elements.

If you want to add one of the backgrounds to an existing scene, choose File➪Apply Scene Wizard. A dialog box appears warning you that existing lights will be replaced to achieve the lighting effects you select. Click on OK to launch the Scene Wizard. To create a new scene based on a wizard backdrop, choose File➪New and then click on the Use Scene Wizard radio button.

Either way, the Scene Wizard dialog box, shown in Figure 18-8, appears. Click on the icon for the type of backdrop you want to use, and then click on the Next button. You can then choose from an entire ready-made backdrop or put together a custom backdrop using a selection of prefab backgrounds and lighting designs. After selecting the options you want to use, click on the Done button to see the results.

You don't see the entire scene in your workspace; only objects that can be manipulated appear. The remaining elements in the scene appear when you render the object, as described next. For example, compare the scene in

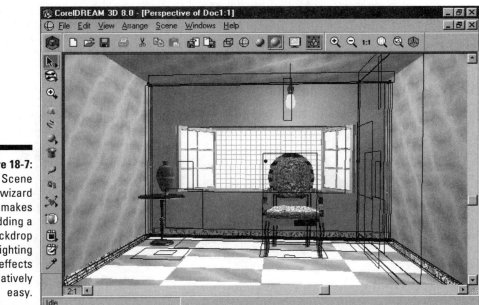

Figure 18-7:
The Scene wizard makes adding a backdrop and lighting effects relatively easy.

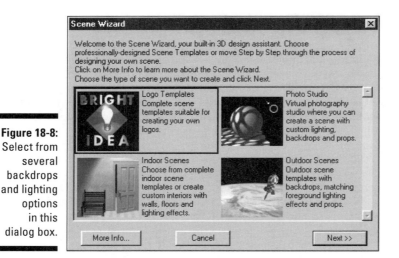

Figure 18-8:
Select from several backdrops and lighting options in this dialog box.

Figure 18-7 with the final, rendered scene in Figure 18-9. The sky behind the open windows and the shadows on the wall appear only in the rendered version.

If you apply a complicated backdrop to your scene and your existing objects are at the back of the workspace, backdrop objects may obscure the existing objects. To save yourself the headache of having to relocate your objects — not an easy prospect in a crowded scene — move your objects to the front of the workspace before adding a backdrop from the Scene wizard. You can then more easily select and reposition the existing objects.

Figure 18-9:
My final scene, rendered at 160 dpi and adjusted in Photo-Paint.

The End of the 3-D Highway

When you finish a drawing in CorelDraw, you print it. When you finish editing a photograph in Photo-Paint, you print it. You can also print your 3D creations, but the process is more involved.

A 3-D drawing is so vast and complex that printing it would take far too long. So, you must perform an intermediate step called *rendering,* in which Dream 3D converts the drawing to pixels and saves it as a separate image file.

Before rendering, it's a good idea to save your drawing to disk. Although Dream 3D saves the rendered image to a separate file, you don't want to lose your work if something goes wrong.

Here's how to render a 3-D drawing:

1. **Choose Scene⇨Render Settings.**

   Up comes the Rendering Settings dialog box, which enables you to specify the resolution of the final image.

2. **Set the scene dimensions.**

   Enter the final size of the drawing in the Width and Height option boxes. You can change the unit of measure by using the pop-up menus next to the option boxes. Select the Keep Proportions check box if you want to maintain the original proportions of the drawing.

3. **If you have a specific resolution in mind, enter it in the Resolution option box.**

   Or, if you want Dream 3D to suggest a resolution for you, enter the resolution of your final output device in the Resolution option box, select the Best Resolution radio button, and click on the Estimate button. For example, if you're going to print your image on a 600-dpi laser printer, enter 600 into the Resolution option box.

4. **Select the Render Time radio button and click on the Estimate button.**

   Dream 3D estimates the amount of time required to create the image. In all likelihood, you're looking at several minutes. Complex scenes with lots of objects can take more than an hour. Images with higher resolutions take longer as well.

5. **Click on OK.**

6. **Choose Scene⇨Render⇨Low Res Preview.**

   Dream 3D begins generating a preview of the drawing in a new window. If you don't like how things look, close the image by clicking on the Close button, or choose File⇨Close and make the necessary changes. If you do like the image, close it and proceed to the next step. Either way, you don't need to save the preview, so click on the No button when the save message comes up.

7. **Choose the Perspective option from the bottom of the <u>W</u>indows menu.**

   Dream 3D has the irritating habit of returning you to the wrong window after rendering. Choose Perspective (followed by the name of your drawing) to get back to the work area.

8. **Press Ctrl+R.**

   This command tells Dream 3D to begin rendering your drawing according to the settings in the Rendering Settings dialog box. The process may take a long time, so be patient. If you decide to skip it for now, press Esc to cancel the rendering or right-click the rendering area and select Abort from the pop-up menu that appears.

   You don't have to sit on your hands while you wait for Dream 3D to complete the image. Thanks to Windows 95, you can keep working in the program or switch to a different program and work in it. Unfortunately, Dream 3D renders more slowly if you make your computer do other stuff, and it may even cause the other program to pause intermittently and, in the worst cases, crash. Despite Windows 95's swell new multitasking capabilities, it's better to let Dream 3D do its stuff unhampered.

   As Dream 3D works, it shows you the parts of the image it has finished.

9. **When the image is complete, save it to disk.**

   Choose <u>F</u>ile⇨<u>S</u>ave or press Ctrl+S. The Save dialog box appears. Enter a name for the image and select a format from the Save as Type pop-up menu. I heartily recommend that you select the Tiff (Cor) (*.TIF) option, but you can select any format you like. Then press Enter or click on the Save button.

If you don't want to go through all this rigmarole and you don't care about a precise size or resolution for your rendered drawing, you can simply choose one of the commands from the bottom portion of the <u>S</u>cene⇨<u>R</u>ender submenu. The submenu contains several options for rendering your scene to various resolutions. Medium resolution should work fine for everyday uses.

After you render a drawing, you can print it by choosing <u>F</u>ile⇨<u>P</u>rint. You can also choose <u>F</u>ile⇨Print P<u>r</u>eview to open the same print preview window offered in CorelDraw and Photo-Paint. (For more information on printing, including how to use the various preview window elements, see Chapter 13.)

Figure 18-9 shows the final chair image after I rendered it at a resolution of 160 dpi and adjusted the brightness and contrast in Photo-Paint as explained in Chapter 17. This scene looks like a combination of a New Age retreat and a prisoner interrogation room.

Part V
The Part of Tens

"NO, THAT'S NOT A PIE CHART, IT'S JUST A CORN CHIP THAT GOT SCANNED INTO THE DOCUMENT."

In this part . . .

Sure, sure, we're all addicted to statistics and sound bites — so much so that no one knows the full story about anything. But I figure what's good enough for Moses is good enough for me. I mean, the guy kept it simple — two tablets, ten factoids — and everybody ate it up. "Thou shalt not kill" kind of sticks in your mind. It has a certain undeniable directness that's downright impossible to argue with. You can toss it out at a party or share it with a friend in a time of need.

> JILL: I swear, Jack's driving me nuts. I'm about ready to strangle the chump in his sleep.
>
> HUMPTY DUMPTY (a friend from a neighboring story line): Now now, Jill. (Wagging finger.) "Thou shalt not kill."
>
> JILL: Oh, right, I forgot about that one. (Considers.) But I can wallop him with my pail, right? It doesn't say anything about walloping folks with a pail, does it?
>
> HUMPTY DUMPTY: No, I believe that's acceptable.

Of course, the following lists don't quite measure up to the Ten Commandments (or Mother Goose, for that matter). In fact, they're more the *Guinness Book of World Records* variety of list. But they're still lots of fun and, wow, talk about memorable! You can even toss them out at a party, assuming that you want to look like a total geek.

Chapter 19

Ten Way-Cool Special Effects

● ●

In This Chapter

▶ Drawing a planet with a ring around it

▶ Morphing between two shapes

▶ Creating a fancy shadow for your text

▶ Making type bulge like a balloon

▶ Wrapping paragraph text around a graphic

▶ Putting your message in the sky

▶ Turning an object into a ghost of its former self

▶ Shuffling the colors in a photograph

▶ Making the pixels beg for mercy

▶ Designing your own repeating pattern

● ●

Some folks characterize CorelDraw as a functional and powerful tool for creating business graphics. They say CorelDraw lets you assemble drawings and edit images in an efficient and timely manner. They add that CorelDraw enables you to store and catalog your graphics quickly and conveniently.

Well, I say bugger. Sure, I guess all that stuff is true, but who gives a rat's fanny? Especially when you consider the real potential of CorelDraw: It enables you to take cheesy little shapes, text, and stock photos and turn them into bizarre artistic monstrosities that overflow with an excess of special effects.

Enticed? That's where this chapter comes in. I hereby invite you to abandon all pretense of good taste and go on a computer graphics binge. Some techniques in the next few pages are based on ideas I cover in other chapters, but don't expect any warmed-over repeats. This is your chance to indulge in some purely frivolous and largely irrelevant special effects.

Draw a Planet with a Ring around It

I'd like to start things off with a razzle-dazzle project. But instead, the following steps tell you how to create something that looks vaguely like the planet Saturn, as in Figure 19-1. Isn't it a beauty? Can't you imagine spying that baby through the viewport of your rocketship? Or perhaps losing communications with an unmanned probe in the vicinity of this gorgeous orb?

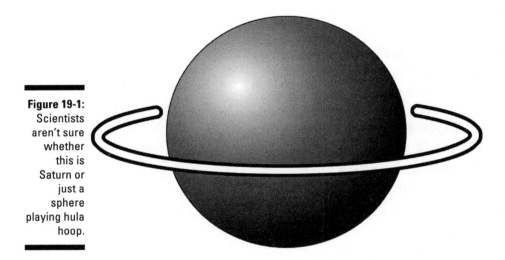

Figure 19-1:
Scientists aren't sure whether this is Saturn or just a sphere playing hula hoop.

1. **Inside CorelDraw, draw a circle.**

   You do this by Ctrl+dragging with the ellipse tool. Saturn is very big, so make your circle nice and big.

2. **Press F11 or select the Fountain Fill icon from the Fill tool flyout menu.**

   The Fountain Fill dialog box appears.

3. **From the Type pop-up menu, select Radial.**

   This setting creates a radial gradation that progresses outward in concentric circles, as in Figure 19-1.

   The way things stand now, the white spot is dead in the center of the gradation, as the preview in the upper-right corner of the dialog box shows. That doesn't look right. It needs to be up and to the left a little, maybe. You can move the white spot using the Horizontal and Vertical options in the Center Offset area.

4. **Enter a value of –20 in the Horizontal option box and 20 in the Vertical option box.**

Or just drag inside the preview in the upper-right corner of the dialog box to move the white spot up and to the left.

5. Press Enter.

CorelDraw exits the dialog box and returns to the sphere, which should look like the one in Figure 19-1 but without the ring.

6. Draw a short, wide oval centered on the sphere.

Using the ellipse tool, Shift+drag outward from the center of the sphere. (Be careful not to drag the center X icon in the bounding box, because doing so will move the sphere.) This new oval represents the planet's rings. Or at least one ring, anyway.

7. Select the second-to-fattest line width from the pen tool flyout menu.

It's the one that's 16 points thick.

8. Select black as your outline color.

The outline color should be black by default. If it's not, just right-click on the black swatch in the color palette.

9. Select the shape tool by pressing F10.

10. Turn the oval into an arc.

The quickest way to do this is to click on the arc icon on the property bar and then enter new values in the Starting and Ending Angle option boxes. Try a starting angle value in the 140 range and an ending angle of about 40. (See Figure 4-9 for a look at these controls.) If necessary, use the X and Y controls to reposition the arc horizontally or vertically on the sphere.

If you prefer, you can create your arc by dragging the node at the top of the oval. First, drag the node down and to the right to create a rift in the outline of the oval. Make sure to keep the cursor outside the oval so that you get an arc instead of a pie. Drag until the outline of the ring no longer overlaps the top portion of the sphere.

By the way, my instruction to drag the node down and to the right assumes that you drew the oval from left to right. If you drew it from right to left, drag down and to the left with the shape tool.

Next, drag the other node down and to the left. Again, keep the cursor outside the oval and drag until the ring no longer overlaps the sphere. You should now have an arc that looks more or less like it circles around the front of the sphere.

11. Press F12 or select the pen icon from the pen tool flyout menu.

The Outline Pen dialog box appears.

12. Select the second Line Caps radio button.

This option is the round cap.

13. **Press Enter to exit the dialog box.**

14. **Press Ctrl+C and then press Ctrl+V.**

    This step copies the arc and then pastes it right in front of the original.

15. **Right-click on the white swatch in the color palette.**

    This step makes the pasted arc white.

16. **Select the 8-point line width from the pen tool flyout menu.**

You could, of course, create a true 3-D sphere in Dream 3D, draw a bunch of really sophisticated rings around it, and make it look just like the real Saturn. But that would take a lot longer. And besides, you'd ruin that special Ed Wood feel of your current planet.

Morph between Two Shapes

CorelDraw enables you to blend a shape filled with one color into a different shape filled with a different color. In essence, the result is a custom gradation, as shown in Figure 19-2. The following steps explain how.

For a different way to create custom gradients, see Chapter 7, which discusses using the interactive fill tool.

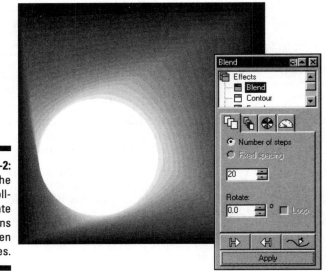

Figure 19-2:
Use the
Blend roll-
up to create
gradations
between
two shapes.

1. **Draw two shapes.**

   For this example, draw a large rectangle with the rectangle tool. Then, using the ellipse tool, draw an oval that fits inside the rectangle.

2. **Select white from the color palette.**

   Because you just finished drawing the oval, it should be selected. So clicking on the white swatch fills the oval with white.

3. **Right-click on the X icon at the top of the color palette.**

   This step deletes the outline from the oval, which is an important step when creating custom gradations. If you don't delete the outline, borders appear between the colors in the gradation. Your oval disappears, but don't freak out; the oval is still there — it's just in temporary hiding.

4. **Select the rectangle with the arrow tool, select black from the color palette, and right-click on the X icon.**

   The rectangle is now black with no outline.

5. **Select both the rectangle and the oval with the arrow tool.**

   Assuming that the rectangle is still selected, you just have to Shift+click on the oval. Or drag around both shapes to surround them with a selection marquee.

6. **Press Ctrl+B.**

   Or choose Effe̱cts⇨Ḇlend to display the Blend roll-up.

7. **Click on the Apply button in the Blend roll-up.**

   CorelDraw automatically creates a gradation between the two shapes, as shown in Figure 19-2.

By default, CorelDraw creates this gradation by generating 20 transitional shapes between the rectangle and oval, each shaped and filled slightly differently. If you want to increase the number of shapes to create a smoother gradation, increase the value in the Steps option box in the roll-up and then click on the Apply button again. Or use the Steps control on the property bar to make your change.

After you create a blend, CorelDraw displays a series of small squares running from the first object in the blend to the second object. These squares represent the steps in your blend.

Another way to create a blend is to use the interactive blend tool, which is the third tool from the bottom of the toolbox, just above the pen tool. Just select the tool and drag from one object to the other.

Create a Shadow for Your Text

Folks invariably ooh and ah when they see the effect shown in Figure 19-3, but it's really easy to create. Here's how:

Figure 19-3:
No program
does type at
dusk like
CorelDraw.

1. **Press the Caps Lock key.**

   This effect works best when you use capital letters only. Lowercase letters sometimes descend below the baseline, ruining the shadow effect.

2. **Create some artistic text.**

   To create artistic text, simply select the text tool (press F8 to do it quickly). Then click in the drawing area and type in one short line of text.

3. **Enlarge the type size to 100 points or so.**

   To enlarge the type, first select the text by dragging over it with the text tool or by using one of the other selection techniques I discuss in Chapter 10. Then choose a new type size from the pop-up menu on the property bar.

4. **Select the arrow tool.**

   Pressing Ctrl+spacebar is the fastest way to select the tool. The text becomes selected.

5. **Press Alt+F9 or choose <u>A</u>rrange⇨<u>T</u>ransform⇨<u>S</u>cale and Mirror.**

   This command displays the Scale & Mirror roll-up.

6. **Click on the vertical mirror icon.**

   This is the icon to the right of the V option box.

You can't use the mirror button on the property bar for this effect. You need to apply the mirroring to a duplicate of your text, as explained in the next step, and the property bar doesn't have an Apply to Duplicate button.

7. Click on the Apply To Duplicate button.

This step creates a duplicate of the text block as it flips the block.

8. Press the down-arrow key until the baselines of the two text blocks align.

In other words, the bottom of the letters in the different text blocks should touch.

9. Click on a light gray color in the color palette.

The flipped text changes to gray.

10. Click on the flipped text block.

The rotate and skew handles appear.

11. Drag the bottom handle to skew the text.

This step makes the shadow appear at an angle. To complete the effect shown in Figure 19-3, I added a rectangle, filled it with light gray, and pressed Shift+PgDn (Arrange⇨Order⇨To Back) to send it to the back of the drawing.

Make Type Bulge Like a Balloon

CorelDraw lets you create type that bulges off the page, as shown in Figure 19-4. This interesting text effect is remarkably easy to create using the Envelope feature:

1. Repeat the first four steps from the preceding section.

Press the Caps lock key, click with the text tool, enter a word or short line of text, increase the type size to 100 points or so, and select the arrow tool.

2. Drag up on the top handle of the text block until it's roughly as tall as it is wide.

The text stretches vertically.

3. Press Ctrl+F7 to display the Envelope roll-up.

Or choose Effects⇨Envelope.

Alternatively, you can select the interactive envelope tool from the interactive blend tool flyout menu and use the controls on the property bar for the following steps. You can skip to Step 5.

4. **Click on the Add New button.**

   This step displays a dotted outline and special handles around the text.

5. **Click on the single-arc icon.**

   It's the second icon below the Add Preset button in the roll-up, and the second icon in the group of envelope mode icons in the middle of the property bar.

6. **Drag the top handle upward, drag the bottom handle downward, drag the left handle farther to the left, and drag the right handle to the right.**

   Don't drag any of the corner handles. Ultimately, you're trying to turn the square confines of the text block into a circle. The text now puffs out like you're viewing it through a fish-eye lens.

Wrap Paragraph Text around a Graphic

You've seen it in national magazines, newspapers, and slick fliers. Now you can join in on the fun. CorelDraw lets you wrap paragraph text around a graphic, which is just the thing for designing nifty documents that'll make your friends and coworkers drool with envy. Just follow these steps:

1. **Create a few lines of paragraph text.**

   To create paragraph text, press F8 to select the text tool. Then drag in the drawing area to create a paragraph text block and enter some text from the keyboard. Any old text will do.

2. **Draw the graphic around which you want to wrap the text.**

   Or import a piece of clip art. If you want to wrap the text around several objects, you may want to group them first by choosing Arrange⇨Group or pressing Ctrl+G. You can alternatively wrap the text around each object individually, which gives you a little more flexibility in layout but is a bit more work.

3. **Right-click on the graphic.**

   CorelDraw displays a pop-up menu of options.

4. **Select the Properties option.**

   It's the one at the bottom of the pop-up menu. The Object Properties docker leaps onto the screen.

   Alternatively, you can select the graphic and press Alt+Enter to display the Object Properties docker.

5. **Click on the General tab and then select the Wrap Paragraph Text check box.**

   Look for the check box on the middle-left side of the panel.

6. **Set the text offset.**

   The *offset* is a fancy name for the distance you want to place between the object and the text.

7. **Click on Apply.**

   CorelDraw wraps the text around the graphic (assuming that the graphic is near the text, of course). If necessary, adjust the text offset and click Apply again to see the text wrap with the new offset.

8. **After you're satisfied with how your text wraps around the graphic, press Alt+F4 to close the dialog box.**

From now on, you can move the graphic anywhere on the page, and all paragraph text — including other text blocks on the page — automatically wraps out of the graphic's way. It's as if the graphic has some kind of force field around it. Too bad you can't apply this feature to yourself and have people wrap out of your way on the subway.

If you don't want to change the offset value, you can turn text wrap on and off for an object by simply right-clicking on the object and choosing Wrap Paragraph Text from the pop-up menu.

Put Your Message in the Sky

You can use the CorelDraw Add Perspective command and Extrude roll-up to create text that appears to zoom across the screen. Figure 19-5 shows an example in which a consumer-oriented message demands the reader's immediate compliance.

Figure 19-5: An important 3-D message solicits the attention of an eager audience.

1. **Create some artistic text.**

   You know the drill: Click with the text tool and begin typing. This time around, you can use lowercase letters if you want to. Furthermore, the type size doesn't matter because you'll end up stretching the type all over the place anyway.

2. **Choose Effects⊅Add Perspective.**

   Four handles appear in the corners of the text block.

3. **Drag the handles until you get the desired effect.**

   Experiment to your heart's content.

4. **Click on red or some other garish hue in the color palette.**

   This step colors the text so that no one will accidentally overlook it.

5. **Press Ctrl+E or choose Effects⊅Extrude.**

   CorelDraw displays the Extrude roll-up so that you can add depth to the text.

6. **Drag the vanishing point to set the direction of the extrusion.**

   The vanishing point is that X you see in the drawing area. To create the effect in Figure 19-5, I set the vanishing point on the left side of the text.

7. **Set the extrusion colors.**

   Click on the Color tab of the roll-up and specify how you want the extruded text to be colored. To create the effect in Figure 19-5, I selected the solid fill radio button and black from the color pop-up menu. Click on Apply to see how your choice looks.

8. **Adjust the Depth value as needed.**

   This value, found on the first tab of the Extrude roll-up, determines how much your text is extruded. Click on the Apply button to see the results of your changes.

9. **Click on the light bulb tab at the top of the Extrude roll-up.**

   You now see the lighting options.

10. **Click on the first light bulb icon on the left side of the roll-up.**

    It's the one with a 1 in it. This step turns on the first light. Drag the little 1 in a black circle down to the lower-right front corner of the box on the right side of the roll-up.

11. **Click on the Apply button.**

    Your text now appears in 3-D. If you want, you can rotate your text in 3-D space by clicking on the Edit button, dragging the big red C on the rotate tab of the roll-up, and then clicking on Apply.

12. **To exit the extrude edit mode, click outside the text with the arrow tool.**

If you accidentally click off the text when you're creating the effect, just click on the Edit button in the Extrude roll-up to continue editing the extrusion.

You can also achieve this effect by using the interactive extrude tool and property bar controls. For more on extruding, see Chapter 9.

Turn Your Object into a Ghost of Its Former Self

In Photo-Paint, you can adjust the opacity of an object in a variety of ways, all of which are illustrated in the spooky "Ghosts of the African Veldt" image in Figure 19-6. In the figure, I adjusted the transparency of the toucan, elephant, and cougar. The two giraffes, part of the original background image, are fully opaque.

Figure 19-6:
I created this haunting scene by adjusting the transparency of the toucan, cougar, and elephant.

Before the zoologists in the crowd start howling and pointing fingers, I want to state that I'm fully aware that cougars are not readily found on the African veldt. But I didn't have an image of a zebra, a lion, or another more appropriate creature lying around. Besides, this is a ghost cougar, and when animals pass out of this world, they get to go wherever they please. This particular cougar always dreamed of going to Africa.

By the way, the cougar, elephant, and toucan in Figure 19-6 are ready-made objects found in the Animals folder of the Objects folder on the third CD-ROM in the CorelDraw 8 package. After opening a background image, open each of the animal files. Then select the arrow tool and drag each animal into the background image window. (After you open the animal files, you see the animals already selected and ready to drag.)

✔ To adjust the transparency of an entire object, as I did for the elephant in Figure 19-6, select the object with the arrow tool. Then adjust the Opacity slider either in the Objects docker (press Ctrl+F7 to display the docker) or on the property bar. The elephant in Figure 19-6 has an opacity value of 49.

✔ The object transparency tool, which is just above the paint tool in the toolbox, applies transparency to your object according to the transparency fill type you choose from the pop-up menu on the property bar or in the Tool Settings roll-up. The Flat option applies uniform transparency to your object, just as if you simply selected the object and changed the Opacity slider as just discussed.

✔ The next six options fade your object into the background by applying a gradient transparency to the object. In the figure, I used the Linear option to fade the toucan into view. When you choose one of these options, Photo-Paint displays transparency controls on your object similar to those you see when using the interactive fill tool or the Edit Fill & Transparency dialog box, both discussed in Chapter 16. Drag these controls to reposition the start, middle, and end points of the transparency and to adjust the angle of the transparency blend. Use the Transparency sliders on the property bar or the option boxes in the roll-up to adjust the level of transparency at the start, middle, and end points.

✔ The Bitmap and Texture options fill your object with a bitmap pattern or texture, respectively. Again, you can use the controls in the roll-up and on the property bar to select a different texture or pattern and adjust the transparency of the fill.

✔ To remove a transparency fill from your object, select the None option from the Type menu in the roll-up or from its counterpart on the property bar.

✔ Turn on the Use Original Transparency option in the roll-up or on the property bar to apply an additional transparency blend to an object that already has a transparency blend applied. Otherwise, the new transparency blend replaces the existing blend.

✔ Turn on the Apply To Clip Mask option in the roll-up or on the property bar to create and apply a transparency blend to a clip mask rather than the original object. This allows you to undo transparency changes, even after saving them, by simply disabling or removing the clip mask from the object. To disable or remove a clip mask, press Ctrl+F7 to display the Objects docker and click on the object whose clip mask you want to change. Then choose Object➪Clip Mask➪Disable to disable it or Object➪Clip Mask➪Remove to remove it. To restore a clip mask you've disabled, choose the Object➪Clip Mask➪Disable command again. You can't restore a clip mask that you've removed — it's deleted, done, gone, outta there.

✔ Using the object transparency brush found on the object transparency tool flyout menu, you can "paint" transparency onto portions of your object. After selecting the cougar in the bottom-left corner of Figure 19-6, I selected the object transparency brush and painted around the outside edges of the animal. The edges of the body are partially transparent and the face is fully opaque. This cougar is trapped between reality and the ghost realm.

✔ When you use the object transparency brush, you can adjust the brush size and shape, as well as control the level of opacity, by using the controls on the property bar or in the Tool Settings roll-up.

The Transparency value controls the amount of transparency you apply with each brush stroke. The Opacity value sets the maximum opacity for the object. No matter how many times you stroke the object, it can't become more or less translucent than the specified Opacity value. If you set the Opacity value to its maximum, 255, areas you touch with the tool become fully opaque. Set both the Opacity and Transparency values to 0, and you make areas you stroke completely transparent. But even though the object appears to have disappeared, it's still hanging around, as you can see if you click on it with the arrow tool. You can restore the object's opacity by using the tool with different Opacity and Transparency values.

Also, if you turn on the Use Original Transparency option, Photo-Paint adds the transparency value of the object transparency brush to the existing transparency of the pixels you stroke. If you turn the option off, Photo-Paint replaces the existing transparency of the pixels you touch with the transparency value set for the tool.

CorelDraw also offers an interactive transparency tool that works similarly to the one in Photo-Paint. Using this tool, you can adjust the transparency of a selected object or block of artistic text. Just select the object and select the interactive transparency tool (it's the fourth one from the bottom of the toolbox). Then choose any option except None from the Type drop-down menu on the property bar.

The Uniform option makes your entire object uniformly translucent; drag the Transparency slider bar on the property bar to change the level of transparency. The Fountain option fills the object with a transparency gradient. Drag the white and black boxes that appear on the object to reposition the angle along with the start and end points of the gradient; use the transparency sliders on the property bar or the midpoint slider on the object to change the transparency level at the beginning and end of the gradient. If you choose the Pattern or Texture option, you can fill your object with a pattern or texture (big surprise there) and then adjust the transparency of the fill by dragging the transparency sliders on the property bar.

Shuffle the Colors in a Photograph

In Photo-Paint, you can apply some serious special effects by using commands that automatically shuffle the colors in an image. Figure 19-7 shows a few examples of these commands, found on the Image➪Transform and Effects➪Color Transform submenus. The labels indicate the commands used, which work as follows:

Original

Invert

Figure 19-7:
An image
subjected
to the
Invert,
Posterize,
and
Psychedelic
commands.

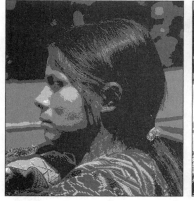

Posterize

Psychedelic

✔ Image⇨Transform⇨Invert — formerly found on the Effects⇨ Color Transform submenu — changes all light colors to dark and all dark colors to light, as in a photographic negative.

✔ Image⇨Transform⇨Posterize, also a former resident of the Color Transform submenu, decreases the number of colors in a selected area to any value between 2 and 32. It's great for creating high-contrast effects.

✔ Effects⇨Color Transform⇨Psychedelic thoroughly jumbles the colors, thus fooling the viewer into seeking medical attention. You can apply this command to color images only.

Make the Pixels Beg for Mercy

Photo-Paint stores its most amazing special effects in the 2D Effects and 3D Effects submenus in the Effects menu. Figure 19-8 demonstrates four effects from the 2D Effects submenu; Figure 19-9 demonstrates one additional effect from that same submenu plus three from the 3D Effects submenu. Although most effects in these submenus are incredibly difficult to apply — sometimes involving specialized selection outlines or other prerequisites — the eight commands demonstrated in the figures are straightforward and produce intriguing, unusual, and occasionally even attractive results.

Edge Detect

Swirl

Figure 19-8:
A few fascinating effects created by using commands from the 2D Effects submenu.

Wet Paint

Wind

Whirlpool

Emboss

Page curl

Pinch/Punch

Figure 19-9: An application of the 2D Effects⇨ Whirlpool command, plus three effects from the 3D Effects submenu.

> ✔ The Edge Detect command traces around high-contrast areas in your image, which is ideal for changing photographs into line art. You can trace with white, black, or the foreground color.
>
> For a really cool effect, set the foreground color to some bright color, such as orange or blue. Then choose Effects⇨2D Effects⇨Edge Detect and select the Other radio button in the Edge Detect dialog box.
>
> ✔ Choosing Effects⇨2D Effects⇨Swirl curls the image toward its center, as if the image were twisting down a drain. Specify the amount of curl by using the two Angle sliders in the Swirl dialog box, and choose whether you want the image to curl in a counterclockwise or clockwise direction by selecting a Direction radio button.

✔ The Wet Paint command melts your image as surely as water melts Wicked Witches of the West. Raise the Percentage value to make the drips stand out more. A positive Wetness value makes the light colors run; a negative value makes the dark colors bleed.

✔ Choose the Wind command to blast the image with a hurricane-force gale. A high Strength value smudges the pixels further. Adjust the Opacity value to mix the blasted pixels in with the original colors in the image. Use the Direction option to control the angle of the wind.

✔ The Whirlpool command brings up one of the most complicated Photo-Paint dialog boxes. Still, you can have fun messing around with the options, and nothing you do can cause any harmful effects until you click on the OK button. Even then, you can press Ctrl+Z to undo the damage. So relax and experiment. The top-left example in Figure 19-9 shows an image created with this effect.

✔ Choose Effects➪3D Effects➪Emboss to make a photograph appear carved out of stone. You can adjust the color of the Emboss effect or select the Original Color radio button to retain the original colors in the image. You can also adjust how deeply the image is carved by changing the Depth value, change the amount of light that shines on the image by using the Level slider, and specify the direction of the light using the Direction control.

✔ Effects➪3D Effects➪Page Curl turns up the corner of your photograph as if it were a curled page. Choose the corner you want to curl by clicking on one of the Adjust icons in the Page Curl dialog box. You can also adjust the size and orientation of the curl; make the curl more or less opaque; and choose a color for the curl and for the background area revealed after you apply the curl.

✔ Pinch/Punch distorts your image inward or outward. A positive Punch/Pinch value (in the Pinch/Punch dialog box) sucks the pixels toward the center. A negative value bows the image outward, as if it were projected on a balloon.

Inside most of the effect dialog boxes, you can switch to a different command on the Effects menu, the Image➪Adjust submenu, or the Image➪Transform submenu by clicking on the Effects button and choosing a command from the resulting pop-up menu. Only the commands on the Effects➪Fancy submenu and the special effects plug-ins that come with Photo-Paint are unavailable from the pop-up menu.

Also, you can click on the Reset button to return the various dialog box options to the settings that were in force when you opened the dialog box. The other dialog box controls, including the hand, zoom, and preview options, work like those I discuss in Chapter 17.

Design Your Own Repeating Pattern

My favorite special-effects command in Photo-Paint wasn't created by Corel. It comes from a company called Xaos (pronounced like *chaos*) Tools. The command, Effects➪Fancy➪Terrazzo, enables you to design totally wild patterns by repeating small portions of your image. Here's how to put this wonderful effect to work:

1. **Choose Effects➪Fancy➪Terrazzo.**

   Photo-Paint displays the busy dialog box pictured in Figure 19-10.

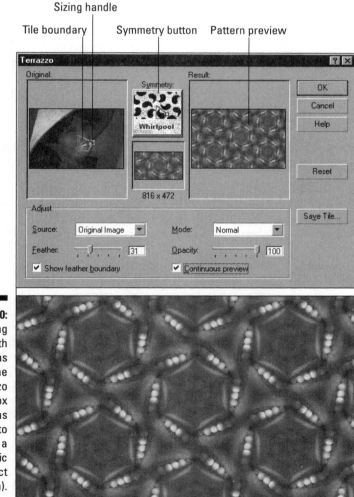

Figure 19-10: By fooling around with the options in the Terrazzo dialog box (top), I was able to create a kaleidoscopic effect (bottom).

2. Click on the Symmetry button in the middle of the dialog box.

Another dialog box appears, offering several ways to repeat your image as a pattern. Select the option that looks interesting — you can always come back and select a different Symmetry option if you change your mind — and press Enter. In Figure 19-10, I selected the Whirlpool option.

3. Edit the pattern tile boundary in the preview to select the area you want to repeat.

Drag the tile boundary to move it. Drag the sizing handle (labeled in Figure 19-10) to stretch or shrink the tile.

4. Adjust the Feather value to soften the transition between tiles.

A low Feather value creates abrupt transitions between one repeating tile and the next; a high value results in soft transitions. Keep an eye on the right-hand preview to see how your changes affect the pattern.

5. Lower the Opacity value if you want to blend the pattern in with the original image.

I just wanted to see the pattern, so I left the value set to 100 percent.

6. Press Enter to apply the pattern.

My completed pattern appears at the bottom of Figure 19-10. Who needs a kaleidoscope when you have Corel Photo-Paint?

If you're working on a speedy computer, you can get immediate feedback in the right-hand pattern preview by selecting the Continuous Preview check box in the Terrazzo dialog box. On a less-powerful computer, the option may slow things down considerably; if you have problems, turn the option off.

Chapter 20

Ten Little-Known, Less-Used Features

*I*n case you haven't figured it out yet, CorelDraw 8 is a grab bag of graphics functions. But like any grab bag, CorelDraw is split between essential capabilities and extravagant, super-complicated excess. This chapter is about the latter. I introduce ten features you'll probably never use, but by gum, you paid for them, so you may as well know about them.

Turning CorelDraw into a Parking Garage

You find layers in just about every drawing program with high-end pretensions, but only a handful of experienced artists use layers on a regular basis. Except for creating master layers (as explained in Chapter 12), I would never recommend layers to anyone who isn't drawing blowouts of manifold exhaust systems, or cancer cell networks, or something equally complicated.

Here's how layers work: Imagine that all the objects in a CorelDraw document are cars. One day you realize you have way too many cars, and you think "How can I sort these cars to make things more efficient?" The answer is to build a multilevel parking garage.

Well, that's layers. By choosing View⇨Dockers⇨Object Manager in CorelDraw, you display the Object Manager docker, which lets you divide your document into a transparent, multilevel parking garage. Each layer contains a bunch of objects fully segregated from objects on other layers.

Unless you specify otherwise, objects on different layers don't look different, and they don't print differently. They're merely organized into separate banks to help eliminate confusion and provide greater control and flexibility. For example, you can hide different layers to get them out of your face; you can print only certain layers to isolate others; you can lock the objects on a layer to prevent accidental alterations; and you can make objects on layers appear in different colors. The icons in the Object Manager docker assist you in determining what's locked, visible, printable, and so on.

Blending between Objects

I mention blending as a way to create custom gradations in Chapter 19. Luckily, there's more to blending than just creating gradations. In fact, blending is one of the most complicated functions in CorelDraw. You display the Blend roll-up by choosing Effects⇨Blend or pressing Ctrl+B. Then you select two objects, click on the Apply button, and watch CorelDraw create a bunch of intermediate objects (called *steps*) between the two. The steps gradually change in form and color as they progress from the first object to the last. You can specify how may steps CorelDraw creates, rotate the steps, make the steps follow a path, and even control the amount of space between steps.

You can accomplish the same feats by using the interactive blend tool and the property bar.

Blending is sort of like morphing — the effect you see when all those faces change into each other at the end of that Michael Jackson video. But instead of each step occurring in a different frame of videotape — creating the effect of a gradual transition — all the steps in CorelDraw appear in the drawing area at the same time. As a result, no one uses blending for any other purpose than creating custom gradations like the one featured in Chapter 19.

Taking the Old Blowtorch to Your Objects

In Chapter 17, I explain that you can manually adjust selection outlines in Photo-Paint. You can add one selection outline to another, delete a chunk from a selected area, or find the intersection of two selection outlines. Well, you can do the same thing in CorelDraw, except with objects.

Suppose that you want to create a snowman. You can take one circle and weld it to another by choosing Arrange⇨Weld. If you want to subtract a small circle from a large circle to create a doughnut, you choose Arrange⇨Trim. And to make a circle with a flat bottom, you can take a circle and a rectangle and choose Arrange⇨Intersection.

Although these are inherently useful commands, CorelDraw handles them in a weird way. First you select just one of the objects you want to add, subtract, or intersect. Then you choose the command to bring up a roll-up. You click on a button in the roll-up — Weld To, Trim, or Intersect With — and then click on the other object. The process would be much easier if you just selected two objects and chose a command to merge them, but simplicity is rarely the Corel style.

Finding Fonts

In Chapter 10, I discuss the basics of working with fonts. Well, if you're hungry for more, you'll be glad to know that CorelDraw 8 offers a new font manager that provides an easy way to find, organize, view, and print the fonts installed on your computer. You can use the font manager also to install new fonts.

You probably won't find yourself turning to this feature very often, but just in case, here's how it works. From the Windows 95 Start menu, choose Programs⇨CorelDraw 8⇨Productivity Tools⇨Bitstream Font Navigator to display the first screen of the Font Navigator wizard. Press Enter, select the icon for your hard disk, and click on the Finish button. Font Navigator searches your hard disk and creates a catalog of all the fonts found on your system. You can then create font groups, view font samples, and install and unistall fonts from within the Font Navigator window.

Backing Your Objects with Data

CorelDraw lets you link data to any object. Select an object and choose View➪Dockers➪Object Data. After the Object Data docker appears, click on the little data icon just below the title bar. The Object Data Manager dialog box appears, sporting a miniature spreadsheet.

Here you can enter any data you want about the selected object. Why on earth would you want to do this? Well, the Corel example is catalogs. If you had a drawing of a rotary combine engine, for example, you might want to write down the name and price of the product. Later you could print this information or export it for use in a different program. Yeah, I'm always wishing I could do that.

Trapping Colors

In Chapter 13, I discuss how to print color separations. Cyan, magenta, yellow, and black primaries are printed on separate pages and reproduced in separate passes. This is the same process used to print the Sunday comics in your local newspaper. Actually, nearly all color newspaper and magazine art is created this way, but the comics are the best example because they invariably have registration problems. Maybe the red in Hagar's beard is printed on Helga's face, or perhaps Robotman's outfit is leaking yellow onto a neighboring panel. These errors are caused by the fact that the cyan, magenta, yellow, and black inks aren't aligned properly.

CorelDraw enables you to compensate for bad registration by overlapping the colors a little. For example, imagine a circle with a cyan fill and a black outline. If the colors don't register exactly right, a gap occurs between the fill and outline colors. CorelDraw can fill in this gap by spreading the colors. The black outline becomes slightly thicker, and the cyan fill becomes slightly larger. This process is known as *color trapping*. To activate the CorelDraw trapping function, do the following:

1. **Press Ctrl+P or choose File➪Print.**

2. **Click on the Separations tab and select the Print Separations check box.**

3. **In the Auto Trapping area, select both the Always Overprint Black and Auto-Spreading check boxes.**

4. **Click on Print to start printing.**

Phew, what a lot of work. On top of that, the trapping options aren't even available for some lower-end printers.

Separating Color Channels in Photo-Paint

In Photo-Paint, you can take a color image and view it as several separate images called channels, each of which represents a primary color. For example, a CMYK image has four channels — one each for cyan, magenta, yellow, and black — just as you have four plates when printing color separations. You can view any of three channels in an RGB image — one each for red, green, and blue, the primary colors of light.

To view the different color channels in an image, press Ctrl+F9 or choose View⇨Dockers⇨Channels. Then click in the column just to the left of a channel name in the image channels list in the Channels docker. Photo-Paint displays the channel as an ordinary grayscale image. To return to full-color view, click just to the left of the Channels item that has the full-color thumbnail. (If you're viewing an RGB item, for example, click next to the RGB Channels item.)

What's the point of all this channel segregation? Well, you can apply a special effect to a single color channel to get a doubly weird effect. In addition, if a color image looks a little fuzzy, it may turn out that only one of the color channels needs sharpening. You may also want to create a psychedelic effect by selecting part of one channel and rotating it independently of the other channels.

Scanning into Photo-Paint or CorelDraw

If you sink a few hundred bucks into a scanner, you can scan images directly into Photo-Paint. And if you also install the CorelScan utility included in Version 8, you can scan directly into CorelDraw as well.

To take a bit of real life and make it appear magically on your computer screen inside Photo-Paint, choose File⇨Acquire Image⇨Acquire. Then click on the Scan button inside the Corel TWAIN dialog box. When the scanner had finished working, your photograph appears on-screen.

Alternatively, you can choose File⇨Acquire Image⇨Acquire from CorelScan inside Photo-Paint or choose File⇨Acquire from CorelScan inside CorelDraw. These commands start the CorelScan wizard, which guides you through the process of scanning your image and then opens the image for you. In CorelScan, you can crop your image, make color corrections, and otherwise improve the quality of the image if you like.

If you don't have a scanner, however, nothing happens. You can try smushing the photograph against the screen, but I don't think Corel has figured out how to make Photo-Paint or CorelDraw read images that way.

Assembling Your Own 3-D Movie Stage

Dream 3D lets you clutter your drawing not only with three-dimensional objects, but also with lights and cameras. Lights shine on the objects so that you can see what's going on. Without lights, you couldn't see anything. The camera controls what Dream 3D renders. Just as the audience at a movie sees what the camera films, your audience sees what Dream 3D's camera shoots.

Dream 3D offers two tools for adding your own lights and cameras. These are the Create Light and Create Camera tools, found roughly in the middle of the toolbox. Lights show up as red cone-shaped objects; cameras appear as blue rectangles. Figuring out which direction the lights or cameras are pointing is virtually impossible unless you're working in the preview or better preview mode, which can be slow on some machines. Moving the lights and cameras around and turning them toward objects is just as difficult.

If, despite these hazards, you want to edit a light, double-click on it. You can then select from different kinds of lights, control the range and brightness, add gels, and generally perform half a dozen modifications that are every bit as bewildering as they sound, if not more so. To switch to a different camera, press Ctrl+E (or choose Scene⇨Camera Settings) and select the desired camera from the Camera pop-up menu. You can even change the lens on the camera from Normal to Telephoto.

Then again, you can accept the Dream 3D default lighting and camera settings and consider yourself lucky that you can draw some halfway decent-looking objects.

Attempting Optical Character Recognition

CorelTrace can recognize the characters in a scanned page and generate a text document you can open in a word processor. This is absolutely the last function that I expected to see worked into a drawing package. It'll be a cold day in Port-au-Prince before you use this function.

Chapter 21

Ten File Formats and Their Functions

CorelDraw supports more file formats than any other graphics program for the PC. This fact means you can create a graphic in just about any program on an IBM-compatible or Macintosh computer and open it or import it into CorelDraw. Likewise, you can export an image from CorelDraw so that it can be opened in just about any program.

The Many Languages of CorelDraw

If CorelDraw were a person, it would be able to speak every language but . . . well, any language I may mention would be politically incorrect, so I'd better keep my mouth shut. Anyway, I've listed several file formats for your reading pleasure.

Native CorelDraw: CDR and CMX

CDR is the native file format, which means that if you just choose File➪Save As and then enter a name, CorelDraw uses the CDR format. This format retains every bit of information about your drawing, including nodes, segments, fills, and layers. Unless you plan to share your drawing with others or open it in another program, stick with this format.

A variation on CDR is CMX, the Corel Presentation Exchange format. Like CDR, CMX saves all information about a drawing. Up until Version 7, Corel stored the clip art that came with CorelDraw in CMX, but now the clip art is stored in CDR.

Encapsulated PostScript: EPS and AI

PostScript is the printer language mentioned in Chapter 13. Encapsulated PostScript (EPS) is a file format that contains a complete PostScript definition of the graphic right in the file. It's as if the artwork contains a little PostScript capsule. When you print an EPS file, the program sends the PostScript capsule to the printer and lets the printer figure it out. The printer must support PostScript to print EPS graphics, however.

The Adobe Illustrator (AI) format is an editable variation on the EPS format. You see, when you import an EPS graphic into a program, you can't edit it. You can just place the graphic on the page and print it. But when you import an AI file into CorelDraw, you can edit every little bit of it. This format is ideal if you want to share artwork with someone who works on a Macintosh. It's also widely supported by Windows programs.

Metafile formats: CGM and WMF

CGM (Computer Graphics Metafile) is a dinosaur-like file format that's certified by the American National Standards Institute. Because CGM predates the EPS format, I prefer it to EPS when I print to non-PostScript printers.

The Windows Metafile Format (WMF) is the rough equivalent of CGM in the Windows environment, though no institutions have come out to certify it. WMF is the format used by the Windows Clipboard. If you plan on transferring a drawing to another Windows program and you'll be printing to a non-PostScript printer, you may want to give WMF a try.

Corel Photo-Paint: CPT and WI

CPT is the Photo-Paint native format. Like other formats covered from here on out — PCX, TIFF, BMP, GIF, JPEG, and PCD — CPT is an image file format. *Image formats* save artwork as pixels, not as objects. Although CorelDraw is perfectly capable of importing these formats, you should not save drawings in these formats unless you want to convert your graphic to pixels.

Saving your images in the CPT format is fine if you're going to be working on your images only inside Photo-Paint 8 or placing them only into a CorelDraw drawing. If you're sharing an image file with someone who uses Photo-Paint 6, save in the Version 6 CPT format.

Keep in mind, however, that if you save your image in any format other than CPT, any objects in the image merge with the background, preventing you from further manipulating them. So you may want to save a backup copy of your image in the CPT format before saving it in another image format.

Images in the Photos folder of the third CorelDraw 8 CD-ROM are stored in the WI (Wavelet Compressed Bitmap) format. This format takes a huge image file and smushes it down to a size that takes up less space on disk. When you open the image, Photo-Paint decompresses it, fluffing all those smushed pixels back up. Anyway, don't save your images in this format unless someone specifically requests it. Instead, use a more widely supported format, such as TIFF or PCX.

PC Paintbrush: PCX

Originally designed for PC Paintbrush, PCX is one of the most widely supported graphics formats on the PC. Recently, this format's popularity has faded. PCX is a great way to swap files with folks who use older programs.

Tagged Image File Format: TIFF

TIFF (Tagged Image File Format) was developed to be the standard image file format, even more of a standard than PCX. Although it still plays second fiddle to PCX in terms of raw support on the PC, TIFF is more likely to be supported by programs running on other kinds of computers, namely the Mac. Furthermore, if you're exporting an image for use in a mainstream desktop publishing program such as PageMaker, QuarkXPress, or CorelVentura, TIFF is the way to go. Generally a more reliable format than PCX, it offers compression options to reduce the size of the image on disk.

Windows bitmap: BMP

BMP is the native format of the little Paint program that comes with Windows. The only reason Corel supports BMP is for importing. I don't recommend exporting to the BMP format unless you're creating graphics that will become part of your computer's system resources — for example, you can use a BMP file as the wallpaper for your Windows desktop.

CompuServe bitmap: GIF

The GIF format was created especially for trading images over CompuServe. GIF offers compression capabilities, but it supports only 256 colors. Before you can save an image in this format, you must convert the image to an 8-bit image using one of the commands in Photo-Paint's Image⇨Convert To submenu.

These days, lots of folks use GIF for artwork they want to post on the Web (as discussed in Chapter 14). One advantage of this format is that you can create what's known as a transparent GIF, which simply means that you can make part of your image transparent so that a portion of your Web page shows through the image.

If transparency isn't an issue, the format discussed next, JPEG, may be a better choice because it lets you save 16 million colors and yet creates smaller files on disk. Use GIF only for high-contrast images, screen shots, and text or for creating transparent GIFs.

Joint Photographic Experts Group: JPEG

JPEG (or JPG) stands for the Joint Photographic Experts Group, the group of folks who came up with the format. JPEG is designed to compress huge images so that they take up much less space on disk. Compression-wise, JPEG wipes the floor with TIFF and GIF. However, you actually lose data when you save to the JPEG format. Usually, the loss is nominal — most users can't see the difference — but it's something to think about.

Generally speaking, you don't need to worry about the JPEG format unless you start creating very large images — say, larger than 400K — with Photo-Paint or Dream 3D. JPEG is also a common format for posting images on the World Wide Web, as discussed in the preceding section and in Chapter 14.

Kodak Photo CD: PCD

CorelDraw and Photo-Paint can import Kodak Photo CD files. Neither program can save to the format because Kodak won't let them. Photo CD is what is known as a *proprietary format*.

In case you haven't heard of it, Photo CD is the latest thing from Kodak, and it's designed for storing photographs on compact discs. You take a roll of undeveloped film to a service bureau and give the technician $30 or so, and the technician scans your photos onto a CD. As long as you own a Photo CD-compatible CD-ROM drive — which means just about every CD-ROM drive manufactured in the last two years — you can then open and edit the images in Photo-Paint. What will they think of next?

Index

IDG BOOKS WORLDWIDE BOOK REGISTRATION

Register This Book and Win!

We want to hear from you!

Visit **http://my2cents.dummies.com** to register this book and tell us how you liked it!

- ✔ Get entered in our monthly prize giveaway.

- ✔ Give us feedback about this book — tell us what you like best, what you like least, or maybe what you'd like to ask the author and us to change!

- ✔ Let us know any other *...For Dummies*® topics that interest you.

Your feedback helps us determine what books to publish, tells us what coverage to add as we revise our books, and lets us know whether we're meeting your needs as a *...For Dummies* reader. You're our most valuable resource, and what you have to say is important to us!

Not on the Web yet? It's easy to get started with *Dummies 101*®: *The Internet For Windows*® *98* or *The Internet For Dummies*,® 5th Edition, at local retailers everywhere.

Or let us know what you think by sending us a letter at the following address:

...For Dummies Book Registration
Dummies Press
7260 Shadeland Station, Suite 100
Indianapolis, IN 46256-3917
Fax 317-596-5498

BESTSELLING BOOK SERIES